PRAISE FOR
GOOD ECONOMICS FOR HARD TIMES

"Excellent…Few have grappled as energetically with the complexity of real life as Esther Duflo and Abhijit Banerjee, or got their boots as dirty in the process…A treasure trove of insight…[Readers] will be captivated by the authors' curiosity, ferocious intellects, and attractive modesty."
—*The Economist*

"Carefully argued and backed with research….*Good Economics for Hard Times* is an effective response to Banerjee and Duflo's more thoughtful critics, some of whom argued that devotion to randomised trials had led to a narrowing of economics, in which complex questions that could not be scientifically tested should simply be set aside. The authors make a convincing case that empirical economics contains answers to many vexing problems, from populism to identity politics, especially when economists are willing to range outside their discipline's confines."
—*Financial Times*

"*Good Economics for Hard Times* lives up to its authors' reputations, giving a masterly tour of the current evidence on critical policy questions facing less-than-perfect markets in both developed and developing countries, from migration to trade to postindustrial blight."
—*Wall Street Journal*

"Their goal is to ground both sides of our national debate in hard evidence, and the process of coming up with ways to do that is pretty interesting in itself…Eager to distance themselves from the previous generation of economists who argued from first principles, Banerjee and Duflo say nothing that smells like special pleading. It would be hard to take umbrage with such studied humility. The authors admit, 'We clearly don't have all the solutions, and suspect no one else does either.' Even so, the prospect of a path towards consensus solutions through iterated experiments is enough to make for a compelling read."
—*National Review*

P9-CJJ-867

"The studies they cite probe hot topics such as climate change, immigration, and the viability of continued economic growth. Banerjee and Duflo synthesize the literature on what is agreed and what is controversial in an accessible, often entertaining way."

—*Nature*

"*Good Economics for Hard Times* makes important policy connections and suggestions.... Banerjee and Duflo explore traditional remedies (tariffs sure aren't the answer, they find, and job retraining and other trade adjustment tools are too narrow and take too long) and suggest some novel ideas... In crafting their carefully reasoned arguments, they marshal evidence assembled over decades from all sorts of areas—the fight against malaria, past efforts at tax reform, previous waves of migration—and propose commonsense solutions."

—*Foreign Policy*

"Lucid and frequently surprising... Banerjee and Duflo's arguments are original and open-minded and their evidence is clearly presented. Policy makers and lay readers looking for fresh insights into contemporary economic matters will savor this illuminating book."

—*Publishers Weekly*, Starred Review

"A canard-slaying, unconventional take on economics.... This might look like yet another conventional state-of-the-world economics book, but it is anything but. It is an invigorating ride through 21st-century economics and a treasure trove of facts and findings."

—*The Times (UK)*

"Not all economists wear ties and think like bankers. In their wonderfully refreshing book, Banerjee and Duflo delve into impressive areas of new research questioning conventional views about issues ranging from trade to top income taxation and mobility, and offer their own powerful vision of how we can grapple with them. A must-read."

—**Thomas Piketty**, professor, Paris School of Economics, and author of *Capital in the Twenty-First Century*

"A magnificent achievement, and the perfect book for our time. Banerjee and Duflo brilliantly illuminate the largest issues of the day, including immigration, trade, climate change, and inequality. If you read one policy book this year—heck, this decade—read this one."

—**Cass R. Sunstein**, Robert Walmsley University Professor, Harvard University, and author of *How Change Happens*

"In *Good Economics for Hard Times*, Banerjee and Duflo, two of the world's great economists, parse through what economists have to say about today's most difficult challenges—immigration, job losses from automation and trade, inequality, tribalism and prejudice, and climate change. The writing is witty and irreverent, always informative but never dull. Banerjee and Duflo are the teachers you always wished for but never had, and this book is an essential guide for the great policy debates of our times."

—**Raghuram Rajan**, Katherine Dusak Miller Distinguished Service Professor of Finance, University of Chicago Booth School of Business

"Banerjee and Duflo move beyond the simplistic forecasts that abound in the Twittersphere and in the process reframe the role of economics. Their dogged optimism about the potential of economics research to deliver makes for an informative and uplifting read."

—**Pinelopi Goldberg**, Elihu Professor of Economics, Yale University, and chief economist of the World Bank Group

"Banerjee and Duflo have shown brilliantly how the best recent research in economics can be used to tackle the most pressing social issues: unequal economic growth, climate change, lack of trust in public action. Their book is an essential wake-up call for intelligent and immediate action!"

—**Emmanuel Saez**, professor of economics, UC Berkeley

GOOD
ECONOMICS
FOR
HARD TIMES

GOOD
ECONOMICS
FOR
HARD TIMES

Abhijit V. Banerjee
& Esther Duflo

PublicAffairs
New York

PublicAffairs
Hachette Book Group
1290 Avenue of the Americas, New York, NY 10104
www.publicaffairsbooks.com
@Public_Affairs

Printed in the United States of America

Originally published in hardcover and ebook by PublicAffairs in November 2019
First Trade Paperback Edition: August 2021

Published by PublicAffairs, an imprint of Perseus Books, LLC, a subsidiary of Hachette Book Group, Inc. The PublicAffairs name and logo is a trademark of the Hachette Book Group.

The Hachette Speakers Bureau provides a wide range of authors for speaking events. To find out more, go to www.hachettespeakersbureau.com or call (866) 376-6591.

The publisher is not responsible for websites (or their content) that are not owned by the publisher.

Editorial production by Christine Marra, *Marra*thon Production Services. www.marrathoneditorial.org

Book design by Jane Raese
Set in 12-point Granjon

Library of Congress Cataloging-in-Publication Data has been applied for.

ISBN 978-1-61039-950-0 (hardcover), ISBN 978-1-5417-6287-9 (ebook), 978-1-5417-8894-7 (trade paperback)

LSC-C

PRINTING 2, 2022

To our children, Noemie and Milan,
in the hope that they grow up
to a more just and humane world,

and for Sasha, who didn't get a chance.

CONTENTS

PREFACE TO THE
PAPERBACK EDITION

January 20, 2021, Paris

Economists seem to have a compulsion to make predictions that are almost doomed to fail. Researchers at the International Monetary Fund, where a large department is devoted entirely to economic forecasting, found that the department had severely underestimated the magnitude of every single one of the major recessions since 1992.[1] To avoid falling into this trap we have made something of an art form of deflecting questions—from taxi drivers, seatmates on planes, audience members, or journalists—about what awaits the economy in the near future.

It was probably therefore pure happenstance that we landed on an uncannily prophetic title for this book. Its first edition came out in November 2019. By March 2020, it was clear that "hard times" were upon the world. In many countries, the book was published in the middle of the hardest time most people could remember.

Of course, being both economists and humans, we had no idea that we were walking into this particular crisis. In late January 2020, if you happened to have been in Cambridge, Massachusetts, you could have spotted us in the MIT cafeteria, listening with some bewilderment to a Chinese colleague telling us what was happening in Wuhan, China. Local officials there were apparently stealing masks intended for other provinces. Roads were being destroyed to prevent people from leaving regions where there were clusters of infection. In late February, we spent the school vacation in New York City, staying with various friends, eating delicious Israeli food while sitting on the floor of a crowded restaurant, oblivious to the fast-spreading virus that would

soon take thousands of lives. Our daughter's birthday party was scheduled for March 15, two days after her school closed its doors "out of an
abundance of caution." We moved the plans for the party to a park,
and finally canceled it on March 14, and that was only because two of
her best friends bailed.

On March 16, the first day of what would turn out to be a very,
very long COVID-19 "vacation," our two children watched a replay
of a 2013 episode of a French kids' science show about the habits of the
influenza virus, in which an infectious disease expert at the renowned
Pasteur Institute calmly announced that "a pandemic with a flu virus,
which is a very contagious virus, would take only a few weeks to diffuse
to the entire world."[2] The expert also said such a pandemic "could be
tomorrow, or it could be in ten years." Well within the ten-year window suggested by the scientist, the worldwide pandemic had arrived,
though it was a coronavirus, not the flu. Any child who had listened
carefully to that science show would have been worried about it—yet
we were not. It dawned on us later that we had become exhibit A for
one of the phenomena we talk about at length in this book but mostly
attribute to other people: the difficulty of taking scientific information
and warnings seriously, if they require us to rethink the assumptions
that underlie our day-to-day lives.

*

A technique used to reveal the structure of a virus is an effective metaphor for the way the year 2020 exposed what ails our world. Scientists
use X-ray crystallography to take X-ray images of the structure of vi-
ruses that are too small for even the most powerful microscopes. The
method was used, for example, to develop a vaccine for the RSV virus,
which provided a template for the development of the Moderna and
Pfizer vaccines for COVID-19.[3] In countless ways, the year 2020 (and
the first months of 2021) performed an X-ray crystallography on our
social and economic ailments.

Despite the early chatter about the pandemic being a great leveler,
in fact it crystallized the tragic inequality that exists both within and
across countries. In the United States, black people were three times as
likely to be affected by COVID-19, and four times as likely to die of
it, when we adjust for age. This is not because African Americans are

less careful: data we collected online from approximately twenty thousand people showed that, in September 2020, black Americans were actually more likely to wear masks and practice social distancing than whites (particularly white Republicans). Despite these precautions, they suffered more from COVID-19 at least in part because they tend to have the kinds of jobs that are more likely to put them at risk, and because the treatments they got when they fell ill were less likely to be top notch. At the same time, whereas for the top quartile of earners employment bounced back to pre-pandemic levels by September, it was down 20 percent for the bottom quartile. Thanks to vigorous stock market rallies, the richest Americans became ever richer during the pandemic, while the rest of the country went the other way.

Meanwhile, many low- and middle-income countries moved to lock down their economies more or less at the same time as those in the West did, partly because they were scared by the dire early pronouncements about the impact of the pandemic in low-income settings from Western epidemiologists. As it turned out, those predictions were often off by an order of magnitude, and thankfully the epidemic so far has not been as bad in Africa and India as it has been in Europe and the Americas. Unfortunately, however, the measures taken to contain it have already been wreaking their own kind of havoc. As economic activity slowed down and jobs vanished as a result of the lockdown, the rich countries spent 20 percent of their GDP on fiscal stimulus to minimize economic distress. By contrast, the poorest economies spent just 2 percent.[4] The results have been some of the deepest recessions ever known in modern times (India's GDP fell by almost a quarter) and a dramatic increase in global poverty. Schools were closed and remained closed nearly a year later in many countries; routine healthcare collapsed, largely because of the focus on COVID-19, with the result that childhood immunization in a number of countries is down to levels not seen since the 1990s. This will have generational consequences. Consumed by their own internal crises, and hobbled by the lack of leadership from the United States, the rich countries have been unable to react to these cumulating disasters with anything near the kind of help that was needed. Despite the last couple of decades of falling global poverty, the crystallographic image highlights just how easily things can fall apart for the world's most disadvantaged.

In the United States, the killing, in quick succession, of three un-armed black Americans—Ahmaud Arbery, Breonna Taylor, and George Floyd, two of them by police officers—shined an X-ray beam on systemic racism. While it surely came as no surprise to most black people that it is dangerous to be black (and especially young, male, and black) in today's America, the massive protests that followed the death of George Floyd in May 2020 seem to have animated a generation of young people of all races. Almost ten years ago, their older brothers and sisters had protested against economic inequality, declaring them-selves to be the "99 percent" against the 1 percent. The battle cry was even more fundamental this time: "Black Lives Matter." Neither the issue nor the movement was new, but its wide acceptance beyond the black community was. It quickly spread beyond the universities and the mainstream media to the corporate sector, and many leading com-panies declared that they, too, were opposed to racism. While it is easy to be cynical about such solemn declarations, they might prove binding in the current climate of heightened scrutiny.

The pandemic also acted as a reminder that when the going gets really tough, we need the government. The chapter in this book titled "Legit.gov" describes how the idea that the government is mostly the problem rather than the solution evolved out of the Reagan-Thatcher "revolutions" to become a premise of all too many policy discussions. The pandemic demonstrated, better than we ever could, just how wrongheaded this idea is. Only the government (local or national) can impose a mask mandate, force businesses to close, borrow trillions to bail them and their employees out when they are forced to close, and organize and fund the kind of amazing research effort that delivers a vaccine in a few months. Much has been made of the difference be-tween the performance during the first phase of the COVID-19 pan-demic of countries and states led by women—such as Angela Merkel of Germany, Jacinda Arden of New Zealand, Mette Frederiksen of Denmark, and K. K. Shailaja of the Indian state of Kerala, where she was the health minister. They kept the case count low and the mor-tality even lower in comparison to other countries through a combi-nation of decisive containment measures and efficient and emphatic treatment. In Kerala, a state that has a population nearly the size of Canada, the daily death toll never went beyond twenty-five.[5]

Without taking away anything from their individual performances, it is probably no coincidence that these women all came to power in places that take the business of governing seriously. As we noted in the book, that meant their bureaucracy was well respected and competent. It also meant that they were largely trusted to do their best to respond to the pandemic. This was critical, because acting against something like COVID-19 required decisive steps that would impose costs on many to protect those who were at risk. People needed to be tested, masks needed to be worn, curfews had to be respected, social distancing had to be enforced. As the experience of the United States underscored, all those tasks are harder in a climate of suspicion where many people worry that they are being misled or tricked, and therefore use every excuse to fight back, which impedes quick and decisive action. The result can be, as the United States reminds us, hundreds of thousands of unnecessary deaths, though in the case of the US there was the additional complication that the Trump administration and many state governments found it politically expedient to refuse to acknowledge the magnitude of the problem, mostly because they believed the message would be unpopular. Generally, countries with higher trust in government had fewer COVID-19 deaths.[6] And consistent with that idea, a twenty-three-country study found that those with higher trust in government were significantly likelier to wash their hands, avoid crowded places, and make personal sacrifices to stop the spread of the virus.[7]

Indeed, it is clearly easier to make sacrifices when we are confident the government will compensate us. Compensation for the economic damage of the pandemic rapidly became a key part of government responses throughout the rich world. In fact, the issue of just and adequate compensation presents a clear example of one of the key economic ideas running through this book, but also an instance of the blinding power of ideology among those who equate economics with the intuitions they vaguely remember from Economics 101. Very early in the pandemic, there was a consensus in the economics profession, stretching from left to right, that rapid action was needed to help businesses and households face the pandemic. Even Glenn Hubbard, a former chairman of the Council of Economic Advisors under George W. Bush, and very far from an extremist of the left, worked to persuade Republican senators to line up behind a huge relief program.

He, like many others, was worried that in the absence of such help, the necessary (but hopefully temporary) induced coma of the economy would morph into a massive demand crisis. The persuasion worked, and the CARES Act passed, offering a multipronged package to support businesses and individuals. One part of the package was a temporary weekly unemployment allowance of $600, which prevented an increase in poverty and allowed the economy to start humming again when the restrictions lifted in the summer. Remarkably, this weekly allowance was independent of how much people were making before being laid off, which meant that some people earned more from their unemployment allowance than they made from work before they lost their jobs. Although the financial aid was temporary (and not nearly as painless and efficient as the massive wage-replacement program that was unleashed in Europe at the same time), it was still unprecedented in recent US history: generous and unconditional support offered with no questions asked.

The knee-jerk reactions against such untoward generosity started almost immediately: Chuck Grassley, the (Republican) chairman of the Senate Finance Committee, complained that the payment would discourage work. However, economists, grounded at home and desperate to be useful, had already begun gathering the data to look at the effect of CARES on labor supply. Several independent studies released over the next few months all concluded the same thing: despite the high and uniform subsidies, the CARES Act had not discouraged work.[8]

We were not particularly surprised. A lesson running through this book is that people's important labor choices are not driven purely by financial incentives. We believe that people want to work, and a more generous support when they are not working does not usually persuade them to stay home if the option to work exists, even when the work is unpleasant or downright dangerous. It is true that other economists interpreted the results quite differently: they argued that since the help was temporary, the incentives to quit in these uncertain times were fairly minimal, and therefore not much could be learned from this experience about what would happen in more normal contexts.[9] But almost no one in the community of academic economists really disagreed with the main fact: the CARES Act had helped keep the US economy afloat during the hard times, and it had not come at the cost of subsidizing laziness. The studies, however, did nothing to quell the chorus of concerned pundits. The *Wall Street Journal*'s opinion page announced that it was "Economists versus common sense" ("If you pay people not to work, fewer will work. Except at Yale it seems").[10] And the aid was allowed to lapse. When Congress finally voted on a new package in December 2020, the extra unemployment support was missing, even though aid targeted to the poor would have been much better than the one-time $600 checks sent to almost everyone that were included in the package.

Even Donald Trump, despite his general indifference to the well-being of anyone outside his immediate family (if that), understood that the December package was inadequate. He pushed for a larger check, signaling and perhaps aggravating the rift between his base and the "very serious Republicans" in Congress, which culminated in Senate Majority Leader Mitch McConnell's house being vandalized and spray-painted with the words "Mitch kills the poor."

This particular act of "radical tantrum" (as McConnell described his garage graffito), of course, paled next to the much more dramatic tantrum that was to follow a few days later on January 6, 2021, when a group of Trump supporters, members of right-wing militias, and conspiracy theorists left a Trump rally to go attack the US Capitol, where congressional representatives and senators were debating and counting electoral votes to put the final stamp on the election of Joe Biden. They were driven by the lie, nourished by Trump and his supporters in the media and the Republican party in the teeth of all evidence, that the election had been "stolen" and Joe Biden's victory was fraudulent.

That this myth could be so widely believed shows the extent of the breakdown of social communication. But the sense of betrayal that millions of white people associated with the election is only a symptom of a broader sense of having been played. Ultimately, so many people could be lied to only because they were willing to listen, and that could only happen because for them, reality has become too hard to contemplate. They have come to understand that the very serious Republicans have been using them all this while to promote their own policy goals, and that in the pursuit of these goals those politicians were perfectly willing to abandon the poor. At this point their rage against the very serious Republicans is probably as profound as their fear of Democrats and socialists. This is why the vice president, Mike Pence, went so quickly from a friendly face to a direct target of the attack. He embodied, like so many of his Republican colleagues, the persistent lack of any real improvement in the conditions of life of so many Americans, despite the promise to make America great again.

*

Put into focus this way, the challenges the world faces are truly terrifying to contemplate. Optimists by nature, we have struggled at times to find a silver lining in the series of events that has unfolded since the early spring of 2020. And yet, just as it was necessary to magnify the pathogen manyfold to understand its structure and be able to develop a vaccine for coronavirus, perhaps we needed to understand the shape of what we are facing to be able to deal with it.

In the aftermath of the storming of the Capitol on January 6, it became easy to forget that the year 2021 had started on a good footing. Multiple vaccines were developed at record speed, building on decades of publicly funded research and months of hard work in partnership between the government and pharmaceutical companies. The United States had a new presidential administration that represented a decisive break from the preceding four years.

Nevertheless, there is no denying the daunting scale of the challenges facing the United States, which are very similar to the challenges faced by much of the rest of the world: not only do we need to end the COVID-19 pandemic; we urgently need to proactively manage the consequences of global climate change, and we need to revamp democracy.

Perhaps the message on Mitch McConnell's door shows us the way. Mostly unwittingly, the elites in the US have indeed been killing the poor, softly before COVID and more obviously since. The combination of stagnant wages, poor social protection, unaffordable healthcare, unhealthy hyperprocessed foods, an epidemic of legal and illegal opiates, and the everyday pain of being poor in a society that judges people by their economic success seems to have led to falling life expectancy among white, nonelite Americans, something that has no parallel in the rest of the developed world.[11] Paradoxically, a ray of hope may be emerging from the fact that the poor understand this and see that an effective government has the means to step in and stop the killing, if the politicians in charge have the will.

There is, in fact, at least one issue that commands overwhelming bipartisan support among the voters, if not politicians. Although Joe Biden lost Florida to Trump in the 2020 election, during the same election a proposition to increase the minimum wage in that state from $8.56 to $15 was adopted with a 60 percent supermajority. Increasing the federal minimum wage to that level was proposed in Joe Biden's first recovery package. It might not survive the arcane legislative process, but regardless, it is a dramatic turn of events for a policy idea that was considered fringe until fairly recently, and that Barack Obama did not consider when he came to office because his economic advisors persuaded him that it would be bad for the economy. Perhaps the slow recovery from the 2008 crisis, the popular revolt culminating in Trump's election, and the refusal to accept the 2020 results, together with the COVID-19 crisis, managed to finally shatter the stranglehold of "basic" economics. Higher minimum wages, massive levels of deficit financing (in a crisis), and public debt levels that were unthinkable till recently suddenly became acceptable and responsible tools of economic management.

The minimum wage increase is emblematic of the kind of policies around which a saner political conflict, based on economics rather than identity, could reemerge. An increase in the minimum wage will disproportionately benefit black and brown communities: a study of the impact of the 1967 introduction of the minimum wage in the United States has shown that it is responsible for at least 20 percent of the convergence between black and white wages in the US between 1960 and 1970, without leading to loss in employment.[12] The rise will also likely help scores of poorer white people whose standard of living has not improved for decades. Corporate profits will likely decline somewhat, so it is not surprising that the business associations have been vocal opponents of the measure, and that Republican senators are now balking. This is a debate we should welcome.

The most visible measure of the rescue package proposed by the Biden administration is a onetime direct payment to (almost) everyone. It is not obvious that direct payments make the most sense from a purely economic standpoint; as we discuss in this book, we are generally in favor of universal cash transfers in poor countries, but not in rich countries, where we have enough information to target our assistance much better. But their symbolic importance is undeniable.

But with this, perhaps more than with his speeches for unity, Joe Biden extends an olive branch to all those who voted for Donald Trump—and who would also have voted for the minimum wage increase if it had been proposed in their state. With a check of $1,400, Joe Biden's package "completes" the payment to reach the $2,000 that Trump wanted Congress to enact. In a way, Biden executes what Trump was prevented from doing by the very serious Republicans, but also what Obama was barred from accomplishing by the very serious Democrats.

Biden reportedly is a student of Franklin Delano Roosevelt, and there is clearly a sense, much more now than when he was running against Elizabeth Warren and Bernie Sanders during the Democratic primaries, that he and his economic team want to use the occasion to push a more progressive package than any administration has pushed since, if not Roosevelt, then at least Lyndon Johnson. In particular, the proposed bill contains a refundable child credit, which, if it persists beyond the pandemic relief, would represent an unprecedented transfer to poor families. With Biden's party holding only a narrow majority in the Senate, his proposals may or may not fully succeed. But defeat in the process of trying to enact a truly pro-poor agenda, along the lines of what we describe in this book, would already be more valuable than success in enacting a more conventional ("modern Democrat"–style) economic agenda, as long as it is accompanied by a realignment of political interests with economic interests, with the poor of all races joining a common fight against wanton inequities. *For this, it is important not to be subtle*. Biden needs to continue to advocate for direct redistribution, via, among other things, a high minimum wage, cash transfers to poor families and children, a more generous social protection and unemployment system, and a much more progressive tax code (including a wealth tax) to pay for all of it. Not everyone will agree, but the fault lines will be clear, and the argument over them will be much healthier for America than a fight between nonwhites and some members of the "elite" on one side, and the "true Americans" on the other.

As urgent as the fight against climate change is, it is only after they are persuaded that the government is acting in their interest that most

Americans will agree to play their part in it. Like the battle against COVID-19, this fight will require changes and sacrifices, at least in the short run. And those who lose need to be confident that they will be compensated. Today, this confidence is mostly absent, and that is why a winning political strategy is to deny the existence of climate change (and the need to pay for it). A silver lining from recent history is that Trump's strategy of COVID denial may have persuaded at least a few people that denying a problem because it requires uncomfortable adjustments does not make it go away—it makes it deadlier.

Some might think we are wide-eyed optimists to believe that a realignment of the political divide along the more traditional rich-poor lines (as against the current black-white, woke-cancel, Christian-other, urban-rural divides) could happen, or that the government will be able to regain the trust of the people. The media today is fascinated by just how many outlandish ideas some of the participants in the January 6 attack appear to believe. How is it possible, we are told, that people who espouse the kinds of tales spun by QAnon could just go back to the pedestrian reality of a fight over the minimum wage? But one of the most important lessons from this book is that people should never be assumed to *be* what they say or even believe at a given point in time. Our preferences, and even our own strong sense of identity, are much more of the moment than they appear.

Ordinary men and women are rarely completely unmoored from reality. In September 2020, we worked with dozens of Boston doctors of different ethnicities to record straightforward informational videos about COVID. The messages they carried were direct, and they simply reinforced what everyone else had been saying about the importance of social distancing and wearing masks. Our study sample of nearly twenty thousand people was equally distributed between blacks and whites across the entire United States. Among whites, we had Democrats, Independents, and Republicans. Some received bland videos on exercise, nutrition, and sleep, while others got to listen to an informational COVID video. There was a strong sense in the media at the time that self-protection against COVID had become a political issue, and we were wondering whether messages from such a diverse group of people from the East Coast would be ignored in some parts of the country.

We found instead that while black and white Democrats were generally more likely to wear masks and keep their distance than white Republicans, the doctors' messages were equally persuasive across all groups. Neither the race of the doctors, nor the emphasis on the differential burden of the disease, nor a statement from the American Medical Association that denounced racism as a health hazard seems to have encouraged either black people to pay more attention or white people to stop listening. Straightforward, actionable information was listened to and acted upon.[13]

A language of politics that focuses on simple, easy-to-follow information that everyone can understand and respond to is an important part of the remedy for these hard times.

PREFACE

Ten years ago we wrote a book about the work we do. To our surprise, it found an audience. We were flattered, but it was clear to us that we were done. Economists do not really write books, least of all books human beings can read. We did it and somehow got away with it; it was time to go back to what we normally do, which is to write and publish research papers.

Which is what we were doing while the dawn-light of the early Obama years gave way to the psychedelic madness of Brexit, the Yellow Vests, and the Wall—and strutting dictators (or their elected equivalents) replaced the confused optimism of the Arab Spring. Inequality is exploding, environmental catastrophes and global policy disasters loom, but we are left with little more than platitudes to confront them with.

We wrote this book to hold on to hope. To tell ourselves a story of what went wrong and why, but also as a reminder of all that has gone right. A book as much about the problems as about how our world can be put back together, as long as we are honest with the diagnosis. A book about where economic policy has failed, where ideology has blinded us, where we have missed the obvious, but also a book about where and why good economics is useful, especially in today's world.

The fact that such a book needs to be written does not mean we are the right people to write it. Many of the issues plaguing the world right now are particularly salient in the rich North, whereas we have spent our lives studying poor people in poor countries. It was obvious that we would have to immerse ourselves in many new literatures, and there was always a chance we would miss something. It took us a while to convince ourselves it was even worth trying.

We eventually decided to take the plunge, partly because we got tired of watching at a distance while the public conversation about core economic issues—immigration, trade, growth, inequality, or the environment—goes more and more off-kilter. But also because, as we thought about it, we realized the problems facing the rich countries in the world were actually often eerily familiar to those we are used to studying in the developing world—people left behind by development, ballooning inequality, lack of faith in government, fractured societies and polity, and so on. We learned a lot in the process, and it did give us faith in what we as economists have learned best to do, which is to be hard headed about the facts, skeptical of slick answers and magic bullets, modest and honest about what we know and understand, and perhaps most importantly, willing to try ideas and solutions and be wrong, as long as it takes us toward the ultimate goal of building a more humane world.

CHAPTER 1

MEGA: MAKE ECONOMICS GREAT AGAIN

A woman hears from her doctor that she has only
half a year to live. The doctor advises her to marry
an economist and move to South Dakota.

WOMAN: "Will this cure my illness?"
DOCTOR: "No, but the half year will seem pretty long."

WE LIVE IN AN AGE of growing polarization. From Hungary
to India, from the Philippines to the United States, from the
United Kingdom to Brazil, from Indonesia to Italy, the public conversation between the left and the right has turned more and more into a
high-decibel slanging match, where harsh words, used wantonly, leave
very little scope for backtracking. In the United States, where we live
and work, split-ticket voting is at its lowest on record.[1] Eighty-one
percent of those who identify with one party have a negative opinion of the other party.[2] Sixty-one percent of Democrats say they view
Republicans as racists, sexists, or bigots. Fifty-four percent of Republicans call Democrats spiteful. A third of all Americans would be disappointed if a close family member married someone from the other
side.[3]

In France and India, the two other countries where we spend a lot
of time, the rise of the political right is discussed, in the liberal, "en-
lightened" elite world we inhabit, in increasingly millenarian terms.
There is a clear feeling that civilization as we know it, based on democracy and debate, is under threat.

1

As social scientists, our job is to offer facts and interpretations of facts we hope will help mediate these divides, help each side understand what the other is saying, and thereby arrive at some reasoned disagreement, if not a consensus. Democracy can live with dissent, as long as there is respect on both sides. But respect demands some understanding.

What makes the current situation particularly worrying is that the space for such conversations seems to be shrinking. There seems to be a "tribalization" of views, not just about politics, but also about what the main social problems are and what to do about them. A large-scale survey found Americans' views on a broad spectrum of issues come together like bunches of grapes.[4] People who share some core beliefs, say about gender roles or whether hard work always leads to success, seem to have the same opinions on a range of issues, from immigration to trade, from inequality to taxes, to the role of the government. These core beliefs are better predictors of their policy views than their income, their demographic groups, or where they live.

These issues are in some ways front and center in the political discourse, and not just in the United States. Immigration, trade, taxes, and the role of government are just as contested in Europe, India, South Africa, or Vietnam. But views on these issues are all too often based entirely on the affirmation of specific personal values ("I am for immigration because I am a generous person," "I am against immigration because migrants threaten our identity as a nation"). And when they are bolstered by anything, it is by made-up numbers and very simplistic readings of the facts. Nobody really thinks very hard about the issues themselves.

This is really quite disastrous, because we seem to have fallen on hard times. The go-go years of global growth, fed by trade expansion and China's amazing economic success, may be over, what with China's growth slowing and trade wars igniting everywhere. Countries that prospered from that rising tide—in Asia, Africa, and Latin America—are beginning to wonder what is next for them. Of course, in most countries in the affluent West, slow growth is nothing new at this point, but what makes it particularly worrying is the rapid fraying of the social contract that we see across these countries. We seem to be back in the Dickensian world of *Hard Times*, with the haves facing off against the increasingly alienated have-nots, with no resolution in sight.[5]

Questions of economics and economic policy are central to the present crisis. Is there something that can be done to boost growth? Should that even be a priority for the affluent West? And what else? What about exploding inequality everywhere? Is international trade the problem or the solution? What is its effect on inequality? What is the future on trade—can countries with cheaper labor costs lure global manufacturing away from China? And what about migration? Is there really too much low-skilled migration? What about new technologies? Should we, for example, worry about the rise of artificial intelligence (AI) or celebrate it? And, perhaps most urgently, how can society help all those people the markets have left behind?

The answers to these problems take more than a tweet. So there is an urge to just avoid them. And partly as a result, nations are doing very little to solve the most pressing challenges of our time; they continue to feed the anger and the distrust that polarize us, which makes us even more incapable of talking, thinking together, doing something about them. It often feels like a vicious cycle.

Economists have a lot to say about these big issues. They study immigration to see what it does to wages, taxes to determine if they discourage enterprise, redistribution to figure out whether it encourages sloth. They think about what happens when nations trade, and have useful predictions about who the winners and losers are likely to be. They have worked hard to understand why some countries grow and others don't and what, if anything, governments can do to help. They gather data on what makes people generous or wary, what makes a man leave his home for a strange place, how social media plays on our prejudices.

What the most recent research has to say, it turns out, is often surprising, especially to those used to the pat answers coming out of TV "economists" and high school textbooks. It can shed new light on those debates.

Unfortunately, very few people trust economists enough to listen carefully to what they have to say. Right before the Brexit vote, our colleagues in the UK desperately tried to warn the public that Brexit would be costly, but they felt they were not getting through. They were right. No one was paying much attention. Early in 2017, YouGov conducted a poll in the UK in which they asked: "Of the following, whose opinions do you trust the most when they talk about their field of expertise?" Nurses came first. Eighty-four percent of people polled trusted them. Politicians came last, at 5 percent (though local members of Parliament were a bit more trusted, at 20 percent). Economists were just above politicians at 25 percent. Trust in weather forecasters was twice as high.[6] In the fall of 2018, we asked the same question (as well as several others about views on economic issues, which we make use of at various points in the book) to ten thousand people in the United States.[7] There again, just 25 percent of people trusted economists about their own field of expertise. Only politicians ranked lower.

This trust deficit is mirrored by the fact that the professional consensus of economists (when it exists) is often systematically different from the views of ordinary citizens. The Booth School of Business at the University of Chicago regularly asks a group of about forty academic economists, all recognized leaders in the profession, their views on core economic topics. We will often refer to these in the book as the IGM Booth panel answers. We selected ten questions asked of the IGM Booth respondents and posed the same questions to our survey respondents. On most of these issues, economists and our respondents were completely at odds with each other. For example, every single respondent in the IGM Booth panel disagreed with the proposition that "imposing new US tariffs on steel and aluminum will improve Americans' well-being."[8] Just over one-third of our respondents shared this view.

In general, our respondents tended to be more pessimistic than the economists: 40 percent of economists agreed with the proposition that "the influx of refugees into Germany beginning in the summer of 2015 would bring economic benefits to Germany over the succeeding decade," and most of the rest were uncertain or did not give an opinion (only one disagreed).[9] In contrast, only a quarter of our respondents agreed, and 35 percent disagreed. Our respondents were also more likely to think the rise of robots and AI would lead to widespread unemployment, and much less likely to think they would create enough extra wealth to compensate those who lost out.[10]

This is not because economists are always more in favor of laissez-faire outcomes than the rest of the world. A prior study compared how economists and a thousand regular Americans answered the same twenty questions.[11] They found economists were (much) more in favor of raising federal taxes (97.4 percent of economists were in favor, compared to 66 percent of regular Americans). They also had much more faith in the policies pursued by the government after the 2008 crisis (bank bailouts, the stimulus, etc.) than the public at large. On the other hand, 67 percent of regular Americans but only 39 percent of professional economists agreed with the idea that CEOs of large companies were overpaid. The key finding is that, overall, the average academic economist thinks very differently from the average American. Across all twenty questions, there is a gaping chasm of 35 percentage points between how many economists agree with a particular statement and how many average Americans do.

Moreover, informing respondents about what prominent economists think of those issues does nothing to change their point of view. For three questions where the experts' view was markedly different from that of the public, researchers varied the way they asked the question. For some respondents, they first stated, "Nearly all experts agree that . . ." before posing the question; for others they just asked the question. It made no difference in the answers they got. For example, on the question of whether the North American Free Trade Agreement increased the average person's well-being (to which 95 percent of economists answered yes), 51 percent of respondents answered yes if they were provided with the economists' view, and 46 percent when they were not. A small difference at best. From this, it seems a large part of the general public has entirely stopped listening to economists about economics.

We don't for a moment believe that when economists and the public have different views, economists are always right. We, the economists, are often too wrapped up in our models and our methods and sometimes forget where science ends and ideology begins. We answer policy questions based on assumptions that have become second nature to us because they are the building blocks of our models, but it does not mean they are always correct. But we also have useful expertise no one else has. The (modest) goal of this book is to share some of this expertise and reopen a dialogue about the most urgent and divisive topics of our times.

For that, we need to understand what undermines trust in economists. A part of the answer is that there is plenty of bad economics around. Those who represent the "economists" in the public discourse are not usually the same people who are part of the IGM Booth panel. The self-proclaimed economists on TV and in the press—chief economist of Bank X or Firm Y—are, with important exceptions, primarily spokespersons for their firms' economic interests who often feel free to ignore the weight of the evidence. Moreover, they have a relatively predictable slant toward market optimism at all costs, which is what the public associates with economists in general.

Unfortunately, in terms of how they look (suit and tie) or the way they sound (lots of jargon), the talking heads are hard to tell apart from academic economists. The most important difference is perhaps in their willingness to pronounce and predict, which unfortunately makes them all the more authoritative. But they actually do a pretty poor job of predicting, in part because predictions are often well-nigh impossible, which is why most academic economists stay away from futurology. One of the jobs of the International Monetary Fund (IMF) is to forecast the rate of growth of the world economy in the near future. Without a whole lot of success, one might add, despite its team of many very well-trained economists. The *Economist* magazine once computed just how far the IMF's forecasts were off on average over the period 2000–2014.[12] For two years from the time of prediction (say, the growth rate in 2014 predicted in 2012), the average forecast error was 2.8 percentage points. That's somewhat better than if they had chosen a random number between –2 percent and 10 percent every year, but about as bad as just assuming a constant growth rate of 4 percent. We suspect these kinds of things contribute substantially to the general skepticism of economics.

Another big factor that contributes to the trust gap is that academic economists hardly ever take the time to explain the often complex reasoning behind their more nuanced conclusions. How did they parse through the many possible alternative interpretations of the evidence? What were the dots, often from different domains, they had to connect to reach the most plausible answer? How plausible is it? Is it worth acting upon, or should we wait and see? Today's media culture does not naturally allow a space for subtle or long-winded explanations.

Both of us have had to wrangle with TV anchors to tell our full story (often to have it edited out of what gets shown), so we recognize why academic economists are often unwilling to take on the responsibility of speaking out. It takes a lot of effort to be heard properly, and there is always the risk of sounding half-baked or having one's careful words manipulated to mean something quite different.

There are of course those who do speak out, but they tend to be, with important exceptions, those with the strongest opinions and the least patience for engaging with the best work in modern economics. Some, too beholden to some orthodoxy to pay attention to any fact that does not square with it, repeat old ideas like a mantra, even though they have long been disproved. Others are there to pour scorn on mainstream economics, which it may sometimes deserve; but that often means they are unlikely to speak for today's best economic research.

Our sense is that the best economics is frequently the least strident. The world is a sufficiently complicated and uncertain place that the most valuable thing economists have to share is often not their conclusion, but the path they took to reach it—the facts they knew, the way they interpreted those facts, the deductive steps they took, the remaining sources of their uncertainty. This is related to the fact that economists are not scientists in the sense physicists are, and they often have very little absolute certainty to share. Anyone who has watched the comic TV series *The Big Bang Theory* knows that physicists look down on engineers. Physicists think deep thoughts, while engineers muck around with materials and try to give shape to those thoughts; or at least that's how the series presents it. If there were ever a TV series that made fun of economists, we suspect we would be several rungs below engineers, or at least the kind of engineers who build rockets. Unlike engineers (or at least those on *The Big Bang Theory*), we cannot rely on some physicist to tell us exactly what it would take for a rocket to escape the earth's gravitational pull. Economists are more like plumbers; we solve problems with a combination of intuition grounded in science, some guesswork aided by experience, and a bunch of pure trial and error.

This means economists often get things wrong. We will no doubt do so many times in this book. Not just about the growth rate, which is mostly a hopeless exercise, but also about somewhat more limited questions, like how much carbon taxes will help with climate change, how CEOs' pay might be affected if taxes were to be raised a lot, or what universal basic income would do to the structure of employment. But economists are not the only ones who make mistakes. Everyone gets things wrong. What is dangerous is not making mistakes, but to be so enamored of one's point of view that one does not let facts get in the way. To make progress, we have to constantly go back to the facts, acknowledge our errors, and move on.

Besides, there is plenty of good economics around. Good economics starts with troubling facts, makes some guesses based on what we already know about human behavior and theories elsewhere shown to work, uses data to test those guesses, refines (or radically alters) its line of attack based on the new set of facts, and eventually, with some luck, gets to a solution. In this, our work is also a lot like medical research. Siddhartha Mukherjee's wonderful book on the fight against cancer, *The Emperor of All Maladies*, tells a story of combining inspired guesswork with careful testing, and many rounds of refinement, before a new drug gets to the market.[13] A big part of the economist's work is very much like that. As in medicine, we are never sure we have reached the truth, just that we have enough faith in an answer to act on it, knowing we may have to change our minds later. Also like in medicine, our work does not stop once the basic science is done and the core idea is established; the process of rolling out the idea in the real world then begins.

At one level, one could think of this book as a report from the trenches where that research happens: what does the best economics of today tell us about the fundamental issues our societies are grappling with? We describe how today's best economists think about the world; not just their conclusions but also how they got there, all the while trying to separate facts and pipe dreams, brave assumptions and solid results, what we hope for and what we know.

It is important that in this project we be guided by an expansive notion of what human beings want and what constitutes the good life. Economists have a tendency to adopt a notion of well-being that is often too narrow, some version of income or material consumption. And yet all of us need much more than that to have a fulfilling life: the respect of the community, the comforts of family and friends, dignity, lightness, pleasure. The focus on income alone is not just a convenient shortcut. It is a distorting lens that often has led the smartest economists down the wrong path, policy makers to the wrong decisions, and all too many of us to the wrong obsessions. It is what persuades so many of us that the whole world is waiting at the door to take our well-paying jobs. It is what has led to a single-minded focus on restoring the Western nations to some glorious past of fast economic growth. It is what makes us simultaneously deeply suspicious of those who don't have money and terrified to find ourselves in their shoes. It is also what makes the trade-off between the growth of the economy and the survival of the planet seem so stark.

A better conversation must start by acknowledging the deep human desire for dignity and human contact, and to treat it not as a distraction, but as a better way to understand each other, and to set ourselves free from what appear to be intractable oppositions. Restoring human dignity to its central place, we argue in this book, sets off a profound rethinking of economic priorities and the ways in which societies care for their members, particularly when they are in need.

That said, on any single issue we will cover in the book, or perhaps all of them, you may well come to a different conclusion than we do. We hope to persuade you not reflexively to agree with us, but to adopt a little bit of our methods and share some part of our hopes and fears, and perhaps by the end, we will really be talking to each other.

CHAPTER 2

FROM THE MOUTH
OF THE SHARK

MIGRATION IS BIG NEWS, big enough to drive the politics of much of Europe and the United States. Between President Donald Trump's imaginary but enormously consequential hordes of murderous Mexican migrants and the anti-foreigner rhetoric of the Alternative for Germany, the French Rassemblement National, and the Brexit crew, not to mention the ruling parties in Italy, Hungary, and Slovakia, it may be the single most influential political issue in the world's richest countries. Even politicians from the mainstream European parties are struggling to reconcile the liberal traditions they want to uphold with the threat they see across their shores. It is less visible in the developing world, but the fights over Zimbabwean refugees in South Africa, the Rohingya crisis in Bangladesh, and the citizenship bill in Assam, India, have been equally frightening for those who are its targets.

Why the panic? The fraction of international migrants in the world population in 2017 was roughly what it was in 1960 or in 1990: 3 percent.[1] The European Union (EU) on average gets between 1.5 million and 2.5 million non-EU migrants every year from the rest of the world. Two and a half million is less than one half of one percent of the EU population. Most of these are legal migrants, people with job offers, or those who arrive to join their families. There was an unusual influx of refugees in 2015 and 2016, but by 2018 the number of asylum seekers to the EU was back to 638,000, and only 38 percent of the requests were granted.[2] This represents about one for every twenty-five hundred EU residents. That's it. Hardly a deluge.

10

Racist alarmism, driven by a fear of the intermingling of races and the myth of purity, doesn't heed facts. A survey of 22,500 native respondents from six countries where immigration has been a defining political issue (France, Germany, Italy, Sweden, the United Kingdom, and the United States) revealed massive misperceptions about the number and composition of immigrants.[3] For instance, in Italy, the actual share of immigrants in the population is 10 percent, but the average perception of that share is 26 percent.

Respondents starkly overestimate the share of Muslim immigrants, as well as the share of immigrants coming from the Middle East and North Africa. They believe immigrants are less educated, poorer, more likely to be unemployed, and more likely to live on government handouts than they actually are.

Politicians stoke these fears by abusing the facts. In the run-up to the 2017 French presidential election, Marine Le Pen frequently claimed that 99 percent of immigrants were adult males (58 percent were), and that 95 percent of migrants who settled in France were "taken care of by the nation" because they wouldn't work in France (in reality, 55 percent of migrants in France were in the labor force).[4]

Two recent experiments show this is a winning electoral tactic, even in a world of systematic fact-checking. In one study in the United States, researchers worked with two sets of questions. One set aimed to solicit respondents' *opinions* about migration, the other their *factual knowledge* of the numbers and characteristics of migrants.[5] Those who answered the fact-based questions first, before being asked their opinion (and thus reminded of their own distorted perceptions about migrants) were significantly more likely to be against immigration. When they were told the true numbers, their sense of the facts changed, but not their bottom-line views on immigration. In France, a parallel experiment found something similar. People deliberately exposed to Marine Le Pen's false claims were more likely to want to vote for her.[6] Sadly, this persisted after her statements were fact-checked in front of them. Truth did not sway their opinions. Simply thinking about migration makes people more parochial. The facts aren't allowed to get in the way.

There is an important reason why facts are ignored, and it is based on a piece of economics seemingly so utterly self-evident that many find it impossible to think past it, even when the evidence says the opposite. The economic analysis of immigration often comes down to a seductive syllogism. The world is full of poor people who would obviously earn a lot more if they could find their way here (wherever that might be), where things are clearly much better; therefore, given half a chance, they will indeed leave wherever they are and come to our country, and this will drive down wages and make most of us already here worse off.

What is remarkable about this argument is its faithfulness to the standard exposition of the law of supply and demand, as taught in high school economics. People want more money and therefore will all go wherever wages are highest (supply goes up). As the demand curve for labor slopes down, the rise in the labor supply will lower wages for everyone. The migrants may benefit, but the native workers will suffer. This is the sentiment President Trump tries to capture when he insists the country is "full." The reasoning is so simple it can fit on the back of a very small napkin, as in figure 2.1.

The logic is simple, seductive, and wrong. First, wage differences between countries (or locations, more generally) actually have relatively little to do with whether or not people migrate. While there are obviously many people desperate to get out from wherever they are, as we will see, the enduring puzzle is why so many others *don't* move when they can.

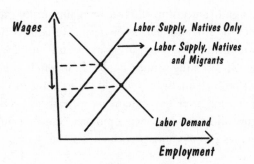

FIGURE 2.1 "Napkin economics." Why immigrants must make the rest of us poorer.

Second, there is no credible evidence that even relatively large inflows of low-skilled migrants hurt the local population, including members of the local population most like the migrants in terms of skills. Indeed, migration seems to make most people, migrants and locals, better off. This has a lot to do with the peculiar nature of the labor market. Very little about it fits the standard story of supply and demand.

LEAVING HOME

The British Somali poet, Warsan Shire, wrote:

> no one leaves home unless
> home is the mouth of a shark
> you only run for the border
> when you see the whole city running as well
> your neighbors running faster than you
> breath bloody in their throats
> the boy you went to school with
> who kissed you dizzy behind the old tin factory
> is holding a gun bigger than his body
> you only leave home
> when home won't let you stay.[7]

She was clearly onto something. The places people seem most desperate to leave—countries like Iraq, Syria, Guatemala, and even Yemen—are far from being the poorest in the world. Per capita income in Iraq, after adjusting for differences in cost of living (what economists call *purchasing power parity*, or PPP), is about twenty times that in Liberia, and at least ten times as high as in Mozambique or Sierra Leone. In 2016, despite a dramatic fall in income, Yemen was still three times richer than Liberia (there is no data for more recent years). Mexico, President Trump's favorite target, is an upper-middle-income country with a much praised and widely imitated welfare system.

Those trying to get out of such places probably don't face the grinding extreme poverty the average Liberian or Mozambique resident faces. It is more that they find life intolerable because of the collapse of everyday normality: the unpredictability and violence brought upon them by the drug wars in Northern Mexico, the horrible military Junta in Guatemala, and the civil wars in the Middle East. A study from Nepal found that even bad years in agriculture didn't drive many Nepalis out of the country.[8] In fact, fewer people left in bad years because they could not afford the trip out. It is only when the violence from Nepal's long-standing Maoist insurgency flared up that people started leaving. They were running from the mouth of the shark. And when that happens, it is almost impossible to stop them, because in their minds there is no home to return to.

Of course, there is also the opposite: the ambitious migrant who needs to get out at all costs. This is Apu, the protagonist of *Aparajito*, the second of Satyajit Ray's wonderful Apu trilogy, caught between his lonely mother in their village home and the many exciting possibilities offered by the city.[9] This is the migrant from China who works two jobs and scrimps and saves so his children one day can go to Harvard. We all know such people exist.

And then there are the people in the middle, the vast majority who don't face extreme internal or external compulsions to move. They do not seem to go chasing after every extra dollar. Even where there are no border checks and no immigration agents to dodge, they stay where they are, in the countryside, for example, despite the large wage gaps that exist *within the same country*, between rural and urban areas.[10] In Delhi, a survey of slum dwellers, many of them recent migrants from Bihar and Uttar Pradesh, the two enormous states to the east of Delhi, found that after paying for housing, the average family lived on slightly over $2 a day (at PPP).[11] This is much more than the bottom 30 percent in those two states, who live on less than $1 a day at PPP. Yet the rest of the very poor people (of whom there are about a hundred million) have not opted to move to Delhi and more than double their earnings.

It is not only in developing countries that people do not move to take advantage of better economic conditions. Fewer than 350,000 Greeks are estimated to have emigrated between 2010 and 2015, at the height of the economic crisis that shook their country.[12] This represents at most 3 percent of Greece's population, despite the fact that the unemployment rate was 27 percent in 2013 and 2014, and Greeks, as members of the EU, are able to work and move freely within Europe.

THE MIGRATION LOTTERY

But maybe there is no puzzle here; maybe we overestimate the benefits of migration. An important general problem in assessing the benefits of migration is that we usually only focus on the wages of those who chose to move, and not on the many reasons that made them do so, and the many things that made it possible for them to do so successfully. Those who migrate may have special skills or unusual stamina and would therefore earn more, even if they had stayed home. While migrants do many things that do not require particular skills, their jobs often involve hard, backbreaking work calling for great stamina and patience (think of construction or fruit picking, the jobs many migrants from Latin America do in the United States). Not everyone can do it day after day.

Therefore, one cannot naively compare the earnings of migrants with the earnings of those who remain in their home location and conclude, as many cheerleaders for more migration have, that the benefits of more migration must be enormous. This is what economists call an *identification problem*. To be able to claim a difference in wages is *caused* by the difference in the location and nothing else, we need to establish an exact connection between the cause and the effect.

One easy way to do this is to study visa lotteries. Winners and losers in a lottery tend to be identical in every way except for this one piece of luck, and therefore the difference in earnings resulting from winning the visa lottery cannot be due to anything other than the change of location it facilitates. Comparing winners and losers of the New Zealand visa lottery, for applicants from the tiny South Pacific island of Tonga (most of them quite poor), a study found that within one year of moving, winners more than trebled their income.[13] At the other end of the earnings spectrum, Indian software professionals who got to work in the United States because they won the visa lottery made six times more money than their peers who stayed in India.[14]

LAVA BOMBS

The problem with these numbers is also what makes them easy to interpret: they rely on comparisons among those who *applied* for visa lotteries. But those who don't apply may be very different. They may have little to gain from migrating, say, because they do not have the right skills. There are, however, some very revealing studies of people forced to move by an act of pure chance.

On January 23, 1973, there was a volcanic eruption in the Westman Islands, a prosperous fishing archipelago off the coast of Iceland. The Westman Islands' fifty-two hundred inhabitants were evacuated within four hours and only one person died, but the eruption lasted for five months, and lava destroyed about one-third of the houses on the islands. The houses destroyed were those on the eastern part (directly in the flow of the lava), plus some houses elsewhere that were hit by random "lava bombs." There is no way to build a house that resists lava, so destruction was entirely determined by location and bad luck. There seemed to be nothing out of the ordinary about the eastern neighborhood; destroyed houses had the same market value as nondestroyed houses, and their inhabitants were the same kinds of people. This is what social scientists call a *natural experiment*: nature has thrown the dice, and we can safely assume there was nothing different ex ante between those who had their houses destroyed and those who did not.

But there was an important difference afterward. Those whose houses were destroyed were given cash corresponding to the value of their houses and land, which they could use to rebuild or buy another house, or to move wherever they pleased. Forty-two percent of those whose houses were destroyed chose to move (and 27 percent of those whose houses were not destroyed moved anyway).[15] Iceland is a small but well-organized country, and using tax and other records it is possible to follow the long-term economic trajectories of all the original inhabitants of the Westman Islands. Impressively, exhaustive genetic data also allows matching to their parents every descendant of those caught in the eruption.

Using this data, researchers found that for anybody who was under twenty-five at the time of the eruption, losing a house led to *large economic gains*.[16] By 2014, those whose parental houses were destroyed earned over \$3,000 per year more than those whose parental houses were not destroyed, even though not all of them moved. The effect was concentrated on those who were young when it happened. This is partly because they were more likely to have attended college. It also seems that having to move made it more likely they found a job they were good at instead of just becoming fishermen, the one thing most people do in the Westman Islands. This would have been much easier for a young person who had not yet invested years in learning fishing. Still, people needed to be forced out (by the random munificence of the lava); those who kept their houses mostly remained, as many generations before them had, fishing and getting by.

An even more remarkable example of this kind of inertia comes from Finland in the years just following the Second World War. As a result of fighting on the losing German side in the war, Finland was forced to cede a substantial part of its territory to the Soviet Union. The entire population of that area, some 430,000 people, 11 percent of the nation's population, had to be evacuated and resettled in the rest of the country.[17]

Before the war, the displaced population was, if anything, less urbanized and less likely to have formal employment than the rest of Finland's people, but was otherwise very similar. Twenty-five years on, in spite of the bruises this hurried and chaotic exit must have left, the displaced population was richer than the rest, mainly because they were more likely to be mobile, urban, and formally employed. Being forced to move seemed to have loosened their moorings and made them more adventurous.

That it takes a disaster scenario or a war to motivate people to gravitate to a location with the highest wages shows economic incentives on their own are often not sufficient to get people to move.

DO THEY KNOW?

Of course, one possibility is that poorer people are simply unaware of the opportunity to improve their economic situation by moving. An interesting field experiment in Bangladesh makes it clear this is not the only reason they don't move.

There is no legal barrier to migration within Bangladesh. Yet, even during the lean season, commonly referred to as *monga* ("season of hunger") when there are very few opportunities to earn money in rural areas, few people migrate to the cities, which offer low-skill employment opportunities in construction and transportation; or even to neighboring rural areas that may have a different crop cycle. To understand why and to encourage seasonal migration, researchers decided to try out different ways of encouraging migration during monga in Rangpur in the north of Bangladesh.[18] Some villagers were randomly selected by a local nongovernmental organization (NGO) to either receive information about the benefits of migration (basically what the wages were like in the cities), or the same information plus $11.50 in cash or credit (this amount was roughly the cost of travel to the city and a couple of days of food), but only *if they migrated*.

The offer encouraged about a quarter (22 percent) of all households who would not have otherwise done so to send out a migrant. Most of those who migrated succeeded in finding employment. On average, those in the group who left earned about $105 during their migration, far more than they would had they stayed home. They sent or brought back $66 of that money to the families they left behind. As a result, the families who sent an extra migrant consumed on average an amazing 50 percent more calories; these families went from near starvation to a comfortable level of food consumption.

But why did the migrants need the extra push from the NGO to decide to make the trip? Why was near starvation not enough of an impetus?

In this case, it is very clear that information was not the binding constraint. When the NGO provided a randomly chosen group of people with information about the availability of jobs (but no incentive), the information alone had absolutely no effect. Moreover, among the people given the financial support who chose to make the trip, only around half went back during the next monga season, despite their personal experience of finding a job and making money. For these people, at least, it could not be skepticism about the job opportunities that held them back.

In other words, despite the fact that those who do migrate, forced or otherwise, gain economically, it is hard to take seriously the idea that most people are just waiting for an occasion to give up everything and head to a richer country. Given the size of the economic rewards, there are many fewer migrants than we would expect. Something else must hold them back—we will return to this puzzle later. Before we come to that, it is useful to understand how the labor market for migrants functions, and in particular whether the gains migrants make arise at the expense of the natives, as many seem to believe.

LIFT ALL THE BOATS?

This question has been the object of a vigorous debate in the economics profession, but overall the evidence seems to suggest even large bouts of in-migration have very little negative impact on the wages or employment prospects of the population the immigrants join.

The debate continues mainly because it is not usually easy to tell. Countries restrict migration, and in particular they are less likely to let people in when the economy is doing badly. Migrants also vote with their feet, and their natural tendency is to go where there are better options. For a combination of these two reasons, if you plotted the wages of nonmigrants in cities against the share of migrants in cities, you would find a nice upward-sloping line; the more migrants, the higher the wages. Good news for the pro-migration view, but perhaps entirely spurious.

To find out the real impact of immigration on the wages of the natives, we need to look for changes in migration that are not a direct response to the wages in that city. And even that may not be enough, because both current residents and firms also vote with their feet. It could be, for example, that the influx of migrants drives out so many native workers from the city that wages do not fall for those who stay behind. If we looked only at the wages of those natives who chose to stay in the cities where migrants settled, we would entirely miss the pain of those who decided to leave. It is also possible the new migrant population attracts firms into a city at the cost of other cities, and we could miss the cost to the workers in those other cities.

A clever attempt to get around some of these issues is David Card's study of the Mariel boatlift.[19] Between April and September of 1980,

125,000 Cubans, mostly with little or no education, arrived in Miami, after Fidel Castro unexpectedly gave a speech authorizing them to leave if they wished to. The reaction was immediate. The speech was delivered on April 20 and by the end of April people were already leaving. Many of the boatlifted settled permanently in Miami. The Miami labor force increased by 7 percent.

What happened to wages? To find out, Card took what has come to be called a "difference in differences" approach. He compared the evolution of wages and the rate of employment of prior residents in Miami, before and after the arrival of the migrants, to the same trajectory for residents in four other "similar" cities in the United States (Atlanta, Houston, Los Angeles, and Tampa). The idea was to see if the growth in wages and jobs for all those already in Miami when the Marielitos showed up fell behind the growth in wages and jobs of comparable residents in those four other cities.

Card found no difference, either immediately after the immigrants arrived or some years later; the wages of natives were not affected by the arrival of the Marielitos. That was also true when he specifically looked at the wages of Cuban immigrants who had come over before this episode, who were probably the most similar to the new wave of Cuban arrivals and hence the most likely to be adversely affected by a new influx of immigrants.

This study was an important step toward providing a robust answer to the question of the impact of migration. Miami was not chosen for its employment opportunities; it was just the closest landing point for the Cubans. The boatlift was unexpected, so workers and firms did not have a chance to react to it, at least in the short run (the workers by leaving, the firms by moving in). Card's study was very influential, both for its approach and for its conclusion. It was the first to show the supply-demand model might not directly apply to immigration.

No doubt as a result, the study was also extensively debated, with multiple rounds of rebuttals and counter-rebuttals. Perhaps no other single empirical study in economics has generated quite so much back and forth, and so much passion. A long-standing critic of the Mariel boatlift study is George Borjas, a vocal supporter of policies to shut out low-skilled migrants. Borjas reanalyzed the Mariel episode, including a larger set of cities for comparison and focusing specifically on non-Hispanic male high school dropouts, on the grounds they were the group we should be most concerned about.[20] In that sample, he found that wages started going down very steeply in Miami after the boatlift arrived, compared to what was happening in the comparison cities. But a subsequent reanalysis showed these new results once again get reversed when data about Hispanic high school dropouts (who would seem to be the most obvious people to compare Cuban migrants with, but are for some reason omitted by Borjas) and women (again omitted by Borjas for no clear reason) are included.[21] Moreover, studies continue to find no wage or employment effects when comparing Miami to a different set of cities where wages and employment were on very similar trends to Miami before the boatlift.[22] Borjas however remains unconvinced, and the debate over the Mariel boatlift continues.[23]

If you are not entirely sure of what to make of all this, you are not alone. To be blunt, it does not help that no one on either side ever changes their mind, and that opinions seem aligned with political views. Either way, it seems unreasonable to hang the future of migration policy on one episode that occurred thirty years ago in one city.

Fortunately, inspired by Card's work, a number of other scholars tried to identify similar episodes where migrants or refugees were sent to a place with little warning and no controls over where they should go. There is a study examining the repatriation to France of Algerians of European origin resulting from Algeria's independence from France in 1962.[24] Another study looked at the impact of massive immigration from the Soviet Union to Israel after the Soviet Union lifted the emigration restriction in 1990, which increased Israel's population by 12 percent in a space of four years.[25] Yet another looked at the impact of the large influx of European immigrants into the United States during the age of the great migration (1910–1930).[26] In all of these cases, the researchers found very little adverse impact on the local population. In fact, sometimes the impacts were positive. For example, the European migrants to the United States increased overall employment in the native population, made it more likely natives would become foremen or managers, and increased industrial production.

There is also similar evidence from the more recent influx of refugees from all over the world on the native population in Western Europe. One particularly intriguing study looks at Denmark.[27] Denmark is a remarkable country in many ways, and one of them is that it keeps detailed records of each member of its population. Historically, refugees used to be sent to different cities without regard for their preferences or their ability to find a job. All that mattered was the availability of public housing and the administrative capacity to help them settle down. Between 1994 and 1998, there was a large influx of immigrants from countries as diverse as Bosnia, Afghanistan, Somalia, Iraq, Iran, Vietnam, Sri Lanka, and Lebanon, and they ended up sprinkled, more or less randomly, across Denmark. When the policy of administrative placement was abandoned in 1998, migrants most often went where their co-ethnics were already located. Therefore, the places where the first group of migrants from, say, Iraq had landed more or less by pure chance are where the new Iraqi migrants headed. As a result, some places in Denmark ended up getting a lot more migrants than others, for no good reason other than at some time between 1994 and 1998, they had spare capacity for resettlement.

This study came to the same conclusion as the historical ones. Comparing the evolution of wages and employment of less-educated natives in cities subject to this chance influx of migrants to those in other cities, it found no evidence of negative impacts.

Each of these studies suggests low-skilled immigrants generally do not hurt the wages and employment of the natives. But the level of rhetorical fervor in the current political debate, never mind whether it is supported by the facts, makes it hard to see past the politics of the people involved in the debate. Where, then, is there a calm, methodical voice to be found? Readers interested in the delicate art of consensus building in the economics profession may want to peruse page 267 of the (free) report on the impact of immigration edited by the US National Academy of Sciences, the most respected body for academics in the country.[28] From time to time, the National Academy of Sciences convenes panels to summarize the scientific consensus on an issue. The panel for the immigration report had some fans of immigration and some immigration skeptics (including George Borjas). They had to make sure to cover the good, the bad, and the ugly, and their sentences often thread a long-winded path, but their conclusion is as close to unequivocal as you are ever going to get from a group of economists:

"Empirical research in recent decades suggests that findings remain by and large consistent with those in The New Americans National Research Council (1997) in that, when measured over a period of more than 10 years, the impact of immigration on the wages of natives overall is very small."

WHAT'S SO SPECIAL ABOUT IMMIGRANTS?

Why does the classic supply-demand theory (the more of something you have, the lower the price) not apply to immigration? It is important to get to the bottom of this question, because even if it is clearly true that low-skill wages are unaffected by immigration, unless we know *why*, we will always wonder if there was something special about these circumstances or the data.

There are a number of factors that turn out to be relevant, which the basic supply-demand framework sweeps under the rug. First, the influx of a new group of workers will typically shift the demand curve to the right, which will help undo the effect of the downward slope. The newcomers spend money: they go to restaurants, they get haircuts, they go shopping. This creates jobs, and mostly jobs for other low-skilled people. As illustrated in figure 2.2, this tends to increase their wages and perhaps thus compensate for the shift in the labor supply, leaving wages and unemployment unchanged.

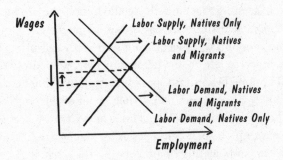

FIGURE 2.2 Napkin economics redux. Why more migrants do not always lead to lower wages.

In fact, there is evidence that if the demand channel is shut down, migration may indeed have the "expected" negative effect on natives. For a short period of time, Czech workers were allowed to work across the border in Germany. At its peak, in the border towns of Germany, up to 10 percent of the workforce was commuting from the Czech Republic. There was very little change in wages for natives when this happened, but there was a large drop in native employment because, unlike all the other episodes we discussed above, the Czechs went back home to spend their earnings. Therefore, the knock-on effects on labor demand in Germany did not happen. The immigrants may not produce growth for their new communities unless they spend their earnings there; if the money is repatriated, the economic benefits of immigration are lost to the host community.[29] We will then find ourselves back in the case of figure 2.1, where we are traveling the downward-sloping labor demand curve without a shift in labor demand to compensate.

A second reason why low-skilled migration might push up the demand for labor is that it slows down the process of mechanization. The promise of a reliable supply of low-wage workers makes it less attractive to adopt labor-saving technologies. In December 1964, Mexican immigrant farm laborers, the *braceros*, were kicked out of California, precisely on the grounds that they were depressing wages for native Californians. Their exit did nothing for the natives: wages and employment did not go up.[30] The reason is that as soon as the braceros were thrown out, farms in places that used to rely heavily on them did two things. First, they mechanized production. For example, for tomatoes, harvesting machines that could double the productivity per worker had existed since the 1950s, but adoption was very slow. In California, adoption rates went from near 0 percent in 1964, exactly when the braceros left, to 100 percent in 1967, while in Ohio, where there had been no braceros to speak of, adoption did not change at all during those years. Second, they switched out of the crops for which mechanization was not available. This is how California, at least temporarily, gave up on such delicacies as asparagus, fresh strawberries, lettuce, celery, and pickling cucumbers.

A third, closely related point is that employers may want to reorganize production to make effective use of the new workers, which can create new roles for the native low-skilled population. In the Danish case we discussed above, Danish low-skilled workers eventually benefited from the influx of migrants, in part because it enabled them to change their occupations.[31] Where there were more migrants around, more native low-skilled workers upgraded from manual to nonmanual jobs and changed employers. While doing so, they also shifted to jobs with more complex tasks and that required more communication and technical content; this is consistent with the fact that the immigrants hardly spoke Danish when they first arrived and could not be rivals for these jobs. The same kind of occupational upgrading also happened during the great European migration to the United States in the late nineteenth and early twentieth centuries.

More generally, what this suggests is that low-skilled natives and immigrants do not have to compete directly. They may perform different tasks, with immigrants specializing in tasks requiring less communication and natives in tasks that do. The availability of immigrants may actually encourage firms to hire more workers; the immigrants perform the simpler tasks, and the natives switch to complementary, more rewarding tasks.

Fourth, another way in which migrants complement rather than compete with native labor is they are willing to perform tasks natives are reluctant to carry out; they mow lawns, flip burgers, attend to the needs of babies or sick people. So when there are more migrants, the price of those services tends to go down, which helps the native workers and frees them to take on other jobs.[32] Highly skilled women, in particular, are more likely to be able to go out to work when there are many migrants around.[33] The entry of highly skilled women to the labor market in turn boosts demand for low-skilled labor (childcare, catering, cleaning) at home or in the firms they manage or run.

The effects of migrants will also crucially depend on who the migrants are. If the most enterprising move, they may start businesses that create jobs for the natives. If they are the least qualified, they might have to join the undifferentiated mass that native low-skilled workers will have to compete against.

Who migrates typically depends on the barriers migrants have to overcome. When President Trump compared the migrants from "shithole countries" to the good ones coming from Norway, he most probably did not know that a long time ago Norwegian immigrants were part of the "huddled masses" Emma Lazarus talked about.[34] There is actually a case study of Norwegian migrants to the United States during the age of mass migration, in the late nineteenth and early twentieth centuries.[35] At the time, there was nothing to stop migration, other than the price of passage. The study compared the families of migrants to the families where nobody migrated. It found migrants tended to come from among the poorest families; their fathers were substantially poorer than average. So, by one of the cute ironies historians (and economists) delight in, Norwegian migrants were exactly the kinds of people Trump would instinctively prefer to keep away. In his eyes, they would have been the "shithole people" of their day.

In contrast, those who migrate out of poor countries today need to have the money to afford the cost of travel and have the grit (or the advanced degrees) required to overcome a system of immigration control typically loaded against them. For this reason, a lot of them bring exceptional talents—skills, ambition, patience, and stamina—that help them become job creators, or raise children who will be job creators. A report by the Center for American Entrepreneurship found that, in 2017, out of the largest five hundred US companies by revenue (the Fortune 500 list), 43 percent were founded or co-founded by immigrants or the children of immigrants. Moreover, immigrant-founded firms account for 52 percent of the top twenty-five firms, 57 percent of the top thirty-five firms, and nine of the top thirteen most valuable brands.[36] Henry Ford was the son of an Irish immigrant. Steve Jobs's biological father was from Syria, Sergey Brin was born in Russia. Jeff Bezos takes his name from his stepfather, the Cuban immigrant Mike Bezos.

And even among those not so special to start with, the fact of being an immigrant, in a foreign location, without the social ties that make life richer but also impose limits on the single-minded pursuit of one's career, can liberate one to try something new and different. Abhijit knows of many middle-class Bengali men who, like him, had never washed their own dishes before leaving home. But, finding themselves short of money and long on time in some British or American town, they ended up bussing tables in a local restaurant and discovered they quite liked doing something more hands-on than the white-collar job they had imagined for themselves. Perhaps the reverse happened to the Icelandic would-be fishermen who, thrown into an unfamiliar place where many more people were going to college, decided it might not be such a bad idea after all.[37]

So one very big problem with the supply-demand analysis applied to immigration is that an influx of migrants increases the demand for labor at the same time it increases the supply of laborers. This is one reason why wages do not go down when there are more migrants. A deeper problem lies in the very nature of labor markets: supply-demand is just not a very good description of how they really work.

WORKERS AND WATERMELONS

Traveling around Dhaka, Delhi, or Dakar in the early morning, you will sometimes notice groups of people, mostly men, crouching on the sidewalks near important crossings. They are job seekers, waiting to be picked up by someone who needs them for work, often in construction.

For a social scientist, what is striking, however, is how rare these physical labor markets are. Given there are nearly twenty million people in the greater Delhi area, one might imagine every street corner would have such an assemblage. In fact, one has to look around to find them.

Signs advertising jobs are also relatively rare in Delhi or Dakar. There are lots of ads on websites and employment portals, but most of those jobs are well out of the reach of the average rural goatherd. By contrast, in Boston the subway is full of announcements for job opportunities, but the ads challenge prospective employees to solve some seemingly impossible riddle to prove their intelligence. They want workers but they don't want to make it too easy for them. This reflects something very fundamental about labor markets.

Hiring is different from buying, say, watermelons in a wholesale market, for at least two reasons. One is that the relationship with a worker lasts a lot longer than the purchase of a bag of watermelons; you can switch suppliers next week if you don't like the melon you got. But even where the laws don't make it difficult to fire a worker, firing is unpleasant at best, and potentially dangerous if the disgruntled employee becomes enraged. Therefore, most firms will not hire just anyone willing to work for them. They worry whether the worker will show up for work on time, whether the work will be up to snuff, whether they will fight with their colleagues, insult an important client, or break an expensive machine. Second, the quality of a worker is harder to judge than that of watermelons (which professional watermelon sellers are apparently very good at assessing[38]). Despite what Karl Marx had to say, labor is no ordinary commodity.[39]

Firms therefore need to put in some effort to know whom they are hiring. In the case of more highly paid workers, this means they spend time and money on interviews, tests, references, and so forth. This is costly both for the firms and the workers, and seems to be universal. In Ethiopia, a study found that just applying for a midlevel clerical job took several days and repeated journeys. Each application cost the would-be applicant a tenth of the monthly wage he would earn and had a very low probability of leading to a hire, one reason why few people applied.[40] For this reason, in the case of lower-paid workers, firms often skip the interview and rely on the recommendation of someone they trust. Relatively few firms hire those who just walk in and ask for a job, *even if they say they would accept a lower wage*. This of course flies in the face of the standard supply-demand framework. But it is too costly to be put in a position where the employer might want to get rid of a worker. In a striking example, researchers trying to find firms in Ethiopia willing to randomize whom they hired, approached over three hundred firms before they found *five* that were willing to join the experiment.[41] These were jobs where no specific skills were needed, but the firms still wanted to retain some control over whom they hired. Evidence from other studies in Ethiopia suggests 56 percent of firms insist on work experience even for blue-collar jobs,[42] and it is also common to ask for a referral from an employer.[43]

This has several important implications. First, established workers are much more secure from competition from newcomers than a pure supply-demand model would have us believe. Their current employer knows them and trusts them; incumbency is a huge advantage.

From the point of view of a migrant this is bad news. To make matters worse, there is a second implication. Think of what an employer can do to punish a worker who is not performing; at worst he can fire the employee. But firing will only be adequate punishment if the job pays enough for the worker to really want to keep it. As the future Nobel Prize–winner Joe Stiglitz pointed out many years ago, firms would not want to pay their workers the minimum the workers would accept, precisely to avoid being in the position captured by that old Soviet joke: "They pretend to pay us, we pretend to work."

This logic says that the wage the firm must pay to get workers to work typically has to be high enough that being fired actually hurts. This is what economists call the *efficiency wage*. As a result, the wage difference between what firms pay their established workers and what they would need to pay a newcomer may not be very large, because they cannot risk the consequences of paying a newcomer too little.[44]

This makes the incentive to employ a prospective migrant even weaker. Moreover, employers are also reluctant to have large differences in wages within their establishments, for fear of lowering morale. Evidence suggests that workers hate inequality within firms, even if the inequality is related to productivity, at least when the link between pay and productivity is not immediately obvious and transparent.[45] And unhappy workers do not make for a productive workplace. This contributes to why native workers are not quickly replaced by cheaper immigrants.

This discussion fits nicely with another finding from the Czech migration study mentioned before: job losses for natives were not actually losses; they were, rather, lower gains (compared to regions of Germany where Czechs did not go).[46] German firms did not replace their existing staff with Czech migrants. Those already employed in Germany still had the benefit of familiarity. What happened was that instead of hiring new native workers whom they did not know, German firms sometimes hired Czechs whom they also did not know.

The view that there is not much scope for migrants to get the jobs natives already hold, even by offering to do them for lower wages, also helps us understand why immigrants often end up in jobs natives do not want, or in cities no one wants to go to. There, they are not taking jobs from anyone; those jobs would remain unfilled if there were no migrants willing to take them.

THE SKILLED SET

So far we have been talking of the impact of unskilled migrants on natives. But even those who oppose unskilled migration are usually in favor of skilled migrants. Many of the arguments we made to explain why low-skilled migrants do not compete with low-skilled natives do not apply to skilled ones. For one, they are typically paid much more than the minimum wage. There may not be a need to pay them an efficiency wage because their jobs are exciting, and getting a chance to do them and doing them well would be its own reward. Therefore, there is paradoxically more scope for a skilled migrant to undercut the wages of the natives. Second, for skilled workers, the employer cares relatively more about the exact skill set of the person being hired than about the applicant's personality or reliability. Most hospitals hiring a nurse, for example, will focus primarily on whether the applicant meets the legal requirements for the job (in particular, whether they have taken and passed the nursing board exam). If a foreign-born nurse with the right certification is available for less, the hospital has little reason not to go for that nurse. Moreover, no one hires such workers without a series of interviews and tests, putting unknown workers on the same footing as familiar or connected ones.

Therefore, it is no surprise that in the United States one study finds that, for every skilled, qualified foreign nurse employed in a city, there are between one and two fewer native-born nurses.[47] In part this is because native-born students facing competition from nurses born and educated abroad are unwilling to sit for the nursing board exam in their states.

Therefore, despite widespread support for it, including from people like President Trump, the immigration of skilled workers is more of a mixed bag from the point of view of its impact on the domestic population. It helps low-skilled natives, who benefit from cheaper services (most doctors who serve the poorest corners of the United States are migrants from the developing world) at the cost of worsening the labor market prospects of the domestic population with similar skills (nurses, doctors, engineers, and college teachers).

WHAT CARAVAN?

The myths about immigration are crumbling. There is no evidence low-skilled migration to rich countries drives wage and employment down for the natives; nor are labor markets like fruit markets, and the laws of supply and demand do not apply. But the other reason immigration is so politically explosive is the idea that the numbers of would-be immigrants are overwhelming, that there is a flood of strangers, a horde of foreigners, a cacophony of alien languages and customs waiting to pour over our pristine monocultural borders.

Yet, as we saw, there is simply no evidence the hordes are waiting for a chance to descend on the shores of the United States (or the United Kingdom or France) and need to be kept out by force (or a wall). The fact is that unless there is a disaster pushing them out, most poor people prefer to stay home. They simply aren't knocking on our door; they prefer their own countries. They don't even necessarily want to move as far as their local capital city. People in rich countries find this so counterintuitive that they refuse to believe it, even when faced with the facts. What explains it?

WITHOUT CONNECTIONS

There are many reasons why people don't move. All the things that make it hard for new immigrants to compete with long-term residents for jobs also discourage them from moving. For one, as we saw, it is not easy for an immigrant to find a decent job. The one exception is where the employer is a relative or a friend, or a friend of a friend, or at least a co-ethnic: someone who either knows or at least understands the migrant. For that reason, migrants tend to head to places where they have connections; finding a job is easier and they have help to land on their feet in the city. Of course, there are all kinds of reasons why the employment prospects of migrants from the same location will be correlated over time; for example, if a village produces great plumbers, both recent and previous generations of migrants will be employed, and employed in plumbing. But the pull of kinship is stronger. Kaivan

Munshi, a professor at the University of Cambridge, and perhaps not coincidentally a member of the small and very tightly connected community of Zoroastrian Indians otherwise known as Parsis, demonstrated that Mexican migrants explicitly seek out people they might know.[48]

He observed that, regardless of opportunity in the United States, bad rains (disasters) have pushed people out of Mexico. When the rains failed in a particular village, a group of people left to seek other opportunities. Many of them ended up in the United States, with the result that a subsequent migrant from the same village would have connections in the US who were securely employed and able to help him or her find a job. Kaivan predicted that if one compares two villages in Mexico that have the same weather this year, *but one of them had a drought several years ago* (causing some villagers to emigrate) *while the other did not*, it will be easier for a resident of the village with the past drought to find a job (and also to find a better job) than for the resident of the village without the past drought. He expected to see more migrants, more employed migrants, and better-paid migrants. This is exactly what the data showed. Network connections matter.

The same applies to the resettlement of refugees; the ones most likely to find employment are those sent to a place with many older refugees from the same country.[49] Those older refugees usually do not know their new countrymen, but they still feel compelled to help.

Connections are obviously useful for those who have them, but what happens to those who don't? They will clearly be at a disadvantage. In fact, the presence of some people who come with recommendations can ruin the chances for everyone else. An employer used to workers coming with recommendations is likely to be suspicious of anyone without one. Knowing that, anyone who can get a recommendation would rather wait to get it (maybe some connection to a prospective employer will emerge; maybe a friend will start a business), and only those who know no one will ever recommend them (perhaps because they are actually not good workers) will go around knocking at doors to find a job. But then the employer would be right in refusing to talk to them.

The market in this situation is *unraveling*. In 1970, George Akerlof, another future Nobel laureate, but then just a fresh PhD, wrote a paper, "The Market for 'Lemons,'" in which he argued that the market for used cars might just shut down because people have an incentive to sell off their worst cars. That sets off the kind of self-confirming reasoning we saw in the case of newcomers to the labor market; the more suspicious buyers become of the old cars being sold, the less they will want to pay for them.[50] The problem is the less they want to pay, the more the owners of good used cars will want to hold on to them (or sell their cars to friends who know and trust them). Only those who know their car is about to collapse will want to sell on the open market. This process by which only the worst cars or the worst employees end up on the market is called *adverse selection*.[51]

Connections are supposed to help people, but the fact that some have access to them and others do not may actually shut down a market that would function just fine if no one had connections. The playing field is level if there are no connections. Once some people have connections, the market can unravel, with the consequence that most people become unemployable.

THE COMFORTS OF HOME

Abhijit once asked migrant respondents in Delhi slums what they liked about living in the city.[52] They liked many things; there were more options to give their children a good education, health care was better, finding a job was easier. The one thing they did not like was the environment. This is no surprise. Delhi has some of the vilest air in the world.[53] When asked about which problems in their living environment they wanted fixed first, 69 percent mentioned drains and sewers, and 54 percent complained about garbage removal. The combination of choked drains, absent sewers, and piled-up garbage are often what gives the slums in India (and elsewhere) their distinctive odor, somewhere between acrid and putrescent.

For obvious reasons, many slum dwellers hesitate to bring their families with them. Instead, when it all becomes unbearable, as it must fairly quickly, they go home. In rural Rajasthan, the typical villager who migrates from the village to earn money comes back once a month.[54] Only one out of ten migration episodes lasts more than three months. This means migrants tend to stay close to their home village, which probably limits the kinds of jobs they can get and the kinds of skills they acquire.

But why do they need to live in slums, or worse? Why don't they rent themselves something a bit better? Often, even if they can afford it, the option doesn't exist. In many developing countries, there are often several missing rungs in the quality ladder of housing. The next thing to a slum might be the nice little flat entirely out of reach.

There is a reason for this. Most third-world cities lack the infrastructure they need to serve their population. According to a recent report, India alone needs 4.5 trillion US dollars in infrastructure investment between 2016 and 2040, while Kenya needs 223 billion and Mexico 1.1 trillion.[55] This means the relatively small parts of most cities with decent-quality infrastructure are always hugely in demand and have astronomically high land prices. Some of the most expensive real estate in the world, for example, is in India. Starved of investment, the rest of the city develops in haphazard ways, with the poor often squatting on whatever land happens to be unoccupied, whether or not it has sewer connections or water pipes. Desperate for a place to live but worried they can be evicted any day because it's not their land, they build makeshift housing that sticks out like scars on the urban landscape. These are the famous third-world slums.

Making matters worse, as Ed Glaeser has argued in his wonderful book *Triumph of the City*, are city planners who resist building dense neighborhoods of high-rises for the middle class, aiming instead for a "garden city."[56] India, for example, imposes draconian limits on how high buildings can be, much stricter than what is found in Paris, New York, or Singapore. These restrictions result in massive urban sprawl and long commutes in most Indian cities. The same problem also shows up in China and many other countries, albeit in a less extreme form.[57]

For the would-be low-income migrant, this set of bad policy choices creates an unenviable trade-off. He can crowd into a slum (if he is lucky), commute many hours a day, or resign himself to the daily misery of sleeping under a bridge, on the floor of the building where he works, in his rickshaw or under his truck, or on the pavement, protected perhaps by the awning of a shop. If that is not discouraging enough, for reasons already discussed, low-skilled immigrants know that, at least to start out, the jobs they can get are the jobs nobody else wants. If you happen to be dropped somewhere without a choice you may take them on, but it is hard to get excited about abandoning friends and family and going to the end of the world to sleep under a bridge, clean floors, or bus tables. It is only the migrants with the ability to think past the immediate obstacles and pain, and contemplate a steady climb from busboy to restaurant chain owner, who typically take it on.

The attraction of home goes beyond creature comforts. Poor people often live very vulnerable lives. Their incomes tend to be volatile and their health precarious, making it very useful to be able to call on others for help when needed. The more connected you are, the less exposed you will be if something bad happens. You might have a network where you are going, but your network is probably deeper and stronger where you grew up. You (and your family) may lose access to that network if you leave. As a result, only the most desperate or the very well off who can afford the risk will leave.

Comfort and connections play the same limiting role for would-be international migrants, only much more so. If they leave, they must often leave alone, abandoning everything familiar or dear to them for many years to come.[58]

FAMILY TIES

The nature of life in traditional communities may be another important drag on migration. The Caribbean economist Arthur Lewis, one of the pioneers in the field of development economics and the 1979 Nobel laureate, made the following simple observation in a famous paper published in 1954.[59] Suppose jobs in the city pay $100 a week. In the village there are no jobs, but if you work on the family farm then you get your share of the farm income, which is $500 a week, but there are four of you, so each makes $125 a week. If you go, your brothers won't share with you. Why would you go, especially if the hours are the same and the work is equally unpleasant? Lewis's insight was that this argument stands whether or not you are needed on the farm. Suppose the output on the farm would be the same $500 whether or not you worked there, but you could add $100 to the family's total kitty by going off to the city. You won't do it because it does not help you; you will end up with your $100 and your three brothers will get to share the farm's $500. Of course, today it may not be a farm; a family taxi business would be just as likely to keep you at home.

What Lewis was pointing out is that everyone in the family would be better off if, for example, they could promise you $50 from the farm for being away, so that your total take is $150, and your three brothers can each enjoy $150 as well. But maybe they cannot; maybe such promises are easily forgotten. Once you are gone, maybe they will deny you were ever part of the family business. So you stay on to enforce your claim. And as a result, Lewis thought, the speed of integration of the rural workforce into the more productive urban sector, be it domestically or abroad, will be too slow. There is too little migration in Lewis's scenario.

The more general point here is that network connections, of which the family is a specific example, are designed to solve specific problems, but it does not mean they promote the general social good. It turns out, for example, that parents who worry about being abandoned in old age may strategically underinvest in the education of their children to make sure they do not have the option of moving to the city. In the state of Haryana, not too far from Delhi, researchers teamed up with firms recruiting for back-office processing jobs to provide information about these opportunities to villagers.[60] The jobs required two things: moving to the city and a high school education. For girls, the parental response to the advertising campaigns was unambiguously beneficial; compared to girls in villages that did not get the information campaign, girls in campaign villages were better educated, married later, and perhaps, more remarkably, were better fed and taller.[61] For boys, however, there was no increase in education on average; boys expected to leave the village to earn money benefitted from the intervention, much like the girls, but boys whose parents wanted them to stay home and take care of them ended up getting *less* education. The parents, in effect, chose to handicap their sons to keep them at home.

SLEEPLESS IN KATHMANDU

In the experiment where villagers were offered $11.50 to go and explore the job market in one of the big cities of Bangladesh, many participants ended up so much better off that they should have been happy to pay out of pocket to get the opportunity.[62] However, there were still a few who would have ended up worse off if they'd had to pay for the trip themselves: the ones who did not find a job and went back empty handed. Most people do not like risk, and those close to subsistence level especially so, since any loss could push them into starvation. Is that why so many people prefer not to try?

The problem with this explanation is that another option for potential migrants would be to save up $11.50 before making the trip. Then if they failed to find a job they could go home, and they would be no worse off than if they had not saved and not tried, which is what most of them seem to do. Moreover, the evidence suggests they do save for other things, and $11.50 is very much within their range. So why don't they? One possible reason is they overestimate the risks. A study from Nepal highlights this.

Today, more than a fifth of Nepal's male working-age population has been abroad at least once, mostly for work. Most of them work in Malaysia, Qatar, Saudi Arabia, or the United Arab Emirates. They typically go for a couple of years, with an employment contract tied to a specific employer.

This is a setting where one might imagine the migrants would be very well informed about the potential costs and benefits of migrating, since one needs a job offer to get a visa. Yet the Nepalese government officials we met expressed concerns the migrants did not know what they were getting into. They had inflated expectations about earnings, the officials told us, and had no idea how bad living conditions could be abroad. Maheshwor Shrestha, a Nepalese PhD student of ours, decided to investigate whether these officials were right.[63] He placed himself with a small team in the passport office in Kathmandu, where potential migrants went to apply for their passports. He interviewed more than three thousand of these workers, asking them detailed questions about what they thought they would be paid, where they were going, and what they thought of the living conditions abroad.

Maheshwor found these would-be migrants were in fact somewhat overoptimistic about their earnings prospects. Specifically, they overestimated their earning potential by around 25 percent, which could be for any number of reasons, including the possibility that the recruiters who provide job offers lied to them. But the really big mistake they made was that they vastly overestimated the chance of dying while they were abroad. A typical candidate for migration thought that out of a thousand migrants, over a two-year stint, about ten would come back in a box. The reality is just 1.3.

Maheshwor then gave some of the potential Nepali migrants information about the true wage rate or the actual risk of dying (or both). Comparing the migration decisions of those he informed that of to those he did not (just because his random procedure did not pick them), he found strong evidence the information was useful. Those provided information on wages lowered their expectations, while those provided information about mortality revised their estimates downward as well. Moreover, they acted on what they had learned; when he checked on them several weeks later, those who received the wage information were more likely to be still in Nepal. Those provided with information on mortality, on the other hand, were more likely to have left. Moreover, because the extent of misinformation about mortality was so much more severe than the misinformation about wages, those who got both pieces of information were more likely to have gone. Therefore, on average, contrary to what the Nepalese government believed, misinformation was keeping the migrants home.

Why did people systematically overestimate the risk of dying? Maheshwor offers an answer, showing that a single death of someone from a particular district (a small area) in Nepal significantly reduces migration flows from that district to the country where the death happened.[64] Clearly, potential migrants pay attention to local information. The problem seems to be that when the media reports deaths from a particular region, it does not simultaneously report the number of migrant workers from that region. So the workers have no idea of whether it was one death out of a hundred or a thousand, and in the absence of this information, they tend to overreact.

If people don't have the right information in Nepal, with its many employment agencies, vast flows of workers in and out, and a government genuinely concerned about the welfare of its international migrants, one can only guess at how confused most potential migrants are elsewhere. Confusion could of course go either way, dampening migration, like in Nepal, or boosting it if people are overoptimistic. Why then is there a systematic bias against going?

RISK VERSUS UNCERTAINTY

Perhaps the exaggerated sense of mortality Maheshwor's respondents reported should be read as a metaphor for a general sense of foreboding. Migration, after all, is leaving the familiar to embrace the unknown, and the unknown is more than just a list of different potential outcomes with associated probabilities, as economists would like to describe it. In fact, there is a long tradition in economics, going back at least to Frank Knight, of distinguishing between quantifiable risk (50 percent probability this happens, 50 percent that happens) and the rest, what Donald Rumsfeld memorably called the "unknown unknowns,"[65] and Knightian economists call *uncertainty*.[66]

Frank Knight was convinced humans react very differently to risk and uncertainty. Most people don't like dealing with the unknown unknowns, and will go to great lengths to avoid making decisions in cases where they do not know the exact contours of the problem.

From the point of view of the would-be migrants in rural Bangladesh, the city (and of course any foreign country) is a morass of uncertainties. In addition to not knowing how the market will value their particular sets of skills, they also need to worry about where to find potential employers, whether they face competition for their services or exploitation at the hands of a single employer, the kinds of references they will need, how long it will take to find a job, how they will survive until then, where they will live, and so on. They have little or no experience to guide them; the probabilities have to be made up. It is therefore not surprising that many potential migrants tend to hesitate.

THROUGH A GLASS DARKLY

Migration is a plunge into the unknown, which may make people particularly reluctant to undertake it, even if they could in principle save up to cover the various financial contingencies involved. It is uncertain rather than risky. Additionally, there is good evidence that people particularly hate mistakes of their own making. The world is fraught with uncertainties, many of which people have no control over. These vagaries make them unhappy, but perhaps not as unhappy as making an active choice that ends up, purely as a result of bad luck, making them worse off than if they had done nothing. The status quo, the outcome of letting things be, serves as a natural benchmark. Any loss relative to that benchmark is particularly painful. This concept was named *loss aversion* by Daniel Kahneman and Amos Tversky, two psychologists who have been incredibly influential in economics. (Kahneman won the Nobel Prize in economics in 2002 and Tversky would probably have as well, but for his untimely demise.)

Since their original work, a vast literature has demonstrated the existence of loss aversion and its ability to explain many apparently strange behaviors. For example, most people pay a huge premium on their home insurance plans to get a low deductible.[67] This allows them to avoid that painful moment when, after some accident has damaged their house, they have to pay a large sum out of pocket (the high deductible). By comparison, the fact that they may be paying a lot extra now (to get the policy with the low deductible) is painless because they will never discover if it was a mistake. The same logic also explains why gullible buyers often end up with outrageously expensive "extended warranties." In essence, loss aversion makes us extremely worried about any risk, even small, that is a consequence of our active choice. Migration, unless everyone else is doing it, is one of these active choices, and a big one; it is easy to imagine many will be chary of trying.

Finally, failure in migration is something people take personally. They have heard too many success stories, admiringly told, to not feel that failure would reveal something about them to themselves, if not to the world. In 1952, Esther's grandfather, Albert Granjon, a veterinarian running a slaughterhouse in Le Mans, France, took his wife and four young children to Argentina, then a journey of several weeks

by boat. He was inspired by a desire for adventure, and had the somewhat vague plan of forming a partnership for raising cattle with some
acquaintances. That plan collapsed less than a year after the family's
arrival. The conditions on the farm were harder than he had thought
and he fought with his business partners, who complained he had not
brought enough money to fund the venture. The young family found
itself in the middle of nowhere in a country they did not know, with no
income. Returning to France would have been relatively easy at that
point. In the booming postwar years, Esther's grandfather could have
easily found a job. He had two solidly middle-class brothers who could
have paid for the return voyage. But he chose not to. His wife, Eve-
lynne, told Esther many years later that coming back empty handed,
having begged his brothers for the price of the passage, was an unac-
ceptable loss of face. So the family toughed it out, living for over two
years in dire poverty, made worse by a misplaced sense of superiority
vis-à-vis the natives. The children were not allowed to speak Spanish at home. Violaine, Esther's mother, completed her entire schooling
through a French correspondence course—she never went to school
in Argentina—and spent her spare time doing chores, fixing holes in
the cloth sandals the children wore. The family's financial situation
improved only when Albert finally got a job running an experimental
farm for Institut Mérieux, a French pharmaceutical company. They
would stay in Argentina for over ten years before going on to Peru,
Colombia, and Senegal. Albert went back to France after his health
deteriorated (though he was still quite young), but by then his career
trajectory could plausibly be described as a successful adventure. Still,
the hardscrabble life surely had taken a toll, and he died shortly after
his return.

The fear of failure is a substantial disincentive for embarking on
a risky adventure. Many people prefer not to try. After all, most of
us want to protect an image of ourselves as intelligent, hard-working,
morally upright individuals, both because it is simply not pleasant to
admit we might in fact be dumb, lazy, and unscrupulous, but also because maintaining a good opinion of ourselves preserves our motivation to keep trying in the face of whatever life throws at us.

And if it is important to hold on to a certain self-image, then it also
makes sense to burnish it. We do this actively by filtering out negative

information. Another option is to simply avoid taking actions that have at least some chance of rebounding badly on us. If I cross the road to avoid passing by a beggar, I won't have to reveal to myself that I lack generosity. A good student may fail to study for an exam in order to have a ready-made excuse that will preserve his perception of being intelligent, should he not do well. A would-be migrant who stays home can always maintain the fiction he would have succeeded had he gone.[68]

It takes an ability to dream (Albert, Esther's grandfather, was seeking adventure rather than escaping from a bad situation), or a substantial dose of overconfidence, to overcome this tendency to persist with the status quo. This is perhaps why migrants, at least those not pushed out by desperation, tend to be not the richest or the most educated, but those who have some special drive, which is why we find so many successful entrepreneurs among them.

AFTER TOCQUEVILLE

Americans are supposed to be the exception to this rule. Most of them are willing to take risks and move toward opportunity, or at least that has always been the myth. Alexis de Tocqueville was a nineteenth-century French aristocrat who saw America as a model of what a free society could be. For him, restlessness was one of the things that made America special: people moved all the time, both across sectors and across occupations. Tocqueville attributed this restlessness to the combination of a lack of hereditary class structure and a constant desire to accumulate.[69] Everyone had a shot at striking it rich, and therefore it was their responsibility to follow the opportunities wherever they might be.

Americans still believe in this American dream, though as a point of fact, heredity plays a *greater* role in the fortunes of today's Americans than it does in Europe.[70] And that may have something to do with America's declining restlessness. For at the same time as they were becoming less tolerant of international migration, Americans became less mobile themselves. In the 1950s, 7 percent of the population used to move to another county every year. Fewer than 4 percent did in

2018. The decline started in 1990 and accelerated in the mid-2000s.[71] Furthermore, there is a striking change in the pattern of internal migration.[72] Until the mid-1980s, rich states in the US had much faster population-growth rates. Sometime after 1990, this relation disappeared; on average, rich states no longer attract more people. High-skilled workers continue to move from poor states to rich states, but now low-skilled workers, to the extent they still move, seem to be moving in the opposite direction. These two trends mean that since the 1990s, the US labor market has become increasingly segregated by skill level. The coasts attract more and more educated workers, while the less well educated seem to concentrate inland, particularly in the old industrial cities in the east like Detroit, Cleveland, and Pittsburgh. This has contributed to the divergence in earnings, lifestyles, and voting patterns in the country and a sense of dislocation, with some regions left behind as others pull ahead.

The pull of Palo Alto, California, or Cambridge, Massachusetts, for highly educated software or biotech workers is not surprising. Wages are higher for educated workers in those cities, and they are more likely to find friends and the amenities they enjoy.[73]

But why don't less-well-educated workers follow them? After all, lawyers need gardeners, cooks, and baristas. The concentration of educated workers should create a demand for uneducated workers and encourage them to move. And this is the United States where, unlike in Bangladesh, almost everyone can afford the bus fare across the state, or even across the country. The information is much better and everyone knows where the boomtowns are.

Part of the answer is that the wage gain from being in a booming city is lower for workers with only a high school degree than for high-skilled workers.[74] But this can only be a part of the reason. There is a wage premium for low-skilled workers too. According to websites that post salaries online, a Starbucks barista makes about $12 an hour in Boston and $9 in Boise.[75] This is less than the gains for high-skilled workers, but still not negligible (and, in addition, in Boston they get to have an attitude).

However, precisely because there is such demand from the growing numbers of high-skilled workers, housing costs have exploded in Palo

Alto and Cambridge and other similar places. A lawyer and a janitor would both earn much more in New York than in the Deep South, although the difference between the wages in New York and in the Deep South would be higher for the lawyer (45 percent) than for the janitor (32 percent). But housing costs are only 21 percent of a lawyer's wages in New York, while they are 52 percent of a janitor's. As a result, the real wage after subtracting the cost of living is indeed much higher for the lawyer in New York than in the Deep South (37 percent), but the opposite is true for the janitor (he would make 6 percent more in the Deep South). It makes no sense for a janitor to move to New York.[76]

The Mission District in San Francisco has become a symbol of this phenomenon. Until the late 1990s, the Mission District was a working-class neighborhood dominated by recent Hispanic immigrants, but its location made it attractive to the young workers of the tech industry. Average rents for one-bedroom apartments have been going up steeply, from $1,900 in 2011 to $2,675 in 2013 and $3,250 in 2014.[77] Today, the average rent of an apartment in the Mission District puts it entirely out of reach for someone earning minimum wage.[78] The "Mission yuppie eradication project," a last-ditch effort to drive tech workers away by vandalizing their cars, drew considerable attention to the gentrification of the Mission District, but ultimately was doomed.[79]

Of course, more houses can be built near booming cities, but it takes time. Moreover, many of the older cities in the United States have zoning regulations designed to make it hard to build up or build densely. Buildings cannot be very different from what exists, property lots have to be a minimum size, and so on. This makes it harder to transition to high-density neighborhoods when housing demand goes up. As in the developing world, this presents the new migrant with a rather dire set of choices: live far away from work or pay through the nose.[80]

Recent growth in the United States has been concentrated in locations with strong educational institutions. These places also tend to be the older cities with expensive and hard-to-expand stocks of real estate. Many are also more "European" cities, which tend to have stronger incentives to preserve their historical endowment against the forces of development, and hence have restrictive zoning regulations and high rents. This might be one reason why the average American is not moving to where the growth is happening.

If a worker loses his job because his region is hit by an economic downturn, and he contemplates moving to get a job elsewhere, the real estate question gets even more complicated. As long as he has his house, even if its resale value may be very low, at least he can live in it. If he doesn't own the house, it is still true that he will benefit more from the fall in rents resulting from the meltdown in the local economy than a high-skilled worker, since housing is a larger part of his budget.[81] The collapse of the local housing market that typically accompanies a downturn therefore tends to, perversely, keep the poor from going other places.

There are other reasons to stay put even if opportunities are scarce at home and better elsewhere; childcare, for one, is expensive in the United States, due to a combination of strict regulations and lack of public subsidies. For someone with a low-wage job, buying childcare at market price is often out of the question; the only recourse is grandparents or, failing that, other relatives or friends. And unless you can get them to come with you, moving is out of the question. This was less of an issue when most women did not work and could provide the childcare, but in today's world it can be a clincher.

Moreover, the job may not last. Job loss leads to eviction, and then it is hard to get another job if you don't have an address.[82] In such times, family also provides a safety net, both financial and emotional; unemployed young people move back to their parents' house. Among unemployed men in their prime working age, 67 percent live with their parents or a close relative (up from about 46 percent in 2000).[83] It is easy to understand why one might be reluctant to leave that comfort and security behind and move to a different city.

For people who just lost a job in, say, manufacturing after spending most of their career working in their hometown for a single employer, all this is compounded by the trauma of having to start over again. Instead of going from comfortable employment to graceful retirement as many of their fathers did, they are being asked to reset their expectations, move to a town where no one knows them, and start at the bottom of the ladder in a job they never imagined they would have to do. No wonder they'd rather stay put.

THE COMEBACK CITIES TOUR

If it is hard for people to move from distressed areas, why aren't jobs coming to them? Surely firms could take advantage of the newly available labor force, lower wages, and lower rents in the counties where other firms have closed. This idea has been floated. In December 2017, Steven Case, the billionaire co-founder of AOL, and J. D. Vance, the author of *Hillbilly Elegy,* a lament for America's lost heartland, started the investment fund Rise of the Rest. It was funded by some of the best-known billionaires in America (from Jeff Bezos to Eric Schmidt), to invest in states traditionally overlooked by tech investors. A bus tour (the Comeback Cities Tour) took a group of Silicon Valley investors to places like Youngstown and Akron, Ohio; Detroit and Flint, Michigan; and South Bend, Indiana. The fund promoters were quick to point out this was not a social impact fund, but a traditional money-making venture. In the *New York Times*, when reporting on the trip[84] and the fund itself,[85] many Silicon Valley investors emphasized the congestion, the insularity, the high cost of living in the Bay Area, and the great opportunities in the "heartland."

But for all the chatter, there were reasons to be skeptical. The size of the fund was only $150 million—pocket money for people in this group. Bezos backed the venture, but not enough to put Detroit on the shortlist of possible headquarters for Amazon's HQ2. The hope clearly was to create some excitement, to get some enterprise started, and to start some buzz around the early investors to encourage others. It worked for Harlem, so why not for Akron? Except that Harlem is in land-scarce Manhattan, with all its excitement and its many amenities. The Harlem revival was bound to happen one day. We are less optimistic about Akron (or South Bend or Detroit). It is difficult for those places to provide the kinds of alluring amenities most young affluent people look for these days: nice restaurants, glitzy bars, and cafes where they can buy overpriced espressos from high-minded baristas. In other words, there is a chicken and egg problem: young educated workers will not come unless these amenities exist, but the amenities cannot thrive unless there are enough workers like them around.

In fact, firms in almost every industry tend to be clustered. Suppose you threw darts at random on a map of the United States. You'd find the holes left by the darts to be more or less evenly distributed across the map. But the real map of any given industry looks nothing like that; it looks more as if someone had thrown all the darts in the same place.[86] This is probably in part because of reputation; buyers may be suspicious of a software firm in the middle of the cornfields. It would also be hard to recruit workers if every time you needed a new employee you had to persuade someone to move across the country, rather than just poach one from your neighbor. There are also regulatory reasons: zoning laws often try to concentrate dirty industries in one place, and restaurants and bars in another. Finally, people in the same industry often have similar preferences (techies like coffee, financiers show off with expensive bottles of wine). Concentration makes it easier to provide the amenities they like.

Clustering, for all these reasons, makes sense, but it means it is that much harder to start small and grow. Being the one biotech firm in Appalachia is always going to be hard. We hope the Comeback Cities Tour succeeds, but we are not holding our breath (or buying real estate in Detroit).

EISENHOWER AND STALIN

The real migration crisis is not that there is too much international migration. Most of the time, migration comes at no economic cost to the native population, and it delivers some clear benefits to the migrants. The real problem is that people are often unable or unwilling to move, within and outside their country of birth, to take advantage of economic opportunities. Does that suggest that a forward-looking government should reward people who move and perhaps even penalize those who refuse to?

This might sound outlandish, given that the current conversation is mostly focused on how to limit migration, but in the 1950s the governments of the United States, Canada, China, South Africa, and the

Soviet Union were all heavily involved in more or less forced relocation policies. Those policies often had unstated but brutal political goals (suppression of troublesome ethnic groups being one), but they tended to be cloaked in the language of modernization, which emphasized the economic deficiencies of traditional economic arrangements. The modernization agenda in developing countries has often taken inspiration from these examples.

There is also a long tradition in developing countries of governments using price and tax policies to benefit the urban sector at the cost of the rural. Many countries in Africa in the 1970s created what they called agricultural marketing boards. This was a cruel joke, since many of the boards were intended to *prevent* the marketing of produce so the board could buy it at the lowest prices, thereby stabilizing prices for city dwellers. Other countries, like India and China, banned exports of farm products to keep prices where urban consumers wanted them. A by-product of these policies was to make agriculture unprofitable, encouraging people to leave their farms. Of course, these policies hurt the poorest people in the economy, the small farmers and the landless laborers, who may not have had the wherewithal to move.

This unfortunate history should not, however, blind us to the economic rationale for promoting migration. Mobility (internal and international) is a key channel through which standards of living can even out across regions and countries, and regional economic ups and downs can be absorbed. If workers move, they will take advantage of new opportunities and leave regions hit by economic adversity. This is how an economy can absorb crises and adapt to structural transformation.

For those of us (including most economists) who already live in the richer countries and the most successful cities, it seems so obvious that we have it so much better where we are that we assume everyone else would want to come. For economists, the economic magnetism of successful places is largely a good thing. For city dwellers in developing countries or the residents of rich countries, on the other hand, the assumption that the whole world will be drawn to their areas is a scary prospect. They imagine masses of people coming and fighting them for the scarce resources they have, from jobs to spots in public housing to parking spaces. That central concern, that migrants lower wages and employment prospects for natives, is misplaced, but the fear of overcrowding, especially in the half-built cities of the third world, is not entirely unwarranted.

The fear of being overwhelmed is also what gives rise to worries about assimilation. If too many people with a different culture come (from country cousins moving within India to Mexicans settling in the United States), will they assimilate or will they change the culture? Or, for that matter, will they assimilate so well that their culture will vanish, leaving us all with a uniform globalized tasteless blend? A utopia of perfect and instant movement in response to any difference in economic opportunities might become its own dystopia.

But we are nowhere near such a utopia/dystopia. Far from being irrepressibly attracted by economically successful places, people struggling where they are often prefer to stay home.

This suggests that encouraging migration, both internal and external, should indeed be a policy priority, but that the right way to do it should be not by forcing people or distorting economic incentives, as has been done in the past, but by removing some of the key obstacles.

Streamlining the whole process and communicating it more effectively, so workers have a much better understanding of the costs and rewards of migration, would help. Making it easier for migrants and their households to send money back and forth to each other would also help by making migrants less isolated. Given the outsized fear of failure, offering migrants some insurance against failure would be a possibility. When this was offered in Bangladesh, the effects were almost as large as the effect of offering a bus ticket.[87]

But the best way to help (and therefore perhaps encourage) migrants while making locals more accepting is probably to ease their integration. Offering housing assistance (rent subsidies?), pre-migration matching to a job, help with childcare arrangements, and so on would ensure that any newcomer quickly finds a place in society. This applies both to internal and international mobility. It would make those who hesitate more likely to make the trip and allow them to become more quickly a part of the normal existing fabric of the host communities. We are almost in the opposite situation now. With the exception of the work done by some organizations to help refugees, nothing is really done to make it easy for someone to adjust. International migrants face a real obstacle course to get the right to work legally. Internal migrants have no place to stay and often struggle to land their first job, even when there seem to be many opportunities.

Of course, we cannot forget that the politics of the response to migration is not just one of misunderstood economics, but also one of identity politics. There is nothing new in the disconnect between economics and politics. US cities that received the most European migrants in the golden age of European migration benefited economically from them. But despite that, immigrants triggered widespread and hostile political reactions. Cities cut taxes and public spending in response to immigration. Within public spending, the cuts were particularly deep for services that made interethnic contact more likely (like schools) or those that helped low-income immigrants (such as sewerage, garbage collection, etc.). In cities that got the most migrants, the vote share of the Democratic Party, which supported immigration, declined and more conservative politicians, in particular those who supported the National Origins Act of 1924 (which put an end to the era of unrestricted immigration to the US) were elected. Voters were reacting to the cultural distance between them and the new migrants; at the time Catholics and Jews were considered irremediably alien, until of course they assimilated.[88]

The fact that history repeats itself does not make it less unpleasant the second or third time around. But perhaps it helps us understand better how to react to this anger. We will return to this question in chapter 4.

Ultimately, we also need to remember that many people, regardless of any incentives on offer, will choose not to move. This immobility, which runs against every economist's instinct of how people should behave, has profound implications for the entire economy. It affects the consequences of a wide range of economic policies, as we will see throughout this book. We will see in the next chapter, for example, that it partially explains why international trade has been much less beneficial than many hoped, and in chapter 5 we will discuss how it affects economic growth. This requires a rethinking of social policy that takes this immobility into account, something we will attempt in chapter 9.

CHAPTER 3

THE PAINS FROM TRADE

I N EARLY MARCH 2018, President Trump signed new tariffs on steel and aluminum, surrounded by steelworkers in their hard hats. Shortly after, the IGM Booth panel, which we talked about in the introduction, asked its roster of experts, all senior economics professors at top economics departments, Republicans and Democrats, whether "imposing new US tariffs on steel and aluminum will improve Americans' welfare." Sixty-five percent "strongly" disagreed with the statement. All the others merely "disagreed." No one agreed. No one was even unsure.[1] When asked the additional question of whether "adding new or higher import duties on products such as air conditioners, cars, and cookies (to encourage producers to make them in the US) would be a good idea," once again all of them agreed it would not be.[2] Paul Krugman, the standard-bearer of liberal economics, likes trade but so does Greg Mankiw, a Harvard professor who headed the Council of Economic Advisors under President George W. Bush and a frequent critic of Krugman's views.

In contrast, in the United States the general public opinion about trade is mixed at best, and more often than not these days, negative. On the steel and aluminum tariffs, opinions were split. In a survey conducted during the fall of 2018 where we asked a representative sample of Americans exactly the same question as in the IGM Booth panel, only 37 percent of people either disagreed or strongly disagreed with Trump's proposal to increase tariffs. Thirty-three percent agreed.[3] But, more generally, the sentiment seems to be, both on the right and on the left, that the United States is too open to goods from other countries. Fifty-four percent of our respondents agreed that using higher tariffs to encourage producers to produce in the US would be a good idea. Only 25 percent disagreed.

Economists mostly talk about the gains of trade. The idea that free trade is beneficial is one of the oldest propositions in modern economics. As the English stockbroker and member of Parliament David Ricardo explained two centuries ago, since trade allows each country to specialize in what it does best, total income ought to go up everywhere when there is trade, and as a result the gains to winners from trade must exceed the losses to losers. The last two hundred years have given us a chance to refine this theory, but it is a rare economist who fails to be compelled by its essential logic. Indeed, it is so rooted in our culture that we sometimes forget the case for free trade is by no means self-evident.

For one, the general public is certainly not convinced. They are not blind to the gains of trade, but they also see the pains. They do see the advantages of being able to buy cheap abroad, but worry that, at least for the direct victims of cheaper imports, the gains are swamped by the costs. In our survey, 42 percent of respondents thought low-skilled workers are hurt when the United States trades with China (21 percent thought they are helped), and only 30 percent thought everyone is helped by the fall in prices (27 percent said they thought everyone was hurt).[4]

So is the public simply ignorant, or might it have intuited something the economists have missed?

STAN ULAM'S CHALLENGE

Stanislas Ulam was a Polish mathematician and physicist, one of the co-inventors of modern thermonuclear weapons. He had a low opinion of economics, perhaps because he underestimated economists' capacity to blow up the world, albeit in their own way. Ulam challenged Paul Samuelson, our late colleague and one of the great names in twentieth-century economics, to "name me one proposition in all of the social sciences which is both true and non-trivial."[5] Samuelson came back with the idea of comparative advantage, the central idea in trade theory. "That this idea is logically true need not be argued before a mathematician; that it is not trivial is attested by the thousands of important and intelligent men who have never been able to grasp the doctrine for themselves or to believe it after it was explained to them."[6]

Comparative advantage is the idea that countries should do what they are *relatively* best at doing. To understand how powerful the concept it, it is useful to contrast it to *absolute advantage*. Absolute advantage is simple. Grapes don't grow in Scotland, and France does not have the peaty soil ideal for making scotch. Therefore, it makes sense that France should export wine to Scotland, and Scotland should export whisky to France. Where it gets confusing is when one country, like China today, looks like it's pretty much better at producing everything than most other countries. Wouldn't China simply swamp all markets with its products, leaving other countries with nothing to show for themselves?

David Ricardo argued in 1817 that even if China (or in his era, Portugal) was more productive at everything, it could not possibly sell everything, because then the buyer country would sell nothing and would have no money to buy anything from China or anywhere else.[7] This implied that not all industries in nineteenth-century England would shrink if there was free trade. It was then evident that if any industries in England were to shrink because of international trade, it should be the least productive ones.

Based on this argument, Ricardo concluded that even if Portugal was more productive than England at producing *both wine and cloth,* once trade between them opened up, they would nonetheless end up specializing in the product for which they had a *comparative advantage* (meaning where their productivity was high *relative to their productivity in the other sector:* wine for Portugal, cloth for England). And the fact that both countries make the goods they are relatively good at making and buy the rest (instead of wasting resources producing a product ineptly) must add to the gross national product (GNP), the total value of goods people in each country can consume.

Ricardo's insight underlines why there is no way to think of trade without thinking about all the markets together. China could win in *any single* market and yet there is no way for it to win in *every* market.

Of course, the fact that GNP goes up (both in England and in Portugal) does not mean there are no losers. In fact, one of Paul Samuelson's most famous papers purports to tell us exactly who the losers are. Ricardo's entire discussion assumed production required only labor, and all workers were identical, so when the economy became richer everyone benefitted. Once there is capital as well as labor, things are not that simple. In a paper published in 1941, when he was just twenty-five, Samuelson set out the ideas that remain the basis of how we are taught to think about international trade.[8] The logic, once you understand it, as is often the case with the best insights, is compellingly simple.

Some goods require relatively more labor than others to produce and relatively less capital; think of handmade carpets versus robot-made cars. If two countries have access to the same technologies of production for both goods, it should be obvious the country relatively abundant in labor will have comparative advantage in producing the labor-intensive product.

We would therefore expect a labor-rich country to specialize in labor-intensive products and move out of capital-intensive ones. This should raise the demand for labor compared to when there was no trade (or more restricted trade), and therefore wages. And, conversely, in a relatively capital-abundant country, we should expect instead that the price of capital goes up (and wages go down) when it trades with a more labor-abundant partner.

Since labor-abundant countries tend to be poor, and laborers are usually poorer than their employers, this implies freeing trade should help the poor in the poorer countries, and inequality should fall. The opposite would be true in rich countries. So opening trade between the United States and China *should* hurt US workers' wages (and benefit Chinese workers).

That does not mean the workers in the United States must necessarily end up worse off. This is because, as Samuelson showed in a later paper, the fact that free trade raises GNP means there is more to go around for everybody, and therefore even workers in the United States can be made better off *if society taxes the winners from free trade and distributes that money to the losers*.[9] The problem is that this is a big "if," which leaves workers at the mercy of the political process.

BEAUTY IS TRUTH, TRUTH BEAUTY[10]

The Stolper-Samuelson theorem (as this result is now widely known in economics, after Samuelson and his co-author, Stolper) is beautiful, at least as much as any theoretical result in economics is beautiful. But is it true? The theory has two clear and encouraging implications, and one that is less encouraging. Opening up to trade should increase GNP in all countries, and in poor countries inequality should go down; however, in rich countries, inequality can go up (at least before any redistribution the government might undertake). The slight problem is that the evidence more often than not refuses to cooperate.

China and India are often portrayed as the poster children for trade-fueled growth in GNP. China opened up its markets to trade in 1978, after thirty years of communism. For most of those thirty years, China barely acknowledged the world market. Forty years later, it is the world's exporting powerhouse, about to seize the position of the world's biggest economy from the United States.

India's story is less dramatic, but perhaps a better example. For about forty years, until 1991, its government controlled what it called the "commanding heights of the economy." Imports required licenses that were at best grudgingly granted and in addition required the importer to pay import duties that could *quadruple* the price of the imports.

Among the things essentially impossible to import were cars. Foreign visitors to India would write about the "cute" Ambassador, a barely updated replica of the 1956 model of the Morris Oxford, a British sedan of no particular distinction, that was still the most popular car on Indian roads. Seat belts and crumple zones were entirely unknown. Abhijit can still remember his one ride in a 1936 Mercedes-Benz (this must have been in 1975 or thereabouts), and the sense of exhilaration from being in a car with a genuinely powerful engine.

Nineteen ninety-one was the year after Saddam Hussein's invasion of Kuwait that eventually led to the First Gulf War. This resulted in the interruption of oil flows out of Iraq and the Gulf, and sent oil prices through the ceiling. It delivered a huge shock to India's oil import bill. Coming at the same time as the war-driven exodus of Indian émigrés from the Middle East, who therefore ceased sending money to their loved ones at home, the country experienced a massive foreign exchange shortage.

India was forced to seek help from the International Monetary Fund (IMF), an opportunity the IMF was waiting for. China, the USSR, Eastern Europe, Mexico, and Brazil, among others, had begun to take serious steps toward letting markets decide who should produce what. India at the time was the last of the big holdouts, an economy that continued to adhere to the anti-market ideology fashionable in the 1940s and 1950s.

The deal the IMF offered would change all that. India could have the funds it needed, but only if it opened its economy to trade. The government had no choice. The import and export licensing regime was abolished, and import duties came down very quickly from an average of nearly 90 percent to something closer to 35 percent, in part because many of the leading figures in the economic ministries had long desired a chance to do something like this, and they were not going to let the opportunity pass.[11]

There were, unsurprisingly, many who predicted this would lead to disaster. Indian industry, raised behind high tariff walls, was too inefficient to compete with the rest of the world's powerhouses. The Indian consumer, starved of imports, would go on a binge and bankrupt the economy. And so on.

Remarkably, the dog hardly barked. After a sharp drop in 1991, by 1992 GDP growth was back at its 1985–1990 trend of about 5.9 percent per year.[12] The economy did not collapse, nor did it dramatically take off. Overall, during the period 1992–2004, growth inched up to 6 percent and then jumped to 7.5 percent in the mid-2000s, where it has remained, more or less, ever since.

So should India be counted as a shining example of the wisdom of trade theory, or something closer to the opposite? On the one hand, that growth weathered the transition smoothly, echoing the predictions of trade optimists. On the other hand, that growth took more than a decade to accelerate after 1991 seems disappointing.[13]

WHEREOF ONE CANNOT SPEAK, THEREOF ONE MUST BE SILENT[14]

This particular debate has no real resolution. There is only one India with its one history. How would anyone know whether pre-1991 growth would have continued had there been no crisis and the trade barriers not been brought down in 1991? To complicate matters, trade was being liberalized gradually starting in the 1980s; 1991 just sped that up (a lot). Was the big bang necessary? We will never know unless we are allowed to rewind history and let it go down the other path.

Unsurprisingly, however, economists find it very hard to let go of this sort of question. The issue is less about India per se. There is no way around the fact that there was a large shift in Indian growth, at some point in the 1980s or 1990s, associated with the move from socialism (of sorts) to capitalism. The growth rate before the mid-1980s was around 4 percent. Now it is closer to 8 percent.[15] Such changes are rare and what is especially rare is that the change seems to have been sustained.

At the same time, inequality increased dramatically.[16] Something very similar, if perhaps even more dramatic, happened in China in 1979, in Korea in the early 1960s, and in Vietnam in the 1990s. It is clear that the kind of extreme state control these economies operated under before liberalization was very effective at keeping inequality down, but at a high cost in terms of growth.

Where there is much more disagreement, and therefore more scope for learning, is about the best way to run an economy once a nation gives up extreme government control. How important is it to get rid of the remaining tariff protections India holds on to, which are significant barriers to trade, but nothing like what there was before? Will that further speed up growth? What will happen to inequality? Will the Trump tariffs derail growth entirely in the United States? And will they actually help the people he is purportedly trying to protect?

To answer such questions economists often compare countries. The basic idea is simple: some countries (like India) liberalized trade in 1991 but others more or less like them did not. Which groups grew faster in the years immediately after 1991, in absolute terms or perhaps relative to their pre-1991 growth rates? Those who liberalized, those who had always been open, or those who stayed closed all along?

There is a voluminous literature on this question, perhaps not surprisingly given the importance of free trade among economists and its popularity in the business press. The answers run the gamut from very positive assessments of the effect of trade on GDP to much more skeptical positions, though it must be said that there is little or no evidence for strongly negative effects.

The skepticism comes from three distinct sources. First, reverse causality. The fact that India liberalized trade, whereas another similar country did not, might reflect that India was ready for the transition, and would have grown faster than its comparator *even without the change in trade policy*. In other words, was it growth (or the potential for growth) that caused trade liberalization, and not the other way around?

Second, omitted causal factors. Liberalization in India was part of a much bigger set of changes. Among them was the fact that the government essentially stopped trying to tell business owners what they should produce and where. There was also a more nebulous but perhaps equally important shift in the attitude of the bureaucracy and the political system toward the business sector: the idea that business was a legitimate pursuit of honest people, something that could even be "cool." It is essentially impossible to separate the effects of all these changes from that of trade liberalization.

Third, it is hard to know what in the data constitutes trade liberalization. When the tariffs are 350 percent, there are no imports, so cutting them quite a bit might change very little. How do we distinguish relevant policy changes from irrelevant posturing? Moreover, such sky-high taxes invited defiance; people found creative ways to get around them. In response, the governments would often set up arcane rules to trap violators. A lot of these things changed when the country liberalized, but different bits changed at different speeds in different countries. How do we decide which country liberalized more, given that different countries chose different reforms?

All these are issues that make cross-country comparisons particularly fraught. The reason why different researchers get different answers about the effect of trade policy on growth has a lot to do with the different choices they make on each of these issues—how to measure changes in trade policy and which of the many possible sources of confusion about causality one is willing to tolerate.

For this reason, it is very hard to have a lot of faith in the results. There are always going to be a million ways to do cross-country comparisons, depending on exactly which brave assumption one is willing to swallow.

The same constraints get in the way of being able to test the other prediction of the Stolper-Samuelson theory. Does inequality fall in poorer countries when they open up to trade? There are relatively few cross-country studies on this subject, reflecting a pattern we will see again and again. Trade economists have tended to stay away from thinking about how the pie is shared, despite (or perhaps because?) Samuelson's early warning that, in rich countries at least, trade could come at the expense of the workers.

There are exceptions, but not ones that inspire confidence. A recent research report by two members of the IMF's staff finds that countries that are close to many other countries, and as a result trade more, tend to be both richer and more equal. They ignore the inconvenient fact that Europe is where there are many small countries that trade a lot with each other, and those countries tend to be both richer and more equal, but probably not primarily because they trade a lot.[17]

One other reason to be skeptical of this rather optimistic conclusion is that it flies in the face of what we know from a number of individual developing countries. In the last three decades, many low- to middle-income countries have opened up to trade. Strikingly, what happened to their income distribution in the following years has almost always gone in the opposite direction of what the basic Stolper-Samuelson logic would suggest. The wages of the low-skilled workers, who are abundant in these countries (and should therefore have been helped), fell behind relative to those of their higher-skilled or better-educated counterparts.

Between 1985 and 2000, Mexico, Colombia, Brazil, India, Argentina, and Chile all opened up to trade by unilaterally cutting their tariffs across the board. Over the same time period, inequality increased in all those countries, and the timing of these increases seems to connect them to the trade liberalization episodes. For example, between

1985 and 1987, Mexico massively reduced both the coverage of its import quota regime and the average duty on imports. Between 1987 and 1990, blue-collar workers lost 15 percent of their wages, while their white-collar counterparts gained in the same proportion. Other measures of inequality followed suit.[18]

The same pattern, liberalization followed by an increase in the earnings of skilled workers relative to the unskilled, as well as other measures of inequality, was found in Colombia, Brazil, Argentina, and India. Finally, inequality exploded in China as it gradually opened up starting in the 1980s and eventually joined the World Trade Organization (WTO) in 2001. According to the World Inequality Database team, in 1978 the bottom 50 percent and the top 10 percent of the population both took home the same share of Chinese income (27 percent). The two shares starting diverging in 1978, with the poorest 50 percent taking less and less and the richest 10 percent taking more and more. By 2015, the top 10 percent received 41 percent of Chinese income, while the bottom 50 percent received 15 percent.[19]

Of course, correlation is not causation. Perhaps globalization per se did not cause the increase in inequality. Trade liberalizations almost never take place in a vacuum; in all these countries, trade reforms were part of a broader reform package. For example, the most drastic trade policy liberalization in Colombia in 1990 and 1991 coincided with changes in labor market regulation meant to substantially increase labor market flexibility. Mexico's 1985 trade reform took place amid privatization, labor market reform, and deregulation.

As we mentioned, India's 1991 trade reform was accompanied by the removal of the industrial licensing regime, capital market reforms, and a general shift of power and influence to the private sector. China's trade liberalization was of course the capstone of the massive economic reform undertaken by Deng Xiaoping, which legitimized private enterprise in an economy where it had been almost forbidden for thirty years.

It is also true that Mexico and other Latin American countries opened up exactly at the time when China was also opening up, and therefore they all faced competition from a more labor-abundant economy. Perhaps that was what hurt the workers in these economies.

Showing anything definitive about trade by just comparing countries is difficult, because both growth and inequality could depend on so many different factors, trade being just one of those ingredients, or indeed an effect rather than a cause. There have, however, been some fascinating within-country studies that do throw a shadow over the Stolper-Samuelson theorem.

THE FACT THAT COULD NOT BE

Looking at different regions within countries clearly reduces the number of potential things going on at the same time that might obscure the effects of trade; there is usually a single policy regime, a shared history, and common politics, making the comparisons more convincing. The problem is that the central predictions of trade theory, by their very nature, encompass every market and region in the economy, and not just the ones where imports come in or exports take off.

In the Stolper-Samuelson view of the world, there is one unique wage for every worker with the same skills. A worker's wage does not depend on his sector or region, but only on what he brings to the table. This is because the steelworker in Pennsylvania who loses his job because of foreign competition should move immediately to wherever he can find a job, to Montana or to Missouri, to plating fish or making fisher-plates. After brief transitions, all workers with the same skills will earn the same.

If this were true, then the only legitimate object of comparison for learning about the impact of trade would be the entire economy. We would not learn anything by comparing workers in Pennsylvania with workers in Missouri or Montana because they would all have the same wage.

Rather paradoxically, therefore, if one believes the assumptions of the theory, it is almost impossible to test it, since the only impact one observes is what happens at the country level, and we just demonstrated the many pitfalls of cross-country comparisons and country case studies.

However, as we saw with migration, labor markets tend to be *sticky*. People do not move even when labor market conditions would suggest they ought to, and as a result wages are not automatically equalized across the economy. There are in effect many economies inside the same country and it is possible to learn a lot by comparing them, as long as the changes in trade policy affecting these subeconomies are not all the same.

One young economist, Petia Topalova, who was a PhD student at MIT at the time, decided to take this idea seriously, and to start from the premise that people may be stuck, both in a place and in a line of trade. In an important paper, she studied what happened in India after the massive trade liberalization of 1991.[20] It turned out that even though we think of "India liberalizing," there were very different changes in trade policy that affected different parts of the country. This is because, even though eventually all the tariffs were brought down to more or less the same level, since some industries were much more protected than others to start with, there were much bigger *reductions* in tariffs for some industries. Moreover, India has over six hundred districts that differ enormously in the kinds of businesses they are home to. Some are mainly agricultural; others have steel plants or textile factories. Since different industries fared differently, the liberalization led to very different reductions in tariffs in different districts. Topalova constructed, for each Indian district, a measure of how much it was affected by liberalization. For example, if one district mainly produced steel and other industrial manufacturing products, whose tariff dropped from almost 100 percent to about 40 percent, she would say this district was strongly affected by liberalization. If another district just grew cereals and oilseeds, whose tariff essentially did not change, it was almost unaffected.

Using this measure of exposure, she looked at what happened before and after 1991. The national poverty rate dropped rapidly in the 1990s and 2000s, from about 35 percent in 1991 to 15 percent in 2012.[21] But, against this rosy backdrop, greater exposure to trade liberalization clearly slowed poverty reduction. Contrary to what the Stolper-Samuelson theory would tell us, the more exposed a particular district was to trade, the *slower* poverty reduction was in that district. In a subsequent study, Topalova found that the incidence of child labor dropped *less* in districts more exposed to trade than in the rest of the country.[22]

The reaction to her findings in the economics profession was surprisingly brutal. Topalova ran into a barrage of very unfriendly comments suggesting she had the wrong answer, even if her methods were correct. How could trade actually increase poverty? The theory tells us trade is good for the poor in poor countries, so her data had to be wrong. Despite eventually getting offers to join very good economics departments, Topalova took a job at the IMF, which, somewhat paradoxically given the IMF had pushed for the massive liberalization in the first place, was more open-minded about her research than the academic community.

Topalova also chose not to submit her pathbreaking paper to the top economic academic journals despite the fact that it eventually inspired a literature dedicated to the debate. There are now many papers applying Topalova's approach in other contexts and, incidentally, finding the same results in Colombia, Brazil, and, as we will see below, eventually the United States.[23] It was only several years later that she got some measure of vindication from academic economists when her findings won the Best Paper Award from the journal in which the paper had been published.

THE STICKY ECONOMY

Topalova had always insisted she had no intention of claiming anyone had been hurt by the trade liberalization. Since she was comparing regions within the same country, all she could say was that some areas (those most affected by trade) were less successful in reducing poverty than others. This is entirely consistent with the possibility, which her paper is careful to underline, that the tide of liberalization had lifted all boats, just some more than others. And her work does not imply that inequality increased in India as a whole, just that it went up more in the more trade affected districts. In fact, because the places most touched by liberalization tended to be somewhat richer to start with, the fact that they did not fare particularly well after liberalization, paradoxically, reduced countrywide inequality. In other papers, Topalova and her colleagues demonstrated some clearly positive economy-wide consequences of the Indian trade liberalization. For example, Indian firms, challenged to find new markets, started introducing new products they could now sell abroad. Moreover, the fact that they could import cheaper and better inputs, indeed ones they could not even find in India before, meant they could make new products for the domestic and international markets.[24] This increased their productivity and, along with other reforms undertaken by the government in the early 1990s (and some luck with worldwide growth), contributed to the rapid growth of the Indian economy since the 1990s.

Nevertheless, it is easy to see why trade economists felt threatened by Topalova's paper. The benefits of trade in traditional theory come from the reallocation of resources. The very fact that Topalova finds any difference between more exposed and less exposed districts tells us resources (workers, but also capital) do not move easily, as we noted earlier. If they did, wages everywhere would have been more or less the same. And she is not the only one to find this; a number of other studies also found very little evidence of resource reallocation.[25] But once we give up on the idea that people and money will chase opportunities, how do we hold on to our faith that trade is good?

If workers are slow to move across district boundaries, it is plausible they are also slow to move from one kind of job to another. This is entirely consistent with what we know about labor markets. In India, Topalova found the negative effect of trade liberalization on poverty was exacerbated in states where strict labor laws made it very difficult to fire workers and shrink unprofitable firms, allowing profitable ones to take their place.[26]

There is also a body of solid evidence showing that, at least in developing countries, land does not easily change hands. Capital also tends to be sticky.[27] Bankers are slow to cut credit to firms that are not doing well, but also to lend to those firms that are doing well, for the interesting reason that many credit officers, the people who make lending decisions, are terrified of being held responsible for loans that go bad. The easiest way to avoid this is to make no decision; just rubber-stamp whatever decision has been made in the past, by someone else, and let yet another person deal with the loans in the future. The one exception, unfortunately, is when loans are about to fail—then bankers actually give the ailing firms new loans to pay back their old ones, in the hope of postponing the default and perhaps benefitting from a reversal of fortune. This is the phenomenon, in banking parlance, of "evergreening" loans, one of the main reasons why so many banks with seemingly impeccable balance sheets suddenly wake up to a looming disaster. Sticky lending means existing firms that should have been put out of their misery continue to hang on. At the same time, it also means new businesses have a hard time raising capital, especially in the middle of the uncertainty that comes with, say, a trade liberalization, because the loan officers shy away from taking on new risks.

Given these various forms of stickiness, it is plausible that when bad news arrives in the form of greater competition from outside, instead of embracing it and moving resources to their best possible use, there is a tendency to hunker down and hope the problem will go away on its own. Workers are laid off, retiring workers are not replaced, and wages start to drift down. Business owners take a big hit on their profits, loans get renegotiated, all in order to preserve as much as possible of the status quo ex ante. There is no improvement in efficiency, just a fall in the earnings of everyone associated with the industries that lose their protection.

This might seem extreme, but Topalova finds something like this in the Indian data. For one, there was very little migration out of the districts affected by liberalization.[28] Even within a region, resources were slow to move among industries.

More strikingly still, this was true *within* firms. Many firms in India produce more than one product, so one would expect firms to close down product lines competing with cheaper imports and reorient production toward products facing less of a disadvantage. There is nothing to stop this even where labor laws make it hard to fire people, but Topalova's research found very little "creative destruction." Firms never seem to discontinue a product line that has become obsolete. Perhaps it is because the managers find the transition process costly: workers need to be retrained, new machines need to be purchased and installed.[29]

PROTECTION FOR WHOM?

These internal barriers notwithstanding, resources did eventually move (at least in some countries) and exports are a big part of the remarkable success stories of East Asia in particular. Despite what you hear from President Trump and others, it was not because rich countries were naively welcoming. Rich countries heavily regulate imports, which have to meet strict safety, labor quality, and environmental standards.

It has been argued that regulations often serve to keep imports out. California avocado producers successfully lobbied for a complete federal ban on Mexico Hass avocados from 1914 until 1997. This was on the grounds of keeping Mexican pests out, despite the facts that Mexico is territorially adjacent and that pests do not require visas to cross the border. In 1997, the federal ban was lifted but remained in effect in California until 2007. More recently, researchers found that during the 2008 crisis in the United States, the Food and Drug Administration suddenly became more likely to refuse, on food-safety grounds, shipments of imported foods coming from developing countries; for exporters from developing countries, the cost associated with shipments being refused quadrupled during the period! Obviously, the quality of shipments from Mexico could not have changed because of the subprime crisis in the United States, but because demand for avocados went down, it became all the more valuable to keep them out to protect local growers.[30] Domestic pressures for protection mount during bad times and safety regulations are often used as an excuse to protect the domestic producers.

That said, some of these standards also reflect genuine consumer preferences for safety (e.g., some Chinese toys have been found to contain lead), the protection of the environment (e.g., pesticide use in agricultural products), or the condition of workers (e.g., child labor). Indeed, the success of the Fairtrade branding shows that many consumers are willing to pay more to intermediaries who can assure them that a product meets some environmental and ethical standards. And, partly inspired by this, many well-known brand names these days impose quality standards over and above any regulatory requirements, making it even harder for new exporting countries to enter.

WHAT'S IN A NAME?

There is something else quite specific about developing countries trying to be the next China that adds to all these challenges.

The World Trade Organization established an Aid for Trade initiative in 2006, and as of mid-2017, over \$300 billion had been disbursed for various programs to help developing countries trade.[31] Behind all such initiatives and funding is the belief that trade is a route out of poverty for these countries. A project from Aid to Artisans (ATA), a US-based NGO helping producers of handmade products in developing countries to access international markets, allowed researchers to put that assumption to the test.[32]

In October 2009, ATA received funding to implement a new program in Egypt. The program followed a standard procedure. First, ATA looked for a suitable product that appealed to high-income markets and was produced in the country relatively cheaply. The research team helped ATA identify the ideal product: carpets. Handmade rugs are an important source of employment in Egypt, and there is demand for them in the US.

Second, ATA had to find a location. They chose Fowa, a town located two hours southeast of Alexandria that is home to hundreds of small firms producing a specific type of rug. A typical firm in Fowa is a one-man (never woman!) operation; the owner operates a single loom out of his home or a shed.

Third, ATA always works through a local intermediary firm with on-the-ground knowledge, which receives the order and finds small-scale producers to manufacture the products. The hope is that ATA will work in the country for some years but then pull out, leaving the intermediary strong enough to keep the project going and growing. A big appeal of the town of Fowa, from this point of view, was the presence of a natural intermediary, Hamis Carpets. Hamis was already marketing many of the carpets produced in the town, although for the most part they were not exported.

Hamis Carpets and ATA then set out to decide what kind of carpets to make, find the buyers, and generate orders. That took a lot of effort. ATA brought the CEO of Hamis to the United States for a training course, hired an Italian consultant to design rug samples, and showcased Hamis's products in every gift fair and to every importer they knew. Despite all this, it was only after one and a half years of searching for customers that Hamis Carpets secured its first significant export order, from a German buyer.

From this point on, business picked up. Between 2012 and 2014, orders arrived rapidly, and five years after the project had started total orders exceeded $150,000. A US NGO with good contacts and financing, a fearless team of very committed and talented young researchers, and a solid firm with a good domestic reputation took five years to get a decent amount of orders, enough to give sufficient work to occupy thirty-five small firms. Without the external push from ATA, it probably would not have been possible for the local intermediary to make this work.

Why was it so difficult? A large part of the problem seems to be that from the point of view of a foreign buyer (often a large retailer or online store with a brand name), buying from a small carpet manufacturer in Egypt is a gamble. For them quality is critical. Customers expect it; they want flawless carpets. So is timing. If the carpets are not ready for the launch of the new spring collection, the sellers take a big hit. Finally, there is no way to pass the entire risk back to the manufacturer. While it is possible to refuse to pay the manufacturers if quality is low or there is a delay, what the retailer can claw back by returning carpets or refusing to pay is peanuts relative to the reputational loss (think of irate buyers' web posts about the low quality of products from Wayfair) or the cost of missing the spring collection deadline. In principle, firms can also agree on penal damages (the manufacturer agrees to pay a certain large amount of money for every day of delay, say), but good luck collecting from a small-town Egyptian firm that could vanish overnight. Nor is it feasible for the retailer to check every single carpet to avoid any reputational risk; it would cost way too much in staff time.

Another possibility might be to offer the products so cheaply that consumers were willing to accept the risk of some defects, knowing they could always send the carpet back. Why stake reputation on delivering a product as close to perfection as possible? Why not lower expectations along with prices?

It turns out this does not always work, because in many cases the price cannot go low enough for consumers to waste their time with a product they don't trust. We once purchased a DVD player in Paris. When it came, we realized the flap through which one puts in the DVD was stuck. After about an hour spent trying to make it work, and another hour looking for technical help on the manufacturer's site, we went online to chat with a nice Amazon employee who offered a full refund. To get the refund we had to drop the DVD player off at a grocery store near us.

The first time Abhijit went to the grocery store, the shop owner refused to take the player because they had too many Amazon shipments. The second time, the owner made him wait twenty-five minutes before taking the package, because he was getting another consignment of packages at the same time that he needed to log. In the meantime, we bought another DVD player from a different retailer (we were in a rush since we wanted it for our daughter's birthday). Unfortunately, when it came we realized it would not work with the television in our apartment. We attempted to return it through the product's website, but since the purchase had not yet been logged as completed, it was not possible until a few days later. At the time of writing, the second DVD player sits, nicely repacked but unreturned, on the table in our entryway. Meanwhile, we gave up on buying a DVD player. Esther's father lent us one.

Why this long story about our misadventures with a DVD player? It drives the point home that for the ultimate consumer, time is money, as is reliability, and it's money we will never recover. It is not like Amazon will pay Abhijit his hourly wage for his two trips to the grocery store or the two hours spent trying to fix the machine.

Or think about the pretty T-shirt you bought cheap on some website, which infected the entire wash with its brilliant blue color. Who will compensate you for the $100 blouse that now has blue stains across the front? Or for the time it took you to find that blouse by rummaging through every consignment store in the Village?

This is why Amazon goes to great trouble to maintain its reputation for excellent service. In some cases, for example, they protect the customer's time by not requiring they return the defective product. For the same reason, Amazon then wants to deal with a producer it can totally trust, ideally a company they have dealt with before, or at least one with a reputation for good products and good service. For both customer and retailer, time is money.

The structure of global inequality is such that the kind of customers in the West who would buy a handmade carpet or a hand-printed T-shirt (labor-intensive products for whose manufacture poor countries have a comparative advantage) are often so much richer than the makers that any savings from a new entrant offering cheaper prices will be insufficient to compensate the customer for their lost time or the ruin of a favorite blouse.

Take the example of an Egyptian manufacturer trying to compete with China on T-shirts. Average monthly wages in China are $915, while those in Egypt are about $183.[33] Assuming a work-week of forty hours, the hourly wage in China is about $5 an hour, while in Egypt it is $1. So the saving in labor cost to hand print a T-shirt that takes an hour to make (a very, very nice T-shirt) in Egypt rather than in China is at most $4. In fact, it is probably much less since T-shirt makers tend to pay a lot less than the average wage. As buyers, many of us would happily pay the extra $4 for the peace of mind its quality assures. Amazon knows that. Why would it pay to experiment with the unknown guy in Egypt when it has a known and reliable supplier in China?

In the case of the Egyptian carpets, an intermediary (in fact, two: ATA and Hamis Carpets) was needed because it was impossible for each individual carpet weaver to build a reputation. They were just too small. Hamis at least had the volume needed to establish a track record of identifying good producers and monitoring their work effectively, and thereby establishing a reputation for quality. It was also in a position to teach them to improve their quality: the exporting firms improved quality very quickly and were soon much better technically than similar firms that had lost the lottery for being included in the study. But since no one outside Egypt knew Hamis, it is no surprise that hardly anyone initially wanted to deal with it or give it a chance to build a reputation.

Making matters worse, when Hamis finally got the chance to export, it had the reverse problem to deal with. A foreign buyer might also be tempted to misbehave: to not pay for an order or change their mind on what they wanted. Hamis had to be the trusted intermediary on both sides. For example, one buyer had asked the carpets be given an antique look by bathing them in tea and sprinkling them with acid. Unfortunately, when they received the carpets, they hated the result and blamed the manufacturer.

In such cases, Hamis was caught between a rock and a hard place. It could try to push back against the buyer, but there was never going to be adequate documentation of all the back-and-forth before the order was filled ("Yes, there was an email, but remember what we said on the phone"). So Hamis would be put into a he said–she said situation where, being a new player and from Egypt to boot, it was unlikely matters would turn out well. On the other hand, the manufacturers in Egypt felt they had done what they were asked to do and would be very upset if they did not get paid. They could not afford not to be. In the end, Hamis often had to absorb the losses.

We first encountered the pain of establishing a reputation in the nascent Indian software industry in the late 1990s. Software in India initially developed around the southern city of Bangalore, then a sleepy town known for its pleasant climate (and now a sprawling metropolis with impossible traffic). Indian firms specialized in customized products for specific clients. If a company wanted a new accounting software, they could get a standard one customized for them, or they could get one built from scratch by an Indian firm.

India had several clear advantages in this sector: a supply of graduates from engineering colleges well known for their excellence, good internet access, English as a first language, and a different time zone, which allowed software engineers to work on different shifts from their American clients. The infrastructure needs were minimal: an office, a small team, a few computers. In Bangalore, this was made even easier by the establishment, as early as 1978, of Electronic City, an industrial park reserved for firms in what would later be called the infotech sector, which came with an assured supply of electricity and reliable communication lines.

All this made it relatively easy for anybody with the right diploma and a willingness to work hard to hang up their shingle and establish themselves as a software firm. But surviving in the industry was not easy.

In the winter of 1997–1998, we asked the CEOs of over a hundred Indian software firms about their experiences with their most recent two projects. For CEOs of young firms, life was unglamorous and hard. A client would specify what they wanted, the firm would try their best to build it, but the client would often claim it was not exactly what they had requested. The CEOs almost always felt the client had changed their mind, but the client typically took the view that the firm had not understood the requirements. In any case, for the most part disagreeing was futile, since the deal with young firms almost always involved a contract where they got paid a fixed amount irrespective of the amount of work done, and only when the buyer was satisfied.

We suspect the choice of this type of contract reflected the buyer's sense that it was taking a risk by contracting with an unknown supplier in faraway India. Consistent with this interpretation, as firms matured and presumably became better known, we saw a switch from fixed-price contracts to cost-plus contracts, where the buyer paid for whatever time and materials it cost the seller to produce the software.[34] Our story also explains why the relatively few cases where a young firm got a cost-plus contract tended to be when the firm had already done a project for the client and therefore had established a reputation.

One of the young CEOs we met was exhausted. He felt he was working night and day on uninteresting projects (and their endless adjustments) just to stay afloat. He had recently taken up a Y2K project, which meant hunting through thousands of lines of code to eliminate dates written in the form "1/1/99" rather than in the form "1/1/1999." There were dire warnings of the disasters that would ensue if computers started thinking the year was 2099. Companies were rushing to fix their databases.

The work was predictable—there was relatively little risk of a disastrous cost overrun—but mind numbing. The CEO was considering shutting down and joining a bigger firm. The life of slogging through mindless projects, haggling with clients who did not know what they wanted, and constantly wondering whether he could pay his rent was not what he had signed up for when he launched his dream of software entrepreneurship.

Young firms lacking a reputation need to start with deep pockets. Although people often refer to Infosys, started in 1981 by seven engineers with $250 borrowed from the first CEO's wife and now the third-largest software company in India, it is probably not a coincidence that India's two biggest software firms today are Wipro, owned by a family that had a successful cooking-oil business before branching out into software, and Tata Consultancy Services (TCS), part of the large industrial Tata Group that produces everything from salt to steel.

Of course, it took more than money. In these two cases there was also someone with vision and talent. But clearly money helped.

Having a name also helps. It is no accident that Gucci, originally a high-end leather goods producer, now sells everything from car seats to perfume, and that Ferrari, which started with sports cars, now sells eyeglasses and laptops. Buyers of Gucci perfumes or Ferrari laptops probably don't expect particularly innovative products from those brand names. They are going, rather, for the assurance Gucci and Ferrari value their good names too much to sell low-quality products, and perhaps the bragging rights that come with buying something clearly expensive.

THE WORLD OF NAMES

The value of a brand name is that it wards off competition. That the buyers are so much richer than the producers makes it very important for the seller or the intermediary to focus on quality rather than price. What makes, for any potential new entrant, the challenge of undercutting the incumbent even harder is that the price paid to the supplier tends to be a small part of what a good-quality product is worth to the buyer. Indeed, branding and distribution costs are often much larger than manufacturing costs. For many items, the cost of production is no more than 10–15 percent of the retail cost. This means a more efficient producer can do very little to affect the final price of the product in proportional terms. Cutting his cost of production by 50 percent would only reduce the overall cost of putting the product in the hands of the buyer by at most 7.5 percent.

That could still be a significant amount of money, but as a large literature has demonstrated, proportional changes are what buyers seem to care about. In a classic experiment, one group was asked whether they would drive twenty minutes to save $5 on a $15 calculator and another group whether they would do the same for a $125 calculator. Twenty minutes is twenty minutes, and $5 is $5, but the answers were very different: "68 percent of the respondents were willing to make an extra trip to save $5 on a $15 calculator; only 29 percent were willing to exert the same effort when the price of the calculator was $125." The point is that $5 is a third of $15 but only 4 percent of $125, which is why they switch in one case but not the other. Consumers are unlikely to switch sellers to save 7.5 percent.[35]

What this means is China's prices can increase quite a bit without anyone really noticing. Moreover, there is no reason for these prices to significantly increase anytime soon. China is a big country with a lot of very poor people willing to take jobs at current wages, so costs will remain low. Countries like Vietnam and Bangladesh that aspire to be the next China, the supplier of every kind of cheap manufacture to the world, might spend a long time waiting in the wings. And it is a bit frightening to imagine just how long that could be for Liberia, Haiti, and the Democratic Republic of the Congo, which would like to inherit the same mantle one day, once Bangladesh and Vietnam are too rich to want it.

The outsized role of reputation means international trade is not just about good prices, good ideas, low tariffs, and cheap transportation. It is very difficult for a new player to enter and take over a market, because they start without reputation. This along with the stickiness of labor means the easy flow of people and moneys that free trade is meant to leverage, and which the Stolper-Samuelson thesis is based on, does not work nearly as well on the ground.

THE COMPANY YOU KEEP

To make matters worse for, say, a new country trying to get into the fray, it is not only your own name that counts. Japanese cars are known to be well built, Italian cars are famous for being stylish, German cars are great to drive. A new Japanese entrant, like Mitsubishi when it first entered the US market in 1982, probably benefitted significantly from the success of older Japanese brands. Conversely, buyers are unlikely to want to try out a car produced in Bangladesh or Burundi, even if it is supposedly made to the most exacting standards, the price is low, and the reviews are good. God knows, they will wonder, what might go wrong in a few years. And they may well be right. It is possible that it would take many years of experience producing for the domestic market to know how to make a good car. That is how Toyota, Nissan, and Honda got started.

However, suspicion of newcomers can also turn into a self-fulfilling prophecy. If almost no one buys the car, the company will collapse and customer service will cease. Or if everybody expects the Egyptian rugs to fade, then they will sell for very little money and therefore it would not pay for entrepreneurs in Egypt to invest in producing higher quality rugs. It's a vicious cycle.[36]

The curse of low expectations can be very hard to overcome. Even if a firm chooses to deliver the highest-quality products, sufficiently pessimistic buyers will assume it is just a matter of time before the quality goes down. This is where it can be very useful to have the right connections: someone who knows you and will vouch for you.

It is no accident that ethnic Indians and Chinese who lived and worked in Western countries played an important role in their native countries' transition when they returned home. They used their reputation earned and business cards collected to assure buyers (often firms where they had already worked) that things would be okay.

The presence of some success stories can set off a virtuous cycle. Buyers tend to flock to firms that have had one successful breakthrough, reassured by the fact that others have continued to do business with them. Most young sellers who get an order, recognizing this is their one chance to break the vicious cycle of low expectations, will try their best to deliver when given a chance.

For example, in the rose export market in Kenya,[37] local producers work with intermediaries to export their roses to Europe. Neither the buyer nor the seller in this industry can rely solely on formal contracts to enforce good behavior. Roses are very perishable, so upon receiving a shipment a buyer could always claim the roses were not of an acceptable quality and refuse to pay. But, on the other hand, the seller could also claim the buyer somehow spoiled the roses to avoid paying. This means that establishing a reputation for reliability is important. During a period of political unrest in Kenya after the disputed presidential election of 2007, when workers were scarce and transportation was dangerous, new producers who were yet to establish a reputation went to great lengths to continue delivering to their buyers. Some even hired armed guards to protect their roses during delivery. The buyers stayed happy and the Kenya rose market survived the unrest.

Of course, even such desperate measures may not always save your skin. The overall reputation of the industry matters, and it may take only a few bad eggs to ruin the reputation of an otherwise high-quality industry. Governments, recognizing this, have tried to find ways to penalize individual producers who cheat on quality. In 2017, the Chinese government decided these penalties needed to be upped. *China Daily* quoted Huang Guoliang, director of the administration's quality supervision department: "Current law generally imposes administrative penalties on violators of product quality law, which are too lenient . . . A system under which violators of the law would suffer *devastating consequences* would act as a deterrent [italics added]."[38]

The best-case scenario in this world of fragile and interconnected reputations is often an "industrial cluster," a concentration of firms in the same industry in one location, all benefiting from the reputation associated with the cluster.

There have been knitwear factories in Tirupur in India since 1925, and throughout the 1960s and 1970s, the industry grew, producing mainly the white cotton tank tops Indian men wear under their shirts. In 1978, an Italian garment importer, a Mr. Verona, was desperately looking for a large shipment of white T-shirts. The association of garment exporters in Mumbai directed him to Tirupur. Happy with his first lot, he came back for more. In 1981, the first major European chain, C&A, followed him to Tirupur. Its exports were still only $1.5 million until 1985. Then they grew exponentially. By 1990, Tirupur's export volumes had passed $142 million.[39] Exports peaked at $1.3 billion in 2016, though the industry is now facing severe pressure from China, Vietnam, and other recent entrants to the market.[40]

China has scores of very large specialized manufacturing clusters ("socks city," "sweater city," "footwear capital," etc.). For example, the Zhili cluster in Huzhou has more than ten thousand enterprises producing children's wear, employing 300,000 workers. In 2012, it was responsible for 40 percent of the GDP of its region. The United States has clusters too, some better known than others. Boston has a biotech cluster. Carlsbad, near Los Angeles, specializes in golf equipment, and Michigan has clocks.[41]

The organization of the garment industry in Tirupur reveals the value of a name. The whole industry is organized around jobbers, subcontractors who take care of one or more stages of the production process, or even do all the stages for part of a shipment. The jobbers are the invisible people. Buyers deal instead with a smaller number of known names who secure orders and then distribute them among the jobbers. The advantage of this model of production is that it allows production at a very large scale, even if no one has the wherewithal to invest in a single immense factory. Everyone invests what they can and leave it to the intermediaries to put the pieces together. This is another reason why the industry needs to be clustered.

A similar system operates in many large exporting clusters throughout the developing world, where the reputation of some secures the employment of many others. Intermediaries, just like Hamis Carpets in Egypt or the sellers in Tirupur, mediate the relationship with foreign buyers. They have a lot to lose if there is a problem with quality from any of the jobbers and therefore take care of quality control. And while there can be a lot of teething pain, as we saw in the case of Hamis, the eventual rewards are probably quite decent.

Interestingly, this system may be changing. A substantial part of the business model of two of the world's most successful companies, Amazon and Alibaba, is to insert themselves in place of these intermediaries by allowing individual producers to build their own reputations on their sites, for a price of course, thereby not requiring certification from the intermediary. This is why after you receive a package ordered through Amazon Marketplace, you get repeated entreaties for feedback from Amazon sellers. It is in pursuit of these ratings that they are selling you the socks or the toy for an absurdly low price. Their hope is that one day they will have ratings both numerous and high enough that they can name their price. Of course, it will take some time for these new marketplaces to cement their reputations as guarantors of quality (and they may yet fail). Until they succeed, it is essentially impossible for an isolated producer in the third world to start competing on the international market, however good its product is and however low its prices are.

WAS IT WORTH $2.4 TRILLION?

The Italian maverick Marxist, Antonio Gramsci, once wrote: "The old is dying and the new cannot be born; in this interregnum all manner of morbid symptoms appear."[42] He could have well been writing about the post-liberalization world. As we saw, there are many very good reasons why resources tend to be sticky, especially in developing countries, and breaking into export markets is hard. One consequence of this fact is that trade liberalization anywhere may not be as much of a slam dunk as is often implied by economists. Wages may go down instead of up, even in labor-abundant developing countries where workers should benefit from trade, because everything that labor needs to be productive—capital, land, managers, entrepreneurs, and other workers—is slow to shift from the old job to the new one.

If machines, money, and workers continue to be used in the old sectors, there will be many fewer resources moving to the potential exporting sectors. In India, the effect of the 1991 liberalization was not a massive and sudden change in import and export volumes. Between 1990 and 1992, the openness ratio (the sum of all the imports and exports, as a percentage of the GDP) only increased a little bit, from 15.7 percent to 18.6 percent. But eventually both imports and exports went up, and India today is actually *more* open than China or the United States.[43]

Resources eventually moved and new products started being produced. And since existing producers benefitted from being able to import what they needed more easily, what they produced was of better quality and more saleable outside. The software industry, for example, benefited from the ability to import smoothly the hardware they needed, and software exports boomed. Indian firms were quick to switch to imports when they became cheap. Moreover, they also eventually introduced new product lines (for domestic and international use) to take advantage of those cheaper imports. But it took time.[44]

There is some evidence for the view (held by many policy makers) that the best way to speed up this process is to adopt "export promotion policies," that help exporters export more. All the East Asian success stories of the postwar era—Japan, Korea, Taiwan, and most recently China—have used one strategy or the other to help exporters speed up their expansion. Most observers believe China, for example, systematically undervalued its exchange rate throughout the 2000s (until about 2010) by selling renminbi and buying foreign currencies to keep its products artificially cheap against the competing products sold in dollars.

In 2010, Paul Krugman called China's policy the "most distortionary exchange rate policy any major nation ever followed." It was not cheap: China already owned $2.4 trillion in reserves and it added $30 billion to it per month.[45] Given how good the Chinese were at exporting and just how frugal Chinese consumers are, China has a natural tendency to sell more than it buys, and this ought to have pushed the exchange rate up and choked off export growth. The policy prevented this from happening.

Was the promotion of exports good economics? It is possible that it did help the exporters by raising their profits in renminbis (if you sell your shoes for the same number of dollars, the lower the exchange rate, the more local currency you get for them). This made it easier for them to afford to keep the dollar price of their exports low, which encouraged foreigners to buy Chinese, and thereby helped build the reputation of Chinese products. It also helped the exporters accumulate more capital and hire more new workers.

On the other hand, it was at the expense of Chinese consumers who paid for those overvalued imports (this is the flip side of having a weak currency). It is not easy to say what would have happened if the policy had not been adopted. First, the Chinese government also adopted a range of other policies that also favored exporters. China continued to remain competitive when it stopped manipulating its currency after 2010. Second, even if exporters had expanded more slowly, the domestic market might have grown faster and absorbed the surplus. China even today only exports about 20 percent of its GDP; the rest goes to local production.

Even if export promotion did work for China—and it could have—the same strategy is unlikely to work for too many other countries, at least in the near future. The problem in part is China itself. Its success and its enormous size make it harder for others to succeed. The sheer fragility of the process of acquiring a reputation, the critical importance of the right connections, and all the breaks needed to succeed also make us question whether trying to break into international trade is the way forward for the average poor country.

THE CHINA SHOCK

J. D. Vance's 2016 book *Hillbilly Elegy* is a lament on behalf of America's left-behind people, though reading it, one senses the author's deep ambivalence about how much to blame the victims.[46] Part of the economic hollowing out of the parts of Appalachia the book is set in occurred due to trade with China. The fact that poor people got hurt is what we would expect from the Stolper-Samuelson theorem: in rich countries it is the workers who suffer. What is surprising is how geographically concentrated the suffering ends up being. The left-behind people live in left-behind places.

The approach taken by Petia Topalova to examine the impact of trade liberalization on India's districts was replicated in the United States by David Autor, David Dorn, and Gordon Hanson.[47] China's exports are heavily concentrated in manufacturing, and within manufacturing they are concentrated in specific classes of products. For example, within the apparel sector, sales of some goods in the US, such as women's nonathletic footwear or waterproof outerwear, are completely dominated by China, but for other goods, such as coated fabrics, almost nothing comes from China.

Between 1991 and 2013, the United States was hit by the "China shock." China's share of world manufacturing exports grew from 2.3 percent in 1991 to 18.8 percent in 2013. To examine its labor market impacts, Autor, Dorn, and Hanson constructed an index reflecting the exposure of each US *commuting zone* to the China shock. (A commuting zone is a cluster of counties constituting a labor market, in the sense that it is possible to commute between them for a job.) The index is built on the idea that if Chinese exports to countries other than the US of a specific commodity are particularly high, implying China is generally successful in that industry, the commuting zones in the US producing that particular commodity will be hurt more than those producing another commodity. For example, since China's growth in female nonathletic footwear was particularly rapid after China's accession to the WTO, a commuting zone producing lots of footwear in 1990 would be more affected by the China shock than a commuting zone producing mostly coated fabrics, where China was not so present. So the China shock index measures the vulnerability of a region's industrial mix to China's strength by weighing each product type by China's import to the EU.

US commuting zones fared very differently depending on what they happened to produce. Those zones more affected by the China shock experienced substantially larger reductions in manufacturing employment. More strikingly, there was *no* reallocation of labor to new kinds of jobs. The *total* number of jobs lost was often larger than merely the number of jobs lost in the industries that were hit, and rarely less. This is presumably a consequence of the clustering effect we talked about. Those who lost their jobs tightened their belts, further reducing the economic activity in the area. Nonmanufacturing employment did not pick up the slack. If it had, we would have seen an increase in nonmanufacturing employment in the most affected regions. In fact, for lower-skilled workers, the increase in nonmanufacturing employment in affected commuting zones was *lower* than in other regions. Wages also declined in these areas compared to the rest of the country (and this was a period of stagnant wage growth overall), especially for low-wage workers.

Despite the fact that there were neighboring commuting zones essentially unaffected by the shock (and zones that actually benefitted, say, by importing certain components from China), workers did not move. The working-age population did not decline in the adversely affected commuting zones. They had no work.

This experience is not unique to the United States. Spain, Norway, and Germany all suffered similarly from the impact of the China shock.[48] In each case the sticky economy became a sticky trap.

CLUSTERF**K!

The problem was exacerbated by the clustering of industries. As we already saw, there are many good reasons for industries to cluster, but one potentially negative consequence is that a trade shock may hit with particular violence, potentially affecting all the firms concentrated in the region. In one single year, between October 2016 and October 2017, exports in Tirupur, the Indian T-shirt cluster, went down 41 percent.[49]

This can set off a downward spiral. Laid-off workers spend less in local businesses, such as shops and restaurants. The value of their houses declines, sometimes catastrophically, since to a large extent the value of my house depends on how nicely *your* house is maintained. When most of a neighborhood starts to go down, everyone goes down together. Households with larger declines in housing wealth experience a tightening of their credit limit and their ability to refinance, which further reduces their consumption.[50] This hits the shops and the restaurants, and some of them end up closing. The disappearance of these amenities, the dearth of nice neighborhoods, and the catastrophic decline in the local tax base that makes it harder to provide water, schools, lights, and roads can eventually make an area so unattractive that it becomes impossible to revive. No new firm will want to move there to take the place of those that have died.

This logic applies just as much to the manufacturing clusters in the United States as it does to those in India or China. Tennessee, for example, had a large concentration of clusters producing goods directly competing with China, from furniture to textiles. The closure of these firms has produced a series of ghost towns. Bruceton, Tennessee, which was profiled in the *Atlantic*, had been home to the factory of the Henry I. Siegel Company (H.I.S.). At its peak, H.I.S. made jeans and suits in three giant plants, employing seventeen hundred people. It started winding down in the 1990s. In 2000, it laid off its last fifty-five workers. Afterward, according to the *Atlantic* article,

> this town has struggled to figure out how to survive. The three giant H.I.S. plants in town are empty, their windows broken, their paint peeling. A few new manufacturing operations have come, but they've also left. One by one, the businesses on the main streets of Bruceton and neighboring town Hollow Rock have closed, leaving modern-day ghost towns. In downtown Bruceton, the bank is gone, the supermarket and the fashion store have closed, and there's a parking lot where

there used to be another supermarket. All that's left is a pharmacy where seniors come to get their prescriptions filled.

The neighboring town of McKenzie lost its pajama factory and a shoe company in the 1990s. It is still trying to convince new businesses to come. Whenever the town hears a new factory wants to move, city employees call the decision maker and try to sell the town to them. They have had some interest, but no taker yet. The *Atlantic* article goes on:

> One reason they may not be getting bites, Holland [the town's mayor] says, is because of the town's depressing Main Street. One company was going to locate in McKenzie, but when executives showed up to town and saw empty businesses on Main Street, they decided it wasn't a place they wanted their families to live. . . . "They said it looked like an atomic bomb went off, so they just kept walking. . . . They didn't even give it a second chance."[51]

This is not a reason to try to prevent clustering, since the gains from clustering are potentially very large, but a warning to be willing to step in and deal with what happens when the cluster unravels.

FORGET THE LOSERS

Even though they clearly overestimated the extent to which the market would take care of those directly affected by trade, trade theorists have always known some people *would* get hurt. Their response has always been that since many people do benefit, we should be willing and able to compensate those who are negatively affected.

Autor, Dorn, and Hanson looked at the extent to which the government stepped in to help the regions ill-affected by trade with China. They found that while they received somewhat more money from public programs, it was much too little to fully compensate for the lost incomes. For example, comparing the residents of the most affected commuting zones to those of the least affected, incomes per adult went down by $549 more in the former, whereas government welfare payments went up by only approximately $58 per adult.[52]

Furthermore, the composition of these transfers may have contributed to worsen the situations of the workers who lost their jobs. In principle, the primary program to help newly unemployed workers who have lost their jobs due to trade is the Trade Adjustment Assistance (TAA) program. Under the TAA, a qualifying worker can extend unemployment insurance for up to three years as long as they receive training to work in other sectors. They may also get financial help to relocate, to search for jobs, or to get health care.

TAA is a longstanding program, in place since 1974, and yet it provided a minuscule share of the already small transfers toward the affected counties. Of the $58 in additional transfers that went to the more affected regions, only twenty-three extra *cents* came from TAA. A very big part of what did grow was disability insurance; out of every ten workers who lost their jobs due to trade, one went on disability insurance.

The huge increase in disability insurance is alarming. It is unlikely that trade had a direct effect on the physical health of these workers, especially since the most physically demanding jobs were those that typically disappeared. Some workers were undoubtedly depressed; for others, disability insurance became a strategy they had to adopt to survive. Either way, unfortunately, going to disability is usually a one-way street out of employment. For example, research on a veterans' program that newly recognized diabetes as a reason to claim disability for those exposed to Agent Orange showed that for every hundred veterans who entered the disability program as a result of the policy change, eighteen dropped out of the labor force for good.[53] In the United States, those who join the disability rolls rarely leave them,[54] partly because being classified as disabled hurts their employment prospects. Having to adopt disability after a trade shock to pay the bills is likely to push some people who could have otherwise found a new job out of the labor force entirely.

For workers who need to resort to disability benefits to survive, being classified as disabled adds insult to injury. When they go on disability, workers who have spent their lives in a physically demanding job lose not only their occupation, but their claim to dignity. So not only did the United States not come close to compensating the workers who lost out, but what little help people could get through the existing social protection apparatus seemed designed to make them feel denigrated.

Partisan politics has played a role in this disaster. When someone who has lost their job needed healthcare, a recourse was supposed to be Obamacare. Unfortunately, many Republican states like Kansas, Mississippi, Missouri, and Nebraska decided to make a show of resisting the federal government by denying their citizens this option. This pushed some people to apply for disability status in order to get healthcare. Indeed, after the adoption of the Affordable Care Act (a.k.a. Obamacare), disability claims increased by 1 percent in states that refused to expand Medicaid, while they decreased by 3 percent in expansion states.[55]

But the causes run deeper. US politicians are wary of subsidizing specific sectors (since others would feel slighted and would lobby for their own protection), which is probably partly the reason why TAA has remained such a small program. Economists have also traditionally been unwilling to embrace place-based policies ("help people, not places" as the slogan goes). Enrico Moretti, one of the few economists who has actually studied such policies, actively dislikes them. For him, channeling public funds into regions doing poorly is throwing good money after bad. Blighted towns are meant to shrink while others take their place. It is the way of history. What public policy needs to do is to help people move to the places of the future.[56]

This analysis seems to give too little weight to the facts on the ground. As we know, the same reasons that make clusters develop also mean they fall apart quickly. Theoretically, the obvious response to this wholesale unwinding ought to be for a lot of people to leave, but as we saw already, they don't. At least not nearly fast enough. Instead, when their county was hit by the China shock, fewer people got married, fewer had children, and of the children who were born, more were born out of wedlock. Young men—and, in particular, young white men—were less likely to graduate from college.[57] "Deaths of despair" from drug and alcohol poisoning and suicides skyrocketed.[58] These are all symptoms of a deep hopelessness once associated with

African American communities in inner cities of the United States but are now replicated in white suburbs and industrial towns up and down the Eastern Seaboard and the eastern Midwest. A lot of this damage is irreversible, at least in the short run. The school dropouts, the drug and alcohol addicts, and the children growing up without a father or a mother have lost a part of their futures. Permanently.

IS TRADE WORTH IT?

Donald Trump decided the solution to the negative effect of trade was tariffs. He welcomed a trade war. It started in the first few months of 2018, with new tariffs on aluminum and steel. Trump then talked about $50 billion in tariffs on Chinese goods, and then when China retaliated, suggested another $100 billion.

The stock market tumbled on the announcement, but the basic instinct that we should close our economy and, in particular, defend it against China is shared by many Americans on both sides of the aisle.

Meanwhile, economists were jumping up and down. They evoked the specter of the "worst ever tariff," the Smoot-Hawley Tariff Act, which precipitated a global trade war in 1930 by imposing tariffs on twenty thousand goods imported into the United States. The Smoot-Hawley bill coincided with the onset of the Great Depression, and although it may or may not have caused it, it certainly gave sweeping tariffs a bad rep.

The idea that more trade is good (on balance) is deeply engrained in anybody who went to graduate school in economics. In May 1930, over a thousand economists had written a letter encouraging President Hoover to veto the Smoot-Hawley bill. And yet there is something else economists do know but tend to keep closely to themselves: the aggregate gains from trade, for a large economy like the United States, are actually quantitatively quite small. The truth is, if the US were to go back to complete autarky, not trading with anybody, it would be poorer. But not *that* much poorer.

Arnaud Costinot and his longtime collaborator Andrés Rodríguez-Clare managed to make themselves infamous in the community of trade economists for making that point. In March 2018, they released a timely new article, "The US Gains from Trade," with the following prescient first paragraph:

> About 8 cents out of every dollar spent in the United States is spent on imports.
>
> What if, because of a wall or some other extreme policy intervention, these goods were to remain on the other side of the US border? How much would US consumers be willing to pay to prevent this hypothetical policy change from taking place? The answer to this question represents the welfare cost from autarky or, equivalently, the welfare gains from trade.[59]

This article builds on a line of research they developed over several years, both together and with others, and on decades of research in trade. The key idea is that the gains from trade depend primarily on two things: how much we import and the extent to which these imports are influenced by tariff, transportation costs, and the other costs of trading internationally. If we import nothing, clearly it does not matter if we erect a wall and stop importing. Second, even if we import a lot, if we stop doing so when import prices increase even a little bit, because it becomes a little more expensive to bring the goods here, it must mean we have many available substitutes at home, so the value of imports is not that high.

COMPUTING THE GAINS FROM TRADE: A SLIGHTLY TECHNICAL ASIDE

Building on this idea, we can compute the gains from trade. If the United States only imported bananas and produced apples, it would be fairly easy. We could look at the share of bananas in consumption, and the extent to which consumers were willing to switch between apples and bananas as the prices of bananas and apples changed. (These are what economists call *cross-price elasticities*.) In fact, the United States imports products in about eighty-five hundred categories, so to do this calculation properly, we'd need to know the cross-price elasticity between every product and the price of every other product around the world—apples and bananas, Japanese cars and US soybeans, Costa Rican coffee and Chinese undershirts—making this approach unfeasible.

But in fact we don't actually need to look at products one by one. We can get reasonably close to the truth by assuming all imports are a single undifferentiated good that is either directly consumed (imports represent 8 percent of US consumption) or used as input for US production (another 3.4 percent of consumption).[60]

To get the final gains from trade, we need to know just how sensitive our imports are to trade costs. If they are very sensitive, it means it is easy to replace what we import with things we produce locally, and it is not very valuable to trade with other countries. If, on the other hand, the value remains unchanged even as the costs change, it means we really like what we buy abroad, and trade increases welfare a lot. There is some guessing involved here, since we are in fact talking about a good that does not exist, a composite of thousands of widely differing products. The authors therefore present the results for a range of situations, going from a scenario where traded goods can very easily be substituted with domestic goods (leading to gains of trade of 1 percent of GDP) to one where it is very difficult to substitute them (leading to an estimate of 4 percent of GDP).

SIZE MATTERS

Costinot and Rodríguez-Clare's preferred estimate is that the gains from trade are about 2.5 percent of GDP. This is really not a lot. The US economy grew 2.3 percent in 2017,[61] so one year of decent growth could pay for sending the US economy into complete autarky, in perpetuity! Did they get something wrong in their calculations? One can argue with many of the details, but the order of magnitude has to be right. Simply put, despite its openness to trade, the US import share (8 percent) is one of the lowest in the world.[62] So the gains from international trade to the United States cannot be that large. Belgium, a small open economy, has an import share of above 30 percent, so there trade matters much more.

This is not so surprising. The US economy is very large and very diverse, and therefore capable of producing much of what is consumed there. Moreover, a lot of consumption is of services (everything from banking to house cleaning) not typically traded internationally (yet). Even the consumption of manufactured goods involves a significant share of locally produced services. When we buy an iPhone assembled in China, we also pay for US design and local advertising and marketing. The phone is sold in shiny Apple stores built by local firms and manned by local tech lovers.

We should not be carried away by the US example, however. Large economies like the United States and China have the skills and the capital to produce most things at a very high level of efficiency somewhere in the country. Moreover, their internal markets are large enough to absorb production from many factories in many sectors operating at the appropriate scale. They would lose relatively little by not trading.

International trade is much more important for smaller and poorer countries, like those in Africa, Southeast Asia, or southeastern Europe. Skills there are scarce and so is capital, and the domestic demand for steel or cars is unlikely to be big enough, given that incomes are low and populations are small, to sustain production at scale. Unfortunately, it is precisely those countries that face the biggest barriers to becoming players in the international market.

But for larger developing countries like India, China, Nigeria, or Indonesia, the bigger problem is often internal integration. Many developing countries suffer from a lack of internal connectivity. Nearly a billion people worldwide live more than a mile from a paved road (one-third of them are in India), and nowhere near a train line.[63] Internal politics sometimes add to that. China has excellent roads, but Chinese provinces have found ways to discourage domestic firms from importing goods from the rest of the country.[64] And until the recent introduction of unified taxes on goods and services in India, each state had the power to set its own tax rates, and often used them to favor local producers.

IS SMALL BEAUTIFUL?[65]

But perhaps the very idea of comparative advantage is overrated, and even small countries can live in autarky. Or to push the logic even further, perhaps every community can learn to produce what it needs.

This idea has a long and somewhat infamous pedigree. During the Great Leap Forward in China, Chairman Mao argued, among other things, that industrialization could be willed to happen in every village, and that steel could be produced in backyard steel furnaces. The project failed miserably, but not before peasants melted down their pots and pans and plowshares to comply with the chairman's wishes, and busied themselves producing steel while fields remained fallow and crops rotted on the ground. Many China observers think this might have contributed to the Great Chinese Famine of 1958–1960, when upward of thirty million people died.

The idea of self-sufficient village communities was also the centerpiece of Gandhi's economic philosophy. His vision of a society clothed in homespun and living mainly off the land had a durable effect on Indian economic policy in the post-independence era. Until the WTO forced India to do away with the policy in 2002, 799 goods, from pickles to fountain pens, dyes, and many items of clothing, were reserved for tiny firms that could be set up in villages.

The problem of course is that small is not beautiful. A minimum scale is required to allow firms to employ specialized workers or to use high-productivity machines. In the early 1980s, Abhijit's mother, Nirmala Banerjee, an economist with quite left-wing views, surveyed small firms in and around Kolkata, and was astounded by just how unproductive they were.[66] Later evidence confirmed her insight. In India, small firms are much less productive than larger ones.[67]

But firms can only be large if the market is large. As Adam Smith wrote in 1776: "The division of labour is limited by the extent of the market."[68] This is why trade is valuable. Isolated communities cannot have productive firms.

Indeed, national integration via railroad has had transformative impacts in many economies. In India, between 1853 and 1930, the British colonial administration oversaw the building of nearly forty-two thousand miles of railroad in India. Before the railways, commodities were transported by bullocks on dirt roads, and could travel at most twenty miles per day. Railroads could transport these same commodities almost four hundred miles in a day, at a much lower cost, and with less risk of spoilage. Inland regions all but cut off from the rest of the country got connected.[69] The railroad network dramatically reduced trade costs. The transportation cost per mile traveled was nearly two and a half times higher for roads than for railroads. And places brought together by railways started to trade more and became richer; the value of agricultural production increased 16 percent faster in districts that got a train line, relative to those that did not.

The United States was another large country integrated through a vast network of railroads at about the same time. Although the role of railroads in the development of the US economy has been controversial, recent research suggests agricultural land value would have been 64 percent lower in the absence of railroad construction.[70] These land prices embody all the gains farmers expected from better connections with other counties. And the gains came in large part from the ability to specialize in what each region was good at. Between 1890 and 1997, agriculture became more and more locally specialized. Farmers increasingly chose the crop that each field (due to its climate, soil, etc.) was ideally suited for, which led to large gains in overall agricultural productivity and income.[71]

Poor internal integration also makes economies sticky, eliminating the gains from international trade for the common men and women, or even turning them into losses. Bad roads discourage people from taking new jobs in cities. In India, the unpaved roads connecting villages to main roads have been shown to be a deterrent for rural dwellers to get nonagricultural jobs outside their villages.[72] Bumpy rides add so much to the final price of goods that consumers in remote villages enjoy almost no benefits from international trade. In Nigeria and Ethiopia, by the time imported goods arrive at those villages, if they make it at all, they are unaffordable.[73] Poor transportation, both for inputs and for the final products, erode the cost advantages of a cheap labor force. Internal connections must improve for international integration to be beneficial.

DON'T START THAT TRADE WAR

The examples and analyses in this chapter come from cutting-edge research conducted by the most respected departments of economics, yet the main conclusions may seem to put us at odds with decades of conventional wisdom. While every economics undergraduate learns there are large aggregate gains from trade, and that everybody can be made better off as long as we can redistribute those gains, the three main lessons from this chapter are decisively less rosy.

First, the gains of international trade are fairly small for a large economy like that of the United States. Second, while the gains are potentially much larger for smaller and poorer countries, there is no magic bullet. Just as we saw in the chapter on migration that opening a border widely would not be enough to get everyone to move, removing trade barriers is not enough to ensure new countries can join the party. Declaring trade is free is not the magic bullet for development (or even for trade). Third, the redistribution of gains from trade has proven extremely tricky, and people negatively affected by trade have suffered, and are still suffering, a great deal.

Taken together, the exchange of goods, people, ideas, and cultures made the world much richer. Those lucky enough to be in the right place at the right time, with the right skills or the right ideas, grew wealthy, sometimes fabulously so, benefitting from the opportunity to leverage their special gifts on a global scale. For the rest, the experience has been mixed. Jobs were lost and not replaced. Rising incomes have paid for more new jobs—as chefs and chauffeurs, gardeners, and nannies—but trade has also created a more volatile world where jobs suddenly vanish only to turn up a thousand miles away. The gains and the pains ended up being very unequally distributed and they are, very clearly, starting to bite back at us; along with migration they define our political discourse.

So do protectionist tariffs help? No. Reintroducing tariffs now will not help most Americans. The reason is simple: one of our main argument so far has been that we need to worry about transitions. Many of those displaced by the China shock never really recovered because the sticky economy meant they could not move sectors or regions to get back on their feet, and the resources could not move to them.

But shutting off trade with China now will clearly create a new set of displacements and many of those new losers will be in counties we have not yet heard anything about, simply because they are doing just fine. Indeed, among the 128 products on which China announced tariffs on March 22 and April 2, 2018, the majority were agricultural: a.p.p. (apples, pears, and pork), rather than apps. US exports in agriculture have risen steadily over the last few decades (from $56 billion in 1995 to $140 billion in 2017). Today a fifth of US agricultural production is exported. And the biggest export destination is East Asia. China alone buys 16 percent of US agricultural exports.[74]

The first-order effect of a trade war with China is therefore likely to be a loss of jobs in agriculture and in the industries supporting it. The US Department of Agriculture estimates that in 2016, agricultural exports were responsible for over a million jobs in the United States, almost three-quarters of which were in the nonfarm sector.[75] The five states with the largest share of agricultural employment are California, Iowa, Louisiana, Alabama, and Florida.[76] For precisely the same reasons people who lost their manufacturing jobs in Pennsylvania were not able to get other jobs near home, these agricultural jobs will not be replaced by manufacturing jobs in the region. And we know from everything we have seen in this chapter and the previous one that just as manufacturing workers did not move when their jobs were lost, farm workers would probably not move. Alabama and Louisiana are two of the ten poorest states in the United States,[77] and a trade war would throw them under the bus.

For the United States, a trade war would not be the end of the world as we know it. But while it may save some jobs in steel, it would likely cause significant new damage to others. The US economy will be fine. Hundreds of thousands of people will not.

IF NOT TARIFFS, WHAT?
EASE MOBILITY, ACCEPT IMMOBILITY

Since the main problem with trade is that it creates many more losers than the Stopler-Samuelson theory suggests, it seems any solution should involve either limiting the number of losers by helping them move or change jobs, or finding a way to compensate them better.

One side benefit of the negative effect of trade being so concentrated is that we actually know where to look for the victims. Why not target some help directly to the workers in industries that lost out to the China shock? Indeed, this was the idea behind the Trade Adjustment Assistance program. The TAA pays for training (up to $10,000 a year) and the trained workers get up to three years in unemployment benefits, precisely to give them some time to land on their feet. The only problem, as we saw, is that the program remained tiny.

Sadly, this was not because TAA was ineffective as a concept; it was just severely underfunded. To qualify for the program, a worker must petition the Department of Labor. A caseworker is then allocated the worker's file and tasked with determining whether in this case the job in the worker's former firm disappeared because of competition from imports, the offshoring of jobs, or ripple effects from the trade-induced distress of other companies that either bought from or sold to that firm.

A complex judgment goes into this decision, and some caseworkers are much more willing than others to rule in favor of the worker and allocate them aid. One study makes the case that the assignment of a petition to a particular caseworker, and therefore the eventual judgment, is more or less random.[78] Using a database of 300,000 petitions, it compares workers assigned to more or less lenient caseworkers. Workers assigned to more lenient caseworkers are more likely to receive the TAA and therefore more likely to be trained, move sectors, and earn more money. Overall, workers awarded TAA initially had to forego $10,000 in earnings (since they could not work while they got the training), and the government spent some money for the training, but over the next ten years the retrained worker earned $50,000 more than the untrained worker. It took ten years for the salary levels of the retrained and untrained workers to converge. This was thus a worthwhile investment for them, although not one they could undertake without the government's support, since getting a bank loan for this purpose would have been very difficult.

So why was an effective program like the TAA underfunded and underused? Partly because neither policy makers nor the public knew it worked until that study came out, quite recently. This probably reflects the lack of interest in these kinds of policies among trade economists. Economists also don't like programs that rely so much on a judgment call; they worry about potential abuse. At a political level, spending large sums of money on trade adjustment would have made it more explicit that trade adjustment costs are in fact large, and this may not have been palatable.

One obvious path is therefore to expand a program like the TAA, making it both more generous to individuals and more easily awarded. For example, the revamped TAA could be modeled on the GI bill, paying enough for someone who is a "veteran" of a trade shock to get a new start with their education. The GI Bill provides up to thirty-six months of education benefits, pays for full tuition at public schools, and up to $1,994 toward tuition for a full-time student (and a pro-rated rate for part-time programs), as well as a stipend for housing.[79] The new TAA could be something like that, combined with extended unemployment insurance for the duration a person is in school. And since we know there are strong local market effects from trade disruptions, the TAA could be more generous in regions known to have been particularly affected by trade shocks, to avoid sending the affected labor markets into a downward spiral.

More generally, much of the hardship caused by trade is related to the immobility of both people and resources. The free movement of goods across borders is not matched by movement within countries. All the solutions we discussed at the end of chapter 2 to encourage internal migration, and the seamless integration of movers (subsidies, housing, insurance, help with childcare, etc.) would help in adjusting to trade shocks.

But it is also clear that mobility, TAA induced or not, is not the ideal solution for all workers. Some may not want to, or not be able to, be retrained; others may not want to change their job, particularly if this involves moving. This may be especially true for older workers. For them retraining would be difficult, and they might be less likely than younger workers to find a new job afterward. Indeed, a study found that after mass layoffs, older workers find it very difficult to find another job. Two and four years after losing their job, men and women swept in a mass layoff at age fifty-five were at least twenty percentage

points more likely to be unemployed than those lucky enough to escape job loss at fifty-five.[80] This kind of job loss has a permanent effect
on younger workers as well, but the impact is nowhere near as large.[81]

Older workers who get fired also tend to be those who spent a long
career working at a particular job. For them, the work they do provides a sense of pride and identity and defines the place they have in
their communities. It is difficult to compensate them with an invita-
tion to be trained to do something entirely different.

Why not then offer to subsidize firms adversely affected by trade
(particularly those located in the most affected regions) as long as they
keep employing older workers? Larry Summers (the head of the National Economic Council from 2009 to 2012) and Edward Glaeser have
recently argued for a payroll-tax reduction in some specific areas.[82] A
tax reduction may, however, be insufficient to convince a firm to keep
its employees if it has become uncompetitive. By being more specific
about the sector and the areas, and by restricting the program to already employed workers between the ages of fifty-five and sixty-two
(when they can claim social security and retire), it would be possible to
spend much more money on each person, possibly compensating the
firm for more than the cost of a full-time worker if that is what it takes.
That won't save every firm, but it might preserve a significant amount
of employment where it matters the most, prevent communities from
falling apart, and be part of the necessarily long transition to a new
path. The right way to pay for this is to use general tax revenue. To the
extent we are all benefitting from trade, we should collectively pay for
the cost. It makes no sense to ask agricultural workers to lose their jobs
just so steelworkers can keep theirs, which is what tariffs accomplish.

Of course, the proposal is not without practical difficulties. Affected firms would need to be identified, and there would certainly
be lobbying and attempts to circumvent the rules. The proposal may
be seen as a form of trade protection and run afoul of WTO rules.
But these issues could be solved. The principle of identifying firms
that have been subject to trade shocks is already accepted by the TAA
program, which has developed a mechanism to adjudicate claims. To
avoid casting it as trade protection, the provision could be extended to
jobs lost due to technological disruptions.

The overarching takeaway is that we need to address the pain that goes with the need to change, to move, to lose one's understanding of what is a good life and a good job. Economists and policy makers were blindsided by the hostile reaction to free trade, even though they have long known that as a class workers were likely to suffer from trade in rich countries and benefit from it in poor countries. The reason is they have taken it for granted that workers would be able to move jobs or places, or both, and if they were not able to do this, it was somehow their failing. This belief has colored social policy, and set up the conflict between the "losers" and the rest that we are experiencing today.

CHAPTER 4

LIKES, WANTS,
AND NEEDS

THE INCREASINGLY OPEN EXPRESSION of unvarnished animus toward people of different race, religion, ethnicity, and even gender has become the staple of populist leaders throughout the world. From the United States to Hungary, from Italy to India, leaders who offer little more than racism and/or bigotry as their policy platform are becoming a defining feature of the political landscape, a ground force that shapes elections and policies. In the United States, in 2016, the degree to which a person deeply identified as white was one of the strongest predictors of support for Donald Trump among Republicans, much more than, for example, economic anxiety.[1]

The vicious vocabulary our leaders employ daily legitimizes the public expression of views some people probably had already, but were rarely spoken or acted upon. In one instance of everyday racism, a white woman in a supermarket in the US called the police on a black woman whom she suspected, on the basis of a phone conversation she was overhearing, was trying to sell food stamps—and in the process rather tellingly exclaimed, "We are going to build this wall." On the face of it, the comment made no sense: the accused was an American citizen who belonged on the same side of the hypothetical wall as her white critic.

But of course we all know what she meant. She was expressing her *preference* for a society free of people different from her, with President Trump's metonymic wall separating the races. This is why the wall has become such a flashpoint in American politics, an image of what one side dreams of and the other fears.

Preferences, at one level, are what they are. Economists make a sharp distinction between preferences and beliefs. Preferences reflect whether we prefer cake or cookies, the beach or the mountains, brown people or white. Not when we are ignorant of the merits of each and may therefore be swayed by information, but when we know everything we could possibly need to know. People can have wrong beliefs but they cannot have wrong preferences—the lady in the supermarket can insist she is under no obligation to make sense. Yet it is worth trying to understand why people have such views before we sink deeper into the morass of racism, especially because it is impossible to think about the policy choices we will confront in this book without getting a handle on what these preferences represent and where they come from. When we discuss the limits of economic growth, the pain of inequality, or the costs and benefits of protecting the environment, there is no way to avoid dealing with the distinction between what individuals need and what they want, and how society at large should value those desires.

Unfortunately, traditional economics is ill-equipped to help us here. The attitude in mainstream economics has been very much one of tolerance of people's views and opinions; we may not share them, but who are we to pass judgment? We can shout out the facts to make sure people have the right information, but only they can decide what they like. Moreover, there is often a hope the market will take care of the problem of bigotry. People who happen to have petty, narrow-minded preferences should not survive in the marketplace, since being tolerant is good business practice. Take, for example, a baker who does not want to bake cakes for same-sex weddings. He will lose sales from all same-sex weddings, which will go to other bakers. They will make money; he will not.

Except it does not always work that way. Bakers who don't want to bake for same-sex weddings don't go bankrupt, in part because they win support from like-minded people. Bigotry can be good business, at least for some, and it seems to be good politics as well. As a result, economics in recent years has had to reckon with preferences, and we have gained some useful insights about how we might be able to get out of this mess.

DE GUSTIBUS NON EST DISPUTANDUM?

In 1977, in a famous piece titled "De Gustibus Non Est Disputandum" (usually translated as "There Is No Accounting for Tastes"), Gary Becker and George Stigler, Nobel Prize winners and founders of the Chicago school of economics, made an influential case for why economists should avoid getting entangled in trying to understand what lies behind preferences.[2]

Preferences are part of who we are, Becker and Stigler argued. If, after we go over all the information we have, two of us still disagree on whether vanilla is better than chocolate or polar bears are worth saving, the presumption ought to be this is something intrinsic to who we each are. Not a whim or a mistake or a response to social pressures, but a considered judgment reflecting what we value. While they recognized that this is surely not always true, they argued that it is still the best place to start when we set out to understand why people do what they do.

We have some sympathy for the idea that people's choices are *coherent*, in the sense of being thought out rather than a collection of random acts of whimsy. It is both patronizing and wrong-headed, in our view, to assume people must have screwed up just because we might have behaved differently. And yet society routinely overrules people's choices, especially if they are poor, supposedly for their own good, for instance when we give them food or food stamps rather than cash. We justify this on the grounds we know better what they really need. To partially combat this attitude—only partially, because we don't deny there are many misjudgments in the world—in our book *Poor Economics* we took some pain to argue that the choices of the poor often make more sense than we give them credit for.[3] For example, we told the story of a man in Morocco. After he made a compelling case that he and his family really did not have enough to eat, he showed us his largish television with a satellite connection. We might have suspected the television was just an impulse purchase he had subsequently regretted. But that was not at all what he said. "Television is more important than food," he told us. His insistence made us ask how this could make sense, and once we went down that road it was not that hard to see what was behind this preference. There was not much to do in the village, and given he was not planning to emigrate, it was not clear that better nutrition would buy him much more than a fuller stomach; he was already strong enough to do the little work that was available. What the television delivered was relief from the endemic problem of boredom, in these remote villages where there was often not even a tea stall to relieve the monotony of daily life.

The Moroccan did very much insist his preference made sense. Now that he had the television, any more money, he told us several times, would go to buying more food. This is entirely consistent with his view that televisions serve a greater need than food. But it flies in the face of most people's instincts and many of the standard formulations in economics. Given that he bought a television when there was not enough food in the house, the presumption would be that any extra money in his hands would go even faster down some drain, since he evidently was the sort of person given to irrational impulses. This is at the base of the case against giving money to poor people. And yet, a number of recent studies from across the world, published after we made the case in *Poor Economics* that he knew what he was doing, have found that when randomly selected very poor people get some extra cash from government programs, they do spend a very large fraction of this extra money on food.[4] Maybe after they buy that TV, exactly as the Moroccan man had promised.

So we learned something by being willing to suspend our disbelief and trust that people know what they want. Becker and Stigler however want us to go a step further—to assume preferences are *stable*, in the sense they are not influenced by whatever is going on around us. Neither schools, nor the exhortations of parents or preachers, nor the stuff we read on billboards or on our many screens, in this view, change our true preferences. This rules out conforming to social norms and being influenced by one's peers, like getting a tattoo because everyone else has one, wearing a headscarf because it is expected of one, buying a flashy car because the neighbors have one, and so on.

Becker and Stigler were too good as social scientists not to realize this was not always the case. But they believed it was more useful to ponder why a particular seemingly irrational choice might actually make sense, rather than to close our minds to its potential logic and attribute it to some form of collective hysteria. This view was enormously influential; many, perhaps most, economists bought into this agenda of sticking to what have come to be known as *standard prefer- ences,* meaning preferences that are coherent and stable. For instance, many years ago Abhijit was living in Manhattan and teaching at Prince- eton, and thus often found himself on a train. He noticed people often formed lines at specific places on the platform to wait for their train, but as often as not, the front of the line would be nowhere near a door to the train. It was a fad.

A natural conclusion might have been that people just went with the flow because they preferred doing the same as everyone else. This would have violated the idea that preferences are stable, because their preference for one place on the platform over another depended on how many people were there. To explain why people join fads with- out simply assuming they happen to like behaving like everyone else, Abhijit constructed the following argument. Suppose people suspect that others know something (perhaps the train door will open at a par- ticular spot). They would then join the crowd (perhaps at the cost of ignoring their own information that the train is likely to stop some- where else). But that would make the crowd bigger, and so the next person coming along would see an even bigger crowd and be even more likely to think this conveyed useful information. They might also join the crowd, for the same reason. In other words, what looks like conformity could be the outcome of rational decision making by many individuals with no interest in conforming, but who believe oth- ers might have better information than they. He called it a "simple model of herd behavior."[5]

The fact that each individual decision is rational does not make the outcome desirable. Herd behavior generates *informational cascades*: the information on which the first people base their decision will have an outsized influence on what all the others believe. A recent experiment nicely demonstrates the power of random first moves to generate cas- cades.[6] Researchers worked with a website that aggregates advice on restaurants and other services. Users post comments, and other users add an up- or down-vote. In their experiment, the website randomly chose a small fraction of comments and gave them one artificial up- vote as soon as they were posted. They also randomly chose another small batch to get a down-vote. The positive up-vote significantly increased the probability that the next user also gave an up-vote, by 32 percent. After five months, the comments that had received one *single* artificial up-vote at the beginning were much more likely to get a top grade than those that got a single down-vote. The influence of that original nudge persisted and grew, despite the fact that the posts had been viewed a million times.

Fads, therefore, are not necessarily inconsistent with the paradigm of standard preferences. Even when our preferences do not directly depend on what other people do, the behavior of others can convey a signal that alters our beliefs and our behavior. In the absence of a strong reason to believe otherwise, I might infer from other people's actions that a tattoo does look good, that drinking banana juice will make me slim, and that this harmless-looking Mexican man is really a rapist at heart.

But how can we explain that people will sometimes do things they *know* not to be in their immediate self-interest (for example, getting a tattoo they find ugly or lynching a Muslim man at the risk of being arrested) just because their friends do it?

COLLECTIVE ACTION

It turns out that just as fads can be rationalized by standard preferences, so can sticking to social norms. The basic idea is that those who violate the norm will be punished by the rest of the community. And so will those who fail to punish violators, and those who fail to punish those who fail to punish those who fail to punish, and so on. One of the great achievements of the field of game theory is the *folk theorem*, a formal demonstration that this argument can be made in a logically coherent way and can therefore be a candidate for explaining why norms are so powerful.[7]

Elinor Ostrom, the first and only (until 2019) woman to receive a Nobel Prize in economics, spent her career demonstrating instances of this logic. Many of her examples were drawn from small communities—cheese makers in Switzerland, forest users in Nepal, or fishermen on the Maine coast or in Sri Lanka[8]—who live by a norm about how community members were supposed to behave that everyone stuck to.

In the Alps, for example, Swiss cheese producers had for centuries relied on common ownership of a pasture for cattle grazing. If there had been no communal understanding, this could have led to disaster. The land might have been overgrazed to barrenness since it belonged to no one and everyone had a reason to want to feed their own cows more, potentially at the expense of the others. However, there was a set of clear rules for what cattle owners could and could not do on the common pasture, and those rules were followed because violators were excluded from future grazing rights. Given that, Ostrom argued, collective ownership was actually better for everyone than private property. Dividing the land into small parcels, each owned by a separate person, increases risk, since there is always the possibility of some disease hitting the grass in any given small area.

This kind of logic also explains why, in many developing countries, a part of the land (for example, the forest abutting the village) is always held as common property. As long as the common land is used sparingly, it provides a resource of last resort for those villagers whose own economic plans have hit some headwinds; foraging in the forest or selling grass cut from the common land helps them survive. The intrusion of private property into these settings, generally inspired by economists who don't understand the logic of the context (and love private ownership), has often been a disaster.[9]

It also suggests a selfish reason for why people in villages often seem to help each other out; it is probably partly in anticipation of receiving similar help when they need it.[10] The punishment sustaining the norm is that those who refuse to help will themselves be excluded from the community's help in the future.

Systems of mutual help are vulnerable to collapse if some community members have opportunities outside. Then the risk of being excluded is not that terrifying anymore, making it tempting to default on obligations. Anticipating this, community members may be more reluctant to help, further increasing the temptation to default. The whole system of mutual support may unravel totally, leaving everyone worse off. The community is therefore very alert to, and protective against, behavior that seems to threaten the communal norms.

COLLECTIVE REACTION

Economists have generally emphasized the positive role communities play.[11] But the fact that norms can be self-enforcing does not necessarily make them good. The discipline they impose could be directed toward some reactionary, violent, or destructive cause. A now classic paper showed that both racial discrimination and India's notorious caste system can be sustained by the same logic, *even if no one actually cares about race or caste.*[12]

Suppose no one actually gives a damn about caste, but anyone who crosses caste lines in sex or marriage is charged with miscegenation and treated like an outcast, meaning nobody will marry into their family and no one will befriend or associate with them. And finally suppose that anyone who defies this norm and marries an outcast also becomes an outcast. Then as long as people are sufficiently forward-looking, and that they do want to get married, this will be enough to stop everyone from breaking the rule, however arbitrary everyone feels it is. Of course, this could shift if enough people start defying the norm. But there is no guarantee it will ever happen.

This is very much the story at the heart of *Samskara,* a wonderful 1970 Indian film directed by Pattabhi Rama Reddy, in which a Brahmin (and hence a member of the so-called highest caste) becomes "polluted" by sleeping with a low-caste prostitute. When he suddenly dies, no other Brahmin is willing to cremate him for fear of being polluted by contact with him. His body is left to rot in public. The norm becomes a perversion of the community's rules precisely because the community is stuck in enforcing its own standards.

THE DOCTOR AND THE SAINT

This tension between the community that binds and the community that bullies is of course age old and universal. And it translates into the tension between a state that protects the individual and a state that undermines the community, which is at the heart of a battle ongoing in countries as diverse as Pakistan and the United States. The fight is partly against the bureaucratization and impersonality that come with state interventions, and partly to preserve the right of the community to pursue its own goals. Even if these goals include, as they often do, discriminating against people with different ethnicity or sexual preferences, as well as the enforcement of religious diktats over those of the state (teaching creation science, for example).

In the Indian national movement, Gandhi famously represented the view that the new Indian nation should be based on decentralized self-reliant villages, havens of peace and fellow-feeling. "The future of India lies in its villages," he wrote. His most remarkable opponent in the movement was Dr. B. R. Ambedkar, the man who would eventually draft the Indian constitution. Born into the very lowest caste, not allowed to enter the classroom in the local school, he was so brilliant that he nevertheless ended up with two PhDs and a law degree. He famously described the Indian village as "a sink of localism, a den of ignorance, narrow-mindedness and communalism."[13] For him, the law, the state as its enforcer, and the constitution from which it derived its force, were the best guarantors of the rights of the underprivileged *against* the tyranny of the locally powerful against the community.

The history of independent India has been a reasonable success in terms of integrating the castes. For example, the wage gap between the traditionally disadvantaged castes (SC/STs) and others dropped from 35 percent in 1983 to 29 percent in 2004.[14] This does not look so spectacular, but is more than the improvement in the wage gap between blacks and whites in the United States over a similar time period. In part this is the result of the affirmative action policies Ambedkar put into place, which gave historically discriminated groups privileged access to educational institutions, government jobs, and the various legislatures. Economic transformation also helped. Urbanization, by making people more anonymous and less dependent on their village networks, has permitted greater mixing of the castes. New jobs lowered the importance of the caste network in finding employment opportunities and increased the incentives for young people from lower castes to get educated. In part the village community was also perhaps less bad than Ambedkar had feared. Villages have proven capable of collective action that transcends caste lines, for example, when they embraced universal primary education and free school meals for all children, regardless of caste.

This is not to say the problem of caste has been solved. At the local level, caste prejudice is alive and well. A study of 565 villages in eleven Indian states found that despite legal bans, some form of untouchability continued to be practiced in almost 80 percent of the villages. In almost half of the villages, Dalits (members of the lower castes) could not sell milk. In about a third of them, they could not sell any goods on the local market, they had to use separate utensils in restaurants, and access to water for irrigating their fields was restricted.[15] Furthermore, while traditional forms of discrimination are weakening, upper castes also react with violence to the perceived threat of the economic progress of lower castes. In March 2018, a young Dalit man in the state of Gujarat was killed for owning and riding a horse, something apparently only upper castes are allowed to do.

To complicate matters, a newer pattern of conflict is emerging; caste groups now see each other as closer to equals but also as potential rivals for power and resources.[16] In politics, there is increasing caste polarization in voting; an increasing fraction of the votes of the upper castes go to the Bharatiya Janata Party (BJP), the one party not committed to affirmative action.[17] Other parties have emerged to cater specifically to different caste groups. This polarization has consequences. In Uttar Pradesh, India's most populous state, the complexion of politics changed drastically between 1980 and 1996. Areas dominated by lower castes voted more and more for the two parties identified with the low castes, whereas the areas dominated by upper castes continued to vote for the parties traditionally associated with them. During the same period, corruption exploded. An increasing number of politicians had a case opened against them, some even fighting (and winning) reelection campaigns from jail. Abhijit and Rohini Pande found there was a connection: corruption increased the most in areas where either the upper castes or the lower castes were a large majority.[18] In those areas, as a result of caste-based voting, the candidate of the dominant caste was all but assured to win, even when he was extremely corrupt and the opponent was not. Nothing like that happened in areas where the population was balanced.

At the same time, the importance given to caste loyalty also allows the community to exercise control over its members, often in clear violation of the law of the land. For example, the caste *panchayats* (essentially local caste associations) have actively resisted the state's writ on sex and marriage in the name of tradition. In a grotesque incident in the state of Chhattisgarh, a fourteen-year-old girl who had been raped by a sixty-five-year-old man was advised by the local caste panchayat not to go to the police about it. When she persisted, she was thrashed by some of the elders of the community, both male and female. A strong community can oppress its weakest members (the Dalits yesterday, today the young woman), and the state is largely powerless to stop it, in part because a majority of community members find it in their interest to uphold community control. As long as they conform, the caste collective offers members access to a web of support and comfort in time of need, and while its brutal underside might bother them from time to time, it takes a brave man or woman to take on the entire community.

"BLACK GUY ASKS NATION FOR CHANGE"[19]

This 2008 headline from the satirical newspaper the *Onion* captures just how remarkable Barack Obama's presidential candidacy was for the United States. The play on words highlighted the contrast between the stereotype of a black man as a freeloader (begging for small change) and Obama as an inspirational leader (asking for cultural change). It is easy to forget there were fewer than forty-five years between the Freedom March and the election of the first African American president. Much has changed in race relations in the years since the civil rights movement, a lot for the better. This made it possible for the country to elect Obama, just as the president and the prime minister of India in 2019 were from the erstwhile backward castes, something equally unthinkable forty-five years ago.

On the other hand, while the African American population today is much better educated than it was in 1965, the income gap between white and black men with similar education has been growing and is now as much as 30 percent, more than that between the scheduled castes and the other castes in India.[20] Black Americans have substantially lower rates of upward mobility and higher rates of downward mobility than whites.[21] This clearly is related to the much discussed large gap in incarceration rates between black males and everyone else,[22] but it is also related to a persistent segregation in neighborhoods and schools.

Despite the fact that white males seem to have no reason to feel economically threatened by African Americans, there is evidence of rising (or at least more open) articulation of anti-black sentiments in recent years. According to the FBI, the number of hate crimes rose by 17 percent in 2017. It was the third consecutive year they increased. They started rising in 2015, after a long period when they had been flat or declining. Three out of five hate crimes targeted a person's ethnicity.[23] Nine candidates who were self-described white supremacists or had close ties to white supremacists ran for office in the congressional elections in 2018.[24]

THIS TIME IT'S DIFFERENT

The dominant story in the United States since the 2016 elections, however, is not the mistrust of African Americans, but the open rage against immigrants, which goes well beyond purely economic resentment.

Immigrants do not only "take" "our" jobs; they are "criminals and rapists" who threaten the very survival of whites. Interestingly, within the US the fewer immigrants there are living in a state, the less liked they are. Nearly half of residents in states with almost no immigrants—like Wyoming, Alabama, West Virginia, Kentucky, and Arkansas—believe immigrants represent a threat to American culture and values.[25]

This suggests the worry has more to do with identity than with economic anxiety. The logic seems to be more that in the absence of much contact, it is easy to imagine that the unseen group is fundamentally different.

This phenomenon predated 2016, but Trump's election made it that much easier to talk about openly. In a clever experiment highlighting this, researchers recruited online respondents in eight deep-red states: Alabama, Arkansas, Idaho, Nebraska, Oklahoma, Mississippi, West Virginia, and Wyoming.[26] Just before the 2016 election, they offered respondents a financial incentive to give money to an anti-immigration charity. Specifically, they asked respondents to authorize them to make a $1 donation to the organization on their behalf, and offered to pay them an extra fifty cents if they agreed. For some people the choice was purely private. For some randomly selected others the offer was presented in a way that implied a small chance they would be personally called by a member of the research team to verify their decision—so at least one person would observe their decision and discuss it with them. Before the election, people in this second group were less likely to agree to donate than people who could do it purely privately (34 percent versus 54 percent). But when the same experiment was conducted right after the election, that difference entirely disappeared! The victory of someone who expressed overt anti-immigration views had freed respondents up to openly give money to an anti-immigrant group.

It is perhaps reassuring that previous waves of migrants to the United States experienced similar rejection before they were ultimately accepted. Benjamin Franklin hated the Germans: "Those who come hither are generally of the most ignorant Stupid Sort of their own Nation. . . . Not being used to Liberty, they know not how to make a modest use of it." Jefferson thought the Germans were unable to integrate. "As to other foreigners it is thought better to discourage their settling together in large masses," he wrote, "wherein, as in our German settlements, they preserve for a long time their own languages, habits, and principles of government."[27] America tried to limit Chinese immigration as early as the nineteenth century and it was eventually banned. In 1924, quotas were introduced with the aim of limiting immigration of Eastern and Southern Europeans (Italians and Greeks).[28]

And yet each wave of immigrants eventually was accepted and assimilated. The first names they chose for their children, the occupations they ended up in, the way they voted, and what they bought and ate converged with those of the local population. In turns, the locals adopted the once-foreign first names and foods: Rocky is an American hero and pizza is one of the five basic food groups.

The same phenomenon happened in France. French people rejected the Italians. Then they rejected the Poles. Then they rejected the Spaniards and the Portuguese. Every wave of migrants eventually became integrated, but in each case at first the French believed it was "different this time." By 2016, it was the Muslims' turn to be rejected.

Where do these preferences and attitudes come from? Why do we seem to look for a new enemy even as we become reconciled to the previous one?

STATISTICAL DISCRIMINATION

There are potentially some simple economic explanations for bigoted behavior toward other groups, very much in the spirit of Becker and Stigler's standard model. Intimidation sometimes serves an economic purpose. Between 1950 and 2000, Hindu Muslim riots in India were much more likely to occur in a particular city in a particular year if the Muslim community happened to be relatively well off. And they were less likely to occur if the Hindu community happened to be doing well.[29] This is consistent with detailed accounts of some of the large riots, where Muslim businesses were specifically targeted in the midst of what may have seemed like random violence. Violence is often a convenient camouflage for theft.

It is also true that sometimes individuals feel the need to express intolerance and prejudice (including sentiments they do not actually share) in order to signal fealty to their group. For example, during the Indonesian economic crisis, membership in Koran reading groups increased. The display of intense religiosity was a sign of loyalty to earn a place in a mutual assistance circle.[30] In other contexts, sometimes people keep quiet about racism (and/or sexism), or even echo what they hear because they do not want to lose their jobs or valuable social connections.

And, finally, there is what economists call *statistical discrimination*. We met an Uber driver in Paris who was very enthusiastic about his job. He said that in the old (pre-Uber) days, if a North African man like him was seen driving a nice car, everyone assumed he was either a drug dealer or had stolen the car. Most people believed, correctly, that most normal North Africans tended to be relatively poor and therefore unlikely to be able to afford a new car, and on the basis of that statistical association their presumption was that the *individual* North

African driver of a nice car was a criminal. Now they assume he is an Uber driver, which is clear progress.

Statistical discrimination explains why the police in the United States justify stopping black drivers more often. And how the Hindu majoritarian government of the state of Uttar Pradesh recently explained why so many of the people "accidentally" killed by the state police (in what are called "encounter deaths") are Muslim. There are more blacks and Muslims among criminals. In other words, what looks like naked racism does not have to be that; it can be the result of targeting some characteristic (drug dealing, criminality) that happens to be *correlated* with race or religion. So *statistical* discrimination, rather than old-fashioned prejudice—what economists call *taste-based* discrimination—may be the cause. The end result is the same if you are black or Muslim, though.

A recent study on the impact of "ban the box" (BTB) policies on the rate of unemployment of young black men provides a compelling demonstration of statistical discrimination. BTB policies restrict employers from using application forms where there is a box that needs to be checked if you have a criminal conviction. Twenty-three states have adopted these policies in the hope of raising employment among young black men, who are much more likely to have a conviction than others and whose unemployment rate is double the national average.[31]

To test the effect of these policies, two researchers sent fifteen thousand fictitious online job applications to employers in New Jersey and New York City, just before and right after the states of New York and New Jersey implemented the BTB policy.[32] They manipulated the perception of race by using typically white or typically African American first names on the résumés. Whenever a job posting required indicating whether or not the applicant had a prior felony conviction, they also randomized whether he or she had one.

They found, as many others before them, clear discrimination against blacks in general: white "applicants" received about 23 percent more callbacks than black applicants with the same résumé. Unsurprisingly, among employers who asked about criminal convictions before the ban, there was a very large effect of having a felony conviction: applicants without a felony conviction were 62 percent more likely to be called back than those with a conviction but an otherwise identical résumé, an effect similar for whites and blacks.

The most surprising finding, however, was that the BTB policy substantially *increased* racial disparities in callbacks. White applicants to BTB-affected employers received 7 percent more callbacks than similar black applicants before BTB. After BTB, this gap grew to 43 percent. The reason was that without the actual information about convictions, the employers *assumed* all black applicants were more likely to have a conviction. In other words, the BTB policy led employers to rely on race to predict criminality, which is of course statistical discrimination.

That people are using statistical logic does not, of course, mean they are always drawing the right inferences from it. In one study, researchers asked Ashkenazi Jews (European or American Jews and their descendants) in Israel to play a trust game with Eastern Jews (Asian and African immigrants and their descendants). The trust game is one of the mainstays of experimental economics. It is played by two people, one of whom, the sender, is given a certain amount of money and asked to share some part of it with the other person, the receiver. The amount could be zero and is entirely left to the sender's discretion. However, they are both told that if the sender shares any of it, that shared amount will be tripled and given to the receiver, who then has full control over the money. The receiver has the option of sharing some of his gains with his benefactor but can opt not to do so. The point of this game is to infer what the sender thinks about the receiver; the less selfish the sender believes the receiver to be, the more he should share.

The trust game has been played thousands of times in laboratory settings. Typically, the sender shares half or more of the original amount and gets back more than was sent. Senders are trusting and receivers are trustworthy. This is also what the researchers found when the two players were both Ashkenazi. But things fell apart when the receiver was an Eastern Jew. In that case, the sender shared about half of what would have been sent to an Ashkenazi. As a result, both senders and receivers got less.

It could be that this happens because the Eastern receivers are not trusted to return the gift. Or it could be because they are disliked, and Ashkenazi senders are willing to hurt themselves just to hurt Eastern receivers as well. But when players were asked to just voluntarily give some of their money to a partner with no expectation any of it would come back, they gave about as much to Eastern partners as they did to the Ashkenazi; the source of the different behaviors in the trust game seems to be suspicion rather than animosity.

Interestingly, the suspicion extends to Eastern senders in the trust game. They were no more trusting of their co-ethnics than the others. There seems to be a stereotype of Eastern Jews that everyone has bought into. But the twist is that the stereotype is entirely unfair. There is absolutely no evidence the Eastern players in this game act in a less trustworthy way; their pattern of returning the money is exactly the same as that of the Ashkenazis. The participants in the experiment thought they behaved rationally, but they were being led astray by imaginary suspicions.

SELF-REINFORCING DISCRIMINATION

The ubiquity of self-discrimination, or discrimination against one's own group, was powerfully brought to light by a well-known experiment by the American psychologist Claude Steele, which demonstrated the power of what he called a "stereotype threat." In his original experiment, he found that black students performed comparably with white students when told a test they were taking was "a laboratory problem-solving task."[33] However, black students scored much lower than whites when test takers were told the test was meant to measure their intellectual ability.

Minorities aren't the only ones vulnerable to stereotype threat. Female college students performed better on a hard mathematics test when it included at the beginning the statement "You may have heard that women typically do less well at math tests than men, but this is not true for this particular test."[34] Conversely, white male math and engineering majors who received high scores on the math portion of the SAT (a group of people quite confident about their mathematical abilities) did worse on a math test when told the experiment was intended to investigate "why Asians appear to outperform other students on tests of math ability."[35] These types of experiments have been repeated many times in different contexts to test different types of self-discriminatory prejudice.

Self-discrimination is often self-reinforcing; people perform differently when they are reminded of their group identity, which makes them doubt themselves even more. The same goes for discrimination against other groups. In a now infamous (once famous) experiment in psychology from the 1960s, teachers were tricked into believing one group of their students (a fifth of the class) was gifted and therefore expected to develop much faster than the rest in terms of IQ. In reality, this group was randomly selected and roughly identical to the rest.[36] The students for whom teachers had higher expectations gained twelve IQ points over the course of the year, while the rest gained only eight. The original experiment was criticized for a variety of reasons, including the morality of such interventions, but numerous other experiments have shown the power of self-fulfilling prophecies.

In France, a study of young cashiers in a French grocery store chain, a sizable share of whom were minorities of North African and Sub-Saharan African origin, showed that biased supervisors invested less in the workers they managed.[37] The cashiers worked with different supervisors on different days and had virtually no control over their schedule. The study showed that assignment to a supervisor more or less biased against a minority affected the performance of minority and nonminority workers differently. On days when they were scheduled to work with biased supervisors, minority cashiers were more likely to be absent. When they did come to work, they spent less time working; they also scanned items more slowly and took longer to serve the next customer. Such effects were completely absent for nonminority workers. The reason for the lower performance of minority workers when assigned to a biased manager seemed to be not so much overt hostility (minority workers did not report disliking working with biased supervisors more, or that biased supervisors disliked them) as less-effective management. Minority workers reported, for example, that biased supervisors were less likely to come over to their cashier stations and encourage them to perform better.

Discrimination against women in leadership positions often carries the same flavor of self-fulfilling prophecy. In villages in Malawi, male or female farmers were randomly selected to learn a new technology and teach it to other farmers.[38] Women retained more information from the training, and those who were trained by them and listened to them did in fact learn more. But most farmers did not listen. They assumed women were less able, and therefore paid less attention to them. Along the same lines, when women in Bangladesh were trained to become line managers, they were just as good as men based on an objective assessment of their leadership and technical qualities, but they were perceived as less good by their line workers. And, presumably as a result, the performance of their lines also suffered, perversely confirming the prejudice that they were worse managers.[39] What started as an unjustified preference against women resulted in women actually doing worse through no fault of their own, and this reinforced their inferior status.

CAN AFRICAN AMERICANS PLAY GOLF?

What is strange about these self-fulfilling prophecies is just how predictable they are. It is always a traditionally disadvantaged person who ends up as the victim of a biased, but self-fulfilling prediction; you never hear about white males being systematically underestimated in anything except sports. The bias stems from a stereotype rooted in the social context.

A study of African American and white Princeton undergraduates shows how deep this runs.[40] The students, who had no prior experience of golf, were asked to perform a series of golf exercises of increasing difficulty. In a first experiment, half of them were asked to indicate their race in a questionnaire before they played (the standard way to "prime" race; that is, to bring group identity to the top of the mind), and half were not. All students were then presented the golf exercises as a test of "general sports performance." When race was not primed, white and black students performed very similarly. But once race was made salient, the fact that golf is a "white" sport (this was before Tiger Woods) made the African Americans worsen their performance and the white students improve theirs, creating a large gap between the two.

In a second experiment, researchers did not prime race, but instead the students were randomly assigned to one of two treatments.[41]

In both groups, the instructions said the exercises would become increasingly challenging. In one group, the instructions said the test was designed to measure personal factors correlated with natural athletic ability. Natural athletic ability was defined as "one's natural ability to perform complex tasks that require hand-eye coordination, such as shooting, throwing, or hitting a ball or other moving objects." In the other, the same test was presented as measuring "sports intelligence," or "personal factors correlated with the ability to think strategically during an athletic performance." In the "natural ability" condition, the African Americans did much better than the whites. In the "sports intelligence" condition, the whites did much better than the African Americans. Everyone, including the blacks themselves, had bought into the stereotype of the African American natural athlete and the white natural strategic player. And this was at Princeton . . .

It is hard to square this evidence with the Becker-Stigler construct of coherent and stable preferences. It seems clear that the way the groups thought about themselves (and others) was a product of these largely ephemeral social constructs of "sports intelligence" and "natural ability" and their supposed connection to race.

ACTING WHITE

Becker and Stigler want us to stay away from the social context behind preferences, but the social context keeps creeping back in. We have preferences not only about what to eat or where to live, but also about who we should spend time with.

We avoid people we are suspicious of, move to neighborhoods where there are more of us. In turn, this segregation affects life chances and breeds inequality. When a neighborhood is mostly poor and black it also gets fewer resources, and all of this has lasting influences on the lives of the children who grow up there. When black people moved to white towns in the north between 1915 and 1970, during what is known as the Great Migration, whites moved away, often leaving behind worse schools, declining infrastructure, and fewer job opportunities.[42]

These neighborhoods became poorer and more derelict, more crime prone, and less and less conducive to economic success. The chance for a black kid to move from the bottom quintile to the top quintile of the distribution of income is much lower in neighborhoods abandoned by the whites during the Great Migration than in others.[43] There are obviously many factors at play, but one of them is that people consciously and unconsciously end up playing by the rules of their neighborhoods. Violence becomes the norm in a neighborhood where it is expected, just as taking five courses when four are required is the norm for MIT undergraduate students.

In a clever experiment illustrating the power of these norms, a group of mostly Hispanic high school students in Los Angeles were offered the option to sign up for a free SAT prep.[44] Some students, chosen at random, were told their choice would remain a secret, while some of them were led to believe their choice might become public. In non-honors classes, the latter group of students were less likely to sign up for the course (61 percent versus 72 percent), presumably because they did not want their friends to find out they had academic aspirations.

It is true that the folk theorem could explain what is going on here. Perhaps it is true that students would be dropped by all their friends if they found out the students were nerds, and anyone who talked to them would also be excommunicated. But it is not accidental that this norm has taken hold with Hispanic students, where there is a history of resenting the norms of white culture, sometimes with very good reason; these Hispanic boys and girls, it seems, were worried about "acting white." That worry has deep roots in their history. We never hear of Asian kids in the United States who have adopted a habit of avoiding their friends who work too hard. In the Becker-Stigler world, since the norms are norms only because people have submitted to them, there is no reason why Hispanic students would not sometimes turn out to be hard working and the Asians the slackers. It is history and the social context that seem to be guiding us toward one norm rather than the other.

LET'S TRY TO ACCOUNT FOR TASTES[45]

To investigate the way the social context influences us, researchers at the University of Zurich recruited a group of bankers as experimental subjects and asked them to flip a coin ten times and report online the outcomes they got.[46] They were told that if they had more than a threshold number of heads (or tails) they would get twenty Swiss francs (about $20) for each extra head (or tail) they reported. Nobody checked whether or not they reported accurately, which created a very strong incentive to cheat.

The key comparison was between those who, before the experiment began, were asked about their favorite leisure activity, highlighting their role as a "regular" person, and those questions about their role as a banker, effectively highlighting their banker identity. Those made to think of themselves as bankers reported many more heads, so many more that it could not have been pure chance. The estimated cheating rate went from 3 percent for those thinking of themselves as regular people to 16 percent for those thinking of themselves as bankers.

This was not because the bankers were better at figuring out how to do well in the game; everybody in the game was a banker, and what got highlighted about them (banker or not) was chosen at random. But being reminded of their profession seems to have brought out a different moral self, one more willing to cheat.

In other words, people seemed to act as if they had multiple personalities, each with different preferences. The context picks the personality that gets to decide in a particular situation. In the Swiss experiment, the context was whether or not the person saw himself as a banker, but in life it is often the people we are with, the schools we went to, what we do for work or for play, the clubs we belong to, and the clubs we would like to belong to that form us and shape our preferences. We economists, in our fealty to standard preferences, have tried very hard to keep all of that out, but it is increasingly obvious this is a hopeless quest.

MOTIVATED BELIEFS

Once we begin to acknowledge that our beliefs and even what we take to be our deep preferences are determined by context, many things fall into place. One important insight comes from the Nobel Prize–winner Jean Tirole's work with Roland Bénabou on motivated beliefs.[47] They argue that a big step toward understanding beliefs is not taking them too literally. Our beliefs about ourselves are shaped in part by our emotional needs; we feel terrible when we disappoint ourselves. The emotional value we put on beliefs about ourselves also leads us to distort our beliefs about others; for example, since we want to shield ourselves from our own prejudices, we couch them in the language of objective truth ("I have nothing against North African cashiers, but they would not respond to my encouragement anyway, so I don't bother").

We don't like changing our minds because we don't like to admit we were wrong to begin with. This is why Abhijit insists it is always the software's fault. We avoid information that would force us to confront our moral ambiguities; we skip over news about the treatment of migrant children in detention centers to avoid thinking about the fact we have supported a government that treats children in this way.

It is easy to see how we may get trapped by these strategies. We don't like to think of ourselves as racists; hence, if we have negative thoughts about others, it is tempting to rationalize our behavior by blaming *them*. The more we can persuade ourselves migrants are to blame for bringing their children with them, the less we worry about the children in their little cages. Instead, we look for evidence that we are right; we overweight every piece of news, however thin, that supports our original position, ignoring the rest.

Over time, the instinctive defensive reaction we started from is replaced by a carefully constructed set of seemingly robust arguments. At that point, we start feeling that any disagreement with our views, given how "solid" the arguments are, has to be either an insinuation of moral failure on our part or a questioning of our intelligence. That's when it can get violent.

Recognizing these patterns has a number of important implications. First, obviously, accusing people of racism or calling them the "deplorables," as Hillary Clinton famously did, is a terrible idea. It assaults people's moral sense of themselves and puts their backs up. They immediately stop listening. Conversely, one can see why calling egregious racists "fine people," and emphasizing there are bad people "on both sides," as President Trump did, is clearly an effective strategy (however morally reprehensible) to gain popularity, since it makes those who make these remarks feel better about themselves.

It also explains why facts or fact-checking don't seem to make much of a dent on people's views, at least in the short run, as we observed in chapter 2, in the context of migration. It remains possible that in the longer run, when the initial "How dare you challenge my beliefs?" reaction fades, people will adjust their views. We should not stop telling the truth, but it is more useful to express it in a nonjudgmental way.

Since most of us like to think we are decent people, forcing someone to affirm their own values before exercising a judgment involving others might reduce prejudice. Psychologists these days encourage parents to tell their children not that they *should* be nice, but that they *are* nice, and all they have to do is to behave in conformity with their natural kindness. That applies to all of us.

This strategy is more likely to work when self-esteem is not already battered. Part of the problem low-income whites face in areas where anti-immigrant and anti-black sentiments are the strongest is that in some observable ways their lives come very close to their own caricature of how those despised "others" live. In 1997, William Julius Wilson wrote in the context of what was happening in the black community that "the consequences of high neighborhood joblessness are more devastating than those of high neighborhood poverty . . . Many of today's problems in the inner-city ghettos—crime, family dissolution, welfare, low levels of social organization, and so on—are fundamentally a consequence of the disappearance of work."[48]

Twenty years later, J. D. Vance wrote in *Hillbilly Elegy:* "Wilson's book spoke to me. I wanted to write him a letter and tell him that he had described my home perfectly. That it resonated so personally is odd, however, because he wasn't writing about the hillbilly transplants from Appalachia—he was writing about black people in the inner cities."[49]

That Wilson's description of the social problems in black neighborhoods applies so well to white communities in the Rust Belt now literally adds insult to injury. Since the perception of their own worth is tied to a sense of superiority with respect to blacks and migrants, the convergence in social circumstances exacerbates the poor white American's sense of crisis.

There are two ways to proceed to restore the sense of self. One is denial (for instance: "We can afford to be resolutely anti-abortion since none of the girls in our community ever get pregnant"). The other is increasing the distance between us and them by turning the other into a caricature. For a white person who has to be on disability because it is the only way to get welfare, it is not sufficient anymore to say a black or Latino single mother must be a welfare queen; that was a Reagan-era insult. Now that white people have to be on welfare as well, the insult has to be ratcheted up; she must be a gang member.

This underscores why we need social policies to reach beyond economic survival and try to restore the dignity of those whose occupations are threatened by technological progress, trade, and other disruptions. The policies must effectively counterbalance the loss of self-confidence; old-fashioned government handouts are not going to work by themselves. What is needed is a wholesale rethinking of the social policy apparatus, the subject of chapter 9.

COHERENT ARBITRARINESS[50]

We know that people will go to great lengths to avoid evidence that would force them to revise their opinions on what they consider to be their core value system (including their opinion about other races or immigrants), because it is so related to their views of themselves. Unfortunately, it does not follow that people are particularly thoughtful about forming those initial opinions.

In one of the most famous experiments in the field of behavioral economics, Daniel Kahneman and Richard Thaler chose college students randomly to receive a mug or a pen. Immediately following the gifts, they offered to buy them back from the newly endowed mug and pen owners. At the same time, they also offered those who did not get a mug or a pen the opportunity to buy what they did not get. Strikingly, the price at which the newly endowed sellers were willing to part with their mugs or pens was often two to three times greater than what those who did not have the pen or mug wanted to pay for them.[51] Since who ended up with a mug or a pen was entirely random, there was absolutely no reason why the arbitrary act of being chosen to get one of them would create such a divergence in valuations. The difference in the bids must have been because those who ended up with a mug started liking their mug more, while those who got a pen did the same with the pen, suggesting there is relatively little intrinsic or deep about how people value things like mugs and pens.

An even more dramatic form of arbitrariness was revealed by another experiment. Students were asked to bid on trackballs, wine bottles, and books. Before bidding, they were asked to write down the last two digits of their social security number with a dollar sign in front of it and *imagine* it was a possible price for the product they had. They obviously knew their social security number had nothing to do with the price of a wine bottle, but nevertheless they were influenced by the "price" they had written down. Students with social security numbers ending in the number eighty or larger bid between 200 percent and 350 percent more for the same good than those whose social security numbers ended in a number less than twenty. In most other ways, they still behaved according to the standard model: for example, they were less willing to buy as the price went up and were most likely to buy cheaper items. But they seemed to have no idea how much these products were worth to them in absolute terms.[52]

But of course mugs and pens are not immigrants and Muslims. Are we really seriously implying this arbitrariness applies to preferences on these much more serious issues as well? We are indeed.

ROBBERS CAVE

Something similar shows up in *social preferences*, what economists call preferences that concern other human beings. In 1954, Muzafer Sherif and Carolyn Wood Sherif carried out an experiment in which twenty-two eleven- and twelve-year-old boys were invited to a summer camp in Robbers Cave, Oklahoma.[53] The boys were randomly divided into two groups. Each group spent some time living in a different location of Robbers Cave, so that the groups were initially unaware of each other's existence. Then at some point the two groups were introduced to each other and made to compete, for example, at tug-of-war. This created animosity between the groups, leading to name-calling and attempts to vandalize the other group's possessions. In the final days, the researchers artificially induced a water shortage, making it useful for the two groups to work together. After some initial hesitation, they did so and mostly forgot their animus.

Some version of this experiment has been repeated many times, and the basic insight has proven very robust. Interestingly, the fact that arbitrary labels heavily influence our loyalties is true even without the bonding experience the initial isolation provided. Just giving a different name to a randomly chosen group of participants got in-group members to favor their own over the others. This was as true of adults as of eleven-year-olds.

Both parts of the Robbers Cave experiment are important: the fact that it is easy to divide as well as the fact that it is possible to reunite. That it is easy to divide is a strong reason to be extremely frightened by the xenophobes and the cynical manipulators of xenophobia who rule so many countries today. The damage they do is not permanent, but unless it is carefully undone it can leave a terrible scar on a nation. In Rwanda, the Belgian colonialists created the myth of the superior Tutsis and the inferior Hutus out of a more or less homogenous population as a way of securing allies in the process of governing. In the immediate post-colonial period, the Tutsis embraced their purported superiority, much to the resentment of the Hutus, and this became a crucial contributory factor to the horrific genocide of 1994.[54]

At the same time, the fact that preferences are not necessarily internally consistent makes attaching ad hominem labels—such as "racist," other "ists," or for that matter "deplorables"—to other human beings suspect, because many people are both racist and not, and their expressions of prejudice are often expressions of pain or frustration. Those who voted for Obama and then Trump may be confused about what each candidate stood for, but to dismiss them as racists after they voted for Trump is both unfair and unhelpful.

HOMOPHILY

Since our preferences are strongly influenced by whom we associate with, social divides are particularly costly because there is very little mixing across these divides; people tend to associate with others like themselves. In US schools, black teenagers mostly associate with blacks, and whites with whites.[55] This is what sociologists call *homophily*. For obvious reasons, this is especially true of those from the largest social group in the school. Those who are a part of a small minority have no choice but to have relatively more friends outside their group.[56]

This does not have to be evidence of intense prejudice. That students in the biggest group do not reach out to outsiders can easily be explained by the fact it is easy for them to meet others like them, and therefore as long as they have a mild preference for their own group, they have no reason to reach out beyond it.

The source of the mild preference does not have to be a negative view of anyone else; it could just be that it is easier to be with people who speak the same language, who share the same gestures and the same sense of humor, who watch the same TV shows and enjoy the same music, or who make the same unstated assumptions about what is appropriate or not. Abhijit, who is from India, is always struck by how easy it is for him to talk to people from Pakistan, notwithstanding the past seventy years of animus between India and that country. The sense of what is funny or what is private (hint: South Asians are nosy), what creates intimacy and what distracts from it, is something, he says, instinctive in all of us South Asians, something partition did not manage to destroy.

The downside to this very natural behavioral pattern becomes evident when we meet people from other groups. We hold back; we walk on eggshells, rationing our human warmth because we worry we might be misunderstood. Or we blunder forward, giving offense when none was intended. Either way, something important gets lost, with the result that we are less likely to communicate smoothly with people from other groups.

This is partly why people mostly marry people like themselves. A little over fifty years after the landmark decision *Loving v. Virginia*, which in 1967 struck down prohibition of interracial marriage in the United States, only about one in six American newly married couples was biracial.[57] In India, 74 percent of families say they believe marriages should be made within castes. Our research suggests this is in part because the men in each caste are looking for women who are the equivalents of their sisters (in other words, the familiar) and likewise for women, and the best place to find such a match is naturally within the group they belong to.[58]

ECHO CHAMBERS AND HOLOGRAMS

Such behavior leads to accidental and probably largely unconscious segregation. We may not realize that if all of us choose to hang out with friends like us, we end up forming entirely separate islands of similar people. This feeds into the intensification of apparently bizarre preferences and/or extreme political views. One obvious downside of sticking to our own is we don't get exposed to other points of view. As a result, differing opinions can persist, even on points of fact such as whether vaccines cause autism or where Barack Obama was born, and even more obviously on matters of taste. We earlier observed that people might rationally choose to suppress their own opinions and join the herd, but of course not being exposed to any opinions outside the herd only makes things worse. We end up with multiple closed groups with contrasting opinions and very little capacity for communicating respectfully with each other. Cass Sunstein, a law professor at Harvard and a member of the Obama administration, describes these as "echo chambers," where like-minded people whip themselves into a frenzy by listening only to each other.[59]

One result of this is extreme polarization on what should be more or less objective facts; for example, 41 percent of Americans believe human activity causes global warming, but the same number either say warming is due to a natural cycle (21 percent) or say there is no warming at all (20 percent). According to the Pew Research Center,[60] public opinion about global warming is deeply segmented along political lines: "Democrats are far more likely than Republicans to say there is solid evidence that temperatures are rising (by a margin of 81% to 58%), and that human activity is the root cause (by 54% to 24%)." That does not mean Democrats are necessarily more pro-science. The scientific consensus, for example, is that GMO foods are not harmful to health, but a strong majority of Democrats think they are and are in favor of labeling them.[61]

Another result of constantly talking to the same people is that the members of a group tend to have shared opinions on most issues. Eclectic political positions become increasingly untenable in the face of a resolute herd, even one that is resolutely wrong. In fact, Democrats and Republicans do not even speak the same language anymore.[62] Matthew Gentkzow and Jesse Shapiro, two economists who are leading scholars of the media, write about members of the US House of Representatives: "Democrats talk about 'estate taxes,' 'undocumented workers' and 'tax breaks for the wealthy,' while Republicans refer to 'death taxes,' 'illegal aliens,' and 'tax reform.' The 2010 Affordable Care Act was 'comprehensive health reform' to Democrats and a 'Washington takeover of health care' to Republicans." It is now possible to predict the political affiliation of a congressman simply by listening to the words they use. Unsurprisingly, partisanship (defined as the ease with which an observer can infer a congressperson's party from a single sentence) has exploded in recent decades. Between 1873 to the early 1990s, it did not change, increasing from 54 percent to just 55 percent during this period. But it increased sharply after 1990; by the 110th session of Congress (2007–2009) it was 83 percent.

This convergence of opinions and vocabulary is precisely why access to Facebook data was so useful to Cambridge Analytica and to political campaigns in the UK and the US. Since most Massachusetts Democrats, for example, have more or less the same views across a wide range of questions and use the same words, it takes just some snippets of our opinions to predict our politics, how we should be targeted, and what types of stories we are likely to like or dislike. And, of course, once real people embrace this cardboard cutout predictability, it becomes that much easier to invent characters, create fake profiles, and inject them into an online conversation.[63]

This insularity also creates an opportunity for skilled political entrepreneurs to present themselves very differently to very different people. During the run-up to the 2014 election for prime minister that he won in a landslide, Narendra Modi in India managed to be at many rallies at the same time by using full-scale, three-dimensional holograms that many voters took to be real. He also managed to be at more than one place in ideological terms. To the generation of globally connected ambitious young urban Indians, he was the embodiment of political modernization (emphasizing innovation, venture capital, and a slick pro-business attitude, and so on); the new entrants into the expanding middle class saw him as the one most likely to uphold their vision of nationalism rooted in Hindu tradition; for the economically threatened upper castes, he was the rampart against the (largely imagined) growing influence of Muslims and lower castes. If members of these groups had met together and each had been asked to describe "their" Modi, their answers would probably have been largely unrecognizable to the others. But the networks in which these three groups operated were sufficiently separate that there was no need for internal consistency.

THE NEW PUBLIC SPACE?

The sharp segmentation of the electorate goes much deeper than just policy disagreements. Americans of different political hues have started to positively hate each other. In 1960, roughly 5 percent of Republicans and Democrats reported they would "[feel] 'displeased' if their son or daughter married outside their political party." By 2010, nearly 50 percent of Republicans and over 30 percent of Democrats "felt somewhat or very unhappy at the prospect of inter-party marriage." In 1960, 33 percent of Democrats and Republicans thought an average member from their own party was intelligent, compared to 27 percent who had the same view about someone from the other side. In 2008, those numbers were 62 percent and 14 percent![64]

What explains this polarization? One of the most important changes since the early 1990s, when partisanship started its sharp increase, is the expansion of the internet and the explosion of social media. As of January 2019, Facebook had 2.27 billion monthly active users globally, while Twitter had 326 million.[65] In September 2014, more than 58 percent of the US adult population and 71 percent of the US online population used Facebook.[66] (That does not include us, so everything we have to say about these networks is second hand.)

Originally, virtual social networks were billed as the new public place, the new way to connect, and hence something that should have reduced homophily. In principle, they provided an opportunity to connect with distant people with whom we shared some specific interest, say in Bollywood movies, Bach cantatas, or raising babies. These people might not have been like us in other ways, offering us a more eclectic choice of friends than what would result from mere physical proximity. They would have had almost nothing to do with each other, so to the extent we would get to exchange views about things other than the precise topic that brought us together, we would all be exposed to a variety of opinions. Indeed, on Facebook, 99.91 percent of the two billion people on it belong to the "giant component," meaning that almost everyone is everyone else's friend of a friend of a friend.[67] There are only about 4.7 "degrees of separation" (the number of "nodes" you have to cross) between any two people in the giant component. This implies that in principle we could easily be exposed to pretty much everyone's views as they travel through the social network.

Nevertheless, virtual social networks have mostly failed to integrate their users on divisive issues. A study of 2.2 million politically engaged users on Twitter (defined as those who followed at least one account associated with a candidate for the US House during the 2012 election period) in the United States finds that while there are roughly ninety million network links among these users, 84 percent of the followers of conservative users are other conservatives, and 69 percent of the followers of liberal users are liberal.[68]

Facebook and Twitter function as echo chambers. Democrats pass on information produced by Democratic candidates, and Republicans do the same for Republicans. Eighty-six percent of first retweets of tweets by Democratic candidates come from liberal voters. The corresponding number for Republicans is an amazing 98 percent. Taking into account retweets, liberals get 92 percent of their messages from liberal sources, and conservatives get 93 percent of their messages from conservative sources. Strikingly, this is not just true of political tweets; for these politically engaged people, the exposure is just as skewed for nonpolitical tweets. Apparently, even to chat about fly fishing on Twitter, people prefer to connect with a fellow liberal or conservative. The virtual community that social networks have created is at best a fragmented public space.

But is there anything specific about social media that causes this polarization? The political strategies to divide the population and plant fake news were invented long before Facebook. Newspapers have always been highly partisan, and political mud-slinging was the bread and butter of the print media in colonial America, and continued into the early days of the American Republic (in the musical *Hamilton*, it is the threat of scurrilous press coverage that forces Hamilton to own up to his affair). The "Republican noise machine" was perfected on cable TV and talk radio in the 1990s, as David Brock powerfully documents in his book bearing that title.[69]

An even more powerful demonstration of just how destructive old media can be comes from the Rwandan genocide. Before and during the genocide, Radio Télévision Libre des Mille Collines (RTLM) called for the extermination of the Tutsis, whom they called "cockroaches," justified it as self-defense, and talked about the supposed atrocities committed by the Rwandan Patriotic Front (or RPF, the Tutsi militia). Villages that RTLM reached experienced significantly more killings than villages it did not due to the mountains blocking radio wave transmissions. Altogether, RTLM propaganda is estimated to be responsible for 10 percent of the violence, or about fifty thousand Tutsi deaths.[70]

Gentzkow and Shapiro computed an "isolation index" for the year 2009 (which in some ways feels like a lifetime ago, but the internet was already quite vibrant) both for online and offline news. This was defined as the difference in the share of news items with a conservative slant a conservative was exposed to and the share of news items with a conservative slant a liberal was exposed to. What they found seemed to suggest polarization was happening offline just as much as it was online. The average conservative's exposure to conservative views online was 60.6 percent of their total news consumption, the equivalent of a person who gets all their news from usatoday.com. The average liberal's exposure to conservative positions was 53.1 percent, at the same level as cnn.com. The isolation index for the internet (the difference between the two) was therefore just 7.5 percentage points, a little bit higher than the isolation index for broadcast news and cable television news, but lower than that for national newspapers. And it was much lower than the segregation of in-person contact. It was already true in 2009 that conservatives had mostly conservative friends, and the opposite for liberals. The isolation index is low because, in their data, both conservative and liberal users visited mostly "centrist" sites, and those most likely to visit extremist sites (like Breitbart) also visited many others, including those with opposite perspectives.[71]

While it is true that polarization has increased among online users, it has also increased in other spheres of life. Indeed, while polarization has increased in all demographic groups since 1996, it increased the most among those sixty-five or older, who are the least likely to be on the internet, and increased the least among the youngest people (those aged eighteen to thirty-nine).[72] Polarization has also increased in traditional news media. A textual analysis of the content of cable news showed that since 2004 the language used by Fox News has become increasingly slanted to the right, while MSNBC has moved to the left.[73] The audiences have also diverged. Until 2008, Fox News had a stable share of about 60 percent Republicans among its viewers. This share increased to 70 percent between 2008 and 2012. Over the years, Fox News became increasingly conservative, which attracted more conservative voters, who in turn pushed it to be even more conservative. This has begun to affect voting patterns. We know this because in some counties in the United States Fox News shows up at a less accessible part of the dial, for purely accidental reasons, and therefore people are less likely to tune in to it.[74] In those counties people are also less prone to vote for conservatives.

So what is it that changed? In Congress, according to Gentzkow and Shapiro, the turning point seems to have been 1994, the year of Newt Gingrich's takeover of the Republican Party and his "contract with America."[75] This was also the first year political consultants played a key role in designing and testing messages, which is something that as social scientists interested in the design and testing of innovations, including in messaging, we find rather disturbing.

NETWORKING NOT WORKING

Even if political polarization did not wait for the internet, it is hard to be entirely sanguine about the effects of the virtual social networks and the internet on our policy preferences, and the ways they are expressed. For one, we don't really know the counterfactual; what would the world be like without these innovations? Comparing those with and without access to the internet, like the young and the old, does not answer this question, for many obvious and less obvious reasons. In particular, the internet is often the place where rumors get manufactured and circulated before they make their way to Fox News, where older people get to hear them. Perhaps younger people are less moved by these rumors because they know the internet is full of errors and exaggerations and can correct for them, whereas older people, used to trusting the booming authority of television anchors, are more gullible.

There are other concerns as well. The first is that the circulation of news on social media is killing the production of reliable news and analysis. Producing fake news is of course very cheap and very rewarding economically since, unconstrained by reality, it is easy to serve to your readership exactly what they want to read. But if you don't want to make things up, you can also just copy it from elsewhere. A study found that 55 percent of the content diffused by news sites and media in France is almost entirely cut and pasted, but the source is only mentioned in less than 5 percent of the cases.[76] If a piece of news produced by a team of journalists is immediately cut and pasted onto many other sites, how does the original source get rewarded for its production? It is no surprise that the number of journalists in the United States has plummeted in the last few years, going from nearly 57,000 in 2007 to almost 33,000 in 2015.[77] There are both fewer journalists in total and fewer journalists per newspaper. The economic model that sustained journalism as a location for "public space" (and correct information) is collapsing. Without access to proper facts, it is easier to indulge in nonsense.

The second concern is that the internet allows for endless repetition. The problem with echo chambers is not just that we are only exposed to ideas we like; we are also exposed to them again and again and again, endlessly, throughout the day. The fake users used to "boost" stories on Facebook plus the real persons paid to "like" content accentuate the natural tendency for some messages to be repeated and acquire a life of their own. The endless repetition whips people into a frenzy (much like the way political demonstrations use repeated chants), making it harder for them to stop and check the stories.

And even if the truth eventually gets out, the many repetitions of a falsehood can raise the salience of a divisive issue and harden extremist views. We remember only the endless talk about Mexicans (who we never trusted in any case) and not the fact that first-generation immigrants, legal or otherwise, are actually less likely to be criminals than native-born Americans.[78] This of course creates a very strong reason to flood the markets with alternative facts. A hundred and fifteen pro-Trump fake news stories that circulated before the 2016 presidential election were viewed thirty million times (pro-Clinton fake news stories also existed, but they were viewed only eight million times).[79]

The third is that the crabbed language of internet communication (which Twitter takes to an extreme) encourages directness and abbreviation, contributing to the erosion of the norms of civic discourse. As a result, Twitter has turned into a lab for trying out the latest nasty pitch. Political entrepreneurs are happy to plant their wildest claims on Twitter and watch them play out, with an eye to whether they have gone too far. If it seems to be working, at least among the targeted group (as measured by retweets or likes, for example), they add it to the pack of potential strategies for the future.

Fourth, there is automatic customization. In 2001, when Sunstein was writing about echo chambers, he was worried about the opportunity users have to choose the news they consume. Increasingly, there is no need to choose. Sophisticated algorithms use machine-learning prediction techniques to try to figure out what we might like based on who we are, what we have searched before, etc. The objective, quite explicitly, is to get people what they like so they spend more time on it.

Facebook came under pressure for the algorithm it used to push stories to users, and in 2018 it promised to reprioritize its feeds, putting posts from friends and family ahead of media content. But you do not need to be on Facebook for this to happen. On Esther's Google home page on July 2, 2018, there was one article from the *Atlantic*, "The Trade Deficit Is China's Problem"; Paul Krugman's latest op-ed in the *New York Times*; one article from the *New York Times* on millennial socialists; one article on the soccer World Cup; one article from the *Boston Globe* on Lawrence Bacow, the new president of Harvard; one article on Simone Veil's burial; a *Huffington Post* article on Senator Susan Collins's view on the choice of the latest Supreme Court justice; and the unavoidable article about the Pixel Watch. There were only two stories she was not obviously interested in: one about a criminal escaping a French prison by helicopter (which turned out to be lots of fun) and a piece on Fox News about Busy Philipps fighting with Delta Air Lines for rebooking her and her child on different flights. That last piece was her entire exposure to right-wing media for the day. Such customization is ubiquitous. Even the National Public Radio app ("NPR One" to the cognoscenti) calls itself "Pandora for Public Radio," referring to the app that gives you the music you like based on what you have listened to in the past. Within the echo chamber for liberal ideas that is NPR, an algorithm will filter for the user exactly what the user likely will want to hear.

This matters because when users actively choose what they are reading, they are at least conscious of what they are doing. They may prefer to read articles from familiar sources, but be sophisticated enough to acknowledge their own biases reflected in those sources. An unusual experiment in South Korea demonstrated that this kind of sophistication is very real. From February to November 2016, two young Koreans created an app offering users access to curated articles from the press on topical issues and regularly asked them their opinions on the articles and on the issues themselves. At first, all users received a randomly selected article about each issue. After a number of rounds, some randomly selected users got to choose the news sources from which they received their articles, while others continued to receive randomly selected articles. The experiment yielded three important results. First, users did respond to what they read: they updated their views in the direction of what was being presented to them. Second, as expected, those given the option chose articles generally aligned with their partisan preferences. Third, however, at the end of the experiment, those who got to choose their articles had updated their preferences more than those who did not, and they had generally updated toward the center! This is the opposite of the echo chamber effect. On balance, the option to choose slanted material made users *less* partisan. The reason is they understood exactly how biased the source they chose was, and partly undid the bias, while being receptive to the information; whereas with randomly assigned stories, users did not recognize the bias and therefore remained skeptical about the content, not changing their opinion much.[80]

It would be very interesting to replicate this experiment in the United States. The effect may also depend on how politically engaged the reader is. It is not entirely clear that many internet readers in the US make a conscious effort to correct the bias in what they read. But this study suggests a key problem of seamless customization: its very seamlessness. Correcting slant requires an understanding of what the source's slant is. When we always read news from the same source, we are familiar with it. But when an algorithm is serving us articles from all over the internet, some of which comes from known sources and some from more unfamiliar corners, and some of which may be entirely fake, we won't know how to read those signals. Moreover, because we have not made the choice ourselves, we may not even remember to make the correction.

RUNNING TOGETHER

As we lose the ability to listen to each other, democracy becomes less meaningful and closer to a census of the various tribes, who each vote based more on tribal loyalties than on a judicious balancing of priorities. The biggest coalition of tribes wins, even if its candidate is a known child molester, or worse. The winner does not need to deliver economic or social benefits even to his own supporters as long as the supporters worry enough about the possibility of takeover by the other side; knowing that, he or she will do their best to stoke those fears. In the worst case, the winner can then use the power gained in this way to take control of the media to shut down any alternative voice, so there is no more competition to worry about. Prime Minister Orbán has successfully done this in Hungary, and many others are not far behind.

Moreover, there is an expanding circle of violence—against blacks, women, and Jews in the United States, against Muslims and lower castes in India, and against immigrants in Europe—that is probably not uncorrelated with the unabashed expressions of vituperation the current polarized climate permits, including by heads of state. The murderous mobs in India and Brazil, and the recent shooters and pipe-bomb senders in the United States or New Zealand seem to all emerge from those vortices of paranoid thinking, where the same falsehoods bounce back and forth. It has not yet reached proportions of a civil war or a genocide, but history suggests that it could.

As we have already seen, our reaction to the other is closely tied to our self-confidence. Only a social policy founded on respect for the dignity of the individual can help make the average citizen more open to ideas of toleration.

There are also possible interventions at the group level. Racism, anti-immigrant views, and the lack of communication across party lines originate, for many people, with an initial lack of contact. Gordon Allport, a professor of psychology at Harvard, formulated what he called the *contact hypothesis* in 1954.[81] This is the idea that under appropriate conditions, interpersonal contact is one of the most effective ways to reduce prejudice. By spending time with others, we learn to understand and appreciate them, and as a result of this new appreciation and understanding, prejudice should diminish.

The contact hypothesis has been intensively studied. A recent review identifies twenty-seven randomized controlled trials (RCTs) investigating Allport's idea. Overall, these studies find that contact reduces prejudice, although the review calls attention to the importance of the nature of the contact.[82]

If this is right, schools and universities are obviously key. They bring together young people from different backgrounds in a single location, at an age when everyone is much more plastic. In one large US university, where roommates were assigned at random, a study found that white students who happened to end up with African American roommates were significantly more likely to endorse affirmative action, and that white students assigned roommates from any minority group were more likely to continue to interact socially with members of other ethnic groups after their first year, when they had full freedom in choosing whom to associate with.[83]

This process of socialization could start even earlier. A policy change in Delhi demonstrated the power of bringing together young children from very different backgrounds. Starting in 2007, elite private schools in Delhi were required to offer places to poor students. In an ingenious study on the impact of this policy change, randomly chosen children were given the responsibility to select teammates for a relay race.[84] Some of them attended schools that had already admitted poor children, and some attended schools that had not done so yet. And, within schools, some children were in study groups with poorer children (based on the first letter of their first name), and some were not. To help them decide who they wanted to partner with in the race, they were all given a chance to observe everyone else run a test race. There was, however, a catch. They had to agree to have a playdate with whomever they picked for their team. The study found that those students from affluent families who had not been exposed to poor students in their school avoided picking them, even when they were better runners, to avoid having to spend time with them. But those who'd had some exposure to children from less-well-off families in their schools, thanks to the new policy, were much more likely to pick the best runner even if the child was from a poor family, because the prospect of a playdate was no longer all that daunting. And those who were in a study group with poor children were even more likely to invite poor child to run and play with them. Familiarity performed its magic.

STUDENTS FOR FAIR ADMISSION VS. HARVARD

One implication of this evidence is that diversity in the student body of educational institutions is valuable in and of itself, because it durably affects preferences. Affirmative action was originally envisioned in the United States partly as compensation for historical injustice, and partly as a way to level the playing field between the whites, who had the advantage of many generations of advanced education, and the rest. But it goes much beyond that. What the twenty-seven RCTs on the effect of contact on tolerance imply is that this mixing is one of the most powerful instruments we have for making society more tolerant and more inclusive. The problem is that affirmative action itself is now a polarizing idea.

In the spring of 2018, New York City struggled with the redesign of the admission system for its elite public schools, which is currently based on an exam and lets in very few Latinos and African Americans. At the same time, Asian Americans were suing Harvard for discrimination, on the grounds that, in order to achieve its diversity goals, Harvard artificially limits the number of Asian American students it admits.

Additionally, the Trump administration has been urging schools to stop taking race into consideration in their admission decisions. The US Supreme Court has so far resisted pressure to forbid any discrimination based on race, but it is not clear how long it will hold out.

In India, the debate is framed in terms of the actual quotas in educational institutions and government jobs for the castes historically discriminated against. These quotas are much resented by the upper castes, resulting in frequent protests and lawsuits challenging the validity of the law, especially on the grounds that a disproportionate share of the reserved slots end up with the more privileged among the lower castes, who perhaps need them less. (They are poetically referred to as the "creamy layer.") The Indian court system has been sympathetic to this complaint, and has made eligibility for the quotas subject to an income qualification: you have to be poor enough to qualify. At the same time, other social groups have been lobbying to be included in the quotas, which would serve to dilute them. As a result, the system of reservations is almost incessantly being fought over somewhere or the other in the country, with not infrequent outbreaks of violence.

The idea of "merit" plays a key role in this debate. At the heart of the argument is the idea that test scores provide an objective measure of merit, a measure of how suitable the candidate is for the job or a place in the university, and therefore affirmative action discriminates against "meritorious" candidates, as they are called in India. Given everything we have seen in this chapter, that seems like a very unlikely proposition. Self-discrimination undermines confidence and test performance. A history of being underestimated, patronized, ignored, or despised by teachers and supervisors because you happen to be from a particular group will make it harder to achieve. Moreover, as we both know, growing up in a household where books are everywhere and dinner table conversation often centers around fine points of mathematics or philosophy, whether or not you always enjoy it, becomes a distinct advantage when you are writing your college essays. A lower-caste candidate who performed as well as Abhijit in the high school leaving exam had to jump through more hoops to get there and is for that reason likely to be more talented.

The fuzziness of the notion of merit was the bone of contention between two first-rate empirical economists, David Card and Peter

Arcidiacono, who were retained by the two sides in the *Students for Fair Admission v. Harvard* trial. On the plaintiffs' side, Arcidiacono argued that Asians must be discriminated against because admitted Asians have higher grades and higher test scores than any other group. In other words, given the same test scores, an Asian student is less likely to be admitted to Harvard than a white student (or an African American).

On the Harvard side, Card had a number of objections to Arcidiacono's analysis, including the point that the objective of diversity in parental background and intended major was legitimate. But the most striking difference came from their interpretations of the "personality rating," meant to capture the candidate's leadership qualities and integrity. Asian students systematically have higher academic and extracurricular ratings, but lower personality ratings, and once we account for that they are no less likely to be admitted than white students.

For Card, this proves there is no discrimination. Arcidiacono contends that the personality rating is exactly the way Harvard discriminates against Asians. In the debate, a rather ironic parallel with history did not go unnoticed. In the 1920s, then Harvard president Abbott Lawrence Lowell attempted to introduce quotas to limit the admission of Jews to the university. This failed, but he put in place the system of "holistic" admission, meaning a system that values personal characteristics beyond grades, which was used to limit the number of Jews. Students for Fair Admission wants to make the case this is happening again.

The debate illustrates the essential treacherousness of the idea of merit, and the very notion of what constitutes quality. On the one hand, "personal qualities" may reflect (perhaps unwittingly) a form of belonging to a club, with secret handshakes not taught in the average public school. The personality rating may indeed be a not so subtle way to keep a certain type of student out (whether or not they are Asian) and ensure the smooth intergenerational transmission of elite status. On the other hand, the fact that among applicants African Americans systematically have higher personality ratings than whites or Asians may well reflect what we mentioned earlier: since admissions at Harvard require a sterling academic record, a child from a disadvantaged background must have quite unusual personal skills to be even considered, especially since the child might have had to survive worse schools and perhaps a more challenging home environment.

There is no evident solution to this problem. As a flagship producer of the next generation of leaders, Harvard clearly needs to find a place for students from all social groups, and a massive overrepresentation of any particular social group relative to its weight in the population is both perhaps undesirable in a democracy and likely to lead to political problems. But we need a more transparent social conversation about the design of affirmative action. The current implementation of affirmative action policies, which dances around the concept of race instead of directly confronting it, is probably not anywhere close to ideal. The Harvard challenge is both inevitable and perhaps desirable in that it makes society confront its own inconsistencies.

From the perspective of the narrow objective of affecting preferences by increasing contact between social groups, the growing resentment of affirmative action poses a problem. Allport's original hypothesis was that contact would reduce prejudice, but only if some conditions were satisfied. In particular, he held that reduced prejudice would result when the contact happened in a setting where there was equal status between the groups in the situation, common goals, intergroup cooperation, and the support of authorities, law, or custom. Extremely contentious integration is unlikely to produce these conditions. For example, if high school students feel they are competing for slots in college and, worse, if they have the impression this competition might be tilted against them, they may come to resent the other group even more.

CRICKET LESSONS

That this is a very real concern is demonstrated by a clever recent study.[85] In the state of Uttar Pradeshin in India, a researcher ran an eight-month-long cricket league involving 800 players, all young men, chosen randomly out of 1,261. In the league, about a third of the players were assigned to homogeneous-caste teams; the others were in mixed-caste teams. Like others, the study found many positive effects of collaborative contact. Compared to those who played on single-caste teams, the young men who played on mixed teams were more likely to be friends with people from other castes after the experiment, and not just those from their teams. When they had a chance to select their teams, they selected better teams for future matches, since they made their choices based on talent, not caste.

But who they played against mattered. Those in teams randomly assigned to play against other-caste teams were less likely to make friends with people from other castes than those who played only against their own caste, or even those who never got to play anyone. Competition undermined contact.

These somewhat less optimistic results make the important point that contact may not be enough to produce tolerance; it may be necessary to have shared goals. Both in 1998 and in 2018, the victory of France's team at the soccer World Cup had exactly this effect on the nation as a whole. In particular, the fact that some of the team's champions grew up and learned their skills in the suburbs of Paris notorious for their dilapidated housing projects and their car-burning riots did create a sense of goodwill and shared purpose. In that moment, everyone could see that the kids from the 93 (as one disadvantaged district in the north of Paris is known) were not all lazy bums who skipped school and committed petty crimes. Behind France's winning *black-blanc-beur* ("black-white-Arab") team was the effort and the discipline of tens of thousands of young kids working hard to make it.

ZONING FOR PEACE

Since there are obvious limits on integration through universities, mixed neighborhoods offer a useful alternative. The problem is that mixed neighborhoods have a proclivity toward being unstable, as Tomas Schelling, who won the Nobel Prize in economics, demonstrated.[86] Suppose homeowners are happy to live in mixed neighborhoods, but not in neighborhoods mostly dominated by another group. Then they must live in fear of the day when, by chance perhaps, a few of their own move out and are replaced by the other. The neighborhood becomes a little less attractive to people like them, and now they all start worrying that if a few more leave, let's say because they are also having the same thoughts, or because they are less tolerant, they will be forced to leave as well. The tension of whether and when that may happen can become unbearable, so anyone who can get out leaves. This is what Schelling called the *tipping point*.

David Card studied the increase in segregation that happened in the United States in the 1970s, 1980s, and 1990s, and it does indeed look like there is this tipping point property.[87] If the fraction of blacks in the neighborhood was less than some number, it remained stable; if it became higher, there was a large outflow of the white population in subsequent years. Chicago, for example, had a particularly low tipping point. If the black population in a neighborhood was less than 5 percent in 1970, it remained at that level afterward, but if it was any more than that the fraction of whites soon plummeted. On average across US cities, Card and his colleagues found tipping points ranging between 12 percent and 15 percent.

The way to prevent the segregation implied by the tipping point logic is to build public housing targeting low-income residents and disperse that housing throughout the city, so there are no "pure" neighborhoods available. In a fancy neighborhood in Paris, where we spent a year, the building next to us was a housing project. The children all attended the same neighborhood school and played in the same park. At that age, they clearly inhabited the same universe. It may not be possible to be as bold as Singapore, where strict quotas ensure some amount of mixing between ethnic groups in every block of residential housing, but it seems possible to reserve a certain fraction of public housing in every neighborhood.

The challenge of implementing such a policy is mostly political. It seems easy enough to imagine how to do it well if the political will is there: spread the public housing around, give everyone a lottery number, have a public lottery every time new housing becomes available, and make it easy to check that the winners get the housing. The difficulty is that public housing in fancy neighborhoods is very tempting for local politicians to use as patronage, but with enough political will it can probably be overcome.[88]

Nevertheless, in the near future, while most poor people still live in low-income neighborhoods, shared schools are another way to integrate the population. For this to happen, children will need to be moved. Busing a large number of children to foster school diversity, as it was done in Boston at some point, is however unpopular, in part for the very good reason that young children do not enjoy being bused. The best idea may be to allow children from designated low-income neighborhoods to attend schools outside their neighborhoods. The METCO program in the United States, which organized the busing of minority children to majority schools, was shown to be beneficial to the minority children without any harm to the test scores of majority children. The latter, who would have mostly spent their lives in largely white enclaves, ended up being exposed to a much more diverse population, which as we have seen durably affects worldviews and preferences.[89]

REARRANGING THE DECK CHAIRS?

The sum total of all our proposals might seem modest in the face of what feels like a tsunami of prejudice. But that would be to miss the main point of this chapter, which is that such preferences are as much part of the symptoms of the malaise as its cause, perhaps more. Prejudice is often a defensive reaction to the many things we feel are going wrong in the world, our economic travails, and a sense that we are no longer respected or valued.

This has four important implications. First, and most obviously, the expression of contempt for those who express racist sentiments, fraternize with racists, or vote for them ("deplorables") serves only to reinforce those sentiments, founded in the suspicion the world no longer respects us. Second, prejudice is not an absolute preference; even so-called racist voters care about other things. North India in the 1990s and early 2000s saw a period of mostly caste-based polarization. However, by 2005 this had run its course. The lower castes who had aligned themselves with explicitly caste-based parties (as against the less transparently caste-based BJP, Prime Minister Modi's party) had begun to question whether they were getting enough from their parties. Mayawati, the leader of one of those parties, decided to rebrand herself as the leader of all poor people, including poor upper castes, and won the 2007 Uttar Pradesh state elections on that basis. She went for broad inclusivity, not narrow sectarianism.

More recently, in the United States we are struck by the curious history of the once much hated Affordable Care Act, or Obamacare. As the signal policy initiative of the much despised black Kenyan Muslim Barack Obama, it was something that many Republican governors refused to have anything to do with, and many refused federal subsidies to expand Medicaid, a key mechanism to extend health care coverage under the Affordable Care Act. Yet by the 2018 midterm election initiatives to expand Medicaid were on the ballot in the deep-red states of Utah, Nebraska, and Idaho. They were approved in all three. Kansas and Wisconsin also elected new Democratic governors who vowed to expand Medicaid where their Republican predecessors had not. This is not because people in these places became Democrats; they still voted for Republican congressmen and senators, often with very conservative views. But on this issue many seem to have decided to ignore the warnings of the Republican establishment and go with their own understanding of what was going to be good for them. Economics trumped Trump.

This is related to our third point. The fact that voters put a premium on race or ethnicity or religion, or even the articulation of racist views, does not have to mean they feel very passionately about them. Voters do realize political leaders choose to play the ethnic or race card when convenient. Part of the reason they still vote for those politicians is they are deeply cynical about the political system, having convinced themselves all politicians are more or less alike. Given that, they might as well vote for the guy who looks or sounds like them. In other words, ethnic or bigotted voting is often just an expression of indifference. But that means it is surprisingly easy to make them change their minds by highlighting what is at stake in an election. In 2007, in Uttar Pradesh, an Indian state famous for its caste-based politics, Abhijit and his colleagues managed to make 10 percent of voters move their vote away from their own caste-party using only a combination of songs, a puppet show, and some street theater—all carrying the simple message "Vote on development issues, not on caste."[90]

Which leads us to our final and perhaps most important point. The most effective way to combat prejudice may not be to directly engage with people's views, natural as that might seem. Instead, it may be to convince citizens it is worth their while to engage with other policy issues. That leaders who promise them a great deal and even make grand gestures toward it may not actually deliver much more than those gestures, in part because doing anything more is not easy. In other words, we need to reestablish the credibility of the public conversation about policy, and prove that it is not just a way to use big words to justify doing very little. And of course we need to try to do what it will take to assuage the anger and deprivation so many feel, while acknowledging it will be neither easy nor quick.

This, as we explained in chapter 1, is the journey we started in this book. We started with the issues where the most is known and understood: immigration and trade. Even there, there is a strong tendency for economists to pronounce on these issues with categorical answers ("immigration is good," "free trade is better") without accompanying detailed explanations and necessary caveats, which massively undermines credibility. We now turn to issues that are much more contentious, even among economists: the future of growth, the causes of inequality, the challenge of climate change.

We will attempt to do the same exercise of demystification for these topics, while recognizing that what we have to say will occasionally be based on more abstract arguments than the ones we have made so far, and somewhat less well grounded in evidence. These issues are nonetheless so central to our view of the future (and the present) that there is no way to talk about how to do better economic policy without embracing them.

In all of this the role of preferences is crucial. It is obviously impossible to talk about growth and inequality and the environment without thinking of needs and wants, and therefore preferences. We have seen that wants may not be needs—people seem to value bottles of wine based on their own social security number rather than the pleasure of drinking—and needs may not be wants—is a television a need or a want? These will of course be central concerns in the coming chapters, implicit and sometimes explicit in the arguments we make and the view of the world we project.

CHAPTER 5

THE END OF GROWTH?

G ROWTH ENDED ON October 16, 1973, or thereabouts, and is never to return, according to a wonderfully opinionated book by Robert Gordon.[1]

On that day, the member countries of OPEC announced an embargo on oil. By the time the embargo was lifted in March 1974, the price of oil had quadrupled. The world economy at this time had become increasingly reliant on oil and was generally facing raw material shortages that were pushing up prices. What followed in the rich countries of the West was a lackluster decade of "stagflation" (economic stagnation accompanied by inflation). Slow growth was supposed to go away but has been with us ever since.

This happened in a world where most citizens of these rich countries had grown up expecting endless and ever-expanding prosperity, where political leaders had grown accustomed to measuring their success in terms of a single yardstick: the rate of growth of the country's gross domestic product, or GDP. And to a large extent this is still the world we live in, and in some sense we are still talking about that pivotal moment in the 1970s. What went wrong? Was there a policy mistake? Can we coax growth to return and stay? What magic button do we need to press? Is China immune to this slowdown?

Economists have been busy answering these questions. Countless books and papers have been written about them. Many Nobel Prizes have been awarded. After all that, what is it that can be said with confidence about how to make rich economies grow faster? Or does the fact so much has been written signal that we really have no idea? And should we even be concerned?

THE GLORIOUS THIRTY

For the thirty-odd years that separated the end of the Second World War from the OPEC crisis, economic growth in Western Europe, the United States, and Canada was faster than it had ever been in history.

Between 1870 and 1929, GDP per person in the United States grew at a then unheard of rate of 1.76 percent per year. In the four years after 1929, GDP per person went down by a catastrophic 20 percent—it is not called the Great Depression for nothing—but it recovered fast enough. The average yearly growth rate from 1929 until 1950 was actually slightly higher than in the previous period. But between 1950 and 1973, the yearly growth rate went up to 2.5 percent.[2] There is more difference than there might appear to be between 1.76 percent and 2.5 percent. It would take forty years for GDP per head to double with a growth rate of 1.76 percent, but only twenty-eight years at 2.5 percent.

Europe had a more checkered history before 1945, partly because of its wars, but after 1945 things really exploded. When Esther was born, late in 1972, France had about four times the GDP per capita than when her mother, Violaine, was born in 1942.[3] This was typical of the Western European experience. GDP per capita in Europe increased by 3.8 percent every year between 1950 and 1973.[4] It's not for nothing that the French call the thirty years after the war *les Trente Glorieuses* ("the Glorious Thirty").

Economic growth was driven by a rapid expansion in the productivity of labor, or the output produced per hour worked. In the United States worker productivity grew at 2.82 percent per year, which meant it would double every twenty-five years.[5] This rise in labor productivity was large enough to more than offset a *decline* in hours worked per head that was going on at the same time. During the second half of the century, the workweek went down by twenty hours in the US and in Europe. And the postwar baby boom lowered the share of working-age adults in the population since the baby boomers were then, well . . . babies.

What made workers more productive? In part, they were becoming more educated. The average person born in the 1880s studied only up to seventh grade, whereas the average person born in the 1980s had on average two years of college education.[6] And they had more and better machines to work with. This was the age in which electricity and the internal combustion engine came to assume their central role.

Making somewhat heroic assumptions, it is possible to guesstimate the contribution of these two factors. Robert Gordon reckons that rising education explains about 14 percent of the increase in labor productivity over the period, and the capital investment that gave workers more and better machines to work with explains a further 19 percent of the increase.

The rest of the observed productivity improvement cannot be explained by changes in things economists can measure. To make ourselves feel better, economists have given it its own name: *total factor productivity,* or TFP. (The famous growth economist Robert Solow defined TFP to be "a measure of our ignorance.") Growth in total factor productivity is what is left after we have accounted for everything we can measure. It captures the fact that workers with the same education level working with the same machines and inputs (what economists refer to as *capital*) produce more output today for each hour they work than they did last year. This makes sense. We constantly look for ways to use our existing resources more effectively. This reflects in part technological progress: computer chips become cheaper and faster, so one secretary can now do in a few hours the work a small team used to do; new alloys are invented; new varieties of wheat that grow faster and require less water are introduced. But total factor productivity also increases when we discover new ways to reduce waste or shrink the time either raw materials or workers are forced to stay idle. Innovations in production methods like chain production or lean manufacturing do that, as does, say, the creation of a good rental market for tractors.

What made the few decades before 1970 extraordinary compared to much of history is that total factor productivity increased particularly rapidly. In the United States, TFP growth was four times faster between 1920 and 1970 than between 1890 and 1920.[7] In fact, it was this rather than growth in education or capital per worker that gave the later period its special mojo. TFP growth in Europe was even faster than in the United States, especially after the war, partly because Europe adopted innovations already developed in the US.[8]

Rapid growth was not only to be seen in national income statistics. By any measured outcome, quality of life was radically different by 1970 compared to what it was in 1920. The average person in the West ate better, had more heat in the winter and better cooling in the summer, consumed a larger variety of goods, and lived a longer and healthier life.[9] With a shorter workweek and earlier retirement, life was no longer quite so dominated by the drudgery of daily labor. Child labor, omnipresent in the nineteenth century, had more or less disappeared in the West. There, at least, children could now enjoy their childhoods.

THE LESS GLORIOUS FORTY

But in 1973 (or thereabouts) it all stopped. On average, over the next twenty-five years, TFP has grown at only a third of the rate achieved in 1920–1970.[10] What started with an economic crisis with a clear start date, and even a set of foreign powers to blame, became the new normal. The persistence of the slowdown was not immediately apparent. Born and bred during the golden age of economic growth, scholars and policy makers initially believed it was a temporary blip, soon to fix itself. By the time it became clear that slow growth was not just an aberration, the latest hope was that a new industrial revolution, spurred by computing power, was right around the corner. Computing power was increasing at a faster and faster speed, and computers were being introduced everywhere, much as electricity and the combustion engine once were. This would surely translate into a new era of productivity growth that would pull the economy with it. And indeed it finally happened. Starting in 1995, we saw a few years of high TFP growth (though still significantly less than in the go-go years). It faded quickly, however. Since 2004, TFP growth and GDP growth both in the United States and in Europe seem to be back to the bad days of 1973–1994.[11] In the United States, GDP growth did pick up in mid-2018, but TFP growth remains slow. Over the year, TFP grew only at an average of 0.94 percent,[12] compared to the 1.89 percent achieved during the 1920–1970 period.

This new slowdown has provoked a lively debate among economists. It seems difficult to reconcile it with everything we hear around us. Silicon Valley keeps telling us we live in a world of constant innovation and disruption: personal computers, smartphones, machine learning. Innovation seems to be everywhere. But how could there be all this innovation without any sign of economic growth?

The debate has revolved around two questions. First, will sustained fast productivity growth eventually return? Second, is the measurement of GDP, at best a bit of an exercise in guesswork, somehow missing all the joy and happiness the new economy is bringing us?

IS GROWTH OVER?

Two economic historians at Chicago's Northwestern University are at the center of this discussion.

Robert Gordon takes the view that the era of high growth is unlikely to come back. We have only met Gordon once. He gives the appearance of being quite reserved; his book, however, is anything but. On the other side is Joel Mokyr, whom we know much better, an enormously vivacious man, with twinkling eyes and a kind word for everybody; he writes with infectious energy consistent with his generally positive outlook on the future.

Gordon has gone out on a limb and predicted economic growth will average a meager 0.8 percent per year over the next twenty-five years.[13] "Everywhere I look," he said during a debate with Mokyr, "I see things standing still. I see offices running desktop computers and software much as they did ten or fifteen years ago. I see retail stores where we are checking out with bar code scanners the same way we did before; shelves are still stocked by humans, not by robots; we still have people slicing meat and cheese behind the counter." Today's inventions, in his view, are simply not as radical as electricity and the internal combustion engine were. Gordon's book is particularly daring. He gleefully takes on the set of future innovations futurologists predict and one by one explains why, in his opinion, none of them would be as transformational as the elevator or air conditioning, and why none would take us back to an era of fast growth. Robots cannot fold laundry. Three dimensional (3D) printing won't affect large-scale manufacturing. Artificial intelligence and machine learning are "nothing new."[14] They have been around at least since 2004 and have done nothing for growth. And so on.

It is clear of course that nothing Gordon says precludes the possibility that something entirely unexpected, perhaps some hitherto unimagined combination of familiar ingredients, will prove to be transformative. It is just his hunch that it won't.

Mokyr, on the other hand, sees a bright future for economic growth, spurred by nations competing to be the leader in science and technology, and the resulting rapid spread of innovation worldwide. He sees the potential for progress in laser technology, medical science, genetic engineering, and 3D printing. To Gordon's claim that nothing much changed in fundamental ways in how we produced in the last few decades, he counters: "The tools we have today make anything that we had even in 1950 look like clumsy toys by comparison."[15] But mostly, Mokyr thinks that the way the world economy has changed and globalized produces the right environment for innovations to bloom and change the world, in ways we cannot even begin to envision. He predicts one factor that will accelerate growth: we will be able to slow down the aging of the brain. Which of course would give us more time to have better ideas. Mokyr, engaging and creative as ever at seventy-two, is a good example for his thesis.

The fact that two brilliant minds come to such radically different conclusions about growth highlights what a vexing topic it has been. Of all the things economists have tried (and mostly failed) to predict, growth is one area where we have been particularly pathetic. To name just one example, in 1938, just as the US economy was going back into high-growth mode after the Great Depression, Alvin Hansen (who was not a nobody; he was the co-inventor of the IS-LM model most students of economics will remember from their first macroeconomics class, and a professor at Harvard) coined the term *secular stagnation* to describe the state of the economy at the time. His view was that the American economy would never grow again because all the ingredients of growth had already played out. Technological progress and population growth in particular were over, he thought.[16]

Most of us today who grew up in the West grew up with fast growth or with parents used to fast growth. Robert Gordon reminds us of our longer history. It is the 150 years between 1820 and 1970 that were exceptional, not the period of lower growth that followed. Sustained growth was virtually unknown until the 1820s in the West. Over the period 1500 to 1820, annual GDP per capita in the West went from $780 to $1,240 (in constant dollars), a paltry annual growth rate of 0.14 percent. Between 1820 and 1900, growth was 1.24 percent, nine times more than in the previous three hundred years, but still much less than the 2 percent it would hit after 1900.[17] If Gordon is right and we end up with a 0.8 percent growth rate, we would simply be returning to the average growth rate over the very long run (1700–2012).[18] This is not the new normal; it is just normal.

Of course, the fact that sustained growth over a long time, the kind we saw over most of the twentieth century, was unprecedented, does not mean it could not happen again. The world is richer and better educated than ever before, the incentives for innovation are at an all-time high, and the list of countries that could lead a new innovation boom is expanding. It could well be the case, as some technology enthusiasts believe, that growth explodes again in the next few years, fueled by a fourth industrial revolution, perhaps powered by intelligent machines capable of teaching themselves to write better legal briefs and make better jokes than humans. But it could also be, as Gordon believes, that electricity and the combustion engine brought about a onetime shift in how much we can produce and consume. It took us some time to reach this new plateau and there was fast growth along the way, but we have no particular reason to expect this episode will repeat itself. Nor, we might add, do we have definitive proof it won't. Mostly, what is clear is that we don't know and have no way to find out other than by waiting.

THE WAR OF THE FLOWERS

Abhijit's parents did not really believe in toys. He spent long afternoons playing war games with flowers. The buds of the ixora, with their long stems and pointy heads, were the enemy, purportedly throwing stones at his foot soldiers, the long and fleshy leaves of the portulaca. The tuberoses were the health workers, operating on the casualties of war with toothpicks and bandaging them with soft petals of jasmine.

Abhijit remembers these as some of the most pleasurable hours of his day. That should surely count as well-being. But none of his enjoyment was captured by the conventional definition of GDP. Economists have always known this, but it deserves emphasis. When a rickshaw puller in Abhijit's native Kolkata takes the afternoon off to spend time with his lady love, GDP goes down, but how could welfare not be higher? When a tree gets cut down in Nairobi, GDP counts the labor used and the wood produced, but does not deduct the shade and the beauty that are lost. GDP values only those things priced and marketed.

This matters because growth is always measured in terms of GDP. The year 2004, when TFP growth, after jump-starting in 1995, slowed down again, is when Facebook began to occupy the outsized role it currently plays in our lives. Twitter would join in 2006 and Instagram in 2010. What is common to all these platforms is the fact that they are nominally free, cheap to run, and wildly popular. When, as is now done in GDP calculations, we judge the value of watching videos or updating online profiles by the price people pay, which is often zero, or even by what it costs to set up and operate Facebook, we might grossly underestimate its contribution to well-being. Of course, if you are convinced that waiting anxiously for someone to like your latest post is no fun at all, but you are unable to kick the Facebook habit because all your friends are on it, GDP could also be overestimating well-being.

Either way, the cost of running Facebook, which is how it is counted in GDP, has very little to do with the well-being (or ill-being) it generates. That the recent slowdown in *measured* productivity growth coincides with the explosion of social media poses a problem, because it is entirely conceivable that the gap between what gets counted as GDP and what should be counted in well-being widened exactly at this time. Could it be there was real productivity growth, in the sense that true well-being increased, but our GDP statistics are missing this entire story?

Robert Gordon is entirely dismissive of this possibility. In fact, he reckons Facebook is probably responsible for part of the productivity slowdown—too many people are wasting time updating their status at work. This seems largely beside the point, however. If people are actually much happier now than they were before, who are we to pass judgment on whether it is a worthwhile use of their time and therefore whether it should be included in well-being calculations?[19]

INFINITE JOY

Can the missing value of social media compensate for the apparent productivity growth slowdown in rich countries? The difficulty of course is that we have no idea how much value to assign to these free products. But we can try to estimate what people would be willing to pay. There are attempts to do this by looking at, for example, how much time people spend browsing on the internet as a proxy for how much they value it. The idea is that people could be working and earning money instead. If we follow this approach, the average annual value of the internet for an American went from $3000 in 2004 to $3,900 in 2015.[20] If we were to add this missing bit to the 2015 GDP, one could explain about one-third of the $3 trillion of "lost output" in that year (compared to what the GDP would have been if the post-2004 slowdown had not happened).[21]

One problem with this way of getting at the consequences of the internet is that it assumes people have the option of working longer hours for more money instead of spending time on the internet. But this is not true for most people with nine-to-five jobs; instead they need to find ways to keep themselves amused (or at least out of trouble) for another eight hours or so every day. If they spend time on the internet, all this means is they like it more than reading a book or hanging out with friends or family. If they are not particularly sociable and don't like books, this is hardly a ringing endorsement; it may be worth much less than $3,900.

However, there is also the opposite problem. Take someone who cannot imagine life without the internet, who needs an hour of Twitter fix every morning. That first hour brings almost infinite joy. But by the end of that hour all the enemies have been nailed, and every clever twist of phrase has been processed and passed on. What is left for the second hour is much more ho-hum, so much so that there is never a third hour. Compare that person with someone who also spends two hours desultorily responding to Facebook posts by or about friends half-forgotten and "friends" they would like to forget. In the data both will show up at the same place, valuing the internet at the price of two hours of time. But obviously they are different, and treating them the same may lead us to vastly underestimate the value of the internet.

Faced with the possibility that we could be either massively over-valuing the internet or the other way around, scholars looked for other ways to measure its value to consumers. In particular, there were several randomized control trials of what happened when the experimenter (with the permission of the participant) blocked access to Facebook (or social media more generally) for a random group of individuals for some relatively short period of time. The biggest of these experiments, which involved more than two thousand participants paid to deactivate Facebook for a month, found that those who stopped using Facebook were happier across a range of self-reported measures of happiness and well-being and, interestingly, no more bored (perhaps less). They seemed to have found other ways to keep themselves amused, including spending more time with friends and family.[22]

When Facebook access was restored after the experiment, those who spent a month without it were slow to return to their Facebook habit, and after several weeks were spending 23 percent less time on the app than they had before the experiment. Consistent with this, the estimate of how much they would need to be paid to give up Facebook for a second month was substantially lower at the end of the first month (after experiencing life without Facebook) than before.

All of this seems very consistent with the view that Facebook is addictive in the sense that it is hard to imagine life without it, but when you do give it up, things are not obviously worse. However, it is interesting that after the month of abstinence, the experimental subjects still wanted to be paid to give up Facebook; they did not simply feel grateful to be rid of it. The researchers assumed this was because they actually missed it, if less than they had expected, and therefore concluded Facebook generates over $2,000 of well-being per user.

How does this square with the fact that getting cut off made people happier on average? In part of course, like all averages, it hides the fact that some people really enjoy Facebook. Moreover, it is likely that what was costly for the participants was in part being the only one among their friends who was now off Facebook, and this inconvenience probably got worse the longer one was absent (it is okay to take a sabbatical from your social connections, but checking out totally is costly). If Facebook did not exist, the problem would not be there.

Where does that leave us? Not quite at a resolution. What we can say with some confidence is that Facebook is not the obvious win for all mankind as its devotees would have it, though people still value it more than they pay for it, at least in the current configuration where all their friends are on Facebook, Instagram, and/or Twitter. Could it be that if we valued these new technologies at their "real value," growth would appear to be much faster? Probably not, based on the evidence at hand.

What we can say with some confidence is that there is nothing in the available evidence promising a return to the kind of fast growth in *measured GDP* that characterized the Trente Glorieuses in Europe and the golden years in the United States.

SOLOW'S HUNCH

This should not come as a complete surprise. Remarkably, at the height of postwar growth, in 1956 Robert Solow wrote a paper suggesting growth would eventually slow down.[23] His basic point was that as per capita GDP goes up, people save more, and therefore there is more money to invest, and more capital available per worker. This makes capital less productive; if there are now two machines in a factory where there was only one, the same workers will have to operate both at the same time. Of course, a single factory can hire more workers if it gets more machines. But the whole economy cannot (assuming migration remains unchanged), once its reserve of underused workers is exhausted. Therefore, the extra machines bought with the additional savings will have to be worked with fewer workers. Each new machine and as a consequence each additional unit of capital will contribute less and less to GDP. Growth will slow down. Furthermore, the lower productivity of capital lowers its financial return, which in turn discourages savings. So eventually people will stop saving and growth will slow down.

This logic operates in both directions. Capital-scarce economies grow faster because new investment is highly productive. Rich economies, which are, in general, capital abundant, tend to grow more slowly because new investment is not as productive. One implication of this is that any large imbalance between labor and capital should get corrected. Economies overabundant in labor grow faster, and since incomes grow faster, savings do as well. So these economies accumulate capital faster and become more capital abundant. By the reverse argument, economies with too much capital relative to labor accumulate capital more slowly.

As a result, a sharp divergence between the rates of growth of capital and the labor force is not sustainable over the long haul because if, say, capital grows faster than the labor force, then the economy will have too much capital relative to labor, which will slow down growth. There can be imbalances in the short run (as we are witnessing today in the United States where the share of the GDP paid to the labor force is falling[24]), but in the long run there is a natural tendency for economies to stay close to a balanced growth path, where labor and capital grow at roughly the same rate, and so does human capital—the part of capital embodied in the skills of the workers, for very much the same reason. Solow argued that GDP (which is after all the product of labor, skills, and capital) would also grow at the same rate as well.

Now, the growth of the effective labor force is determined by past fertility and how much people want to work, both factors that seemed to Solow to be more driven by demography than economics, and therefore more related to a country's history and culture than to the current state of its economy or economic policy. However, there is also the improvement of TFP—if one worker becomes so productive that he can do the work of two, because of improvements in technology, then the effective labor force would have doubled. Solow assumed such transformations were also unrelated to contemporary economics and policies of the country, in effect placing the growth rate of the effective labor force outside the realm of economics. This is why he called it the "natural rate of growth," and from his theory, we know that GDP must also grow at the same rate as the effective labor force in the long run; that is, at the natural rate.

A number of implications follow from Solow's theory. First, growth is likely to slow down after a phase of fast growth that follows a dramatic transformation, once the economy is back on the balanced growth path. This is clearly consistent with what happened to Europe after 1973. After the wartime destructions, capital was scarce and Europe had a lot of catching up to do; by 1973 the era of catch-up growth was over. In the United States, the kind of investment-driven growth Solow had in mind clearly slowed down after the war, but conveniently its place was taken by rapid TFP growth until 1973. Since then, as we already discussed, there has been a slowing trend even in the United States. Interest rates have been falling throughout the West, reflecting, it seems, an abundance of capital, exactly as in the Solow model.

CONVERGENCE?

The second implication of Solow's theory, and perhaps the most striking, is what economists call *convergence*. Countries scarce in capital and relatively abundant in labor, like most poor countries, will grow faster because they have not yet reached their balanced growth path. They can still grow by improving the balance between their labor and capital. As a result, we would expect the difference in GDP per worker across countries to be reduced over time. All else being the same, poorer countries will catch up with their richer counterparts.

Solow himself was careful to stop well short of promising this. If a country has a lot of labor and very little capital, which is how many poor countries start out, then only a fraction of the labor force will be employable at a wage sufficient to ensure their subsistence (there may be nothing for the others to do), and as a result the country will not benefit much from its labor abundance. Convergence, if it happens at all, may be very slow.

Notwithstanding Solow's warnings, this vision of an orderly transition from dire poverty to relative wealth as the countries catch up and then go on to the nirvana of balanced growth, combined with the promise of global convergence in living standards, provided such a comforting narrative for progress under capitalism that it took some thirty years before economists started noticing the model did not fit reality all that well.

To start with, *it is not true that poor countries as a rule grow faster than richer ones*. The correlation between GDP per capita in 1960 and subsequent growth is very close to zero.[25] How does this square with the fact that after the war Western Europe caught up with the United States? Solow had a possible answer. What his model actually says is that countries *that are otherwise identical* will head toward each other. This could be why Western Europe and the United States, which are very similar in many ways, converged toward each other. On the other hand, in Solow's world countries that are naturally thriftier than others and invest more of their output will be richer in the long run. Moreover, for a while, before settling down to grow at the natural rate, initially poor countries that invest more will also grow faster as they converge toward this higher level of GDP per capita.

Could the lack of investment be the one reason the developing world differs from Western Europe and the United States? As we will see, the answer seems to be no.

GROWTH HAPPENS

The third and most radical prediction from Solow's model is that the growth rate of GDP per head among the relatively rich countries, once the economy reaches balanced growth, may not be very different. Essentially, in Solow's world these differences must come from differences in TFP growth, and Solow believed that, at least for these rich countries, TFP growth should be more or less the same.

In Solow's view, as mentioned above, TFP growth just happens— policymakers don't have very much control over it. This was something many economists were not entirely happy about. Given that growth rates are the language in which the league tables of international competition are written, there was something rather off-putting about Solow's refusal to offer some assurance that TFP would be higher for countries that pursue "good" economic policies. Was he just being deliberately quixotic? After all, don't we see many more of the latest technologies being deployed in the richer countries?

This resistance to the idea that a country's balanced growth rate is not easily influenced by policy is perhaps to be expected. But it misses the subtlety of Solow's thinking, in multiple ways. First, Solow is asking what drives technological upgrading in countries *already at the cutting edge.* Presumably the flow of new ideas is a big part of growth for these countries, and it is not clear why ideas should stop at the border. A new product invented in Germany could be simultaneously developed for production in several other countries, possibly by local subsidiaries of the mother company. Productivity would then go up more or less equally in all these countries, even though the invention came from only one of them.

Second, he is talking about growth after countries get to their balanced growth path, and while this might have already happened for some of the richer countries, it is probably a long way away for the ones where capital is still scarce. By the time Kenya or India gets to Solow's balanced growth path, they necessarily would be much richer and be using many or all of the latest technologies. Their current technological backwardness could just be a symptom of their lack of capital.

Finally, and this might be the hardest piece to wrap one's head around, countries on the way to the balanced growth path could actually be upgrading their technologies faster than those already there. Of course, the most showy breakthroughs, the self-driving cars and 3D printers of the day, will always be in the more advanced countries, but most technology upgrading is just moving from day-before-yesterday's technology to yesterday's. This is typically easier than pushing the frontier, precisely because it has already been done and we know exactly how to do it. It is a matter of pulling things off the shelf rather than coming up with something new.

For all these good reasons, Solow deliberately opted to punt on what drives differences between the balanced growth rates of different countries. He simply assumed the rate of improvement in TFP was a product of mysterious forces that had nothing to do with the countries, their culture, the nature of the policy regime, and so on. This meant he had very little to say about what we can do about long-run growth once the process of accumulation of capital has run its writ and the return on capital is low enough. Solow's was what economists call an *exogenous* growth model, where the word "exogenous," meaning driven by outside effects or forces, acknowledges our inability to do anything about the long-run growth rate. Growth, in short, is beyond our control.

GIVE ME A LEVER[26]

It was a combination of the evidence that many poor countries were not growing and the Solow model's inability to say something useful about how to affect long-term growth that eventually made economists look elsewhere. They desperately wanted to be able to say something about what could help countries grow. As Robert Lucas, one of the doyens of the Chicago school of anti-Keynesian macroeconomics and one of the most influential economists of our times, confessed in his much quoted Marshall lecture in 1985, he would like to know "if there is some action a government of India could take that would lead the Indian economy to grow like Indonesia's or Egypt's? If so, what exactly? If not, what is it about the 'nature of India' that makes it so? The consequences for human welfare involved in questions like these are simply staggering: once one starts to think about them, it is hard to think about anything else."[27]

But Lucas had more than just an aspiration to offer. He was also arguing that we are missing something important, and that the reason why India was poor could not all be because of a shortage of skills and capital. He recognized that India had less capital and skills than the United States, maybe because of its colonial history or the caste system. But to explain the enormous difference in GDP per capita between two countries based solely on lack of resources, those resources would have to be extraordinarily scarce. And if they were so scarce they should be very valuable. For example, the one tractor available would be used very intensively on hundreds of fields prepared by thousands of workers; the rental rate on this tractor would be extremely high. Based on this logic, Lucas computed that if the difference in GDP between the United States and India was to be explained by the scarcity of capital in India and nothing else, capital would have to be so scarce that its price (what is paid to the owner of the resources that finance the machines in the economy) would have to be fifty-eight times higher in India than it was in the United States.[28] But in that case why wouldn't all the capital in the United States move to India, he wondered. Since it evidently did not, he concluded the price could not in fact be that high. In other words, the intrinsic productivity of capital must be less in India than in the United States to explain why, despite its obvious scarcity, capital in India does not earn the kinds of astronomical returns that Lucas's computation would predict —or to put it in Solow's terms, TFP must be much lower in India.

Lucas was, perhaps unsurprisingly, being too optimistic about the functioning of markets. We now know that we live in a sticky economy where nothing moves very fast, and certainly not from the United States all the way to India. Nonetheless, some version of his basic insight has been rediscovered by many others who keep hitting up against the TFP puzzle. For one, if you simply try to explain the cross-country variation in GDP by the amount of resources in different countries, you will quickly realize that even though poor countries are indeed desperately short of skills and capital, their GDP per capita is even lower than this lack of resources would predict.[29] In other words, poor countries are poor in substantial part because they make less good use of the resources they have, and even within poor countries some do better than others with the same resources. The question is why?

Paul Romer, a PhD student of Lucas's, was one of the people inspired to respond to Lucas's passionate plea that we have to find a better way to explain growth. What made it a challenge was that Solow's answer rested on perhaps the two most basic ideas in economics. First, that capitalists invest in the pursuit of high returns; when and where returns go down, capital accumulation tends to go down as well. Second, that as capitalists as a class accumulate more and more capital, the productivity of capital becomes lower because there are not enough workers to work with it. In economics this is known as *diminishing returns*. It has a long pedigree. French economist Anne Robert Jacques Turgot, who was briefly France's finance minister and one of the many experts who tried unsuccessfully to head off France's headlong descent into the economic chaos that eventually precipitated the French Revolution, wrote about it in 1767.[30] Karl Marx took it as a premise. As he saw it, this was why capitalism was doomed: the insatiable greed of the capitalist class in the pursuit of more and more capital will drive the return on capital into the ground (in Marxist parlance this is called the "falling rate of profit") and precipitate the crises that eventually end capitalism.[31]

The assumption of diminishing returns makes a certain amount of intuitive sense. What is the point of acquiring new machines if there are no workers to operate them (or new engineers to program them, or salesmen to sell the products)? Of course, there are also counterexamples. Amazon clearly derives a lot of its ability to cut costs from the volume of its sales. Setting up the kind of storage and delivery systems it is famous for would not make sense if there were not a constant flow of demand for everything it sells, and to finance that it needs lots of capital. Amazon at a hundredth of its size could not possibly make money. In fact, Amazon made little or no money until it grew very large, and then profits soared. In July 2018, Amazon's profit reached 2.5 billion dollars.[32]

Economists of Solow's generation were aware of the possibility of increasing returns, which is how economists describe the idea that bigger is better (and the source of Amazon's present dominance). But one obvious implication of increasing returns is that the biggest firms should be the most profitable, and therefore the best situated to undercut the others and push them out of the market. Such markets are doomed to end up with monopolies. This is indeed what is happening with the online retail sector. But while we do see some industries where there are also a small number of dominant players (social networks and hardware stores are both in this category), most important markets—cars, clothes, and chocolate, for example—have many firms. It is for this reason that economists have tended to shy away from theories that rely too heavily on increasing returns.

Romer wanted to stick with the idea that a single firm was still subject to the law of diminishing returns. His insight was that all we need to undo the Solow effect is to be able to assume that *as a whole* an economy with more capital also has a more productive capital stock. This could be true even if every firm faced diminishing returns and there was therefore no tendency for firms to become monopolistic behemoths. To explain how this might happen, Romer invited us to think of the production of new ideas in a place like Silicon Valley, though his paper was written years before Silicon Valley achieved its iconic status.[33] Firms in Silicon Valley are very similar to the firms in Solow's world except in one important way: they use less of what we usually think of as capital (machines, buildings) and more of what economists call *human* capital, essentially specialized skills of different kinds. Many Silicon Valley companies invest in clever people in the hope they will come up with some brilliant and marketable idea, and sometimes this indeed happens.

The usual forces of diminishing returns are present in these companies as well. Too many temperamental geniuses and not enough drudges to manage the cash and make sure the gaming during work hours remains in check, and you have a disaster on your hands. What is different, Romer argues, is the overall environment of the Valley. Ideas can be heard and overheard everywhere, in the coffee shops and wheatgrass bars, in parties and public transport. One stray thought expressed by someone you will never meet again might prompt another, and all of it cumulates into a set of ideas that have remade the world. What matters is not just how many smart people you work with, but also how many smart people you are competing with, or just happen to be around in the Valley as a whole. Silicon Valley, in Romer's theory, is what it is because it brings together the best minds of the world in an environment where they can cross-pollinate each other. The increasing returns here are at the level of the industry, the city, or even the area. Even if every firm faces diminishing returns, doubling the number of high-skilled people in the Valley makes all of them more productive.

Romer argues that the same goes for all successful industrial cities: Manchester in the middle of the eighteenth century, New York and London during various periods of financial innovation, Shenzhen or the Bay Area today. In all of these places, he would claim, the force of diminishing returns that comes from the scarcity of land and labor (labor becomes scarce in part because land is scarce and therefore living in these places is so expensive) was defeated by the exuberant energy that comes out of learning from each other and coming up with new ideas. As a result, high growth can keep going forever as more and more high-skilled people come together, even without help from Solow's mysterious exogenous productivity growth.

Getting rid of diminishing returns at the level of an entire national economy also helps us explain why capital does not flow to India. In Romer's world, capital earns roughly the same return in India and in the United States, even though there is much less capital in India, because the standard law of diminishing returns helping India in Solow's model is compensated for by the faster flow of ideas in richer economies. The question is whether this is just a clever intellectual maneuver, a comforting story we tell ourselves, or whether the force Romer emphasizes looms large in the world.

GROWTH STORIES

Before we get to that, it is worth pointing out something the careful reader might have already noted: as soon as we started talking about the theory of economic growth, the conversation just got a whole lot more abstract. Both Solow and Romer are telling *stories* about what happens to entire economies over long periods of time. To do so, they are telescoping an incredible amount of real-world complexity into as few building blocks as possible. Solow, for example, gives a central role to the idea of economy-wide diminishing returns. Romer, for his part, puts his money on the flows of ideas between firms, but we never get to see the ideas themselves, just their supposed benefits at the level of the entire economy. Given the sheer diversity of occupations, enterprises, and skills that constitute an economy, it is very hard to get a feel (let alone an empirical counterpart) for any of these very broad concepts. Solow wants us to think of what happens in an economy when the total capital available to it goes up. But economies typically don't accumulate capital; individuals do. Then they decide what to do with that capital: whether to lend it out, start a new bakery, buy a new house, and so on. Each such decision changes many things; house prices may go up, bread prices may come down, good pastry chefs may become harder to come by. Solow wants to reduce all that complexity to one change: the change in the availability of labor relative to capital. Likewise, when a city gets an influx of tech people, many things change— you get better espresso, for one, and many low-income residents get pushed out—but Romer highlights just one key thing: the exchange of ideas. Both Romer and Solow may well be right in their guesses about what really matters, but it is difficult to map their abstractions into the real world.

To make matters worse, the data, which has been our main recourse so far, cannot help us very much here. Because the theories operate at the level of entire economies, our tests will need to compare different economies (countries or, at best, cities) rather than individual firms or people. As we discussed in the chapter on trade, this is always a challenge since economies tend to be different from each other in any number of ways, making them hard to compare.

Moreover, even if we were willing to draw conclusions from the comparison of entire economies to each other, it is not clear what we would learn. Take the idea of diminishing returns at the level of the economy. We want to test whether capital is less productive in a country that ends up with some extra capital. The problem once again is that countries don't accumulate capital, individuals do. Those individuals may then invest that capital in firms. Those firms buy machines and buildings and so on, and then try to hire workers to make use of their newly installed capital. This increases competition in the labor market, forcing the firms to settle for fewer workers than they would want, which is what depresses productivity of capital. Now suppose we do observe that an inflow of capital made capital less productive. How can we be sure that the reason this happened is the one Solow has in mind? After all, it could be that the capital was invested in the wrong place and that is what made it unproductive. Or that it was never invested at all. Perhaps if it were invested properly, the return on capital would actually go up (and not down as Solow would have it).

Finally, a lot of the claims in growth economics are about what happens in the long run. In the long run, growth slows down in Solow's world; it does not in Romer's. But how long is long enough? Is it enough to observe a slowdown? Or could that just be a temporary blip, a piece of bad luck to be reversed soon enough?

So at the end of the day, although we will try to stitch together the best evidence for these theories, the result will be tentative. We have already seen that growth is hard to measure. It is even harder to know what drives it, and therefore to make policy to make it happen. Given that, we will argue, it may be time to abandon our profession's obsession with growth. The most important question we can usefully answer in rich countries is not how to make them grow even richer, but how to improve the quality of life of their average citizen. It is in the developing world, where growth is sometimes held back by an egregious abuse of economic logic, that we may have something useful to say, though, as we will see, even that is very limited.

THE MILLION-DOLLAR PLANT

The key ingredient of Romer's happy narrative was the *spillovers*: the idea that skills build on each other and that putting skilled people together in one place makes a difference. Clearly, this is something people in Silicon Valley believe. There are many parts of California prettier than Silicon Valley, and most are cheaper. Why do companies still want to locate there? States and cities in the United States and elsewhere offer large subsidies to attract firms. In September 2017, Wisconsin gave at least $3 billion in fiscal advantages to Foxconn to have it invest $10 billion in an LCD manufacturing plant.[34] This is $200,000 for every job they promised to create. Similarly, Panasonic received more than $100 million to move its North American headquarters to Newark, New Jersey ($125,000 per job), and Electrolux was given $180 million in tax abatements to start a new plant in Memphis, Tennessee ($150,000 per job).[35] The most recent example of this competition was the very visible scramble to attract Amazon's second headquarters, HQ2. Amazon received 238 proposals from different locations before choosing Arlington, Virginia, and New York City.[36] These 237 or 238 cities (depending on whether New York finally withdraws or not) clearly believe in spillovers.

Apparently, Amazon does too. In choosing the location for HQ2, Amazon listed a preference for (among other things) "metropolitan areas with more than one million people" or "urban or suburban locations with the potential to attract and retain strong technical talent."[37]

Amazon's theory seems to be that being in a "thick" market, a market where there are lots of sellers, in this case of skilled labor, is valuable, presumably because it is easier to find, retain, and replace workers.

Romer's theory, you may recall, was more about informal conversations that occur when many people working on related topics are together. There is some evidence for such spillovers. We know, for example, that inventors are more likely to cite patents from other inventors in the same city, suggesting they were more likely to be aware of them.[38]

A variant of Romer's hypothesis that is less specific to Silicon Valley and its imitators is that the presence of more educated people makes everyone else more productive. It turns out, however, that the evidence that we are all becoming more productive as a result of having more educated people around us is not overwhelming. We do observe that everyone earns more in cities where there are more educated people, but this could be for a variety of reasons. Cities with more educated people may also attract more high-paying firms (high-tech firms, more profitable firms, firms that care more about the quality of work, etc.), drawn in by the prospect of being able to find the right kind of workers. The problem is finding instances where the level of education in the population at large goes up significantly without other things (policies, investments, etc.) changing at the same time.

There is clear evidence, however, that cities as a whole can benefit from a large investment. Michael Greenstone, Rick Hornbeck, and Enrico Moretti (who is the author of *The New Geography of Jobs,*[39] which argues that spillovers are the reason why cities are growing and rural areas are not) ask whether cities as a whole benefit from attracting a high-profile plant, much like Amazon's HQ2.[40] To answer this question, their study compared the winners of bidding wars to attract companies to the first runners-up. They find that TFP of the plants already present in the winning county surged, consistent with there being large spillovers—TFP five years after the plants were set up was on average 12 percent higher in places that received the plant than the ones that just missed out, translating into $430 million per year more in earnings for the county. Both wages and employment went up. In many cases, we do not know how much the average state or city spent to attract the plant, but we have some examples. For instance, in the case of the BMW plant that eventually went to Greenville-Spartanburg, South Carolina, over Omaha, Nebraska, the subsidy on offer was $115 million. If they got the average 12 percent benefit, the investment clearly paid off handsomely. This was the argument made in New York City in support of the subsidies to Amazon: that as an investment they were well worth it.[41]

An alternative way to attract businesses to a particular location is to build infrastructure. This is what the Tennessee Valley Authority (TVA) did for Tennessee and its neighboring states over the period 1930–1960, using public funds to build roads, dams, hydroelectric plants, etc. The idea was that infrastructure would attract firms, firms would attract other firms, and so on. Jane Jacobs, one of the most influential American urbanists of the twentieth century, was skeptical. She wrote a piece about it in 1984, called, quite simply, "Why TVA Failed."[42]

But it did not fail. Enrico Moretti and a colleague compared the TVA region with six other areas initially supposed to receive the same type of investment but where, for various political reasons, nothing happened. They found that between 1930 and 1960, the TVA counties generated gains both in agricultural and manufacturing employment relative to this comparison group. It is true that once outside funding for the program stopped in 1960, the gains in agriculture vanished, but the gains in manufacturing persisted and actually continued to intensify all the way until 2000, consistent with a widely held view that spillovers are more important in manufacturing than in agriculture. The effects are substantial; the authors estimate that over the long run the income gains as a result of TVA in the region will be $6.5 billion more than what it cost to set it up.[43]

Does this mean countries can create the conditions for permanently faster economic growth by promoting regional development, perhaps in multiple regions at the same time? There are two reasons why this does not follow. First, it is not enough that the firms gain from the initial investment. They have to gain enough to overcome the usual forces that slow down growth: shortages of land, labor, and skills. Moretti estimates that a 10 percent change in employment today will increase employment in the future by 2 percent, which is not big enough to generate sustained growth over the long term; pretty rapidly the original boost will peter out.[44]

Second, growth in one region is different from national growth because it can happen in part by cannibalizing growth in the rest of the economy, drawing capital, skills, and labor away from other areas. The cities where Amazon eventually locates will grow, but partly that will be at a cost to other American cities. Moretti estimates the two effects might actually net out, with the result that national growth will be more or less unaffected.[45]

Moretti concludes from his reading of this entire literature that regional development is unlikely to be the lever that will help us avoid the end of growth.[46] It is possible his assessment is slightly too pessimistic, but the note of warning is certainly valid. While it may make sense for an individual city to try to lure jobs away from another, this is unlikely to be a large win for a country as a whole, unless it is a very small country (the city state of Singapore, for example) that can grow at the expense of others.

CHARTER CITIES

It is worth emphasizing, however, that this evidence mainly comes from the United States or Europe. It could be that the developing world is quite different in this respect. Certainly, high-quality urban infrastructure is much more concentrated in a few cities in most of these countries, and a case could be made both for building more "high quality" cities and for making the few existing big cities more livable in order to promote economic growth. This is a key policy focus of the World Bank. For example, a 2016 report on urbanization in India[47] highlights "messy" and "hidden" urbanization, dominated by slums and sprawl. In essence, cities grow horizontally, by outgrowing their formal boundaries, rather than vertically through taller and better-quality buildings. In total, 130 million people in South Asia (more than the population of Mexico) live in informal urban settlements. Distances are long, traffic is impossible, and the pollution levels are extraordinary. This makes it more difficult to attract talent to cities, and also limits the effectiveness of cities as places of production and exchange. Better cities could potentially generate entirely new growth opportunities for the countries, without taking any growth away from elsewhere.

Romer's own focus for several years (even before his short and rocky tenure as the World Bank's Chief Economist) was on the cities of the third world. It continues to be a priority of his. He wants these countries to build cities where creative people would want to come together and new ideas would be born out of the cross-pollination. Cities that would be business friendly but also genuinely livable—Shenzhen without the pollution and the traffic. Unusually for a successful academic, he believed and cared enough in his message to set up a nonprofit think tank to help in the creation of what he called "charter cities." These would be giant protected enclaves (Romer wants hundreds of them around the world, each of them hosting eventually at least a million people) that live by Romerian rules within nations that do not. There would be a contract by which the national government agreed that a third-party government, from a developed country, would enforce those rules. So far, there has been just one taker, the government of Honduras, which had plans to set up as many as twenty zones for employment and economic development (ZEDEs). Unfortunately, though it claimed inspiration from Romer's ideas, the Honduran vision seemed closer to the banana enclaves the United Fruit Company and its competitors ran in the first part of the last century, where the company's writ was law. They deviated from the project from the get-go when they decided not to use the oversight of a third-party government. It eventually turned out that the Honduran government was more interested in Romer's name and fame than his counsel, and when it signed a deal with an American entrepreneur with a strong taste for totally unregulated capitalism to develop the ZEDEs, Romer walked out. This story suggests charter cities are unlikely to hold the key to sustained growth in developing countries for the very good reason that the internal political compulsions the charter is intended to hold at bay often have a way of biting back.

CREATIVE DESTRUCTION

To summarize the previous sections, regional spillovers seem real, but based on the limited evidence we have, probably not powerful enough for the task of keeping growth going at the national level. Perhaps anticipating this, Romer had a second story up his sleeve; in that story, growth is driven by firms developing new ideas, which turn into more productive technologies.[48]

Romer was describing a force that ensured technologies would constantly keep improving, and more so in countries pursuing pro-innovation policies. Unlike in Solow's world, technological progress would no longer be some mysterious force we have no control over.

To build a model where there is ongoing innovation and unbridled growth, Romer needed a force to counterbalance what every scientist and engineer knows: the more things have already been invented in the past, the harder it is to find an original idea. To get there, Romer assumed that once produced, new ideas become freely available for others to build on. Knowledge spills over. The advantage of building on previous ideas is that the new inventor is standing on the shoulders of giants. The inventor just needs to tweak the previous invention, not invent something entirely novel. In this way, the growth process can continue unabated.

Romer is a true optimist, as is perhaps evident from his faith that he would be able to entirely ring-fence his charter city project from the notorious politics of Honduras. The same optimism inspires his vision of the innovation process. In his world, new ideas just waft in like the smell of roses on a summer breeze.

In the real world, it seems, the production of new ideas is a much more fraught affair. Many marketable ideas are produced by firms, and firms tend to be possessive of their discoveries. Pharmaceutical companies and software firms, for example, do many things, legal and sometimes not so legal, to acquire and retain control over new ideas. Industrial espionage is a major global industry today, and so is its foil, patent law. A classic paper by Philippe Aghion and Peter Howitt, published a couple of years after Romer's, argued that innovation-led growth was possible even in that much more cutthroat environment.[49] In their world, firms innovate less out of a desire for knowledge than to make sure they get there before the competition. Nevertheless, new ideas do continue to get produced, as long as patent protection does not entirely preclude building on past ideas.

This shift in perspectives is not without its consequences. In Romer's world, innovation is a boon innovators offer the world. They do make some money, but what the economy gets in return is incomparably more valuable because future generations of innovators get to build on it, for free. As a result, Romer in particular wants us to bend over backward to make the world as friendly as possible for innovators— low taxes on profits and capital gains, incubators and innovation cells, patents that protect the innovators' rights as long as possible, and so on.

Aghion and Howitt have a much less romantic view of innovators. Interestingly, Aghion is the rare economist who had a chance to observe the innovative process close at hand. His mother, who was from a French-speaking Jewish family, founded the well-known designer brand Chloé when she moved to France, after being forced to leave her home in Egypt in the early 1950s. The years when Chloé went from being a dressmaker to a global brand were exactly the years of Philippe's growing up. Nevertheless, inspired by Joseph Schumpeter (the Harvard economist of the mid–twentieth century and braggart extraordinaire[50]), Aghion sees innovation as a process of *creative destruction*, in which each innovation involves both creation of the new and destruction of the old.[51] In his world, sometimes the creative dominates, but at other times the destructive holds sway; novelties get created not because they are useful but because they defeat someone's existing patent. Making it more rewarding to innovate might backfire as a result. Innovators may worry that the time interval between the moment they displace the previous incumbent patent holder and the less happy moment they lose their own patent to someone else could be frustratingly short. Patent protection is important to get people to innovate, but it is easy to get too much of it, permitting the incumbents to rest on their laurels. Instead, there needs to be a balance between greenfield innovation and the possibility of adopting other people's ideas.

CUT TAXES

You'll recall that one of the reasons why economists like Lucas were dissatisfied with the Solow model is that it did not provide any direction to an eager policy maker. Romer's model does. Conveniently, the advice is not exactly revolutionary. In particular, for Romer the government needs to get out of the way of stifling incentives to work hard and invent the new technologies that will make everyone more productive. In other words, cut taxes.

Romer is a Democrat in the United States. Or at least that's what the economics rumor mill tells us. His father was a Democrat who was the governor of Colorado. But the idea that low tax rates can affect long-term growth by encouraging innovation is one that US Republicans have come to dearly love. From Reagan to Trump, Republican politicians have consistently promised to cut taxes, and the perennial justification is that they promote growth. Low tax rates are necessary at the top, because the likes of Bill Gates need to be given the incentive to work hard, be creative, and invent the next Microsoft to make us all more productive.

It was not always like that. Top tax rates were above 77 percent for the period 1936–1964, and above 90 percent for about half of that period, mostly in the 1950s under a solidly right of center Republican administration. The top tax rate was brought down to 70 percent in 1965 by a more left-wing Democratic administration, and since then it has drifted down to mid 30 percent. Every Republican administration has tried to cut it down further and every Democratic administration has tried to raise it a little, though always with great trepidation. Interestingly, for the first time in over fifty years, the idea of a top marginal tax rate above 70 percent has gained some traction among Democrats in 2018.

Yet, looking at growth rates since the 1960s, it is evident the low tax rate era ushered in by Reagan did not deliver faster growth. There was a recession in the beginning of the Reagan administration, followed by a catch-up phase when the growth rate went back to normal. Growth rates were a little higher during the Clinton years and declined afterward. Overall, if we take the long-run view (the ten-year moving average, which averages the ups and downs of the business cycle), economic growth has been relatively stable since 1974, remaining between 3 and 4 percent over the entire period. There is no evidence the Reagan tax cuts, or the Clinton top marginal rate increase, or the Bush tax cuts, did anything to change the long-run growth rate.[52]

Of course, as the Republican Paul Ryan, former Speaker of the House of Representatives, pointed out, there is no evidence that they did not. Many other things were happening at the same time. Ryan painstakingly explained to a journalist why all of these things lined up to make tax increases look good and tax decreases look bad:

I wouldn't say that correlation is causation. I would say Clinton had the tech-productivity boom, which was enormous. Trade barriers were going down in the Clinton years. He had the peace dividend he was enjoying. . . . The economy in the Bush years, by contrast, had to cope with the popping of the technology bubble, 9/11, a couple of wars and the financial meltdown. . . . Some of this is just the timing, not the person. . . . Just as the Keynesians say the economy would have been worse without the stimulus [that Mr. Obama signed], the flip side is true from our perspective.[53]

Paul Ryan is right about one thing. Just looking at the variations over time, it is hard to conclude whether there is any causal effect of tax rates on growth. It is indeed possible there is a true relationship, but it is obscured by the many other things that are happening. The same lack of correlation between growth rates and tax rates remains true, however, when we look at changes in taxes across countries. There is absolutely no relationship between the depth of the cut between the 1960s and 2000s in a country and the change in growth rate in that country during the same period.[54]

Within the United States, the experience of individual states is also telling. In 2012, Republican leaders in Kansas passed deep tax cuts, with the promise this would spur the economy. Nothing like that happened. Instead the state went broke and had to cut back on its education budget, the school week was cut to four days, and teachers went on strike.[55]

A recent study from the University of Chicago's Booth School of Business (not a place known for its socialist tendencies) uses a clever trick to answer whether tax cuts that benefit the rich have more or less of a growth effect than tax cuts that benefit the rest of the economy. Different states have very different income distributions, and therefore tax cuts for the rich should have very different consequences in different states. Connecticut, for example, has many more rich people than Maine. Using the thirty-one tax reforms since the war, the study shows that tax cuts benefitting the top 10 percent produce no significant growth in employment and income, whereas tax cuts for the bottom 90 percent do.[56]

One can also directly look at the question of whether high-income earners slack off when taxes are higher. This question can be answered much more precisely than the effects on overall growth, because tax reforms affect different people differently, so it is possible to compare the changes in behavior for people who are more or less affected. The key conclusion from a very large literature, summarized by two of its most respected experts, Emmanuel Saez and Joel Slemrod, is that "there is no compelling evidence to date of *real* economic responses to tax rates at the top of the income distribution."[57]

By now, there seems to be a consensus among a large majority of economists that low taxes on high earners are not guaranteed to, on their own, bring about economic growth. This was reflected in the response of the IGM Booth panel of top economists to the Trump tax cut of 2017. The tax cut provides deep and durable tax cuts for businesses, including a cut in the corporate tax rate from 35 percent to 21 percent. The bill also includes a new top tax rate of 37 percent for the wealthiest Americans (down from 39.6 percent), raises the threshold for top earners, and eliminates the estate tax. It has much smaller tax cuts for the rest of the population, and most of these are meant to be temporary. To the question "If the US enacts a tax bill similar to those currently moving through the House and Senate—and assuming no other changes in tax or spending policy—US GDP will be substantially higher a decade from now than under the status quo" only one person agreed with the statement and 52 percent either disagreed or strongly disagreed (the rest were uncertain or did not answer).[58]

Despite this consensus, a memo from the government's treasury department on the fiscal impact of the bill assumed (without any stated justification) an increase in 0.7 percent in annual growth rates from reducing taxation.[59] How could they get away with a statement that had nothing to do with what anybody seriously believes? One answer, of course, is that it was not the only instance where the administration asserted a non-truth to support its decision. But we suspect that part of the reason the public so easily bought into the idea that tax cuts for the wealthy lead to economic growth is that they have heard this particular message for so many years, from so many prominent economists of a previous era. In those days, evidence was scarce and it was normal to argue from "first principles" based on intuition and no data. The repetition of this mantra by generations of serious economists has given it the soothing familiarity of a lullaby. We still hear it every day from a gaggle of business experts, who even today feel unconstrained by the data. It is now part of the "common sense." When we asked respondents in our survey the question similar to the one asked by the IGM booth panel, 42 percent of respondents agreed or strongly agreed with the proposition the tax cut would increase growth within five years (only one economist did). Twenty percent of our respondents disagreed or strongly disagreed.

It did not help that nine conservative academic economists, mostly with solid reputations but also part of this older generation, wrote a supporting letter to the administration arguing that growth would go up and "the gain in the long-run level of GDP would be just over 3 percent, or 0.3 percent per year for a decade."[60] It was immediately pointed out that this letter was based, once again, on first principles and a very selective reading of the empirical literature.[61] But it was so much in line with what the public and the press expect from economists that it sounded perfectly legitimate.

Once again, this underscores the urgent need to set ideology aside and advocate for the things most economists agree on, based on the recent research. In a policy world that has mostly abandoned reason, if we do not intervene we risk becoming irrelevant, so let's be clear. Tax cuts for the wealthy do not produce economic growth.

DEFORM BY STEALTH

While the tax changes at least are happening in the public eye, there is another very major transformation in the US economy that could have a direct bearing on growth: the increasing concentration of economic activity. The driver of long-run growth, in the Solow and the Romer models, is technological innovation. It is because people constantly invest in new products or new better ways of doing things that TFP grows, and the economy grows with it. But, as Aghion and Howitt reminded us, innovation does not come out of nowhere; someone needs to have a financial incentive to invent something new.

Companies that innovate need access to markets to sell their products. And some evidence suggests this is becoming increasingly difficult for new entrants. At the national level, most sectors (including technology, but not only) are increasingly dominated by a few companies. A 2016 report by the Council of Economic Advisers, for instance, finds that the share of the top fifty corporations in the national revenue of each of their sectors increased across most sectors between 1997 and 2012.[62] This concentration is largely accounted for by a growing share of the "superstars," partly the result of a fairly liberal attitude on mergers in the United States.[63] For example, the share of the top four companies in a sector's revenues has increased in every sector. In manufacturing, the top four accounted for 38 percent of revenues in 1980 and 43 percent in 2012. In retail trade, the share more than doubled, moving from 14 percent to 30 percent.[64]

It is not entirely clear that this increased concentration has been bad for consumers. Depending on the data source and computation methods, some economists find huge increases in markups[65] (the difference between what a firm charges and its costs) but others do not.One thing that has protected consumers is that in the retail sector there has been concentration at the national level but not at the local level. When Walmart or other superstores come to town, they displace some mom-and-pop operations. But this does not make the market less competitive for the final customers and superstores offer more varieties, often at cheaper prices.[66] And Amazon has actually fostered intense competition among sellers on its platform.[67]

But the problem with the increased concentration at the national level is that to the extent it reflects a decline in the competition faced by these behemoths, it may actually lead to reduced innovation because it creates higher barriers for new entrants to disrupt an industry. In the logic of Aghion and Howitt, the promise of (temporary) monopoly power, through a patent, spurs innovation, and this innovation in turn results in the new technologies everyone will eventually be able to use. This is what causes growth. But if monopoly is guaranteed forever anyway, innovation and growth may slow down; a monopolist can sit on their hands and never invent anything new. Some evidence suggests something like this is happening now. In particular, a study found that when a large planned merger and acquisition in a sector narrowly fails to happen for some unpredictable reason (the judge was not lenient enough or the deal fell through), the sector remains more competitive for several years afterward. These sectors with "near misses" see the entry of more new firms, more investment, and more innovation. This result does suggest that the relatively low growth in TFP may in part be explained by the increase in concentration.[68]

GOING GLOBAL

Even if the increase in industry concentration is partly responsible for the slowdown of growth in the United States, it would be unreasonable to conclude that breaking up monopolies will single-handedly restore fast growth. After all, growth has also been sluggish in Europe, and European regulators have been much more aggressive against monopolies. This illustrates, once again, the only clear lesson of the last few decades. We don't understand very well what can deliver permanently faster growth. It just happens (or not).

But if growth in rich countries is not about to explode, what will these countries (and, soon enough, middle-income countries like China or Chile) do with their increasingly abundant capital? The business community, which is sometimes smart enough not to buy into the ideological messaging it offers the rest of us, has been for some years focused on another way out for the abundant capital in its hands. We noticed this about twenty years ago, when, all of a sudden, businesspeople, perhaps sensing they could not count on reliable economic growth in the West, started to quiz us about the countries we knew best, which are all in the developing world. We had become inured to the slightly uncomfortable expression that appeared on the faces of most businesspeople as soon they found out what we do, which is study poor countries—they clearly wanted to find someone else who knew something more useful to them, and were trying to figure out how quickly they could dump us without causing offence. But, suddenly, a couple of decades ago, poor countries became interesting.

They were interesting because some of them were growing fast, and any place growing fast needs investment, and that investment was a potential antidote to the specter of diminishing returns haunting the rich countries' financiers. One way to prevent growth from slowing down is to send capital to the countries where productivity is high. That won't help workers in rich countries, since the production won't take place in their country, but at least national income will keep growing because capital owners will be paid well for their investment abroad.

SOME GOOD NEWS

Of course, for most economists and many businessmen, growth in poor countries is also important because of its implications for human welfare. The last few decades have been rather good for the world's poor. Between 1980 and 2016, incomes for the bottom 50 percent of the world's population grew much faster than the next 49 percent, which includes almost everybody in Europe and the United States. The one group that did even better was the top 1 percent, the rich in the already rich countries (plus an increasing number of superrich in the developing world), who collectively captured an amazing 27 percent of total growth in the world GDP. For comparison, the bottom 50 percent received only 13 percent of global growth.[69]

Nevertheless, perhaps fooled by the fact that they only see the rich getting richer, nineteen out of twenty Americans think world poverty has increased or stayed the same over this period.[70] In fact, absolute poverty rates (the fraction of those living under $1.90 a day at PPP) have been halved since 1990.[71]

This is undoubtedly in part due to economic growth. When people are extremely poor, it takes very little growth in their incomes to lift them up. Thus, even though they often got only the crumbs, those crumbs were enough to push them above $1.90 per person per day.

This might be because the particular definition of extreme poverty we have been using sets too low a bar. But the story of the last three decades is not just one of poverty going down; we also see large and important improvements in the quality of life of the poor. Since 1990, the infant mortality rate and the maternal mortality rate were cut in half;[72] as a result, more than a hundred million child deaths have been averted since 1990.[73] Today, barring major social disruption, nearly everyone, boys and girls, has access to primary education.[74] Eighty-six percent of adults are literate.[75] Even deaths from HIV-AIDS have been declining since their peak in the early 2000s.[76] The gains in income for the poor have not just been paper gains.

The new "sustainable development goals" propose to end extreme poverty (those living under $1.25 a day) by 2030, and it is quite conceivable this target will be met, or at least we will get close if the world continues to grow anywhere near the way it has been growing.

IN SEARCH OF GROWTH'S MAGIC POTION

This shows how important economic growth remains for the very poor countries. For those who believe in either the Solow model or the Romer model, extreme poverty of the kind we still see in the world is a tragic waste, because there is an easy way out. In the Solow model, poor countries have the scope to accelerate their growth by saving and investing. And to the extent poor countries do not in fact grow faster than the richer ones, the Romer model tells us this has to be a consequence of their bad policies.

As Romer wrote in 2008: "The knowledge needed to provide citizens of the poorest countries with a vastly improved standard of living already exists in the advanced countries."

He goes on to offer his growth masala:

If a poor nation invests in education and does not destroy the incentives for its citizens to acquire ideas from the rest of the world, it can rapidly take advantage of the publicly available part of the worldwide stock of knowledge. If, in addition, it offers incentives for privately held ideas to be put to use within its borders—for example, by protecting foreign patents, copyrights, and licenses; by permitting direct investment by foreign firms; by protecting property rights; and by avoiding heavy regulation and high marginal tax rates—its citizens can soon work in state-of-the-art productive activities.[77]

This sounds like the usual right-wing mantra: low taxes, less regulation, less government involvement in general, except perhaps in education and in protecting private property. And by 2008, when Romer wrote this passage, this was familiar ground and we already knew enough to be skeptical.

During the 1980s and the 1990s, one of growth economists' favorite empirical exercises became *cross-country growth regressions*. The game is to use the data to predict growth based on everything from education and investment to corruption and inequality, culture and religion, the distance to the sea or to the equator. The idea was to find what in a country's policies could help predict (and hopefully affect) its economic growth. But that literature eventually hit a brick wall.

There were two problems. First, as Bill Easterly, a vocal skeptic of the ability of "experts" to give any recipe for economic growth, has convincingly shown, growth rates for the same country change drastically from decade to decade without much apparent change in anything else.[78] In the 1960s and the 1970s, Brazil was a front-runner in the world growth tables; but starting in 1980, it essentially stopped growing for two decades, before resuming in the 2000s, and stopping again after 2010. Lucas's poster child for a country that failed to grow, India, started to grow faster more or less exactly when Lucas wrote the famous piece we quoted above, where he was puzzling over why growth in India was so low. For the last thirty years, India has been one of the growth stars of the world. Growth in the countries Lucas wanted India to emulate, Indonesia and Egypt, on the other hand, tanked. Bangladesh, famously described by Henry Kissinger as a "basket case" in the 1970s, has grown at a rate of 5 percent per year or more for most years in the 1990s and 2000s, and at above 7 percent in 2016 and 2017, which puts it among the twenty fastest growers in the world.

Second, perhaps more fundamentally, these efforts to discover what predicts growth make very little sense. Almost everything at the country level is partly a product of something else. Take education, for example, one factor emphasized in the early cross-country growth literature. Clearly education is in part a product of the effectiveness of the government in running schools and funding education. A government good at delivering education is probably good at other things as well; maybe the roads are better in the same countries where teachers show up to work. If we find growth is faster where education is higher, it could be due to these other policies it tends to be bundled with. And of course it is likely that people feel more committed to educating their children when the economy is doing well, so perhaps growth causes education, and not just the other way around.

More generally, both countries and country policies differ in so many different ways that in effect we are trying to explain growth with more factors than the number of countries, including many we may not have thought of or cannot measure.[79] Consequently, the value of these exercises depends very much on how much faith we have in our exact choice of what we put in them. Given that we have very little to justify any of these choices, we think the only reasonable position is to forget the entire project.

That does not mean we have not learned anything. Some of the most surprising results came from efforts to cleanly separate cause and effect. A classic pair of papers by Daron Acemoglu, Simon Johnson, and Jim Robinson (affectionately known as "AJR") contains the most striking of these.[80] They showed that countries where, in the initial years of European colonization, mortality among the early settlers was high still tend to do badly today. AJR argue that is because Europeans preferred not to settle there; instead they set up exploitative colonies where the institutions were designed to allow a small number of Europeans to lord it over vast numbers of natives who labored to grow sugarcane or cotton or to mine diamonds that the Europeans would then sell. By contrast, the places that were relatively empty to start with (think of New Zealand and Australia, for example) and where settler mortality from malaria and other such diseases was low, were the places where Europeans settled in large numbers. As a result, these places got the institutions the Europeans were then developing and that would eventually provide the basis of modern capitalism. AJR show that settler mortality several hundred years ago is an excellent predictor of, say, how business friendly contemporary institutions are in a particular country. And the countries that had low settler mortality once upon a time and are business friendly today tend to be substantially richer.

While this does not prove being business friendly causes growth (it could be the culture the Europeans brought, or the political traditions, for example, or something else entirely), it does imply that some very long-run factors have a lot to do with economic success. This broad insight has been confirmed by a number of other studies, and indeed it is in some ways what historians have always insisted on.

But what does all this tell us about what countries can actually do here and now? We learn that if you want high growth in the modern era, it is useful to have been largely empty and have had less malaria in the period between 1600 and 1900, and to have had large numbers of Europeans settle in your country (though that may have been cold comfort if you happened to be a native resident of the country at the time). Does it mean countries should try to attract European settlers in today's very different world? Almost certainly not. The brutal indifference to local custom and lives that allowed settlers to promulgate their institutions in the pre-modern period is not likely to be available today (thank God for that).

What this *also* does not tell us is whether it would help to set up a particular set of institutions today, because the evidence emphasizes institutional differences that have their roots in events that took place several hundreds of years ago. Does it mean institutions need to be developed over several hundred years for them to be effective? (After all, the US Constitution of today is a very different document than when it was written, enriched by two hundred years of jurisprudence, public debate, and popular involvement.) If so, must the citizens of Kenya or Venezuela just wait?

Moreover, it turns out that among countries at roughly the same level of business friendliness, none of the conventional measures of good macroeconomic policy (such as openness to trade, low inflation, etc.—the kinds of things Romer wanted countries to adhere to) seem to predict GDP per capita.[81] Conversely, while it is true that countries with "bad" policies grow slower, they are also more likely to have "worse" institutions by the measures used in this literature (less business friendly, for example), and therefore it is not clear if they are doing poorly because of policies, or because of some other side effects of their poor institutions. There is little evidence of policies having independent traction, over and above the effects of institutional quality.

What does that leave us with? It seems relatively clear there are things to avoid: hyperinflation; extremely overvalued fixed exchange rates; communism in its Soviet, Maoist, or North Korean varieties; or even the kind of total government chokehold on private enterprise India had in the 1970s with state-ownership of everything from ships to shoes. This does not help us with the kinds of questions most countries have today, given that no one, except perhaps the Venezuelan madmen, seem to be very keen on any of these extreme options. What Vietnam or Myanmar want to know, for example, is whether they should aim to emulate China's economic model, given its stunning success, not whether to follow North Korea.

The problem is that while China is very much a market economy, as are Vietnam and Myanmar, China's approach to capitalism is quite far from the classic Anglo-Saxon model and even its European variant. Seventy-five of the ninety-five Chinese firms on the 2014 Fortune Global 500 list were state owned, though organized like private corporations.[82]

Most banks in China are owned by the state. The government at both the local and the national level has played a central role in deciding how land and credit should be allocated. It also decides who gets to move where and with them the supply of labor to various industries. The exchange rate was kept undervalued for some twenty-five years, at the cost of lending billions of dollars to the United States at almost zero interest rates. In agriculture, the local governments decide who gets the right to use the land, since all land belongs to the state. If this is capitalism, it is surely with very Chinese colors.

Indeed, for all the excitement generated by the Chinese miracle these days, very few economists in 1980 or even 1990 predicted it. Often, at the end of one of our talks someone rises and asks why whatever country we are talking about doesn't just emulate China. Except it is never clear what part of the Chinese experience we are supposed to emulate. Should we start with Deng's China, a dirt-poor economy with comparatively excellent education and healthcare systems and a very flat income distribution? Or with the Cultural Revolution, a valiant attempt to wipe out all cultural advantages of the erstwhile elites and place everyone on an even playing field? Or with the Japanese invasion in the 1930s and its insult to Chinese pride? Or with five thousand years of Chinese history?

A similar puzzle arises in the cases of Japan and South Korea, where the governments initially pursued an active industrial policy (and to some extent still do), deciding what products to push for eventual export and more generally where investments should be made. And Singapore, where everyone had to put a large part of their earnings in a central provident fund, so the state could use their savings to build a housing infrastructure.

In all of these cases, the debate among economists has been whether growth happened because of particular unconventional policy choices, or in spite of them. And in each case, predictably, the discussion has been inconclusive. Did East Asian countries just luck out, or is there actually a lesson to be learned from their successes? Those countries were also devastated by war before they started growing fast, so a part of the fast growth might have been just the natural bounce-back. Those who herald the experience of the East Asian countries to prove the virtue of one approach or the other are dreaming; there is no way to prove any such thing.

The bottom line is that, much as in rich countries, we have no accepted recipe for how to make growth happen in poor countries. Even the experts seem to have accepted this. In 2006, the World Bank asked the Nobel laureate Michael Spence to lead the Commission on Growth and Development (informally known as the Growth Commission). Spence initially refused, but convinced by the enthusiasm of his would-be fellow panelists, a highly distinguished group that included Robert Solow, he finally agreed. But their report ultimately recognized that there are no general principles, and no two growth episodes seem alike. Bill Easterly, not very charitably perhaps, but quite accurately, described their conclusion: "After two years of work by the commission of 21 world leaders and experts, an 11-member working group, 300 academic experts, 12 workshops, 13 consultations, and a budget of $4m, the experts' answer to the question of how to attain high growth was roughly: we do not know, but trust experts to figure it out."[83]

ENGINEERING MIRACLES?

The young social entrepreneurs basking in Silicon Valley's enthusiastic glow have probably not read the Spence report. According to them, we do know what will get the developing world to grow—they just need to adopt the latest technologies, chief among them the internet. Mark Zuckerberg, CEO of Facebook, is a strong proponent that internet connectivity will have a huge positive impact, a sentiment echoed in a hundred reports and position papers. One report from Dalberg (a consulting firm) tells us that "the internet is a tremendous, *undisputed* force for economic growth and social change [italics added]" in Africa.[84]

The fact is evidently so obvious that the report does not bother to cite much solid evidence, which is sensible since there is no such evidence to cite. After all, in developed countries there is no evidence that the advent of the internet ushered in a new era of growth. The World Bank's flagship publication, the *World Development Report*, in its 2016 edition on digital dividends, after much hemming and hawing, concluded that on the impact of the internet, the jury was still very much out.[85]

The internet is just one of the technologies tech enthusiasts believe can be both a commercial success and an engine of growth for poor countries. The list of "bottom of the pyramid" innovations that are supposed to change the life of the poor and power growth from the bottom up is long: clean(er) cookstoves, telemedicine, crank-powered computers, and rapid testing kits for arsenic in water, to name a few.

One common feature a lot of these technologies (though not the internet) share is that they were developed by "frugal" engineers, such as the students at MIT's D-Lab or the entrepreneurs funded by Acumen Fund, a prominent "social" venture capital fund. Behind this and other similar funds is the believable idea that one reason why developing countries are poor is that the technologies developed in the North are not appropriate for them. They use too much energy, too many educated workers, too expensive machines, etc. In addition, they are often developed by monopolies in the North, and the South has to pay a premium to get them. The South needs its own technologies, and for that it needs capital not available from the markets. This may be why growth does not happen on its own in many countries and it's the gap that Acumen Fund tries to fill.

While the Acumen Fund sees itself as an entirely new type of organization, not an aid organization but a venture fund for the poor countries, in a sense its technology-oriented view of growth harks back to the 1960s, when engineers dominated the aid world and went bust trying to bridge the "infrastructure gap," giving large loans to poor countries for building dams and train lines that would allow them to catch up with rich countries. Despite the lack of evidence that this has helped those countries to grow, the fascination for electricity as the source of growth and development has never really gone away. Ecuador is currently under severe financial strain thanks to a loan from China to build a massive dam that was never fully operational. Acumen loans are smaller and they are given to private actors rather than to governments, but the dream is still one where engineers will fix the world's problems. One of Acumen Fund's key sectors is electricity. The ideal source of energy has changed from large dams to power from grain husks, or the sun, and the latest "cool" idea is that it is possible to develop cheaper "off the grid" solutions to reach poor communities; but the focus on electricity goes back fifty years.

It turns out, however, that it is not easy to invent appropriate technologies that are also profitable in a poor country. A good part of what Acumen funds fails. A rule of thumb in the social investing world is that 10 percent of the ventures work out (the rest fold) and only 1 percent reach significant scale. The issue is more that it is difficult to identify those supposedly life-changing new products and services, and efforts to do so often meet a frustrating lack of interest from the people whose lives are supposed to be changed.

Electricity is a case in point. In a recent randomized controlled trial in Kenya, researchers partnered with Kenya Rural Electrification Authority to offer electricity connection at different prices in different communities. The demand fell very sharply as price rose, and villagers were not willing to pay anywhere near what would have been sufficient to cover the cost of connecting to the grid (not to mention building the grid).[86]

The frugal engineering world is littered with many similar disasters, from the $100 laptop to educate the world (which actually costs $200 and has been shown to have no impact on what children actually learn),[87] to cleaner cookstoves that nobody wanted,[88] to various water-filter technologies[89] and innovative latrines.[90] A lot of the problem seems to be that these innovations take place in a void, insufficiently connected to the lives they wish to change. The core ideas are often clever, and it remains possible that one day they will click, but it is hard to place a lot of faith in this prospect.

FISHING WITH CELL PHONES

A central tenet of all the growth theories we have discussed is that resources are smoothly delivered to their most productive use. This is a natural hypothesis as long as markets work perfectly. The best companies should attract the best workers. The most fertile plots of land should be farmed most intensively, while the least productive will be used for industry. People who have money to lend should lend to the best entrepreneurs. This assumption is what allows macroeconomists to speak of the stock of "capital" or "human capital" of an economy, despite the obvious reality that the economy is not one giant machine: as long as resources flow to their best use, each separate enterprise is like one cog in a smoothly operating machine, which spans the entire economy.

But this is often not true. In a given economy, productive and non-productive firms coexist, and resources do not always flow to their best use.

Lack of adoption of available technologies is not just a problem for poor households; it seems to also be a problem in industrial settings in developing countries. In many cases, the best firms in an industry use the latest worldwide technology but other firms do not, even when it seems it would make sense economically.[91] Often, this is because the scale of their production is too small. For example, until recently the typical clothing manufacturer in India was a tailor who made made-to-measure clothes in his one-man workshop, rather than a firm that mass produces. TFP is low not because the tailors are using the wrong technology, but because tailoring firms are too small to benefit from the best technology. In a sense, the puzzle is why these firms exist.

So the problem with technology in developing countries is not so much that profitable technologies are not available and accessible, but that the economy does not appear to make the best use of available resources. And this is true not only of technologies but also of land, capital, and talents. Some firms have more employees than they need while others are unable to hire. Some entrepreneurs with great ideas may not be able to finance them, while others who are not particularly good at what they are doing continue operating: this is what macroeconomists call *misallocation*.

A vivid instance of misallocation comes from the impact of the introduction of cell phones on fishing in the state of Kerala in India. Fishermen in Kerala would go out to fish early in the morning and return to shore midmorning to sell their catch. Before the cell phone, they would land at the nearest beach, where their customers would meet them. The market would run until there were no customers left or the fish ran out. Since the catch varied quite a bit from day to day, there were a lot of wasted fish at some beaches, while at the same time there were often disappointed customers at others. This is a stark example of misallocation. When cell phone connectivity became available, fishermen started to call ahead to decide where to land; they would go where there were lots of customers waiting and not a lot of boats. As a result, waste essentially vanished, prices stabilized, and both customers and sellers were better off.[92]

This first story spawned a second one. The main tool of trade for a fisherman is his boat, and good boats last much longer than bad boats. The technology of making a fishing boat is always the same, but some craftsmen are much better at it than others. Before cell phones, fishermen used to purchase their boats from the nearest boat makers. But when they started to travel to different beaches to sell their fish, they often discovered there were better boat makers elsewhere, and they started to ask them to build their new boats. The result was that the better boat makers got more work and the worst went out of business. The quality of the average boat improved and in addition, because the better boat makers got more work and therefore got to use their existing boat-making infrastructure more effectively, they could lower the price of the boats. Misallocation went down: the workers making boats, the equipment, the wood, the nails, and the ropes that went into a boat were all used more effectively.[93]

What is common to these two stories is that a communication barrier led to misallocation. When communication improved, the same resources were better used, resulting in higher TFP, since more was done with the same inputs.

Misallocation is pervasive in developing economies. Take the city of Tirupur in South India, the T-shirt capital of the country, which we have already encountered in chapter 3.[94] There are two kinds of entrepreneurs in Tirupur: those who come from outside to start a T-shirt-making business, and those born and brought up in the area. The latter are almost uniformly the children of affluent local farming families, the Gounders, looking to do something different with their lives. Those who go there to make T-shirts are generally better at T-shirt making than the locals; many have family connections in the T-shirt business, and perhaps as a result firms run by outsiders make the same number of T-shirts with many fewer machines and their firms grow a lot faster.

But despite being more productive, Abhijit found in a study with Kaivan Munchi, the firms run by the immigrants were smaller in size and had less equipment than the firms run by the locals. The Gounders poured money into the firms run by their children instead of doing the "efficient" thing: lending money to migrants and passing the interest income so earned to their sons. As a result, efficient and inefficient firms could persist in the very same town.[95]

When Abhijit asked them why they preferred to sponsor their sons rather than lend money to the more talented outsiders and live off the proceeds, the Gounders explained they could not be sure of getting their money back. In the absence of a well-functioning financial market, they preferred to give money to their inept sons and get lower but relatively safe returns. It is also probably the case that they felt they had a duty to give their sons not only some hard cash, but also a means to *earn* a decent living.

Family firms are common all over the world (from small farms to large family groups), and they do not always fully adapt to "economic" incentives. Firms are passed on to sons even when daughters would be better at managing them,[96] all the fertilizer in the family goes to one (male) person's plot when it would make sense to use a little bit in all the fields.[97] That is of course true not just of small farms in Burkina Faso or family concerns in India and Thailand, but of the United States as well. Out of 335 CEO successions at family firms a researcher investigated, 122 were "family successions" where the new CEO was a child or a spouse of the current CEO (often a founder or the child of a founder). On the day of the succession, the stock market returns of the companies that appointed an outside CEO went sharply *up*, while the returns of the companies that appointed an inside CEO did not. The market was rewarding the appointment of an outsider. And apparently the market was onto something. Firms that appointed family CEOs experienced large declines in performance in the subsequent three years, compared to firms that promoted unrelated CEOs: their return on assets fell by 14 percent.[98]

What all of this tells us is that we cannot take it for granted that resources will flow to their best use. If they do not within a single family, or within a town, we clearly should not expect them to do so across an entire country. Misallocated resources will in turn lower overall productivity. Part of the reason poor countries are poor is they are less good at allocating resources. The flip side is that it is possible to grow just by allocating the existing resources to more appropriate uses. In the last few years, macroeconomists have spent a lot of effort trying to quantify just how much growth could come from better allocation. This is hard to do perfectly, but the results have been very encouraging. One very prominent estimate suggests that, in 1990, just the reallocation of factors within narrowly defined industries could have increased Indian TFP by 40 percent to 60 percent and Chinese TFP by 30 percent to 50 percent. If we allowed reallocations across broader categories, the estimates would surely be even larger.[99]

And then there is the misallocation we do not see, the great ideas that never see the light of day. Given that venture capital is so much more active in scouting out new ideas in the United States than in India, it is plausible that India is also missing more of these unsung geniuses.

BANKING ON BANKING?

Where does misallocation come from? Indian firms grow much more slowly than US firms, but are also much less likely to shut down.[100] In other words, the United States is an "up or out" economy, where people try something new and either succeed and make it big or fail after a few years. By contrast, the Indian economy is exceedingly sticky: good firms do not grow and bad firms do not die.

These two facts are probably closely related: the fact that good firms cannot grow fast enough also helps explain why bad firms can survive. If the best firms were to grow fast, they would drive down the price of whatever they sold and therefore force out everyone except those efficient enough to make money even when the prices were low. By the same token, they would drive up wages and the cost of raw materials, further discouraging bad firms. In contrast, if they remain small and service only the local demand, a less efficient firm can easily survive in the market next door.

One natural culprit is the capital market. It clearly plays a role in the Tirupur example, where the most productive entrepreneurs in the most productive T-shirt cluster in India cannot borrow enough to catch up in size with the less productive local firms. In India and China, estimates imply that simply reallocating capital across firms would erase most of the TFP gap created by misallocation.[101]

This interpretation dovetails with a generally shared sense that the banking sectors in both China and India have serious problems. Indian banks are famous for trying to avoid lending to anyone except blue-chip borrowers (usually without recognizing that yesterday's blue-chip firms are often today's disaster waiting to happen). Chinese banks have undergone significant reforms since the 1990s, with the goal of allowing for entry of different actors and improving the governance of the state-owned banks, but the "big four" state-owned banks still tend to be all too willing to lend to dubious projects with good political connections.[102] Finding money remains difficult for a young and ambitious entrepreneur with a good idea but no powerful friends.

Indian banks have very much the same problem, and in addition they are reputedly extremely *overstaffed*. Overstaffing means they need to put a large wedge between the rate at which they lend to firms and the savings rate they offer to depositors if they want to break even. As a result, bank lending rates in India are high relative to the rest of the world,[103] even though depositors earn very little interest.[104] This also discourages investment by those who need to borrow to do so and favors those with a rich relative to support them, like the Gounders of Tirupur. Bad banks hurt efficiency from both ends; because of them, savings rates are lower than they could be and savings are poorly managed.

In addition, companies need risk capital, funding that unlike bank funding protects them when they are hit by bad luck. Stock markets do this, but the Chinese stock market is yet to be widely trusted and the Indian one, while older and better run, is still very blue-chip dominated.

Poorly developed land markets are another reason why companies do not grow. In order to grow, a productive firm will need to acquire more land and buildings to make room to accommodate new machines and employees. In addition, land and buildings can be used as collateral for loans. This becomes a huge problem when land markets function poorly. To take a very common example, in many countries ownership of land and property is often disputed. A claims B's land, the land gets placed under court authority, and it typically takes years to settle the dispute. A recent study suggests that in India land and buildings play a big role in misallocation.[105] In fact, in about half the districts in India, more productive firms tend to have *less* land and buildings than the least productive ones! This is likely to be a large problem in many countries where property rights on land are not very clearly defined.

ONE LIFE TO LIVE

But there are other, more psychological, reasons why the best firms are not taking over India, Nigeria, or Mexico. Perhaps the owners like the idea of leaving their son a running business and prefer to avoid the risk of outside control that comes with outside financing; raising money on the stock market, for example, requires setting up an independent board of directors who might get in the way of the succession plans.

And perhaps ultimately the owners do not care enough about growth to put all they have behind that agenda. If no one else is growing fast, they are not at risk of being pushed out. They have a reasonable living and a place to work. Why make it more stressful by trying to grow? A very interesting recent study looks at management gaps in Indian firms.[106] By the norms of what the United States calls good management, firms in developing countries are terribly managed. One might dismiss this as prejudice against other ways of managing. Indians in particular are very proud of their way of doing business on a shoestring, what they call *jugaad*.[107] This requires being inventive in using what you have, and perhaps this is what the managers are doing. But managers are failing in ways that could not possibly make sense for them. For example, trash is allowed to accumulate on the shop floor, to the point that it becomes a fire hazard. Or unused materials are bagged and thrown into an inventory room, but nobody labels or lists them so it becomes virtually impossible to reuse them. When the researchers, one of them a former management consultant, sent (for free) a team of highly paid consultants to work for five months with the managers of a randomly chosen set of these firms, profits went up by $300,000 per firm, which even for these relatively large firms was not chicken feed. Moreover, most of the changes that made this happen were relatively simple things, like labeling inventories and removing trash. It is hard to see why the managers, if they wanted to raise profits, would need this rather expensive external help (the consulting would have cost them $250,000 had they paid for it). They undertake obvious changes if someone points them out and shames them into doing it, but not when left to themselves. It has to be that the owners ultimately don't feel strongly about doing the best they can possibly do.

WAITING FOR FOREVER

Companies also need labor. One might imagine this at least would not be a problem in a labor-abundant poor country, but it is actually not true. Even unskilled laborers in Odisha, one of India's poorest states, hold out for what they think is a fair wage, even if the alternative is not getting a job; workers who accept a lower wage are punished by others.[108]

According to the nationally representative National Sample Survey, in 2009 and 2010, 26 percent of all Indian males between the ages of twenty and thirty with at least ten years of education were not working. This is not because there were no jobs: the fraction of those under thirty with less than eight years of education who were not working was 1.3 percent. And, in fact, the fraction of those with ten years of education *above thirty* who were not working was about 2 percent.[109] We see the same pattern in 1987, 1999, and 2009, so this is not because the young of today are less employable.[110]

There are plenty of jobs, just not jobs these young men want. They will eventually accept jobs they refused to take when they were younger, probably because the economic compulsions become stronger as they age (their parents, who feed and house them now, will retire or pass on; they will want to get married), and the job options shrink (government jobs, in particular, have an age cut-off that is often close to thirty).

Esther found something very similar in Ghana. A little over ten years ago, about two thousand adolescents were identified as having passed the (hard) exam necessary to qualify for higher secondary school in Ghana (corresponding roughly to grades ten to twelve) but had not enrolled in the first trimester for lack of funds.[111] A third of them were randomly selected and offered a full scholarship for their entire time in secondary school. Before they were chosen for the scholarship, Esther and her co-authors asked their parents what they thought the economic benefit of enrolling in secondary school would be. The parents were generally optimistic. On average, they thought a person like their son or daughter could earn almost four times as much if they completed secondary school than if they did not start it. Moreover, they believed these gains would come because of greater access to government jobs, such as teaching and nursing. Not surprisingly, given these beliefs, three-quarters of the kids offered a scholarship jumped at the opportunity and completed secondary school, compared to only about half of the kids who did not get a scholarship. Esther and her colleagues have been following the progress of these adolescents ever since, interviewing them about once a year. They find many positives: the students learned useful things in school and it changed their lives in many ways; they all performed better on a test that measures their ability to apply knowledge to concrete situations; girls waited longer before starting a family and had fewer children.

The not so good news is that the impact on their average earnings was not very large, except for the few who got a government job. The parents were right about one thing: secondary education is indeed essential to get access to the college degrees that allow graduates to get coveted jobs. Secondary school graduates were indeed more likely to be teachers, to have other government jobs, or to have private jobs with benefits and fixed salaries. But where they got it wrong is that although secondary education is *necessary*, it is not *sufficient*. Secondary school scholarship winners (especially the girls) were more likely to go on to college, but the probability was still quite low (16 percent among scholarship winners as against 12 percent in the comparison group). And only a few of them managed to get a government job. The scholarship doubled this probability, but it went from 3 percent to 6 percent; that is, from really, really, small to really small.

Meanwhile, though they were already twenty-five or twenty-six, most of those who had gone to secondary school were still waiting for something better. A substantial fraction were not working at all: only 70 percent of the kids in the sample (treatment and control combined) had earned anything in the last month.

Intrigued by what these young people could be doing instead of working, we visited several of them. Steve, a young, affable, well-spoken man, received us in his home. He had graduated from secondary school over two years before but had not worked since then. He was hoping to go to college and study politics, with the aim of being a radio anchor one day, but his grades on the admission test had been too low so far. He kept retaking it. In the meantime, he was living off of his grandmother's pension. He saw no reason to let go of his dreams yet. He probably will eventually, but as he sees it, he's still young.

The flip side of this is that even in countries with frighteningly high unemployment rates, like South Africa (where 54 percent of those between the ages of fifteen and twenty-four say they are unemployed[112]), companies complain they cannot get the workers they want: workers with some education, a good attitude toward work, and a willingness to accept the wages on offer. In India, the government has invested an enormous amount of public resources on getting workers ready for the jobs the economy is generating. A couple of years ago, Abhijit collaborated with one of these businesses that does vocational training and job placement for the service sector. The company was worried they were not doing particularly well at placing their students. The data confirmed this. Out of 538 young men and women who signed up for a course, 450 completed it. Of those, 179 got job offers and 99 accepted their offers, but after six months only 58 were in the jobs the company had found for them, a hit rate of just over 10 percent. Another 12 were working elsewhere.[113] What were they doing instead, we asked a group of those who had been offered a job but had either never taken it or quit more or less immediately. They were either taking what they called "competitive exams" (to get a government job or a job in a quasi-governmental organization, like a public-sector bank) or studying to complete their bachelor's degree and then apply for a government job. Or just sitting at home, despite the fact that their families could ill-afford that.

Why did they not want the jobs they had been offered? We heard many answers, but it all came down to their not liking them—too much work, too long hours, too much time spent standing, too much going from one place to another, too little pay.

Part of the problem is a mismatch of expectations. The young men and women we interviewed in India grew up in families where post-primary education was still often a novelty; their fathers had on average eight years of schooling, their mothers less than four. They were told that if they studied hard they would get a good job, meaning mostly a desk job or a teaching job. This was closer to the truth in their parents' generation than it is today (especially for historically disadvantaged populations like the lower castes who benefitted from affirmative action). The growth in government jobs slowed and eventually stopped in the face of budgetary pressures,[114] but the population of the educated, even among the historically disadvantaged, kept growing.[115] In other words, the goalposts have moved.

Something similar happened in countries like South Africa, and also in Egypt and other countries of the Middle East and North Africa, which were more developed than India to start with. There, it was not enough to have completed secondary school, but for a while having a bachelor's degree served the same screening function: if you could show your BA degree you would walk into a government job. That is no longer true, but these countries are still producing millions of BAs in subjects like Arabic and political science, for which there is no market anymore. That today's graduates do not have the skills employers want is of course a constant complaint the world over, including in the United States. But the situation is quite extreme in those countries.

The mismatch between reality and expectation is reinforced by the lack of exposure to the real labor market. With Sandra Sequeira, Abhijit evaluated a program in South Africa providing young workers in the townships (the erstwhile black ghettos of the apartheid era) with free transportation to look for jobs far from home. Those randomly chosen to get the transportation subsidy did travel a lot more, but there was no effect on employment. What did change, however, was their perception of the labor market. Almost everyone was too optimistic to start with; the salaries they expected to earn were 1.7 times higher than the actual salaries reported by employed workers similar to them. Being exposed to the actual labor market put a dampener on their expectations, and their wage expectation became closer to the truth.[116]

Labor markets frozen by this kind of radical mismatch are wasting resources. These young people are mostly waiting for jobs they will not get. In India, newspapers frequently write about the mad rush for government jobs; for example, that twenty-eight million people applied for ninety thousand low-level jobs in the government-owned railways.[117]

From the perspective of developing countries, some of these problems are purely self-inflicted. Part of the problem is that there are a small fraction of jobs that are much more attractive than the rest, for reasons having nothing to do with productivity. The best examples are government jobs. In the poorest countries, there is a large gap between the wages of public- and private-sector employees. In the poorest countries, public-sector workers earn more than double the average wage in the private sector. And this is not counting generous health and pension benefits.[118]

This kind of difference can throw the entire labor market into a tailspin. If government-sector jobs are so much more valuable than private-sector jobs, but also very scarce, it is worthwhile for everybody to wait around and queue for those jobs. If the process of queuing and screening entails, as it often does, taking some exams, people may spend most of their working lives (or as much as they are allowed to by their families, anyway) studying for those exams. If the government jobs stopped being quite so desirable, the economy would gain many years of productive labor, wasted in the pursuit of the mostly unattainable. Of course, government jobs are attractive in other countries as well, particularly because they often come with job security. But the wage gap is not quite as large and the queue not nearly as long.

Cutting wages in government jobs would probably be a battle, but it would not be so difficult, for example, to limit the number of times people could apply for government jobs, or to make the age cut-off more stringent. This would avoid the massive waste of everyone waiting around. It could add an element of luck to the job allocation process, but it is not obvious that the resulting allocation would be worse than under the current system, which favors those who can afford to wait. In Ghana, while Steve was twiddling his thumbs, some other young graduates had had to find something to do because they had no one to subsidize their lifestyle. They did not lack imagination: we met a nut farmer, a DJ who specialized in funerals, a preacher in training, and two footballers on a minor league team.

The labor market problems in developing countries are not, however, limited to the outsized attractiveness of the government sector. In Ghana, secondary school graduates are also attracted by a class of private jobs that offers benefits, high wages, and a measure of employment protection. In many developing countries, the labor markets feature this duality: there is a large informal sector without any protection, with many people who are self-employed for lack of better options, and a formal sector where employees are not only pampered but also strongly protected. Some employment protection is of course necessary; workers cannot be at the whim of their employer. But labor market regulations are so stringent that they really put a chokehold on any efficient reallocation of resources.

EVERYONE WAS RIGHT, EVERYONE WAS WRONG

Where does all of this leave us in our understanding of economic growth? Well, Robert Solow was right. Growth seems to slow down as countries get to a certain level of per capita income. At the technological frontier, that is to say in the rich countries, TFP growth is largely a mystery. We do not know what propels it.

And Robert Lucas and Paul Romer were right too. For the poorer countries, convergence is not automatic. This is probably not mainly because of spillovers. It is more that TFP is much lower in poorer countries, to a significant extent because of market failures. And therefore to the extent that business-friendly institutions have something to do with fixing market failures, Acemoglu, Johnson, and Robinson were right too.

And yet all of these economists were also wrong, because they thought of economic growth and of a country's resources as aggregate things (the "labor force," the "capital," the "GDP"), and in doing so they probably missed the key point. Everything we have learned about misallocation tells us we have to step beyond the models and think of *how* the resources are used. If a country starts by using its resources very badly, like China did under communism or India did in its days of extreme dirigisme, then the first benefits of reform may come from moving resources to their best uses. Perhaps the reason why some countries, like China, can grow so fast for so long is that they start with a lot of poorly used talent and resources that can then be harnessed. This is neither Solow's nor Romer's world, in which a country would need either new resources or new ideas to grow. It might also suggest the growth could slow down rapidly, once those wasted resources have all been put to good use, and growth becomes dependent on additional resources. Much is being written about the economic slowdown in China; growth is definitely slowing down and that is probably to be expected. This trend will almost surely continue, whatever Chinese leaders do now. China accumulated resources rapidly, as it had plenty of room to catch up; in the process, the most blatant sources of misallocation were eliminated, which means there is less room to improve now. The Chinese economy relied on exports to provide know-how, investment, and endless (for a while) global demand. But now they are the largest exporter in the world, so they cannot possibly continue to grow their exports much faster than the world is growing. China (and the rest of the world) will have to come to terms with the reality that their era of breathtaking growth is likely coming to an end.

In terms of what is to come, it looks like the United States can relax a bit. In 1979, Harvard professor Ezra Vogel published a book, *Japan as Number One,* that predicted Japan would soon overtake all other countries to become the number one economic superpower. Western countries, he argued, needed to learn from the Japanese model. Good labor relations, low crime, excellent schools, and elite bureaucrats with long time horizons was the new recipe Vogel identified for permanently faster growth.[119]

Indeed, had it continued to grow at its average growth rate over the decade 1963–1973, Japan would have overtaken the United States in terms of GDP per capita by 1985, and in overall GDP by 1998. It did not happen. What happened instead is enough to make one superstitious. The growth rate crashed in 1980, the year after Vogel's book came out. And it never really recovered.

The Solow model suggests a simple reason. Due to a low fertility rate and the near complete absence of immigration, Japan was (and still is) aging rapidly. The working-age population peaked in the late

1990s and has been declining. This means TFP must grow all the more rapidly to keep fast growth going. Another way to say this is that Japan would have to find some miracle for its existing labor force to become more productive, since we still have no reliable way to boost TFP.

In the euphoria of the 1970s, some believed this to be possible, which may explain why people continued to save and invest in Japan in the 1980s, despite the slowdown. Too much good money chased too few good projects in the so-called bubble economy of the 1980s, with the consequence that banks ended up with many bad loans and a huge crisis in the 1990s.

China faces some of the same problems. It is aging fast, partly as a result of the one-child policy, which has proven difficult to reverse. It might still eventually catch up with the United States in per capita terms, but the slowing growth means it will take quite a while. If China slows to 5 percent per year, which is not implausible, and stays there, which is perhaps optimistic, and the United States continues to bounce around 1.5 percent, it will take at least thirty-five years for China to catch up with the US in terms of per capita income. Meanwhile, the Chinese authorities may also want to relax and accept the writ of Solow. Growth will slow.

They are aware of it, and have made a conscious attempt to alert the Chinese people to this fact, but the growth targets they have set may still be too high. The danger is that it could put the leadership in a bind and lead them to make bad decisions in an effort to make growth come back, as Japan did before them.

If a fundamental driver of economic growth is resource misallocation, it opens the door to various unorthodox strategies to make growth happen. Such strategies are meant to respond to the particular way in which resource use in a country is distorted. The Chinese and the South Korean governments did a good job of identifying sectors that were too small and therefore not meeting the economies' needs (they tended to be heavy industry providing basic raw materials to other industries, like steel and chemicals) and directed capital toward them through state investments and other interventions. This might have sped up the transition to efficient resource use.[120]

That it worked in those two countries does not necessarily mean it is something every country should emulate. Economists tend to be very wary of industrial policy, for good reasons. The history of state-directed investments is not one that inspires confidence; judgments are frequently bad even when they are not actually deliberately distorted to benefit someone or some group, which is often. These are "government" failures just as there are market failures, and there are so many instances of these that it would be very dangerous to blindly rely on governments to pick the winners. But there are also so many market failures that it makes no sense either to rely on the market alone to allocate resources to the right use; we need an industrial policy designed that keeps in mind these political constraints.

Another implication of the idea that growth is slowed down by misallocation is that countries like India that are growing fast right now should fear complacency. It is relatively easy to grow fast, starting from a spectacularly messed-up economy, because of the gains from better resource use. In Indian manufacturing there was a sharp acceleration in technology upgrading at the plant level, and some reallocation toward the best firms within each industry after 2002. This appears to be unrelated to any economic policy, and is described as "India's mysterious manufacturing miracle."[121] But it is no miracle. At its root, it is a modest improvement from a dismal starting point, and one can imagine various reasons it happened. Perhaps a generational shift, as control passed from the parents to their children, often educated abroad, more ambitious, and savvier about technology and world markets. Or the effect of the accumulation of modest profits that eventually made it possible to pay for the shift to bigger and better plants.

But as the economy sheds its worst plants and firms, the space for further improvement naturally shrinks. Growth in India, like that in China, will slow. And there is no guarantee it will slow when India has reached the same level of per capita income as China. When China was at the same level of per capita GDP as India is today, it was growing at 12 percent per year, whereas India thinks of 8 percent as something to aspire to. If we were to extrapolate from that, India will plateau at a much lower level of per capita GDP than China. The growth tide does raise all boats, but it doesn't lift all boats to the same level—many economists worry that there may be such a thing as the *middle-income trap,* an intermediate-level GDP where countries get stuck or nearly stuck. According to the World Bank, of 101 middle-income economies in

1960, only 13 had become high income by 2008.[122] Malaysia, Thailand, Egypt, Mexico, and Peru all seem to have trouble moving up.

Of course, there are many pitfalls in any such extrapolation, and India should treat it as what it is: no more than a warning. It is quite possible that India's growth, in spite of all of its problems, has very little to do with some special Indian genius. Instead, it has a lot to do with the flip side of misallocation: the opportunities of being an economy with a large pool of potential entrepreneurs to draw upon and lots of unexploited opportunities.

CHASING THE GROWTH MIRAGE

If this is the right story, India should start to worry about what happens when those opportunities begin to run out. Unfortunately, just as we don't know much about how to make growth happen, we know very little about why some countries get stuck but others don't—why South Korea kept growing but Mexico did not—or how one gets out. One very real danger is that in trying to hold on to fast growth, India (and other countries facing sharply slowing growth) will veer toward policies that hurt the poor now in the name of future growth. The need to be "business friendly" to preserve growth may be interpreted, as it was in the US and UK in the Reagan-Thatcher era, as open season for all kinds of anti-poor, pro-rich policies (such as bailouts for overindebted corporations and wealthy individuals) that enrich the top earners at the cost of everyone else, and do nothing for growth.

If the US and UK experience is any guide, asking the poor to tighten their belts, in the hope that giveaways to the rich will eventually trickle down, does nothing for growth and even less for the poor. If anything, the explosion of inequality in an economy no longer growing has the risk of being very bad news for growth, because the political backlash leads to the election of populist leaders touting miracle solutions that rarely work and often lead to Venezuela-style disasters.

Interestingly, even the IMF, so long the bastion of growth-first orthodoxy, now recognizes that sacrificing the poor to promote growth was bad policy. It now requires its country teams to include inequality in factors to take into consideration when providing policy guidance to countries and outlining conditions under which they can receive IMF assistance.[123]

The key ultimately is to not lose sight of the fact that GDP is a means and not an end. A useful means, no doubt, especially when it creates jobs or raises wages or plumps the government budget so it can redistribute more. But the ultimate goal remains one of raising the quality of life of the average person, and especially the worst-off person. And quality of life means more than just consumption. As we saw in the previous chapter, most human beings care about feeling worthy and respected; they suffer when they feel they are failing themselves and their families. While better lives are indeed partly about being able to consume more, even very poor people also care about the health of their parents, about educating their children, about having their voices heard, and about being able to pursue their dreams. A higher GDP may be *one* way in which this can be given to the poor, but it is only one of the ways, and there is no presumption that it is always the best one. In fact, the quality of life varies enormously between middle-income countries. For example, Sri Lanka has more or less the same GDP per capita as Guatemala but maternal, infant, and child mortality are much lower in Sri Lanka (and are comparable with those in the United States).[124]

DELIVERING WELL-BEING

More generally, looking back, it is quite clear that many of the important successes of the last few decades were the direct result of a policy focus on those particular outcomes, even in some countries that were and have remained very poor. For example, a massive reduction in under-five mortality took place even in some very poor countries that were not growing particularly fast, largely thanks to a focus on newborn care, vaccination, and malaria prevention.[125] And it is no different with many of the other levers for fighting poverty, be it education, skills, entrepreneurship, or health. We need a focus on the key problems and an understanding of what works to address them.

This is patient work; spending money by itself does not necessarily deliver real education or good health. But the good news is that by contrast to growth we know how to make progress here. One big advantage of focusing on clearly defined interventions is that these policies have measurable objectives and therefore can be directly evaluated. We can experiment with them, abandon the ones that do not work, and improve the ones with potential.

The recent history of malaria is a good example. Malaria is one of the biggest killers of small children and a disease preventable by avoiding mosquito bites. Since the 1980s, the number of malaria deaths had been rising every year. At the peak in 2004 there were 1.8 million deaths from malaria. Then in 2005 there was a dramatic turning point. Between 2005 and 2016, the number of deaths from malaria declined by 75 percent.[126]

Many factors probably contributed to the decrease in the number of malaria deaths, but the widespread distribution of insecticide-treated bed nets almost surely played a key role. Overall, the benefits of nets are well established. In 2004, a review of the evidence from twenty-two carefully done randomized controlled trials found that, on average, one thousand more nets distributed contributed to a reduction of 5.5 deaths per year.[127] As we described in *Poor Economics*, however, there was a big debate at the time on whether nets should be sold to beneficiaries (at a subsidized price) or given for free.[128] But an RCT by Pascaline Dupas and Jessica Cohen,[129] replicated since then by several other studies, established that free nets are in fact used just as much as nets that are paid for, and free distribution achieves a much higher effective coverage than cost sharing. Since *Poor Economics* was published in 2011, this evidence eventually convinced the key players that massive distribution was the most effective way to fight malaria. Between 2014 and 2016, a total of 582 million insecticide-treated mosquito nets were delivered globally. Of these, 505 million were delivered in Sub-Saharan Africa and 75 percent were distributed through mass distribution campaigns of free bed nets.[130] The magazine *Nature* concluded that insecticide-treated net distributions averted 450 million malaria cases between 2000 and 2015.[131]

The accumulation of evidence took some time, but it worked. Even the skeptics were convinced. Bill Easterly who in 2011 was an outspoken critic of free bed net distribution, gracefully acknowledged in a tweet that his nemesis Jeff Sachs was more right than he was on this particular issue.[132] The right policy choices were made, leading to tremendous progress against a terrible scourge.

The bottom line is that despite the best efforts of generations of economists, the deep mechanisms of persistent economic growth remain elusive. No one knows if growth will pick up again in rich countries, or what to do to make it more likely. The good news is that we do have things to do in the meantime; there is a lot that both poor and rich countries could do to get rid of the most egregious sources of waste in their economies. While these things may not propel countries to permanently faster growth, they could dramatically improve the welfare of their citizens. Moreover, while we do not know when the growth locomotive will start, if and when it does, the poor will be more likely to hop onto that train if they are in decent health, can read and write, and can think beyond their immediate circumstances. It may not be an accident that many of the winners of globalization were ex-communist countries that had invested heavily in the human capital of their populations in the communist years (China, Vietnam) or countries threatened with communism that had pursued similar policies for that reason (Taiwan, South Korea). The best bet, therefore, for a country like India is to attempt to do things that can make the quality of life better for its citizens with the resources it already has: improving education, health, and the functioning of the courts and the banks, and building better infrastructure (better roads and more livable cities, for example).

For the world of policy makers, this perspective suggests that a clear focus on the well-being of the poorest offers the possibility of transforming millions of lives much more profoundly than we could by finding the recipe to increase growth from 2 percent to 2.3 percent in the rich countries. In the coming chapters, we will go one step further and argue that it may even be better for the world if we did not find that recipe.

CHAPTER 6

IN HOT WATER

I N 2019, IT IS IMPOSSIBLE to think about economic growth without confronting its most immediate implication.

We already know that over the next hundred years the earth will become warmer; the question is by just how much. The costs of climate change would be quite different if the planet got warmer by 1.5°C, or 2°C, or more. According to the Intergovernmental Panel on Climate Change (IPCC) October 2018 report, at 1.5°C, 70 percent of coral reefs would vanish. At 2°C, 99 percent.[1] The number of people directly impacted by the rise in sea levels and the transformation of cultivable land into desert would also be quite different under the two scenarios.

The overwhelming scientific consensus is that human activity is responsible for climate change, and the only way to stay on a course to avoid catastrophe is to reduce carbon emissions.[2] Under the 2015 Paris Agreement, nations set a target to limit warming to a limit of 2°C, with a more ambitious target of 1.5°C. Based on the scientific evidence, the IPCC report concludes that in order to limit warming to 2°C, CO_2 equivalent (CO_2e) emissions[3] would need to be reduced by 25 percent by 2030 (compared to the 2010 level) and go to zero by 2070. To reach 1.5°C, CO_2e emissions would need to go down by 45 percent by 2030 and to zero by 2050.

Climate change is massively inequitable. The lion's share of CO_2e emissions are being generated either in rich countries or to produce what people consume in rich countries. But the greatest share of the cost is, and will be, experienced in poor countries. Does it make it an intractable problem, given that those who must solve it have no strong impetus to do so? Or is there some hope?

THE 50-10 RULE

The IPCC report details everything that would have to be done to cut emissions and limit warming to 1.5°C. Some steps could already be taken; switching to electric cars, constructing zero-emissions buildings, building more trains would all help. But the bottom line is that, even with technological improvements, and even if we could wean ourselves off coal entirely, without any movement toward more sustainable consumption, any future economic growth will have a large direct impact on climate change. This is because as consumption rises we need energy to produce all the things that are consumed. We generate CO_2 emissions not only when we drive our cars, but also when we leave them in our garages, since energy was used in producing the car and the garage. That is true even for electric cars. There are many studies that attempt to look at the relationship between income and carbon emissions. The answer varies with climate, family size, and so on, but the two always track each other closely. The average estimate implies that when your income increases by 10 percent, your CO_2 emissions increase by 9 percent.[4]

This implies that, although Europe and the United States are responsible for a large share of global emissions to date, today's emerging economies (particularly China) are generating an ever-growing share of current emissions. In fact, China is the single largest emitter of carbon. This is, however, largely due to goods produced in China but consumed elsewhere in the world. If we attribute the emissions to where the consumption takes place, North Americans consume 22.5 tons of CO_2e per year per person, Western Europeans 13.1, Chinese 6, and South Asians just 2.2.

Within developing countries, richer people also consume a lot more CO_2 than the poor. The richest people in India and China belong to the select group of the top 10 percent of the most polluting people in the world (and contribute respectively 1 percent and 10 percent to the emissions of this group, or 0.45 percent and 4.5 percent of world emissions). In contrast, the poorest 7 percent of the population in India emit just 0.15 tons of CO_2 per year per person. Overall, we get the 50-10 rule: 10 percent of the world's population (the highest polluters) contribute roughly 50 percent of CO_2 emissions, while the 50 percent who pollute the least contribute just over 10 percent.

The citizens of rich countries and, more generally, the rich worldwide bear an overwhelming responsibility for any future climate change.

BATHING IN THE BALTIC

On a June day sometime in the early 1990s, encouraged by his friend and fellow economist Jörgen Weibull, Abhijit went swimming in the Baltic. He leaped in and instantly jumped out—he claims that his teeth continued to chatter for the next three days. In 2018, also in June, we went to the Baltic in Stockholm, several hundred miles farther north than the previous encounter. This time it was literally child's play; our children frolicked in the water.

Wherever we went in Sweden, the unusually warm weather was a topic of conversation. It was probably a portent of something everyone felt, but for the moment it was hard not to be quite delighted with the new opportunities for outdoor life it offered.

It is in the poor countries that there is no such ambivalence. If the earth warms a degree centigrade or two, residents of North Dakota will mostly feel perfectly happy about it. Residents of Dallas, perhaps a bit less. Residents of Delhi and Dhaka will experience more days that are unbearably hot. As just one example, between 1957 and 2000, India experienced on average five days per year with an average daily temperature above 35°C.[5] Without a global climate policy, it is projected to have seventy-five such days by the end of the century. The typical US resident will experience just twenty-six. The problem is that poorer countries tend to be closer to the equator and that is where the real pain will be felt.

To make matters worse, the residents of poor countries are less equipped to protect themselves against the potential bad effects of hot temperatures. They lack air conditioning (because they are poor) and they work in agriculture, on construction sites, or on brick kilns where air conditioning is not really an option.

What are the likely impacts of the temperature increases that are going to come with climate change on life in these countries? We cannot just compare warmer and colder places to answer this, since these places are also different in a hundred other ways. What allows us to say something about the potential impact of temperature change is that the temperature at a particular location fluctuates, on a given calendar day, from year to year. There are years with especially hot summers, years with particularly cold winters, and nice years when both winters and summers are temperate. The environmental economist Michael Greenstone pioneered the idea of using these year-to-year weather fluctuations to get some understanding of the impact of future climate change. For example, if it was especially hot in one district in India in a particular year, was agricultural production lower in that year compared to the same district in other years, or to other districts where it was not so hot?

There are various reasons to not trust this particular approach blindly. Permanent climate differences will surely spur innovations to limit their impact. We won't pick these up in the effects of year-to-year changes, because innovation takes time. On the other hand, permanent changes may have other costs that don't occur when the change is temporary, such as the draining of the water table. In other words, those estimates could be too small or too large. But as long as the bias in the estimate is the same for rich and poor countries, it is still useful to compare the predictions we get. The general conclusion is that the damage from climate change will be much more serious in poor countries. There will be losses in US agriculture, but the losses in India, Mexico, and Africa will be much larger. In some parts of Europe, such as in the vineyards of the Moselle Valley, there will be more sun warming the vines, and both the quality and quantity of Moselle wine are predicted to increase.[6]

The effect of hot weather on productivity is not limited to agriculture. People are less productive when it is hot, particularly if they have to work outside. For example, evidence from the United States suggests that at temperatures over 38°C, labor supply in outdoor jobs drops by as much as one hour per day, compared to temperatures in the 24°C–26°C range.[7] There are no statistically detectable effects in industries that are not exposed to climate (for example, nonmanufacturing indoor activities). Children have lower test scores at the end of particularly hot school years. These effects are absent where schools have air conditioning, so they affect poorer children the most.[8]

In India, few factories have air conditioning. In a garment factory in India, a study looked at how labor productivity varied with temperature.[9] For temperatures below 27°C–28°C, temperature had a very small impact on efficiency. But for mean daily temperatures above this cut-off (about one quarter of production days), efficiency went down by 2 percent for every one degree Celsius increase in temperature.

Putting everything together, across the entire world, a study finds that it being 1°C warmer in a given year reduces per capita income by 1.4 percent, but only in poor countries.[10]

And, of course, the consequences of a warmer climate are not limited to income. Numerous studies emphasize the danger of hot temperatures for health. In the United States, an additional day of extreme heat (exceeding 32°C) relative to a moderately cool day (10°C–15°C) raises the annual age-adjusted mortality rate by about 0.11 percent.[11] In India, the effect is twenty-five times larger.[12]

LIFE SAVER

The United States experience also illustrates how being richer and more technologically advanced can help mitigate temperature risks. In the United States, the estimates of the mortality impacts of high temperatures in the 1920s and 1930s were six times larger than the estimates for the current period. The difference may be entirely due to the much greater access to air conditioning, a key mechanism through which residents of rich countries adapt to higher temperatures.[13] This explains why in hot years energy demand goes up massively in rich countries. In poor countries, where air conditioning is still rare (in 2011, 87 percent of households in the United States had air conditioning, but only 5 percent of Indians did[14]), we see larger reductions in productivity, and increases in mortality when temperatures go up. In these places, air conditioning could be a critical adaptation tool. It should not be a luxury, but it is.

As poor countries become richer, they will be able to afford more air conditioning. Between 1995 and 2009, the ratio of air-conditioning units to homes in urban China went from 8 percent to over 100 percent (meaning there was more than one AC unit per urban household).[15]

But air conditioning itself aggravates global warming. The hydrofluorocarbon (HFC) gases used in standard air-conditioning appliances have particularly deleterious impacts on the climate; they are much more dangerous than CO_2. This puts us in a rather difficult situation. The very technology that can help to protect people from climate change also accelerates the rate of climate change. Newly available air conditioners that do not use HFC pollute less, but at the moment they are much more expensive. A country like India, which is on the cusp of being able to afford the cheaper air-conditioning appliances, thus faces a particularly ghastly trade-off: saving lives today, or moderating climate change to save lives in the future.

An agreement reached in Kigali, Rwanda, in October 2016, after years of negotiation, illustrates how the world navigates this trade-off (when it does manage to navigate it). The Kigali agreement created three tracks: rich countries, including the United States, Japan, and Europe, will start phasing out synthetic HFCs in 2019; China and a hundred other developing countries in 2024; and a small group of countries, including India, Pakistan, and some Gulf States, will postpone the start date until 2028. While realizing its citizens are both the victims and the cause of global warming, the Indian government took the stance that they prefer to save lives today rather than tackle the problem right now. They are probably banking on the fact that economic growth in the intervening years will put them in a position to afford the more expensive devices (which may also have become cheaper in the meantime) by 2028. But during those ten years, there could be a very rapid spread of old-style appliances in India, especially since the makers of the HFC-based machines will want an outlet for their products, and these will stay operational and continue to pollute for years after 2028. This delay could turn out to be quite costly for the planet.

ACT NOW?

The air-conditioning conundrum is a particularly heart-wrenching illustration of the trade-off India feels it is facing, between the present and the future. More generally, until the Paris Agreement in 2015,

India had simply refused to contemplate limits on its own emissions, arguing that it could not afford to hinder its own economic growth and rich countries should bear the brunt of the adjustment. The position evolved when India ratified the Paris Agreement and came up with a concrete commitment, asking in exchange for some serious financial aid to afford the energy transition, to be financed from an international fund paid for by the rich countries. Although Indian emissions are not a large fraction of world emissions today, India will be a key player moving forward, as its growing middle class consumes more and more. And unlike the United States, a large part of its population will also be directly and severely affected by climate change, so it should be in a good place to understand the costs of today's choices. Its reluctance to act is thus deeply concerning, not only because it has direct impacts, but because it illustrates the dominance of short-term thinking among politicians.

The key question is whether the trade-off is as stark as the Indians (or the Americans, for that matter) seem to believe it is. Do we really have to give up something today? Perhaps we can have our cake and eat it too, if we develop and switch to better technologies that will allow us to curb warming without giving up much by way of our lifestyles. After all, just a few years ago energy experts were sternly telling us that renewable energy sources (solar and wind) were simply too expensive, and it was foolish to invest in them as an alternative to fossil fuel. They are considerably cheaper today, notably due to technological progress in those sectors. Energy efficiency has also considerably improved and could improve more. In 2006, the UK government commissioned the former chief economist of the World Bank, Lord Nicholas Stern, to prepare a report on the economic implications of climate change. The *Stern Review*[16] optimistically concludes:

> Yet despite the historical pattern and the business as usual projections, the world does not need to choose between averting climate change and promoting growth and development. Changes in energy technologies and the structure of economies have reduced the responsiveness of emissions to income growth, particularly in some of the richest countries. With strong, deliberate policy choices, it is possible to "decarbonize" both developed and developing economies on the

scale required for climate stabilization, while maintaining economic growth in both.

Amen to this. Still, it would not quite be free. The Stern report concludes that, assuming a rate of technological progress in the "green sector" based on extrapolating from recent history, it would cost about 1 percent of world GDP annually to stabilize emissions at the level necessary to stave off global warming. But that seems a modest cost to avoid endangering the future of the world as we know it.

One hope is that research and development efforts might respond to incentives.[17] R&D expenditures are strongly influenced by the size of the market for the new innovations they are seeking to finance.[18] So a temporary inducement to research clean alternatives to dirty technologies (in the form of a carbon tax that would make it more expensive to use the old technologies and/or direct subsidies to research clean technologies) could have a snowball effect by creating a demand. The clean technology would become cheaper and therefore more attractive, which would increase the demand for it and hence the returns to research. Eventually, the clean sector would be attractive enough to root out the dirty sector and we would be home free. Our little economic engine could be back on its balanced path with the same growth as before, fueled by wind, water, and the sun. We could even stop all taxes and subsidies to encourage clean energy after a while.

It is easy to see how it could work. It is also frighteningly easy to see how it could *not* work. After all, the dirty technology would still be there. If fewer people used coal and oil, the prices of these inputs would plummet. This would make it very tempting to go back to using them. It is true that because coal and oil are not renewable means their prices will tend to go up over time (as the supplies run down), but there is probably enough coal and oil under the ground to take us to Armageddon. It is hard to be entirely sanguine.

FREE LUNCH?

What the optimists are hoping for is that ultimately there will be a free lunch. Firms and people will save money by adopting the cleaner technologies because research will have made them so much cheaper. Adopting clean technologies would be a win for individuals and a win for the planet. The prospect of a free lunch is always enticing. In fact, it is so enticing that it tends to dominate the climate change conversation. Detailed engineering estimates routinely predict investments that enhance energy efficiency, and pay for themselves in the form of a smaller energy bill. A 2009 McKinsey report, "Unlocking Energy Efficiency in the U.S. Economy," attracted a lot of attention.[19] The report estimated that a "holistic approach" of investment in energy efficiency would "yield gross energy savings worth more than $1.2 trillion, well above the $520 billion needed through 2020 for upfront investment in efficiency measures." In 2013, the International Energy Administration calculated that energy efficiency measures alone could give us 49 percent of the reduction in CO_2e emissions we need, without any other change.[20]

If that is the case, then perhaps we have a relatively easy problem to solve; all we need to do is to bridge this "energy efficiency gap." We need to identify the barriers preventing consumers (and corporations) from undertaking these investments. Perhaps they don't know, perhaps they cannot get a loan to finance the upfront costs, perhaps they are myopic, or perhaps they suffer from inertia.

Unfortunately, when one looks at the on-the-ground performance of those supposedly low hanging fruits rather than predictions of engineering models, there is less good news. The federal Weatherization Assistance Program (WAP) is the largest energy-efficiency program for home users in the United States; it has covered 7 million households in the US since its inception in 1976. Michael Greenstone and a team of economists got a chance to allocate an offer to participate in the program to about seventy-five hundred households, randomly chosen out of thirty thousand in Michigan.[21] The winners were offered over $5,000 in weatherization investments (insulation, window replacements, etc.) at no out-of-pocket cost. The researchers then collected data on winners and losers. The RCT produced three main findings. First, the demand for the program was really low. Despite an aggressive and costly encouragement campaign, only 6 percent of households in the treatment group eventually took up the offer. Second, the energy-use gains were real (the energy bill went down by 10–20 percent for those who took the program up), but were only a third of what was predicted by the engineering estimates, and much lower than the upfront costs. Third, this is not because households reacted to the prospect of a lower energy bill by heating their houses more (the so-called rebound effect); they found no increase in home temperatures. The engineering estimates apparently did not fully apply to real houses in real places; they were much too optimistic.

The gap between the rosy engineering estimates and the truth does not just apply to households. A researcher teamed up with the department of climate change in the government of Gujarat (one of the most industrialized and most polluted states in India) to provide small and medium firms with high-quality energy-efficiency consulting.[22] A random sample of firms received a free energy audit, which gave each firm a list of approved energy-efficiency-enhancing investments the state could heavily subsidize (under a preexisting program). Then a random subset of the firms that got the audits received regular visits from energy consultants to facilitate the adoption. The audits on their own had a limited impact on the adoption of the new technologies. The consulting led to more adoption, but it also changed what firms were doing: they started producing more, which increased their energy demand. Overall, there was no effect on energy consumption, this time because of the rebound effect. Again, the engineers who calculated the potential emission gains from technologies that saved energy were too optimistic in their predictions.

Our sense is that there may not be that many free lunches. Mitigation through better technologies may not do the trick; people's consumption will need to fall. We may have to be content not only with cleaner cars but also with smaller cars, or no cars at all.

THE GREENPEACE ANSWER

This is not what our colleagues in economics like to hear. First, because of economists' ongoing love affair with material consumption as a marker of well-being, and second because they are suspicious of attempts to change behavior, especially when changing preferences is involved. Many economists have a philosophical objection to manipulating preferences.

The reason for this reluctance is the economists' long-standing belief that there is something "true" about people's preferences, and that their actions reflect deep-seated desires. Any attempt to convince people to do something different (such as consume less or consume differently) would then encroach on those preferences. But as we saw in chapter 4, there are really no such things as true well-defined preferences. If people don't know how they feel about something as quotidian as a box of chocolates or a bottle of wine, why do we expect them to have clear preferences about climate change? Or what kind of world their grandchildren should live in? Or whether the people of the Maldives deserve to have their islands washed away by a rising sea? And to know how much are they willing to alter their own lifestyles to prevent those disasters?

Economists typically assume most people would not voluntarily sacrifice anything to affect the lives of unborn people or those who live very far away. But this is probably not true, for example, of you, the reader (or you would have shut this book a long time ago). Or for that matter of most economists themselves. Many of us probably do care about a whole range of outcomes that don't affect us directly, even if we have a hard time assigning money values to them.

The reason this is important is that it changes the way we should think about policy interventions. If everyone has well-defined preferences and acts on them (for example, they don't care at all about the damage to other people), the ideal environmental policy is one that sets a price for damaging the environment but otherwise lets the market do its job. This is the idea behind the carbon tax, which is something most economists, including us, have now embraced. It was key to the work of William Nordhaus, who was rewarded with the Nobel Prize in 2018. Having to pay an explicit price for polluting is certainly something firms take seriously. Allowing firms to buy the right to pollute from other firms that are actually actively reducing pollution, the idea of tradable carbon credits, may also be a good idea because it creates incentives for nonpolluting firms to find ways to actively "unpollute," say, by planting trees. And the revenues from taxes on polluters is useful because we need to pay for new environment-friendly technologies.

But there is a strong case for going beyond carbon credits. Take someone who thinks of themselves as having a strong commitment to fighting climate change but ends up never buying energy-efficient LED lightbulbs. The reason could be that he does not know about LEDs, or that he forgets to buy them when he goes to the shop, or that he cannot make up his mind about just how much a premium he is willing to pay for the LEDs because he has a hard time putting a number on how much he really cares about preventing climate change. Would such a person be better or worse off if the government banned non-LED bulbs?

Or if bans seem too extreme, the government could "nudge" people gently toward choices that are better for the environment. For example, smart meters now afford the possibility of charging higher prices for electricity during peak hours, compensated by lower prices the rest of the time; this would be better for the environment. A recent study in Sacramento, California, found that only 20 percent of users actively chose such plans when they were made available.[23] And yet when a plan like this was made the default for (randomly chosen) users who then had the option of switching back to the traditional plan, 90 percent of them stayed on it, and those who stayed indeed used less energy. What did they truly prefer then, the option they actively chose or the one they did not choose but were willing to stick to? A government may decide that since there is no clear answer to this question, it may as well go with the one better for the environment.

A larger open question is the extent to which energy consumption is a matter of habit. A particular way of consuming could become almost like an addiction simply because this is what people are used to. At the Paris School of Economics, the new "green" building provides very little heating. When we worked there, we were always cold in the winter and spring, and complained regularly about it. But somehow the simple tactic of leaving a thick sweater in the office eluded us for many months. Yet it was really not so difficult. We just were suffering from many years of overheated American offices. And once we had managed to transport the sweater, we did not feel worse off than we would have had the building been warmer. The moral brownie points from doing our bit to save the planet was enough compensation.

Many of the behaviors that influence energy consumption are repeated and habitual: taking the train rather than the car, turning off the lights when leaving a room, and so on. For such behaviors, doing what we have always done in the past is easiest. Changes are costly, but once we switch it is easy to keep going. Even more mechanically, if we buy a thermostat we can set it up once and for all to heat more in the morning and at night and less when we are away. This means today's energy choices also affect future energy consumption. Indeed, there is direct evidence that energy choices are persistent. In an RCT, some randomly chosen households received regular energy reports telling them how much energy they were using relative to their neighbors. The report recipients began to consume less energy than the households that never got them, *even after the reports stopped*. And this seems largely a result of changes in their habits.[24]

If energy consumption is a bit like an addiction, in that using a lot of energy today makes us use a lot in the future, then the appropriate response is high taxes, like those on cigarettes. High taxes would discourage the behavior initially, and then once the proper behavior was learned the taxes could continue to be high without really hurting anyone, since everyone had changed their habits in order to avoid them.

Of course, our energy consumption is not only caused by how we heat, cool, or transport ourselves. Everything we purchase contributes to it. There again, tastes probably do not fall from the sky. Economists have begun to recognize the role of "habits" in our preferences: what we grew up consuming forms our tastes today. Migrants continue to eat what they grew up eating, even when the food that was cheap in their home country is expensive in their new country.[25] Habits mean it is painful, in the short run, to change your behavior. But they can be changed. People even seem willing to modify their behavior in order to get ready for some future change.[26] Thus announcing a *future* tax hike on goods gobbling up energy could be an easier way for people to get used to the idea.

POLLUTION KILLS

Rich countries have the enormous advantage in that much of the energy consumption they need to sacrifice is inessential (driving to the supermarket when you could walk, sticking to your old bulbs instead of switching to LEDs, etc.). Where the rubber really hits the road is in the developing world. In the last two decades, coal consumption has trebled in India and quadrupled in China while declining slightly in the United States and other developed countries. In the decades to come, growth in energy consumption is forecast to be four times higher outside the OECD than within.

But for most Indians, additional consumption and additional energy consumption in particular is not a luxury. The very low energy consumption in rural India today is due to a mode of existence that is often unpleasant and dangerous. They cannot possibly use less, and ought to have a right to use more. In that case, is there a rationale for poor countries to stay completely outside of the climate conversation? Or, at a minimum, to limit any sacrifice to their richest citizens, who have the lifestyles and the emissions of rich Americans?

It is hard to say no. There is certainly something deeply unfair about the world's poor paying for the past and present indulgence of the world's rich. Unfortunately, there are two problems with taking this position. The first, which we already discussed, is that the consequences of a temporary let-off for the developing world may encourage many years of life for the world's most polluting technologies. The temporary let-off may not be that temporary. Most victims will be in the developing world, so people in the developed world may be all too happy to go along with that.

But, second, the real crux of the issue is whether the developing world can afford to continue at its current pollution levels (or grow them), even without the threat of global warming. CO_2e emissions are strongly correlated with something else that directly affects their citizens *today*: air pollution. The environment in China and India has degraded so fast that pollution has become a massive and urgent public health hazard, and it is also becoming worse in other emerging economies.

This pollution kills. In China, coal-fired indoor heating is subsidized on the north side of the river Huai but not on the south, on the grounds that it is colder in the north. One can see a precipitous drop in the quality of the air when crossing the river from south to north. Correspondingly, there is a similar drop in life expectancy.[27] Estimates imply that moving China to the worldwide standard for the concentration of particulate matter in the air would save the equivalent of 3.7 billion years of life.

China's skies are, however, positively pristine compared to those of many big Indian cities. Several Indian cities, including the capital New Delhi, top the list of most air polluted cities on earth.[28] In November 2017, the chief minister of Delhi compared the city to a gas chamber. According to the US embassy's measurements, at that time the air in New Delhi reached pollution levels forty-eight times the guideline value established by the World Health Organization. As in China, this level of pollution is undoubtedly deadly.[29] Admissions to hospitals surge every November when pollution skyrockets. Globally, the Lancet Commission on pollution and health estimates that 9 million premature deaths were caused by air pollution in 2015.[30] More than 2.5 million of those deaths were in India, the most in any single country.[31]

Pollution in Delhi in the winter is due to a combination of several factors (including pure geographical bad luck), but some of it is due to behaviors that could be changed. One important pollutant comes from burning the stubble left after crop-cutting in states neighboring Delhi. The smoke from the burning outside the city is then mixed with various pollutants produced inside the city: dust from construction, exhaust from vehicles, residue from the burning of trash and the open fires the poor use to cook and keep warm in winter.

The smog in Delhi is so bad there is a clear impetus to act immediately. There is no trade-off between the quality of life today and in the future, since people are dying now. The only trade-off is between consuming less or choking. And even this trade-off may be mostly illusory. Two different studies, one involving workers in a textile manufacturing firm in India[32] and one on travel agents in China have shown that on days when ambient pollution is high, productivity is low. So more pollution may mean less consumption.[33]

Delhi is a relatively rich city. City dwellers can easily afford to pay the farmers not to burn their crops, and to instead use machines to bury them and ready the soil for the next planting. The government could ban open fires in the city and create heated rooms where the poor could gather on cold nights. It could replace trash-burning with a more modern trash collection and treatment system. It could ban old

cars (or in fact ban diesel-fueled cars altogether) and introduce congestion pricing or another form of congestion management.[34] It could enforce more vigorously the tough industrial pollution standards on the
books but not typically respected. It could improve the public transportation system. It could shut down or upgrade the large thermal plants
operating within the city. Perhaps none of these would be sufficient
individually, but combined they would surely improve the situation.

None of this is out of reach. For example, a "friends of the court"
brief submitted to India's supreme court suggested that a subsidy of
Rs 20 billion (about $300 million) would be enough for the farmers
of Punjab and Haryana to purchase the equipment needed to prepare
their fields. This is only approximately Rs 1,000 ($14 at the current
exchange rate, a little over $70 at PPP) per inhabitant of greater Delhi.
Surprisingly (and frustratingly), despite the urgency of the bad air, the
political demand for such a response is not overwhelming. Part of the
problem may be that curbing pollution would require a lot of people
to cooperate. But there is also a lack of awareness that air pollution
is a health issue. A recent *Lancet* study found that a large part of the
deaths due to outdoor air pollution can be attributed to the burning of
biomass (leaves, wood, etc.).[35] But a significant part of this biomass is
burnt on indoor stoves, which also generate a tremendous amount of
indoor air pollution. It would therefore seem there would be a strong
private demand for better cooking devices, which would improve both
indoor and outdoor air. But there appears to be no such demand. Study
after study finds that the demand for cleaner stoves is very low.[36] Even
when an NGO distributed cleaner stoves for free, people were not interested enough to get them fixed when they broke.[37] Low demand for
clean air may come from a failure of many of the poorest households to
connect clean air to a healthy, happy, and productive life.

This may change. Slum dwellers asked to compare the conditions
of life in the city to what they had experienced in their villages mostly
reported they preferred Delhi.[38] The only thing they really complained about was the environment and, in particular, the air. In the
winter of 2017–2018, there was finally some outrage in Delhi. School-
children took to the streets when their schools were shut down due to
the dangerously high pollution levels. Even in China, which is not a
democracy, the pressure of public opinion is said to have contributed

to the government's desire to do something about pollution. In India, it may soon become enough of a public issue to lead to some change. The priority should then be to enact policies that will lead to cleaner consumption patterns, even if they come at some cost. The costs may not be very large. In many cases, India would be able to leapfrog to the cleaner technology (e.g., when the poor finally get electricity, they get LED bulbs). In some cases, the new technology may be more expensive than the old (e.g., clean cars may be more expensive than dirty cars). This means the poor will need to be compensated. But the total cost of this is small, and could easily be borne by the elite if the political will was there.

A GREEN NEW DEAL?

With the Green New Deal, the talk of the town in the winter of 2018–2019, Democratic politicians in the United States were trying to link the fight against climate change with an agenda for economic justice and redistribution. They had an uphill political battle in front of them. From Paris to West Virginia and Delhi, fighting climate change is often presented as a luxury for the elites, funded by taxes on the less privileged.

To take an example we encountered firsthand, at the end of 2018 the agitation of the "Yellow Vests" protesting a planned increase in the tax on gasoline closed down the streets of Paris every Saturday, putting the French government under severe strain. Eventually, the tax increase had to be postponed. The argument the Yellow Vest protesters were making was that the increase in the gasoline tax was a way for rich Parisians (who can take the subway to work) to buy themselves a conscience at the cost of people from the suburbs and countryside who had no choice but to drive their cars. They did have a point, given that the same government had removed the wealth tax. In the United States, the specter of a "war on coal" became the rallying cry against the liberal elite, a symbol of their lack of empathy for the poor. And, of course, politicians in the developing world routinely (and rightly) rail against having to pay for previous choices made by rich countries.

The Green New Deal is an attempt to bridge precisely this divide, by emphasizing the fact that building new green infrastructure (solar panels, high-speed railroads, etc.) will both create jobs and help in the fight against climate change. It de-emphasizes the idea of a carbon tax, viewed by many on the left as being too reliant on market mechanisms and, as in France, just another way to make the poor pay.

We understand that a carbon tax is not an easy sell (taxes that hit most people never are), but our view is that it should be possible to make it politically acceptable by making it absolutely explicit that the carbon tax is not a way to raise revenues. The government should structure the carbon tax in a revenue-neutral way, such that tax revenues would be handed back as a compensation: a lump sum to all those at the lower end of the income scale, who would therefore come out ahead. This would preserve the incentive to conserve energy, drive less or drive electric cars, but make it very clear that the less wealthy would not pay for it. Given that energy consumption is a matter of habit, the tax should also be announced well in advance to give people time to get ready for it.

More generally, we are quite aware that it will cost money to prevent climate change and to adapt to the part already on its way. There will have to be investments in infrastructure, and meaningful redistribution to those whose livelihoods are affected. In poor countries, money could help the average citizen achieve a higher quality of life in a way less threatening to the future of the world. (Think of the air-conditioning debate, for example; why doesn't the world simply pay India to leapfrog to the better technology?) Given that the poor do not consume very much, it would not take a lot to help the world's poor consume a bit more, but also get better air and produce less emissions. The richest countries in the world are so rich they can easily pay for it.

The question is to frame the debate in a way that does not pitch the poor in poor countries against the poor in rich countries. A combination of taxes and regulations to curb emissions in rich countries and pay for a clean transition in poor countries may well reduce economic growth in the rich country, though of course we don't know for sure, since we don't know what causes growth. But if much of the cost is borne by the richest in the rich countries and the planet benefits, we see no reason to shy away.

In Delhi and Washington and Beijing, it is in the name of growth that policy makers drag their feet when called upon to enact or enforce pollution regulations. Who benefits from this GDP growth remains an afterthought.

Economists deserve their fair share of the blame for stoking this rhetoric. Nothing in either our theory or the data proves the highest GDP per capita is generally desirable. Yet because we fundamentally believe resources can and will be redistributed, we fall into the trap of always trying to make the overall pie as big as possible. This flies directly in the face of what we have learned over the past decades. The evidence is clear—inequality has risen dramatically in recent years, with searing consequences for societies across the world.

CHAPTER 7

PLAYER PIANO

*P*LAYER *PIANO* WAS the very first novel published by the great American fabulist Kurt Vonnegut.[1] It is a dystopia about a world where most jobs have disappeared. Written in 1952 in the wake of the great postwar expansion of jobs, it was either extremely farsighted or astoundingly misguided, but, either way, it's a perfect novel for our times.

A player piano is a piano that plays itself. In Vonnegut's world, machines run themselves and people are no longer needed. They are provided for, and get to do various forms of make-work, but there is nothing meaningful or useful they can do. As Mr. Rosewater, a character in a later (1965) novel by Vonnegut puts it: "The problem is this: How to love people who have no use?"[2] Or even have them not hate themselves?

The increasing sophistication of robots and the progress of artificial intelligence has generated considerable anxiety about what would happen to our societies if only a few people had interesting jobs and everyone else had either no work or had a horrible job, and inequality ballooned as a result. Especially if this happened because of forces largely out of their control. Tech moguls are getting desperate to find ideas to solve the problems their technologies might cause. But we don't need to contemplate the future in order to get a sense of what happens when economic growth leaves behind the majority of a country's citizens. This has already happened—in the United States since 1980.

ONE FOR THE LUDDITES

An increasing number of economists (and of those who comment on economics) worry that new technologies, such as AI, robots, and automation more generally, will destroy more jobs than they create, making many workers obsolete and causing the share of GDP that goes to pay wages to dwindle. In fact, these days growth optimists and labor pessimists are often the same people; they both imagine future growth will be primarily driven by the replacement of human workers by robots.

In their book *The Second Machine Age*, our MIT colleagues Erik Brynjolfsson and Andrew McAfee offer a bleak view of the impact of digitization on the future of employment in the United States.[3] Digitization, they suspect, will make workers with "ordinary" skills increasingly redundant. As tasks from car painting to spreadsheet manipulation are done by computers or robots, highly educated workers who are adaptable and can program and install the robots will become more and more valuable, but other workers who can be replaced will find themselves without jobs unless they accept extremely low salaries. In this view, artificial intelligence will be the final nail in the coffin of these ordinary workers.

In the first IT revolution, as David Autor has shown, jobs involving routine repetitive tasks were the ones that went.[4] Jobs that required quick judgment and initiative stayed put. The number of typists and assembly-line workers diminished, but executive assistants and burger flippers kept their jobs. This time, many say, it is different. Artificial intelligence means machines can learn as they go and are therefore able to carry out increasingly nonroutine tasks, such as playing Go or folding laundry. In June 2018, a restaurant offering robot-made burgers opened in San Francisco. Humans are still taking the orders and cooking the sauces, but the robots cook the gourmet burgers, such as the *Tumami Burger* ("Smoked oyster aioli, shiitake mushroom sauce, black pepper and salt, pickles, onion, butter lettuce—*Designed by Chef Tu*, Top Chef *Season 15*"[5]), in five minutes and for $6. Esther's sister Annie Duflo, the CEO of a large NGO, does not have a human assistant; she relies exclusively on an AI-powered assistant named Fin. Fin books her hotels and her plane tickets, manages her calendar, and takes care of her travel reimbursements. Annie is, sadly, much happier with Fin than she was with her human assistants. She pays him (her? it?) much less and gets much more reliable service. To be sure, there are some humans behind Fin, but fewer and fewer, and the business model is clearly to move away from them.

The AI revolution is thus poised to hit people across a wide spectrum of jobs. Accountants, mortgage originators, management consultants, financial planners, paralegals, and sports journalists are already competing with some form of artificial intelligence or, if not, will soon. Cynics might say it is precisely because these more high-end jobs are on the line that we are finally talking about this, and they may be right. But AI will also hurt shelf stackers, office cleaners, restaurant workers, and taxi drivers. Based on the tasks they perform, a McKinsey report[6] concludes that 45 percent of US jobs are at risk of being automated, and the OECD estimates that 46 percent of the workers in OECD countries are in occupations at high risk of being either replaced or fundamentally transformed.[7]

Of course, what this calculation misses is that as some tasks get automatized, and the need for humans gets relieved, people can be put to work elsewhere.

So how bad will it be on net? Economists are of course intrigued by this problem, but in this case they have entirely failed to reach a consensus. The IGM Booth panel of experts were asked their opinion of the following statement: "Holding labor market institutions and job training fixed, rising use of robots and artificial intelligence is likely to increase substantially the number of workers in advanced countries who are unemployed for long periods." Twenty-eight percent of respondents agreed or strongly agreed with it, 20 percent disagreed or strongly disagreed, and 24 percent were uncertain![8]

The difficulty is that doomsday (if it is coming) has not arrived. Robert Gordon, whom as we have seen does not think too highly of today's innovations, likes to play "spot the robot" when he travels.[9] For all the talk, he says, it is still a human clerk who checks him in at the hotel, cleans his room, serves his coffee, and so on.

For the time being, humans have not been made redundant. Unemployment in the United States, as we write this book in the first quarter of 2019, is at a historical low and falling.[10] With more and more women joining the labor force, the share of the population in the labor force rose substantially until about 2000 (when it started to plateau or reverse).[11] Jobs were found for all those who wanted to work, despite rapid labor-saving technological progress.

Of course, it is true we are probably just at the very beginning of the process of AI-fueled automation. The sense that artificial intelligence is a new class of technology makes it hard to predict what it might do. Futurologists talk about a "singularity," a dramatic acceleration of the rate of productivity growth fueled by infinitely intelligent machines, although most economists are quite skeptical that we are anywhere close to seeing something like that. But it could well be that if Gordon plays spot the robot in a few years, he will have a more exciting time.

On the other hand, while this particular wave of automation is just starting, there have been others in the past. Like AI today, the spinning jenny, the steam engine, electricity, computer chips, and computer-assisted-learning machinery all automatized and relieved the need for humans in the past.[12]

What happened then is very much what one might have expected: by replacing workers with machines on some tasks, automation has a powerful displacement effect. It makes the workers redundant. This is what happened to the skilled artisans spinning and weaving at the dawn of the industrial revolution. They were replaced by machines. And as is well known, they did not like it one bit. In the early nineteenth century, the Luddites destroyed machines to protest the mechanization of weaving, which was threatening their livelihoods as skilled artisans. The term *Luddite* is now mostly used pejoratively to describe someone who blindly refuses progress, and their example is often used to dismiss concerns about technology creating unemployment. After all, the Luddites were wrong—jobs did not vanish, and wages and living conditions are much higher today than they were then.

Yet the Luddites were less wrong than we might assume. Their particular jobs did vanish in the industrial revolution, along with the jobs of a whole range of artisans. We are told that in the long run everything was fine, but the long run was very long indeed. Real blue-collar wages in Britain were almost halved between 1755 and 1802. Although 1802 was a particularly low year, they were on a declining trend between 1755 and the turn of the century, and it is only at the turn of the century that they started increasing again. They would recover their 1755 level only in 1820, sixty-five years later.[13]

This period of intense technological progress in the United Kingdom was also an era of intense deprivation and very difficult living conditions. The economic historian Robert Fogel showed that boys in England during this period were significantly undernourished compared even to slaves in the US South.[14] The literature of the time, from Frances Trollope to Charles Dickens, describes what was happening to the economy and society with a certain amount of unmitigated horror. Those were Hard Times indeed.

We know that eventually there was a turnaround in the UK. Even as some workers lost their jobs, the labor-saving innovations raised profitability of other inputs, and hence the demand for workers producing them. Improvements in weaving technology, like John Kay's flying shuttle, for example, increased demand for yarn, creating jobs for people to produce yarn. And the burgeoning wealth of those profiting from these innovations increased demand for new products and services in a range of sectors (more solicitors, accountants, engineers, bespoke tailors, gardeners, etc.), which created more jobs.

However, nothing tells us the rebound is guaranteed to happen. There may well be no rebound from the fall in demand for labor resulting from this wave of automation and AI. Sectors that become more profitable may invest in new labor-saving technologies instead of hiring more workers. The new wealth may be used to purchase goods made in another country.

We don't know what will happen this time around, since we haven't seen the very long run yet, but the impact of the current wave of automation (which started in 1990, giving us a perspective of more than twenty-five years) appears so far to be negative. In a study on the impact of automatization, researchers computed, for each region, a measure of *exposure* to industrial robots, capturing the spread of robots in the industries in that region.[15] They then compared the evolution of employment and wages in the most affected areas to that in the least affected areas. The study found, to the surprise of the authors, who had written a previous paper emphasizing the forces that should lead to a rebound,[16] large negative impacts. One more robot in a commuting zone reduces employment by 6.2 workers and also depresses wages. The employment effects are most pronounced in manufacturing and they are particularly strong for workers with lower than a college education, especially those who do routine manual tasks. However, there are no offsetting gains in employment or wages for any other occupation or educational group. These local impacts of robots on employment and wages are reminiscent of the impacts of greater exposure to international trade. They are surprising for the same reasons. As many tasks in a particular industry get automatized, we might have expected displaced workers to find employment in new businesses that would have come to the region to take advantage of the freed-up labor, or to move elsewhere. It is also worrying that the automation of simple tasks did not lead to the hiring of more engineers to supervise the robots. The explanation is probably similar to why competition with China hurt low-skilled workers; in the sticky economy, seamless reallocation is anything but guaranteed.

Even if the total number of jobs does not fall, the current wave of automation tends to displace jobs that require some skills (bookkeepers and accountants) and increase the demand, either for very skilled workers (software programmers for the machines) or for totally unskilled workers (dog walkers, for example), which are both much more difficult to replace with a machine. As software engineers become richer, they have more money to hire dog walkers, who have become relatively cheaper over time, since there is little alternative employment for those with no college education. Even if people remain employed, this leads to an increase in inequality, with higher wages at the top and everyone else pushed to jobs requiring no specific skills; jobs where wages and working conditions can be really bad. This accentuates a trend that has taken place since the 1980s. Workers without a college education have increasingly been pushed out of mid-skill jobs, such as clerical and administrative roles, into low-skill tasks, such as cleaning and security.[17]

LUDDISM LIGHT?

So should we try to stop the push toward automation? There are in fact good reasons to suspect that some of the recent automation is excessive; corporations seem to decide to automate even when robots are less productive than people. Excessive automation reduces GDP instead of contributing to it.

One reason is the bias in the US tax code, which taxes labor at a higher rate than capital. Employers have to pay payroll taxes (used to finance social security and Medicare) on labor, but not on robots. They get an immediate tax rebate when they invest in the robot, since they can often claim "accelerated depreciation" for a capital expenditure, and if they finance it with a loan they also get to deduct the interest from their earnings. This tax advantage gives employers an incentive to automate, even if it would otherwise cost less to keep the workers.[18] Moreover, even without subsidies from the tax code, the many frictions in the labor market may make managers dream of factories without workers. Robots won't demand maternity leave or protest a wage cut in a recession. It is probably not an accident that automation in the retail sector (such as automatic checkout lines) started first in Europe, where the labor unions are stronger.

The increase in industry concentration and monopolies could also reinforce this tendency. A monopolist does not fear competition. It has no reason to constantly reinvent what it is offering its consumers. Therefore, the monopolist will tend to focus more on cost-cutting innovations, which will increase its profit margins. In contrast, a competitive firm might go for a moonshot to try to take over the market.

Now it is true that even if a business adopts a highly productive new technology that displaces labor, the increase in productivity also creates new resources that could be deployed to find new uses for the freed labor. The technologies most dangerous for the workers are what some researchers have described as "so-so" automation technologies; they are just productive enough to be adopted given the distortions in the tax code, and displace workers, but not productive enough to raise overall productivity.[19]

Unfortunately, notwithstanding the grandiose talk about singularities, the bulk of R&D resources these days is directed toward machine learning and other big data methods designed to automate *existing* tasks, rather than the invention of new products that would create new roles for workers, and hence new jobs.[20] This may make economic sense for the companies, given the financial gains in replacing workers with robots. But it distracts researchers and engineers from working on the truly pathbreaking innovations. For example, inventing new software or hardware health workers could use to assist patients in doing their rehabilitation therapy at home after a surgery rather than in a hospital could potentially save insurance companies lot of money, improve well-being, and create new jobs. But the bulk of the automation effort today in insurance firms goes toward searching for algorithms that automate the approval of insurance claims. This saves money but destroys jobs. This emphasis on the automation of existing jobs increases the potential for the current wave of innovation to be very damaging for workers.

That unregulated automation could be bad for workers is also the instinct of most Americans on the right and the left. One place, remarkably, where Republican and Democrat poll respondents agree is in their opposition to letting companies decide how much to automate. Eighty-five percent of Americans would support limiting automation to "dangerous and dirty jobs," with no difference between Democrats and Republicans. Even when the question is posed in a more politically pointed way, asking whether "there should be limits on the number of jobs businesses can replace with machines, even if they are better and cheaper than humans," 58 percent of Americans, including half of Republicans, say yes.[21]

This specific force of automation is exacerbating what is always a concern. When a worker is fired, the firm is done with him, but society inherits the liability of his continued well-being. Society does not want him to starve or his family to be homeless; it wants him to find another job he likes. We fear his anger, especially if it leads to a vote for the many lurking extremists in today's world, whereas the firm does not have to pay for the retraining, the welfare payments, or the social costs of the anger.

This kind of argument has traditionally been used to justify making it difficult to fire workers. Some labor laws, like India's, make it virtually impossible to fire anyone in larger firms. Others, like the French laws, make it difficult and uncertain. The worker can appeal and possibly be reinstated with back pay. The problem with such firing costs is that they can make life very difficult for a manager faced with a nonperforming worker or an urgent need to downsize in order to survive. As a result, firing costs may discourage hiring in the first place, which would exacerbate unemployment.[22]

The alternative to restricting firing or banning the use of robots in some sectors is a tax on robots, large enough to prevent them from being deployed unless the productivity gains are sufficiently high. This is now the subject of a serious discussion. Bill Gates has recommended it.[23] In 2017 the European Parliament considered, but ultimately voted down, a proposed "robot tax," citing concern over stifling innovation.[24] Around the same time, however, South Korea announced the world's first robot tax. The Korean plan reduces tax subsidies for businesses investing in automation and combines it with a tax on outsourcing, so that the tax on robots does not lead to outsourcing.[25]

The problem is that while it is easy to ban self-driving cars (whether or not it's a good idea), most robots do not look like R2-D2 in *Star Wars*. They are typically embedded inside machines that will still have human operators, just fewer of them; how does the regulator decide where the machine stops and the robot begins? A robot tax would likely lead companies to find new ways around it, further distorting the economy.

For some of these reasons, we suspect the current drive toward replacing human actions with robots cannot be prevented from taking a serious toll on the already dwindling stock of desirable jobs for low-skilled workers, first in the rich countries but very soon everywhere. This will add, to a greater or lesser extent, to what the China shock and the other changes described in previous chapters have done to the working class in much of the developed world. It could lead to a rise in unemployment or a multiplication of poorly paid, unstable jobs.

This perspective deeply worries the elites who feel responsible for, and also threatened by, this state of affairs. This is why the idea of a universal basic income has become so popular in Silicon Valley. Most tend to think, however, that robot-induced despair will become a problem in the future, after technologies have improved even further. But the problem of high and rising inequality has already been staring us in the face in many countries, nowhere more so than in the United States. The last thirty years of US history should convince us that the evolution of inequality is not the by-product of technological changes we do not control: it is the result of policy decisions.

SELF-INFLICTED DAMAGE

By the 1980s, not only were the United States and the United Kingdom experiencing lower growth than they were accustomed to, but they also felt continental Europe and Japan catching up. Growth became a matter of national pride. It was important not just to grow but to win the "race" with the other rich countries. After decades of fast growth, national pride was defined by the size of GDP, and its continuous expansion.

For both Margaret Thatcher in the UK and Ronald Reagan in the US, what was to blame for the slump in the late-1970s was clear (though we now know they really had no idea). The countries had drifted too far to the left—unions were too strong, the minimum wage was too high, taxes were too onerous, regulation was too overbearing. Restoring growth required treating business owners better through lower tax rates, deregulation, and deunionization, and getting the rest of the country to be less reliant on the government. As mentioned earlier, the idea that tax rates need to be low to avoid disaster is of recent vintage. In the United States, the top marginal tax rate was above 90 percent from 1951 to 1963. It declined afterward, but remained high. Under Presidents Reagan and George H. W. Bush, top tax rates came down from 70 percent to less than 30 percent. Bill Clinton pushed them back up, but only to 40 percent. Since then they have bounced up and down, as the US presidency passes between Democrats and Republicans, but they have never gone much higher than 40 percent. Lower taxes were accompanied, first under Reagan and then even more strongly under Clinton, by "welfare reform" (in other words, gutting welfare), which was justified both on grounds of principle (the poor must be more responsible and therefore welfare must become workfare) and out of budgetary compulsion (resulting from diminished tax collection). Unions were brought to heel, both by changing the laws and by directly using state power against them (Reagan, famously, called out the army to break an air traffic controllers' strike). Union membership has been in decline ever since.[26] Regulations were made less restrictive, and there was a new consensus that a very compelling justification should be required before the "heavy hand of the government" was allowed to intervene in business.

In the UK, something similar happened. The highest tax rate went from 83 percent in 1978 to 60 percent in 1979 and then to 40 percent, and has remained close to that ever since. The very (too?) powerful unions of the postwar era were taken down with a firm hand—the miner's strike of 1984 was a defining moment of Margaret Thatcher's rule—and have never recovered. Deregulation became the norm, though the integration with regulation-friendly Europe limited how far it could go. The one difference between the UK and the US is that there was never a major attempt to cut welfare (Mrs. Thatcher apparently wanted to, but her cabinet colleagues dissuaded her). Public spending did fall from 45 percent of GDP to 34 percent during the Thatcher years, but it then partially recovered under subsequent governments.[27]

The reason why such radical changes were possible probably had a lot to do with the anxiety that came with slowing growth. Despite the fact that there is no evidence massive tax cuts for the rich promote economic growth (we are still waiting for the promised turnaround in growth in both the US and the UK), at the time the evidence was much less clear. Since growth had stopped in 1973, the natural reaction was to turn to the critics of the Keynesian macroeconomic policies of the 1960s and 1970s, such as the (right-leaning) Chicago school of economics professors and Nobel Prize–winners Milton Friedman and Robert Lucas.

Reaganomics, as the dominant economics of this period came to be called, was quite open about the fact that the benefits of growth would come at the cost of some inequality. The idea was that the rich would benefit first but the poor would eventually benefit. This is the famous trickle-down theory, never better described than by Harvard professor John Kenneth Galbraith, who claimed this was what used to be called the "horse and sparrow" theory in the 1890s: "If you feed the horse enough oats, some will pass through to the road for the sparrows."[28]

Indeed, the 1980s ushered a dramatic change in the social contract in the US and the UK. Whatever economic growth happened since 1980 has been, for all intents and purposes, siphoned off by the rich. Was Reaganomics or its UK version responsible for it?

THE GREAT REVERSAL

In the 1980s, while growth remained sluggish, inequality exploded. Thanks to the outstanding and painstaking work of Thomas Piketty and Emmanuel Saez, the world now knows what happened: 1980 is the year Reagan was elected. It is also almost exactly the year the share of national income that goes to the richest 1 percent reverses fifty years of decline and starts a relentless climb in the United States. In 1928, at the end of the Roaring Twenties, the richest 1 percent captured 24 percent of the income. In 1979, that number was about a third as big. In 2017, the last year to be included at the time of writing, that ratio was almost back where it was in 1929. The increase in *income* inequality was accompanied by a rise in *wealth* inequality (income is what people earn every year; wealth is their accumulated fortune), although wealth inequality has not yet reached its early 1920s level. The top 1 percent wealth share in the United States rose from 22 percent in 1980 to 39 percent in 2014.[29]

The story for the UK is very similar. The turning point, like in the US, is somewhere very close to 1979, the year Mrs. Thatcher took over. Before 1979, the top income share falls steadily from 1920. After 1979, there is a similar rise, interrupted briefly by the global financial crisis of 2009. Unlike in the United States, inequality has not yet reached the 1920s levels, but it does not have that far to go.[30]

In continental Europe the pattern is strikingly different. Before 1920, the top income share in France or Germany, Switzerland or Sweden, the Netherlands or Denmark was not too different from that in the US or UK. But sometime after 1920, inequality crashed in all of these countries, like in the United States, and stayed down, unlike in the United States. There are small ups and downs, and Sweden actually has a significant upswing starting somewhere in the 1980s, but the levels remain very low by US standards.[31]

These data are about *pre-tax income*, before the rich paid taxes and the poor received transfers. Therefore, they do not take into account any attempt to redistribute from the rich to the poor. Since taxes went down in the United States, we might have expected post-tax inequality to increase even more than pre-tax inequality after 1979. One does see a small blip up at the time of the Tax Reform Act of 1986, but for the most part the curves for pre-tax and post-tax income shares track each other.[32] Taxes are important for redistribution, but the increase in inequality is a much deeper phenomenon than a mechanical effect of lower redistribution.

At the same time, around 1980, wages stopped increasing, at least for the least educated. The average hourly wage adjusted for inflation for US workers who were not managers rose through the 1960s and 1970s, reached its peak in the mid- to late-1970s, and then drifted down through the Reagan-Bush years, before slowly turning around. As a result, the average real wage in 2014 was no higher than in 1979. Over the same period (from 1979 to today), the real wages of the least educated workers actually *fell*. Among high school dropouts, high school graduates, and those with some college, real weekly earnings among full-time male workers in 2018 were 10 to 20 percent below their real levels in 1980.[33] If there had been any trickle-down effect of lower taxes, as its advocates claimed, one would expect wage growth to have accelerated in the Reagan-Bush years. But the opposite happened. The labor share (the share of revenues used to pay wages) has continuously declined since the 1980s. In manufacturing, almost 50 percent of sales were used to pay workers in 1982; it had fallen to about 10 percent in 2012.[34]

The fact that this great reversal takes place during the Reagan and Thatcher years is probably not coincidental, but there is no reason to assume Reagan and Thatcher were the reason it happened. Their election was also a symptom of the politics of the time, dominated by anxiety about the end of growth. It is not impossible that if they had lost, whoever won would have gone some distance along the same path.

More importantly, it is not a priori obvious that Reagan-Thatcher policies were the main reason why inequality went up. The diagnosis of what actually happened in this period, with its obvious implications for policy, has been and continues to be an active area of debate within economics, with some, like Thomas Piketty, squarely blaming changes in policies, while most economists emphasize that the structural transformation of the economy, and particular changes in technologies, also had a lot to do with it.[35]

The reason why this is not an easy question is that this was also a period of momentous changes in the world economy. Starting in 1979,

China launched market reforms. In 1984, India started taking baby steps toward liberalization. These countries would eventually become two of the largest markets in the world. Partly as a result, world trade expanded relative to world GDP by about 50 percent over this period,[36] with the consequences we discussed in chapter 3.

The advent of computing was the other characteristic feature of the era. Microsoft was founded in 1975; in 1976, the Apple I was released, followed by the much more widely sold Apple II in 1977; IBM released its first personal computer in 1981. Also, in 1979, NTT launched the first widely distributed handheld cell phone system in Japan. Mostly on the strength of selling cell phones, Apple became the first trillion-dollar company in August 2018.

To what extent do technological change and globalization explain the pattern of increase in inequality in the US and the UK? To what extent did policy, tax policy in particular, play a role?

With computerization came other technological change. This may not have been a revolution in the sense that the steam engine brought in a revolution, as Robert Gordon argued, but like the steam engine and its love child, the internal combustion engine, it killed a lot of jobs. No one probably makes a living by being a typist now, except the three lone men of uncertain age who sit under a tree near where Abhijit grew up in Kolkata, who for a small fee will type in your name and address into government-issued documents. There are few stenographers left. Even in the White House, their days appear to be numbered. And this technological progress was to a large extent skewed against the less qualified.

This skill-biased technological change clearly explains the increase in the return to college education.[37] But it cannot explain what happened at the very top of the income distribution, unless we think skills were suddenly transmogrified just for the very richest. We usually think of skills increasing relatively continuously with education and wage levels. So, if the explosion of top income inequality was just due to technological progress, the widening of the distribution of wages should have been not just for the ultra-rich but also for the merely rich. But, in fact, those making, say, between $100,000 and $200,000 a year have seen their pay increase only slightly more rapidly than the average, while those who are making more than $500,000 have seen their incomes explode.[38]

This suggests that plausible changes in technology are unlikely to explain the stratospheric increase in incomes at the very top. Nor, for that matter, can they explain the difference between United States and continental Europe; technological change has been similar in all rich countries.

WINNER TAKE ALL?

However, technology has also changed the organization of the economy. A lot of the most successful inventions that came out of the high-tech revolution were "winner take all" products; there was no point in being on Myspace when the whole world was on Facebook, and Twitter is meaningless unless someone is retweeting your tweets. Technological innovations have also transformed existing industries, and created large benefits from being connected to industries where they used to be largely absent, like hospitality or transportation. For example, if drivers know that all passengers use a particular ride-sharing platform, they will choose to stay on that one. Conversely, if passengers know that all drivers use a particular platform, that is where they will go. These network effects explain in part the dominance of giant tech companies like Google, Facebook, Apple, Amazon, Uber, and Airbnb, but also of "old economy" behemoths, such as Walmart and Federal Express. In addition, the globalization of demand has increased the value of brands, as rich Chinese and Indian customers can now aspire to the same goods. And the ability to browse, compare, and boast on Facebook has made consumers more aware of differences in prices and quality, but also more sensitive to fads.

The result is a winner-take-all (or if not all, most) economy, in which a few firms capture a large part of the market. As we saw in the chapter on growth, in many sectors sales have become more concentrated, and we see the increasing dominance of "superstar firms." And in sectors that have become more concentrated, the share of revenues going to pay wages has gone down more. This is because those firms, which are monopolies or near monopolies, make more profits, and those tend to be distributed to shareholders. The increase in concentration thus helps explain a part of why wages are not keeping pace with GDP.[39]

The rise of the superstar firms also offers an explanation for why overall wage inequality has been rising: some firms are now much more profitable than others and they pay higher wages. It is also true that profitability is more variable than it used to be, with more clear winners and clear losers, even outside the set of superstars.[40] In fact, in the United States, the increase in inequality between the average salaries at different companies can explain two-thirds of the overall rise in inequality (increase in inequality between workers within the same company explains the rest). A lot of this increase in inequality between firms seems due to changes in who works where; the highest-paid workers in low-paying firms are moving to those that pay more. If one assumes that higher earnings reflect higher productivity (which is probably true on average), then the more productive workers are increasingly working with other high-productivity workers.[41]

This is consistent with a theory in which superstar firms attract both capital and good workers.[42] If more productive people benefit more from being paired with other productive people, then the market should drive such people to come together to form high-productivity firms that would, as a result, have higher wages and salaries than other firms. Moreover, once a firm has invested in a galaxy of talents, the CEO of such a firm is in a position to make a big difference; if he pushes them down the wrong path, he would waste a whole lot of productive capacity. Therefore, such firms should strive to get the best CEO possible even if that requires paying him or her what some may feel is an obscene salary.[43] The rise in top incomes, in this view, is just the flip side of the rise of superstar firms that value getting the best top management and are willing to pay a lot for them.

That the economy is sticky also contributes to the rise in inequality between firms. As production in some sectors gets concentrated in superstar firms, other firms in those sectors all over the country are shutting down (think the local department store versus Amazon), in addition to those that shut down because of the effect of new technology or trade. Since workers do not move out, wage growth in the affected area flattens or gets reversed, and rents do the same. This is good news for the surviving firms in those pockets, especially if their clients are elsewhere. The resulting windfall in profits may lead to greater investment in these companies, but probably not enough to halt the overall decline of the area. In other words, part of the distinction between good firms and bad firms may be purely happenstance. If you are a firm in a failing local economy lucky enough to be able to continue to sell to the national or world economy, you can do very well, at least for a while, until the overall drain in talent from these places, as the young and the ambitious move out, starts to hurt.

In other words, globalization and the rise of the infotech industry, combined with the sticky economy, and no doubt with other important but perhaps more local changes, created a world of good and bad firms, which in turn contributed to an increase in inequality. In this view, what happened may have been unfortunate, but it probably could not have been stopped.

SOMETHING IS NOT ROTTEN IN THE STATE OF DENMARK

But the winner-take-all explanation for the rise in inequality cannot be the whole story either.

The reason is that, like skill-biased technological progress, the explanation ought to apply to Denmark just as much as the United States. But it does not. Denmark is a capitalist country where the share of income going to the top 1 percent was more than 20 percent in the 1920s, just like in the United States. But when it went down it stayed low, and now hovers around 5 percent.[44] Denmark is a small country but it has a number of large and well-known companies, including the shipping giant Maersk; Bang & Olufsen, maker of beautiful consumer electronics products; and the Tuborg Brewery. But its top incomes never went sky high. The same is true of many very different countries in Western Europe and also of Japan.[45] What's different between these countries and the United States?

A part of the answer is finance. The US and UK dominate the "high end" of finance—the investment banks, junk bonds, hedge funds, mortgage-backed securities, private equity, quants, etc.—and this is where many of the astronomical earnings have shown up in recent years. Two finance professors at Harvard Business School (of all places) estimate that investors who use financial market intermediaries pay 1.3 percent of their total investment to their fund manager *every year*, which over the thirty-year horizon of an investor saving for retirement amounts to handing the manager a third of the assets initially invested.[46] A chunk of change, but nothing compared to those who manage the hedge funds, private equity funds, and venture capital funds that epitomize high-end finance, where, at least until recently, you had to pay the managers between 3 percent and 5 percent of the amount invested *every year*. Given that the amount invested is growing steadily, it is no wonder some of these managers are becoming very, very rich.

Financial sector employees are now paid 50–60 percent more than other workers with comparable skills. This was not true in the 1950s, 1960s, or 1970s.[47] This rise in earnings is a big piece of the overall shift in top incomes. In the UK, which is the most finance-dominated large economy, between 1998 and 2007, employees in the financial sector, who represented only about one-fifth of those in the top 1 percent, swallowed 60 percent of the rise in earnings in this group.[48] In the United States, from 1979 to 2005, the share of top incomes going to finance professionals almost doubled.[49] In France, where finance still mostly means banking and insurance, the change in inequality was much smaller in absolute terms. Between 1996 and 2007, the share of national income going to the richest one-tenth of one percent of the population went up from 1.2 percent to 2 percent (it then went down during the financial crisis, but had recovered partly by 2014[50]), but about half of that increase, it is estimated, is due to increasing earnings in finance.[51]

The superstar narrative does not fit finance very well. Finance is not a team sport. It is an industry marked, supposedly, by individual geniuses, people who can spot the particular irrationalities currently infecting the markets or identify the next Google or Facebook before anybody else. But it is hard to see how that explains why an *ordinary* manager in the financial sector is nonetheless paid extraordinary fees, year after year. In fact, most years, actively managed funds do not do any better than "passive funds" that simply replicate the stock market index. In fact, the average US mutual funds *underperform* the US stock market[52]—they seem to have borrowed the language of individual talent but not the talent itself. A large part of the premiums paid to financial sector employees are almost surely pure *rents*; that is, rewards not for talent or hard work but for nothing more than having lucked out in landing that particular job.[53]

These rents, much like the rents from government jobs in poor countries discussed in chapter 5, distort the entire functioning of the labor market. As the 2008 global crisis unfolded, caused in large part by a combination of irresponsibility and incompetence on the part of the masters of finance, a study reported that 28 percent of Harvard college graduates of recent cohorts opted for jobs in finance.[54] That ratio was 6 percent in 1969 and 1973.[55] The reason to be concerned about this is that if some job pays a premium unrelated to its usefulness, like the fund managers earning a fat fee for doing nothing, or the many talented MIT engineers and scientists hired to write software that allows stock trading at millisecond frequencies, then talented people are lost to firms that might do something more socially useful. Faster trading may be profitable because it allows the trader to react more quickly to new information, but given that the reaction time is already seconds or less, it seems implausible that it improves the allocation of resources in the economy in any meaningful way. And hiring the brightest of the bright may be an effective tool for a financial firm to market itself, but if the firm does nothing useful those talents are lost to the world. Maybe in a saner world they would have been writing the next great symphony or curing pancreatic cancer.

There is another problem. The salaries and bonuses of CEOs of the larger corporations are set by board of directors compensation committees, and these committees use the salaries of CEOs at comparable firms as a benchmark. This creates a contagion; if one company (say, in finance) starts to pay its CEO more, others not necessarily in finance feel they have to as well, to keep getting the best. Their CEOs feel undervalued compared to CEOs they play golf with. Consultants who help the CEOs compile a list of what happens in "comparable" firms are very skilled at selecting a sample of particularly high salaries; the high finance salaries tend to infect the rest of the economy as well. The practice of using salary comparisons to negotiate increased compensation has spread far beyond the largest firms, and even beyond the for-profit sector.

This is not helped by the fact that CEOs, everywhere and not just in finance, try very hard to pack boards of directors with people they feel they can control (or people who are only interested in getting paid their director's fees). The result is that CEOs are often rewarded for pure luck; when the stock market valuation of the firm goes up, even if it is due to pure chance (e.g., world crude oil prices went up, the exchange rate moved in the firm's favor), their salary increases. The one exception, which in some ways proves the rule, is that CEOs of companies where there is a single large shareholder who sits on the board (and is vigilant because it is his own money on the line) get paid significantly less for luck than for genuinely productive management.[56]

Stock options probably contributed to the skyrocketing CEO salaries, by normalizing the idea that CEO pay was directly linked to shareholder value and nothing else. In addition, linking managerial pay to the stock market meant that managers' pay was no longer linked to a salary scale within the enterprise. When everyone was on the same scale, CEOs had to grow salaries at the bottom to increase their own. With stock options, they had no reason to increase wages at the bottom, and in fact every reason to squeeze costs. Paternalism, once a feature of the large corporations that demanded loyalty but took care of their own, is now restricted to elite workers in software companies, and is expressed in the form of free food and dry cleaning in exchange for long hours.

One solution to the puzzle posed by Denmark might be that finance is much more dominant in the UK and the US than in continental Europe,[57] and perhaps a more attractive option for those countries' elite graduates. Relatedly, stock options (and stock market–linked compensation more generally) are much more likely to get used in the Anglo-Saxon world, where more people are familiar with the stock market and where most reasonable-sized companies are traded.

TOP TAX RATES AND CULTURAL CHANGE

Low taxes probably played a role as well, as argued by Thomas Piketty. When tax rates on the very top income are 70 percent or more, firms are more likely to decide that paying stratospheric wages is a waste of their money and cut back the top salaries. With these tax rates, the board faces a stark trade-off: at a 70 percent marginal tax rate, a dollar in salary is only thirty cents in the pocket for the manager, versus a whole dollar for the firm. It makes salary less valuable for the CEO, and it becomes cheaper for the board to pay the CEO in other "currencies," such as allowing him to pursue his dream projects. This might not always be what the shareholders want (they want higher profits, not size per se)—economists in the 1960s and 1970s were concerned with empire-building by managers—but could be better for the workers, or the world. For example, the CEO could prioritize growing the firm, being popular with the workers, or pursuing some new product because it is good for the world, even if it is not the best for share value. The shareholders may tolerate this to keep their CEO happy. It might even be part of the reason why workers' salaries were rising when top tax rates were high.

So the point of the very high top tax rates of the 1950s and 1960s, which applied only to extremely high incomes, was not so much to "soak the rich" as to eliminate them. Almost nobody ended up paying the top rates, because those very high incomes had all but disappeared.[58] When the top tax rates went down to 30 percent, ultra-high salaries became attractive again.

In other words, high top tax rates may actually lead to a reduction not just in inequality after taxes, but also in *inequality before taxes*. This is important because, as already discussed, a large part of the reason for the divergence in inequality between Europe and the United States in recent decades comes from pre-tax inequality. And some evidence hints at the possibility that the decline in top tax rates may have something to do with it: at the country level, there is a strong correlation between the size in the cuts in top tax rates between 1970 and today, and the increase in inequality. Germany, Sweden, Spain, Denmark, and Switzerland, where top marginal tax rates stayed high, did not experience sharp increases in top income shares. In contrast, the United States, Ireland, Canada, the UK, Norway, and Portugal cut the top tax rates significantly and experienced large increases in top income shares.[59]

However, beyond tax rates, in the United States it is also likely there was a cultural change that created a social environment in which high salaries were acceptable. After all, how did people in finance manage to convince their shareholders and the world they could be paid that much for their services, if we are correct that they are mostly earning rents?

In our view, beyond the tax cuts, the narrative of incentives that underpinned the Reagan-Thatcher revolution convinced a substantial fraction of the non-rich (and most of the rich who had any doubts about it) that those sky-high salaries were legitimate. Low taxes were a symptom of it, but the ideological shift was even deeper. The rich could go ahead and pay themselves more money than they could ever spend, without raising any hackles, as long as they had "earned" this money. Many economists, with their unconditional love for incentives, played a key role in spreading and legitimizing this narrative. As we saw, many economists remain in favor of high CEO pay today even though they are not opposed to higher taxation across the board. The narrative has spread: even today, while many in the US and the UK clearly resent their own economic situation, they tend to blame immigration and trade liberalization rather than the increasing vacuuming of resources toward the very rich.

Was the basic presumption, that high take-home salaries were essential to encourage the most productive people to do their best and create prosperity for the rest of us, correct? What do we know about the effect of taxes on the effort of the rich?

A TALE OF TWO FOOTBALLS

Europe is a more equal society than the United States, with much lower inequality in pre-tax income, a higher tax burden, and highly progressive taxation. There is one interesting exception to that: payments to top athletes. Major League Baseball in the United States implements a luxury tax, wherein teams are fined if their combined payroll exceeds some amount. A team that goes over the luxury tax threshold for the first time in a five-year period pays a penalty of 22.5 percent of the amount they were over the threshold, and the maximum fine for repeat offenders is 50 percent of the excess. Most other major sports leagues in the United States (the NFL, the NBA, Major

League Soccer, etc.) have salary caps. The maximum that could be paid in total for a team in the NBA in 2018 was $177 million. Not a trifle, but in 2018 the Argentine soccer player Lionel Messi was paid a yearly total of $84 million by his club, Barcelona, way above what would be possible in the US.

Salary caps in professional sports are hardly the product of some Nordic idealism. Clearly, the main rationale of the salary caps is to control costs. It is what a cartel of team owners does to limit how much of the proceeds go to players and, by implication, increase the amount that goes to them. But it has the virtue, and this is the stated reason for the caps, that it ensures some degree of equity between the teams, making the season much more interesting to watch. Unlimited money creates too much inequality, with the result that within a league only a few teams ever have a real chance of winning. In Europe, where Major League Soccer does not have salary caps, some teams (such as Manchester City, Manchester United, Liverpool, Arsenal, and Chelsea in England) spend vastly more than others and enjoy an uncontested domination. So much so that in 2016 the odds against the team of Leicester winning the Premier League championship was five thousand to one, lower than the probability of spotting Elvis alive. Bookmakers lost a combined 25 million pounds when the team, to everyone's surprise, actually won.

There is plenty of opposition to the salary cap in the United States. A *Forbes* article described it as "Un-American," arguing that "based on the capitalist system, spending money on employees (and that's what athletes are in professional sports) should be based on performance and not encumbered by system."[60] Players naturally hate it, resent it as deeply unfair, and have staged multiple strikes to oppose it. Interestingly, the one argument no one makes is that players would play harder if only they were paid a little (or a lot) more. Everybody agrees that the drive to be the best is sufficient.

WINNING ISN'T EVERYTHING[61]

What is true of professional athletes seems to be true of rich people in general.

The question of taxes on rich people took center stage in the political discourse in the United States at the end of 2018. With Alexandria Ocasio-Cortez's proposal of a top marginal income tax above 70 percent and Elizabeth Warren's call to establish a progressive wealth tax, tax policy became one of the core issues at stake for the 2020 presidential election.

Given the longstanding importance of income taxation as a policy issue, it is no surprise there are many studies that look at whether people stop working when their income taxes increase. The authoritative review of the literature by Emmanuel Saez and his colleagues concludes that real work effort does not respond to top tax rates, although effort to evade or avoid taxes does.[62] For example, the Reagan tax cut of 1986 led to a large onetime increase in personal taxable income, which faded quickly. This suggests the increase in taxable income was mainly people bringing their previously hidden incomes into the (now friendlier) tax net rather than an increase in earnings and hence effort. In countries where there are no easy loopholes because taxes apply to all income (with no differential treatment for investment income, labor income, or "fees for being a real estate agent"), taxable income (and therefore the underlying real effort) is insensitive to taxation.

This should make sense. For top athletes, as Vince Lombardi is reputed to have said, "Winning isn't everything, it's the only thing." They are not going to do less than their best because the tax rate just went up. The same probably goes for top CEOs and aspiring top CEOs.

What about the idea that the best firms want the best managers and are willing to pay top dollar for them? Would they be able to do that if taxes were high? The answer is yes. The argument that the best CEO will go wherever he makes the most money works no differently when the government takes 70 percent of the money. The highest-paid job is still the highest-paid job, as long as the tax rate is the same in all firms.

However, high top marginal tax rates may also reduce the lure of the most lucrative, but not necessarily the most socially useful, professions, such as finance. Without the attraction of huge take-home pay, aspiring top managers may prefer to go where they will be the most productive, not where they will make the most money. A silver lining of the 2008 crisis is that it reduced the appeal of the financial sector for the brightest minds; a study of career choices of MIT graduates found those who graduated in 2009 were 45 percent less likely to choose finance than those who graduated between 2006 and 2008.[63] This may lead to a better allocation of talent, and to the extent finance's salary levels infect every other sector, it could further reduce income inequality.

All in all, therefore, it seems to us that high marginal income tax rates, applied only to very high incomes, are a perfectly sensible way to limit the explosion of top income inequality. They would not be extortionary, since very few people will end up paying them; top managers will simply not get these kinds of income anymore. And from all we see, they won't discourage anybody to work as hard as they can. To the extent they affect people's choice of career, it will likely be in a positive direction. This is not to deny the importance of structural economic changes, which have made it increasingly difficult for those with low education to succeed, generating an increase in inequality even within the remaining 99 percent.[64] Addressing this issue will call for other complementary approaches. But we might as well begin by eliminating the ur-super-rich (which really means, in case you feel sorry for them, turning them to merely super rich).

THE PANAMA PAPERS

The other way the rich will surely try to react to a tax rise, however, is by finding ways to not pay taxes.

One thing the absence of caps in European soccer and the resulting astronomical salaries does is encourage players to evade taxes. In 2016, Lionel Messi (who made more than €100 million in 2017) was found guilty on three counts of defrauding tax authorities of €4.1 million and given a suspended jail sentence. In July 2018, the Spanish government and Cristiano Ronaldo signed a deal in which he agreed to pay a fine of €19 million and receive a suspended prison sentence. He was accused of four counts of tax fraud worth €14.7 million, resulting from the use of shell companies outside Spain to hide income made from image rights from 2011 to 2014. Moreover, many of those who do not actually cheat shop around for lower taxes. Comparing countries in Europe that raised or lowered taxes at different points in time, a study found that when the tax rate in a country increases by 10 percent, the number of foreign players goes down by 10 percent.[65] In 2018, Ronaldo left Spain for Italy to lower his tax bill.

The exposé of the so-called Panama papers, which revealed the efforts of Panamanian law firm Mossack Fonseca on behalf of the global plutocracy in setting up hundreds of thousands of shell companies for them to evade taxes, showed just how pervasive tax evasion had become. The list of names included former prime ministers of Iceland, Pakistan, and the UK. Even in famously honest Scandinavia, only 3 percent of personal taxes are evaded on average, but the very rich are much more serious offenders. A study estimated that those in the top 0.01 percent in the wealth distribution of Norway, Sweden, and Denmark evade 25–30 percent of personal taxes they owe.[66]

If taxes go up a lot, so will tax evasion. The question is, by how much? In the short run, the response will surely be substantial. We already mentioned this in the context of the Reagan tax cuts. When taxes go up, we expect to see the reverse: a sharp drop in taxable income as those who can hide their incomes do so right away, but a smaller effect afterward.

In part for this reason, a small number of politicians in the United States and some economists[67] are pushing for a progressive wealth tax applicable on worldwide wealth (in 2019, Elizabeth Warren proposed a 2 percent wealth tax on Americans with assets above $50 million, and a 3 percent wealth tax on those who have more than $1 billion). The idea is not new. After all, most Americans who own a home already pay a tax on the value of their home: the real estate tax they pay to their municipal government. But this tax is regressive. Suppose you own a house worth $300,000 and pay 1 percent property tax ($3,000). Then you will effectively pay 10 percent of your net wealth if you have a mortgage of $270,000 (since your net wealth is then $30,000) but 0.1 percent of your net wealth if you have financial assets of $2.7 million and no mortgage (since your net wealth is then $3 million).

The wealth tax would be progressive and apply to all forms of wealth, not just real estate. The advantage of a tax applied on very high wealth, from the point of view of fighting inequality, is that very wealthy people do not consume the vast majority of the income they derive from their wealth. Instead, they take a small fraction of the wealth income in the form of a dividend, and they plow the rest back into their family trust or whatever structure has allowed their wealth to accumulate. In the current tax codes in most countries, they do not pay any taxes on the amount that goes back into the trust.[68] This is part of the reason why Warren Buffet, as he likes to remind us, pays very little in income taxes.[69] It is difficult to have a redistributive income tax if most of the top incomes are effectively (and legally) shielded from taxation in this way. Moreover the tax advantage gets compounded. The new wealth generates new investment income, most of which is again untaxed for the same reasons, making the rich even richer. A wealth tax on very high fortunes solves this problem. The best way to think about it is not, as the economic press and the politicians try to explain it, as a way for the wealthy to make a special effort to "give back" (though if that makes them feel better maybe it's okay). Instead, it is simply a convenient and administratively (relatively) simple way to ensure they pay a tax on all their income, regardless of what they chose to do with it: someone whose $50 million in wealth makes at least $2.5 million in investment income in the average year. A 2 percent tax on wealth ($1 million) amounts to a 40 percent tax on this income, which is not outrageous.

Unlike estate tax, which got a bad rap after being called the "death tax," the idea of wealth tax is very popular. In 2018, 61 percent of respondents to a poll conducted by the *New York Times* were in favor, including 50 percent of Republicans.[70] So it even may be politically feasible. Yet in recent decades many countries got rid of their wealth tax if they had one, and few countries have put one in place (Colombia is an exception). In France, getting rid of the wealth tax was one of the first actions of the centrist Macron government after his election in 2017. As we saw, this was a very dangerous political move; the abolition of the wealth tax and the attempt to put in place a surcharge on fuel was the original motivation for the Yellow Vest protest movement. In an attempt to quell it, Macron promised a number of giveaways, but did not reinstate the wealth tax.

There are two reasons why wealth taxes are so politically difficult. First, because of effective lobbying. High-net-worth individuals finance the campaigns of politicians on the left and on the right, and few are in favor of wealth taxation, even when they are otherwise quite liberal. Second, it is easy to avoid the taxes, legally or not, particularly in small European countries where people can move or park their wealth abroad. This gives rise to a race to the bottom on tax rates.

We should not lose sight of the fact, however, that all of this happens in part because the world tolerates tax evasion: most tax codes have loopholes galore and the penalties for parking money abroad are ineffective. As we saw, countries with a simple tax code with few loopholes lose less from evasion when taxes go up than the United States.[71] Gabriel Zucman has convincingly argued that there are many relatively straightforward things that would help a lot in limiting tax evasion and tax avoidance. Among his ideas are to create a global financial registry that would keep track of wealth no matter where it is (making it possible to tax wealth no matter where it is parked), to reform the corporate tax system such that the global profits of multinational firms are apportioned to where they make their sales, and to more strongly regulate banks and law firms that help people evade taxes through tax havens.[72]

Identifying a set of steps is of course not sufficient. There needs to be the political will to implement them. The three steps Zucman recommends may be particularly tricky since they involve international cooperation, and the men (yes, almost always men) at the top right now do not seem to be all that able to join together to get things done. Without that, countries may be tempted to engage in a race to the bottom in taxation in the hope of attracting talent and capital. Preferential tax schemes for high-skilled foreign workers have been introduced in Belgium, Denmark, Finland, the Netherlands, Portugal, Spain, Sweden, and Switzerland. In Denmark, for example, high-earning foreigners pay only a 30 percent flat tax for three years (against a top rate of 62 percent for the Danish). This was very effective in attracting high-income foreigners to Denmark, which may be good for Denmark, but bad for other countries. Now they have the choice between taxing their top earners less or pushing them to leave.[73] This tension between country welfare and global welfare in the design of individual income tax policy has loomed large in the debate about tax competition.

But the point is that these are political problems, not economics impossibilities. The spirit of this book is to emphasize that there are no iron laws of economics keeping us from building a more humane world, but there are many people whose blind faith, self-interest, or simple lack of understanding of economics makes them claim this is the case.

CITIZENS UNITED?

From the strict point of view of economic efficiency, therefore, the evidence suggests that nothing stops a government from having a very progressive tax schedule with extremely high top marginal rates. If Denmark can have high taxes on top incomes without all the capital decamping to some neighboring less-taxed country, and all its rich moving to Ireland (or Panama), then for a large and much less globally integrated economy like the United States, from a strictly economic point of view, there is nothing to prevent it from doing the same.

The difficulty of raising top tax rates is a political one. Indeed, we seem to be in the midst of a vicious cycle of concentration of political and economic power. As the rich become richer, they have more interest and more resources to organize society to stay that way, including financing the campaigns of legislators willing to lower taxes at the top. The "Citizens United" decision of the US Supreme Court, which ruled as unconstitutional legislative limits on corporations' ability to fund electoral campaigns, has formally legitimized the unlimited power of money in influencing elections.

But it seems unlikely that this state of affairs can continue unfettered without generating a massive backlash. High tax rates on the top earners are already quite popular. Polling data suggest that 51 percent of voters support a marginal tax rate of 70 percent on income above $10 million.[74] In our survey, more than two-thirds of respondents, who were otherwise not particularly liberal, thought entrepreneurs making more than $430,600 annually (which puts them in the top 1 percent) paid too little in taxes.[75]

To some extent, the recent populist uprising in the United States is the beginning of this backlash. Behind it is a profound sense of disempowerment, a feeling, right or wrong, that the elites always decide, and in any case what they decide makes no difference for the average Joe or Jean. In the United States, Trump, for all his wealth and elite connections, was elected on his promise to undermine business as usual, but the Republicans lined up behind him because they were confident he was as pro-rich as any of them. Indeed he did deliver the tax cut. But it is not clear how long this game of bait and switch can continue without it all exploding. The rich may eventually see that it is in their self-interest to argue for a radical shift toward real sharing of prosperity, or it may end up being imposed on them in even less favorable ways. The reason is that the increase in inequality has been at the root of a deep increase in social anxiety and unhappiness.

KEEPING UP WITH THE JONESES

Social scientists have long suspected that people's sense of self-worth is related to their position in the groups they see themselves as part of—their neighborhoods, their peers, their country. If this were true, inequality would of course directly affect well-being. Given how plausible this seems to us, it has been surprisingly difficult to prove beyond doubt. For example, evidence suggests that, at any given income level, people tend to be less happy when the average income in their locality is higher than their own.[76] But it could be because they live in an expensive neighborhood where everything, from housing to cups of coffee, costs more. In other words, the facts can be explained without reference to inequality per se.

A recent study from Norway shows that increased *awareness* about one's place in the distribution of income increases the extent to which a person's happiness depends on their income.[77] In Norway, tax data has been publicly available many years, but the records were kept as hard copies and were therefore hard to access. This changed in 2001, when they were put online, and it became possible to snoop on your neighbors or your friends with just a few clicks of your mouse. This was very popular, to the point it was dubbed "tax porn," and everyone seemed to know exactly where they stood. What we saw right after the data went online was that the poor were sadder and the rich happier. The awareness of one's place on the totem pole does seem to affect well-being.

In a way, we are all living in some version of the Norway experiment. Bombarded as we are by images of the lives of others on the internet and in the media, it is impossible for those who are stuck to not be aware that the rest of the world looks like it is moving ahead. The flip side of this is the impulse to show the world that we too are able to "keep up with the Joneses" and, if possible, do better than them. This is the logic behind "bling" purchases, designed to show off status. In a recent experiment, an Indonesian bank offered some of its higher-income customers (largely urban and upper middle class) a new platinum credit card.[78] In the control group, customers received an offer upgrade of their existing credit card, with all the benefits of a platinum card except the platinum look. Customers understood the cards had exactly the same benefits, but that did not stop them from liking the platinum card more; 21 percent of those offered the platinum card went for it compared to 14 percent of those offered the nondescript alternative.

Interestingly, the urge to show off is less strong when people feel good about themselves. The experimenters found that simply writing a short essay describing a moment when the person did something she or he was proud of reduced the demand for platinum cards. This creates a vicious cycle, with people who feel economically vulnerable being particularly eager to demonstrate their worth through useless purchases they can ill-afford, and an industry all too ready to provide these services for a handsome fee.

THE AMERICAN NIGHTMARE

Americans have another peculiar problem of their own. Fed a steady diet of the "American dream" along with their breakfast cereals, Americans tend to believe, in spite of everything, that although their society is unequal, it rewards industry and effort. In a recent study, researchers asked people in the United States and in several European countries their views of social mobility.[79] When asked, "Out of 500 families divided in 5 groups of 100, how many of the children born of parents in the poorest group will stay in the poorest group, move one group up, two groups up, or make it to the richest group?" Americans are more optimistic than Europeans. They believe, for example, that out of one hundred poor children, twelve will make it to the richest quintile and only thirty-two will be stuck in poverty. In contrast, the French believe that out of one hundred, nine poor children will make it to the top, and thirty-five will be stuck in poverty.

The rosy American view does not reflect reality today in the United States. Along with the general stagnation at the bottom, intergenerational mobility has declined sharply in the US. Mobility is now substantially *lower* in the United States than it is in Europe. Within the OECD, the child from the bottom quintile most likely to remain stuck in the bottom quintile is from the US (33.1 percent), while the least likely is from Sweden (26.7 percent). The average for continental Europe is below 30 percent. The probability of moving to the top quintile is 7.8 percent in the US, but close to 11 percent on average in Europe.[80]

The places within the United States most likely to cling to the outdated notion of American social mobility, a.k.a. the dream, are actually those least likely to experience it. Americans also generally believe effort is rewarded (with the corollary that the poor must be in part responsible for their own plight), and probably for this reason, those who believe mobility is high also tend to be suspicious of any government effort to address the problems faced by the poor.[81]

When overoptimistic perceptions of mobility clash with reality, there is a strong urge to avoid the awkward truth. The majority of Americans whose wages and income have stagnated, and who confront an ever-widening gap between the wealth they see around them and the financial woes they are experiencing, face a choice between blaming themselves for not benefitting from the opportunities they believe their society offers and finding someone to blame for stealing their jobs. That way lies despair and anger.

By all measures, despair is on the rise in today's America, and it has become deadly. There has been an unprecedented increase in mortality among less-educated whites in middle age and a decrease in life expectancy. Life expectancy declined in 2015, 2016, and 2017 for all Americans. This grim trend is specific to US whites, and in particular to US whites without college degrees: in all racial groups in the US except the whites, mortality is falling. Other English-speaking countries that have pursued a broadly similar social model to the US, namely the UK, Australia, Ireland, and Canada, are also going through a similar change, albeit in slow motion. In all the other wealthy countries, on the other hand, mortality is going down, and going down faster for the uneducated (who had higher mortality to start with) than for the educated. In other words, when the rest of the world saw convergence between mortality levels of the college educated and the rest, the United States went the other way. Anne Case and Angus Deaton have shown that the increase in mortality is due to a steady rise of "deaths of despair" (such as deaths from alcohol and drug poisoning, suicide, alcoholic liver disease, and cirrhosis) among white middle-aged men and women in America, combined with a slowdown in the progress against other causes of mortality (including heart disease). Self-reported health and mental health follow a similar pattern. Since the 1990s, middle-aged whites with low education are increasingly likely to report themselves in poor health, and they are more likely to complain of various pains and aches. They are also more likely to report symptoms of depression.[82]

This is probably not so much a result of low (or unequal) incomes per se. After all, blacks did not fare any better economically over the period, and they are not affected by this trend. And there was no uptick of mortality in Western Europe, even after incomes stagnated during the Great Recession. On the other hand, Russia's mortality exploded after the breakup of the Soviet Union in 1991, and like in the United States, most of the increase was due to changes in mortality from vascular disease and violent deaths (mainly suicides, homicides, unintentional poisoning, and traffic incidents) among young and middle-aged adults.[83]

Case and Deaton also point out that although the increase in mortality in the United States started in the 1990s, it capped a trend that had begun long before that. After the cohort that entered the labor market in the late 1970s, each subsequent cohort fared worse than the preceding one in many different ways.[84] At every age, among less-educated white Americans, each subsequent cohort was more likely to have difficulty socializing, to be overweight, to experience mental distress and symptoms of depression, and to have chronic pain. They were also more likely to kill themselves or die of a drug overdose. It is the accumulated weight of these deprivations that eventually led to the increase in mortality.

Any number of slow-moving factors could have caused this erosion of the well-being of less-educated Americans. Every single one of these cohorts was also less likely than the preceding one to be in the labor force. For those who worked, their real wages were no higher than those of previous cohorts, and sometimes lower, and they were less likely to have a strong attachment to a particular job or company. They were less likely to be married or in stable relationships. All in all, the white non-college-educated working class collapsed after the 1970s, and this was probably a product of the specific kind of unequal economic growth the country experienced.

RAGING AGAINST THE WORLD

The alternative to despair is anger.

Becoming aware of the lack of social mobility does not necessarily make people more willing to support redistribution. In the study we discussed above, after eliciting the views of Americans, the researchers presented some of them with an infographic suggesting mobility was much lower than they thought (and the others with another infographic showing the same data, but with a rosier angle). For respondents who originally identified with the Republican Party, this made them even *less* likely to agree that the government could be part of the solution.[85]

An alternative is to rebel against the system, potentially at great personal cost. In an experiment in Odisha, India, when employees in a firm felt the pay varied arbitrarily, they rebelled by working less hard, and being absent more often, than in comparable firms where the wage was kept constant, and since they were paid a fixed salary for every day they came to work, they hurt themselves by doing so. Workers in firms with unequal pay were also less likely to cooperate to achieve a collective goal tied to a reward. Workers were willing to tolerate pay inequality, but only when it was clearly tied to performance.[86]

In the United States, there is another possible reaction. Because many believe the American market system is fundamentally fair, they must then find something else to blame. If they don't get that job, it must be because the elites have somehow conspired to give it to an African American, a Hispanic, or at one remove, to a Chinese worker. Why would I trust the government of those elites to redistribute to me? More money for the government is more money for "those other guys."

Therefore, when growth either fails or fails to benefit the average guy, a scapegoat is needed. This is particularly true in the United States, but is happening in Europe as well. The natural foils are immigrants and trade. Behind the anti-immigrant views, as we argued in chapter 2, are two misconceptions: an exaggeration of how many migrants are coming in, or about to come in, and a belief in the nonfact that low-skilled immigrants depress wages.

More international trade, as we saw in chapter 3, hurts the poor in rich countries. This has provoked a backlash not only against trade, but also against the existing "system" and the elites. Autor, Dorn, and Hanson found that in US electoral districts more affected by the China shock, moderate politicians were replaced by more extreme ones. In counties originally leaning Democratic, centrist Democrats were replaced by more liberal ones. In counties originally leaning Republican, moderate Republicans were replaced by conservative Republicans. Counties highly affected by trade tended to be in traditionally Republican states, and therefore the overall effect of this was to push many districts toward more conservative candidates. This trend started well before the 2016 elections.[87] The problem of course is that since conservative candidates tend to be against any form of government intervention (and redistribution in particular), they then exacerbated the problem that little was done to compensate those hurt by trade. For example, many trade-affected states governed by conservative Republicans refused federal funds to expand Medicare expansion. And this in turn fueled the resentment against trade.

A similar negative cycle may emerge as people gradually understand that they live in a society that has much more inequality and much fewer opportunities than they previous believed. As in the study mentioned above, they may become even more upset with the government and even less likely to believe it can do something to help them.

This has two implications. First, the obsession with growth at the root of the Reagan-Thatcher revolution, and that no subsequent president has taken issue with, has caused lasting damage. When the benefits of economic growth are largely captured by a small elite, growth can be a recipe for a social disaster (like the one we are currently experiencing). We argued before that we should be wary of any policy sold in the name of growth because it is likely to be bogus. Perhaps we should be even more scared if we think that such a policy might work, because growth will benefit only the happy few.

The second implication is that if collectively we as a society do not manage to act now to design policies that will help people survive and hold on to their dignity in this world of high inequality, citizens' confidence in society's ability to deal with this issue might be permanently undermined. This underscores the urgency of designing, and adequately funding, an effective social policy.

CHAPTER 8

LEGIT.GOV

A RECURRING THEME of this book is that it is unreasonable to expect markets to always deliver outcomes that are just, acceptable, or even efficient. For example, in the sticky economy, government intervention is necessary to help people move when it makes sense, but also sometimes to remain in place without having to give up their livelihood and their dignity. More generally, in a world of skyrocketing inequalities and "winner take all," the lives of the poor and the rich are diverging wildly and will become irremediably different if we allow markets to drive all social outcomes.

As we saw, taxation can be used to rein in inequality at the top of income and wealth distribution. But abolishing the one percent cannot be the end-all of social policy. We also need to find out how to help the rest.

Any innovation in social policy is likely to require new resources. The ultra-rich will probably not be rich enough to finance the entire government, especially if pre-tax inequality goes down, as we hope. Moreover, if history is any guide, they will resist, probably with some success. Others will also need to pay; the experience of many countries shows this is perfectly feasible. The challenge is political. The problem is the eroding legitimacy of the state. The state is perceived as unreliable, or worse, by an increasing majority of the electorate. How can that legitimacy be restored?

TAX AND SPEND?

Democracies raise money through taxation. The overall tax revenues (taking together all levels of government) in the United States in 2017 was just 27 percent of GDP. This is seven points lower than the average in the OECD. The United States was tied with South Korea, and only four other countries in the OECD have lower tax revenues (Mexico, Ireland, Turkey, and Chile).[1]

Any significant public policy effort would require more funding. Even if the United States raises its taxes on the rich to match Denmark's, the overall tax revenue as a share of US GDP will still be much lower than what it was in 2017 in Denmark (46 percent), France (46 percent), Belgium (45 percent), Sweden (44 percent), and Finland (43 percent). One reason is that if US tax rates were raised to those levels, it is possible top incomes would go down a lot because companies would move away from paying astronomical salaries; this might be desirable in itself but would defeat the purpose of raising revenue. In other words, although it might be desirable in terms of limiting inequality, the current proposal to raise income tax rates above 70 percent is unlikely to deliver so much new money to the state.

A wealth tax would raise more revenue as long as steps were taken to reduce evasion. Saez and Zucman estimate that a 2 percent wealth tax on Americans with assets above $50 million (this would affect about seventy-five thousand people), as well as a 3 percent wealth tax on those who have more than $1 billion would raise $2.75 trillion over ten years, or 1 percent of GDP.[2] As we saw, 2 percent wealth tax for those worth more than $50 million is actually more popular than an increase in the marginal income tax rate.[3] But even at the proposed level, it still raises just 1 percent of GDP.

Even in the European countries with high top rates and a wealth tax, the majority of the government's revenues come from taxes on average earners. In other words, the dream of a tax reform that leaves "99 percent of the taxpayers with a lower tax bill" would guarantee that the United States continues to be unable to redistribute much to those falling behind. Tax reform needs to apply not solely to the ultra-rich, but also the merely rich and even the middle class.

As things stand, this is a no-fly zone for US politicians on the left and the right. Proposing to raise taxes on (almost) everyone is not popular. In our survey, 48 percent of respondents thought small business owners paid too much in taxes, and less than 5 percent thought they paid too little. The same was true for salaried workers.[4] The hardest part may be to persuade the average taxpayer in the United States to pay more and get more public services. We suspect economists are partly responsible for people's reluctance to pay taxes, in more than one way.

First, many prominent economists have raised the specter that people will stop working if taxes go up. For example, Milton Friedman, who famously declared: "I am in favor of cutting taxes under any circumstances and for any excuse, for any reason, whenever it's possible."[5] They maintain that high taxes kill initiative and stop growth, even in the face of data that says nothing of the sort. We have already seen that the rich do not stop working when taxes go up. How about the other 99 percent though? Would they retire to the countryside? There is also a voluminous economic literature on the subject that makes it clear they won't.[6]

One of the best examples is from Switzerland. In the late 1990s and early 2000s, Switzerland converted from a system where people paid taxes on the previous two years of income to a more standard "pay as you earn" system. In the old system, taxes due in 1997 and 1998 were based on income earned in 1995 and 1996, taxes due in 1999 and 2000 were based on income earned in 1997 and 1998, and so on. The new system works like that of the United States: estimated taxes due, say, for 2000 are collected throughout the year, then in early 2001 the taxpayer fills out an income tax return and the tax liability is adjusted. To transition to the new system in Switzerland, there had to be a tax holiday. The canton of Thurgau transitioned in 1999. In 1997 and in 1998, taxpayers paid taxes on the income earned in 1995 and 1996. In 1999, they started paying taxes based on income in 1999. To avoid taxing people twice, no taxes were ever levied on the income earned in 1997 and 1998: those were the tax holiday years. Swiss cantons transitioned in different years between 1999 and 2001, so different people got their tax holidays in different years, depending on where they lived. The rebate was temporary and widely known in advance. So while people decided whether (and how much) to work for the year, they already knew they would pay no taxes. This was a perfect opportunity to see whether lowering tax rates made a difference to people's willingness to work; we can just compare labor supply before, during, and after the tax holiday. The answer is it changed *not at all.* There was absolutely no impact on whether people decided to work or not, and no effect on hours worked either.[7]

While the Swiss example is particularly stark, the result is more general. Taxes do not seem to discourage people from working.[8] However, voters may still oppose taxation if they think *others* would stop working if taxes went up. In our survey we asked some of the respondents whether they would stop working, or work less, if taxes were higher. Seventy-two percent said they would absolutely not stop working, and 60 percent said they would work just as much as before. This is very consistent with the data. We also asked the other respondents how they thought the *average person in the middle class* would respond. In that case, only 35 percent of respondents believed the average middle-class person would work as much as before, and 50 percent believed they would stop working.[9] Thus, when judging themselves, Americans are about right, but when they anticipate the behavior of their friends and neighbors, they are much too pessimistic.

IS GOVERNMENT THE PROBLEM?

Another reason why people are reluctant to raise more taxes to get more services is that many people in the United States (but also in the UK and in many developing countries) are skeptical of any intervention by the state. At least since Reagan, we have been fed the mantra that "in this present crisis, government is not the solution to our problem, government IS the problem."[10]

In 2015, only 23 percent of Americans thought they could trust the government "always" or "most of the time." Fifty-nine percent had a negative opinion of the government. Twenty percent thought the government had no tools to improve equality of opportunities between the rich and the poor, and 32 percent thought lowering taxes on wealthy people and corporations to encourage investment would be a better way to improve equality of opportunities than increasing taxes to finance more programs for the poor.[11]

This radical skepticism about government action may be the single biggest constraint on helping those who need it most, paradoxically because many of those people themselves hold precisely these views.

Manpreet Singh Badal, a bright young minister in the Indian state of Punjab, saw his political career stumble over just this issue. Farmers in Punjab get free electricity, and groundwater is free, with the result that everyone over-irrigates their land with the consequence that the water table is falling so fast that in a few years there will be no water to pump out. It is in everybody's interest to reduce water consumption now. Badal's solution was to give everyone a fixed sum of money to compensate them, and then charge them for the electricity so they would not pump any more water than they needed, because the cost would act as a deterrent against excess pumping. From the point of view of economic logic, this is a no-brainer. But it was political suicide. The measure, introduced in January 2010, had to be removed ten months later, and Badal lost his job as finance minister and eventually had to leave his political party. Farmers simply did not trust they would get any money, and the powerful farmers' associations radically opposed the measures. Remarkably, in 2018 Badal, back in government, decided to try again. This time the plan was to *first* give a direct transfer of Rs 48,000 (equivalent to $2823, accounting for purchasing power parity differences) to all farmers directly into their bank accounts, before charging them for electricity by deducting from this same account. The subsidy has been calculated such that at the going rate, a farmer consuming less than 9,000 units of power would come out ahead (the state estimates the average consumption is between 8,000 and 9,000 units). The idea was to make it absolutely clear that this is not a tax in disguise, a sly way to raise money from the farmers. And this time the government moved slowly. They began with a small pilot program, and are now planning a larger RCT to evaluate the impact of this scheme on water consumption and farmers' welfare. Still, farmers remain suspicious. The farmers' union continues to claim that "their real agenda is to discontinue the power subsidy for agriculture."[12]

Why are people so suspicious of the government? A part of it, no doubt, is historical. In India, people have seen too many instances where the government reneged on a pledge. In the United States, there is clearly an ideology of self-reliance, even though for many years it has been based, to a significant extent, on a fantasy—the states in the US where people take the most pride in their autonomy are also the ones most dependent on federal subsidies (Mississippi, Louisiana, Tennessee, and Montana top the list by federal aid as fraction of revenue).[13] In part also, as we suggested earlier, it relates to a distrust of the elite. Government programs are seen as the elite's way of subsidizing everyone but hard-working white (males?). But it doesn't help that there is a background of economist-inspired chatter about waste in government. Mention a government intervention in a roomful of economists and you will hear an unmistakable snicker. Many, perhaps even most, economists believe incentives in government are always messed up, and as a result government interventions, while often necessary, tend to be ham-handed or corrupt.[14]

But bad relative to what? The problem is that there is no substitute for a lot of things the government does (although of course many governments do more things than they should, like running an airline in India or a cement plant in China). When a tornado strikes, when an indigent needs healthcare, or when an industry shuts down, there is usually no "market solution." The government exists in part to solve problems no other institution can realistically tackle. To demonstrate waste in government, *one needs to show there is an alternative way of organizing the same activity that works better*.

There is no doubt waste in governments in most countries. A number of studies from countries like India, Indonesia, Mexico, and Uganda have found that changes in the way governments do things can lead to substantial improvements. For example, in Indonesia simply distributing a card indicating someone was eligible for a program increased the amount of subsidies the poor got by 26 percent. Once they found out what they were eligible for, people were able to better advocate for themselves.[15] On the other hand, as we noted in chapter 5, there is also enormous waste inside private firms, so perhaps good management of resources is harder than we think.

Consistent with this, figuring out how to reduce waste in government turns out to be more difficult than it seems. Simple formulae do not work; privatization, for example, is not a panacea. The limited evidence comparing private and public provision of the same service turns out to be very mixed. Private schools in India are cheaper, but children randomly assigned to a private school have the same low test scores as those who stayed in public schools.[16] Private placement services for the long-term unemployed in France work less well than their public equivalents.[17]

In 2016, the Liberian government transferred the responsibility of running ninety-three government schools to eight different organizations (some NGOs and some for-profit operators) and, remarkably, ran an RCT to evaluate the impact. The results were mixed. Students' results in those schools were somewhat better on average, but the private schools also spent a lot more money per pupil (double what the normal students got), so the playing field wasn't quite level. Moreover, four of the eight organizations did little better than public schools. Bridge Academy, the star provider, had good scores, but only after receiving considerable outside money and dropping all students in excess of their class size cap.[18] Another provider, the US charity More Than Me, got itself embroiled in an egregious sexual abuse scandal.[19] There was no miracle cure.

THE CORRUPTION OBSESSION

Part of the root of the skepticism of government is a widely shared obsession with corruption in government across the world. Perhaps it is because the idea of government officials living the easy life on taxpayers' money offends people, and therefore is often at the heart of political campaigns. The presumption is that if there was enough political will, corruption could be made to go away. There is of course a lot of truth to this. How can you expect corruption to go away when heads of governments are themselves up to their elbows in gravy?

But the view that all it takes to root out corruption is the will to do it misses the key point about the sources of corruption and our ability to control it. It is often precisely because governments do things the market will not touch that they become susceptible to corruption. Take the example of a fine for polluting. The polluter would gladly pay someone in the pollution control office a portion of the fine to make the evidence go away. But would things improve if a profit-maximizing private firm was collecting fines? Probably not, since they like money at least as much. Moreover, as the history of private tax collection ("tax farming") tells us, incentivizing private agents to collect taxes (or fines) runs the risk they will extort those who are not liable as well.

Or consider a slot in the best public schools. It is very tempting for a school official to accept a payment to open a "side door" for a rich but unqualified student, and it is rumored to be a common practice in China's top high schools. But this is not about government per se; it is about rationing. Whenever a good is rationed, the temptation to just pay one's way in is very strong. This was made abundantly clear by the admission scandals that shook elite private universities such as Stanford and Yale in 2019; parents who were wealthy but not wealthy enough to pay the full "price" of back door entry for their offspring (say, a building for the university) worked with a consultant who offered a more affordable side door (e.g., a bribe to the sports coaches).

The broader point is that our social objectives often push us to not follow the market's dictates. There is no pure market solution for collecting fines, and the reason why public schools have low fees and private universities do not charge the price the market would bear is because we want poor but talented kids to be able to get the best opportunities. But whenever anyone tries to get in the way of the market there will be a temptation to cheat. Since it is in the nature of the government's job to interpose itself in front of the market, the fight against corruption in government will be an uphill and continuous battle, even with the best intentions.

Moreover, fighting corruption is by no means costless. In Italy, an umbrella government organization called Consip was set up in reaction to a succession of corruption scandals. Its job was to purchase supplies on behalf of government departments. What it purchased changed from time to time; as a result, sometimes government departments had to provision certain things on their own, while at other times they relied on Consip. When government departments had access to Consip, they used that option most of the time, but it ended up costing the government substantially more for exactly the same products, because usually there was a cheaper version of the product on the market. In other words, the departments could have bought what they needed more cheaply, but they chose not to exercise that option when Consip was available. As a result, on net Consip turned out to be a money loser. Trusting government officials to do what they had always done, without constraining them, would have been a better idea.[20]

Why did almost everyone use Consip when it was available, even though they knew they could get products cheaper elsewhere? Probably because they knew that this way they were protected from any accusation of corruption. There is nothing special about government officials in their desire to check all the boxes to avoid trouble. Doctors in the United States recommend too many tests to avoid malpractice suits, for example. And large companies that use a single mandated travel agent for all their staff travel almost surely lose money on most tickets, since the agent does not search for the best deal. But this limits the risk that employees make money on the side.

This illustrates a broader point. The current fashion in fighting corruption is *transparency,* the idea that the workings of governments should be available for scrutiny by outsiders like independent public auditors, the media, and the public. There is solid evidence that in many situations transparency helps. In particular, informing the ultimate beneficiaries about the difference between what they are entitled to and what they are getting is a powerful instrument for fighting corruption.[21] However, as the Consip example makes clear, there is also a downside to transparency. Monitoring often relies on outsiders limited in their ability to understand the bigger picture or evaluate how well the overall social objectives are being served; the most they can do is to verify that due process is followed. In turn, this means bureaucrats tend to focus a lot on checking off the right boxes to avoid attracting attention. This creates a specific bias toward following the letter of the law, even when its spirit is somewhere entirely different.

Ultimately, the portrayal of bureaucrats and politicians as either bumbling idiots or corrupt sleazeballs, for which economists are probably partly responsible, is deeply damaging.

First, it prompts a knee-jerk reaction against all proposals to expand the government, even when government is clearly needed, like in the United States today. In our survey of US respondents, trust in bureaucrats is as low as trust in economists: only 26 percent of our respondents trust civil servants either "somewhat" or "a lot."[22] This probably explains why so few people think government can be part of the solution.

Second, it affects who wants to work for the government. Attracting qualified people is essential to a well-functioning government. But to a talented young person in the United States, a career in government, given its reputation, is unappealing. Neither of us has ever had an undergraduate about to receive their diploma tell us they were headed to a career in government. This kind of sorting can turn into a vicious cycle. If only the less able work in government, we get an ineffectual government no one of talent would want to join. In France, on the other hand, there is prestige attached to working for the government, and the best and brightest do so.

The image of the government also affects the honesty of those who want to work for it. A study in India replicated the Swiss experiment with bankers we discussed in chapter 4,[23] where participants (in this case, college students) were asked to privately roll a die forty-two times and record what numbers they got each time; the reward was half an Indian rupee for a one, one rupee for a two, one and a half rupees for a three, and so on. Students were free to lie about the numbers they rolled, and roughly the same proportion as in Switzerland did. But, just as those who were reminded of their identity as bankers cheated more in Switzerland, in India students planning to work for the government cheated more.[24] In contrast, when the study was again replicated in Denmark, which is justifiably proud of its social sector, researchers found the exact opposite as in India: those planning to join the government were much *less* likely to cheat.[25]

Third, if it is assumed most people in government are either venal or lazy (or both), it makes sense to try to remove all decision-making power from them (and thereby banish all creativity and all creative people). This has a direct impact on what government officials can do. In a recent experiment in Pakistan, providing a bit more flexibility to the procurement officers of hospitals and schools by giving them some free cash to spend on basic supplies greatly improved their ability to negotiate low prices, leading to big savings for the government.[26]

Putting too many constraints on government officials and government contracts can discourage talent when it is the most needed. Despite the fact that the United States is the world leader in computing, none of the big tech firms chose to bid on contracts to set up the computer system supporting Obamacare. The reason was apparently that there were so many boxes to check off to be a government contractor that very few firms were willing to do it. The Federal Acquisition Regulation has eighteen hundred pages. So, in order to win a government contract, it is more important to be good at paperwork than to be able to do the job.[27] In the development world, the contractors that systematically bid for and win the USAID contracts are known as "Beltway bandits." It is very difficult for other organizations to get a piece of that action, even when they have relevant experience on the ground.

Finally, and perhaps most importantly, the mantra that government is corrupt and incompetent has produced the kind of jaded citizenry who can react to news of shameless corruption among its elected leaders with a shrug, from Washington, DC, to Jerusalem and Moscow. They basically have learned to expect nothing else, and stop paying attention. Perversely, the obsession with petty corruption is breeding room for venality on a grand scale.

AMERICA FIRST?

The United States seems to be at an impasse. Forty years of promising that good things are just around the corner have created an environment where too many people trust no one, least of all the government. The growing economic and political influence of the rich, the result of the pursuit of the elusive elixir of growth, has combined with antigovernment sentiments the rich carefully have cultivated to head off any attempts to rein in their growing wealth. The government is chronically broke because it is politically impossible to raise taxes, and even the most socially minded of the young have become convinced that government is terminally uncool, and so head to private foundations if they do not actually give up and join an "impact" fund, or an unabashedly money-making venture. And yet the only possible way out involves a much expanded role for the government.

It is possible this is also the shape of the future in many other countries. While the rise was less spectacular than in the United States, inequality has also increased in France. Between 1983 and 2014, the average income of the richest 1 percent has risen by 100 percent and that of the richest 0.1 percent by 150 percent. Since GDP growth has been slow, standards of living for most people except the rich have tended to stagnate: over the same period, income increased only by 25 percent (less than 1 percent per year) for the remaining 99 percent.[28] This has fueled growing mistrust of the elite and the rise of the xenophobic Rassemblement National. The recent round of tax reforms undertaken by the centrist Macron government has made tax less progressive: the flat tax was raised, the wealth tax is gone, and taxes on capital have been pared back. The official justification is that this is necessary to make France able to attract capital away from other countries. It may well be true, but it runs the risk of forcing other countries in Europe to cut taxes as well, prompting a race to the bottom. The American experience warns us this may be very hard to reverse. European countries need to cooperate to hold the line on their taxes.

Developing-country governments raise even less money than the United States. The median low-income country raises less than 15 percent of GDP in taxes as compared to nearly 50 percent in Europe (and 34 percent in the OECD on average). To some extent, the underdevelopment of the tax system is a consequence of the nature of the economy; a large part of the economy is taken up by tiny firms or remote farms whose income is hard to verify. But to a large extent the low level of taxation is a political choice. India and China offer an interesting contrast. Historically, most citizens in both countries had too little income for it to be worth taxing them. But as incomes grew, India kept raising the threshold above which people had to pay income taxes—on budget day, when new tax rates are announced, the raised threshold is often headline news. As a result, the share of the population that paid any income tax remained stable around 2–3 percent. In China, where the thresholds were not adjusted, the fraction of the population subject to the income tax went up from less than 0.1 percent in 1986 to about 20 percent in 2008. Income tax revenues in China boomed, from less than 0.1 percent of GDP to 2.5 percent in 2008, while in India they have stagnated at around 0.5 percent of GDP. More generally, tax revenues as a share of GDP have been stable at about 15 percent of GDP in India for many years now, while they are above 20 percent in China, giving China the option to invest more and/or carry out more social spending.[29] The new Goods and Services Tax in India is supposed to help by making it harder to evade taxes, but being a more or less proportional tax on purchases, it has very little redistributive effect.

Moreover, very much like the United States, India has not been very successful in using taxation to limit the ballooning of top-income pre-tax inequality. According to the World Inequality Database, the share of the top 1 percent of income in India's GDP increased from 7.3 percent in 1980 to more than 20 percent in 2015. In China, where there was a bit more effort, it still went up, but by less, from 6.4 percent to 13.9 percent.[30]

The interesting counterexample here is Latin America, for many years the example everyone used for growth with exploding inequality (which then turned into inequality with no growth), where the recent decades have seen a significant reduction in inequality. This was partly driven by rising commodity prices, but also in part by policy interventions, higher minimum wages, and large-scale redistribution in particular.[31]

The way redistribution was expanded in those countries is instructive. The political opposition to transfer programs in Latin America is couched in terms of the moral and psychological consequences of giveaways, much like the US conversation about welfare is dominated by the fear of abuse and laziness. From the beginning, Santiago Levy, an economics professor who played a very important role in setting up Progresa, the transfer program in Mexico that provided the blueprint for many others, was very conscious of the need to get buy-in from the right.[32] The program emphasized a social quid pro quo. The transfers were quite explicitly conditional: the families had to take their children to the doctor and send them to school to get the money. A randomized controlled trial proved that those given access to the program had better child outcomes.[33] Probably as a result, these programs have proved durable. For decades, successive governments have sometimes changed the name of the program (Progresa became Oportunidades and then Prospera) but not much else. In 2019, the new left-wing Mexican government seems to be on the way to replace the program with a similarly generous program with fewer strings attached.

In the meantime, the conditional cash transfer program (CCT) had been imitated all over the region and beyond (all the way to New

York City). Originally, most of the programs adopted similar condi-tionalities, and often paired the programs with RCTs. These series of experiments had two impacts. First, they demonstrated nothing ter-rible happens when one gives cash to the poor. As we will see in the next chapter, they don't drink it all and they don't stop working. This was instrumental in shifting the public perception on redistribution all over the developing world. In the 2019 elections in India, both major parties, for the first time, made a cash transfer to the poor a central element of their platform. Second, as countries started to experiment with the model and try out variants of it, it became clear the poor don't need as much handholding as the design of the original CCTs implied. There has been a complete turnaround in the public conversation on redistribution, and the Progresa experiment and its successors contrib-uted a lot to it.

The battle against growing inequality has not been permanently won even in Latin America. The top tax rates remain low and top incomes are not systematically going down (since 2000, in the World Inequality Database, they are completely flat in Chile, rising in Co-lombia, bouncing all over the place in Brazil).[34] But the experience of Progresa highlights the notion that careful program design will be key to breaking open the seeming impasse in the United States and similar issues that might come down the pike elsewhere.

Figuring this out may be one of the greatest challenges of our time. Much greater than space travel, perhaps even than curing cancer. After all, what is at stake is the whole idea of the good life as we have known it. We have the resources. What we lack are ideas that will help us jump the wall of disagreement and distrust that divides us. If we can engage the world seriously in this quest, and the best minds in the world to work with governments and NGOs and others to redesign our social programs for effectiveness and political viability, there is a chance history will remember our era with gratitude.

CHAPTER 9

CASH AND CARE

MANY VISITORS TO the northern Indian city of Lucknow visit a gigantic eighteenth-century Indo-Islamic monument in the middle of the old city called the Bada Imambara. It is unusual among buildings from that period, being neither a fort nor a palace, nor a mosque nor a mausoleum. Guides tell many stories about it inflected, no doubt, to suit the tastes of the audience—Abhijit was told it was a part of the kingdom's defense against the encroaching British Raj, despite not looking remotely like a fort. In fact, it was built by the king of Awadh, Asaf-ud-Daula, in 1784 to provide jobs to his starving subjects because crops had failed.

There is one story about this project that stuck in Abhijit's memory. It is claimed the project took much longer than it should have because what the workers built during the day, the elites destroyed at night. The idea was to give the elites, who also lived off agriculture and were therefore starving like the rest, a way to earn enough to survive. Being aristocrats, they would rather die than let it be known to the public that they had fallen into such dire straits, hence the artifice of the nightly effort.

Whatever one makes of the wanton snobbery that made this necessary, and indeed whether or not it actually happened, the story makes an important point. It is easy to forget, especially in a crisis, the need to protect as far as possible the dignity of those being helped. Asaf-ud-Daula, to his credit, did not. Or at least that's how history remembers him.

We will argue that this tension between cash and care should be one of the central concerns in the design of social policy. In the current debate, at one extreme there are those who believe the best we can do for people who have not flourished in the market economy is to hand them some cash and walk away, leaving them to find their own way in the world. At the other extreme stand those who have little faith in the ability of the poor to take care of themselves, and as a result either want to abandon them to their fate or intrude heavily into their lives, restricting their choices, punishing those who do not fall in line. One side acts as if the self-esteem of the beneficiaries of public programs is not an issue; the other side either does not care or believes it is the price they need to pay if they want public help. And yet the desire to be respected is often a reason why support for social interventions is lacking even among those who need them, and also a reason why these policies fail. In this chapter we explore the implications of this particular perspective on the design of social policies.

DESIGNER SOCIAL PROGRAMS

There is nothing more designer these days, at least among social programs, than universal basic income (UBI). Elegant in its simplicity, it is the midcentury modern of welfare, popular among Silicon Valley entrepreneurs, media mavens, certain kinds of philosophers and economists, and the odd politician. UBI imagines the government paying everyone a substantial guaranteed basic income (the amount of $1000 a month has been floated for the United States), irrespective of their needs. This amount would be small change for Bill Gates, but quite a bit of money for someone out of a job, allowing them, if it comes to that, to go through their entire life without paid employment. Silicon Valley likes it because they worry their innovations may cause lots of dislocations. Benoit Hamon, the socialist candidate to replace François Hollande as the president of France, tried to use it to revive his doomed campaign; Hillary Clinton mentioned it occasionally (she lost too); there was a referendum about it in Switzerland (but only a quarter of the voters voted for it); in India, it recently showed up in an official finance ministry document, and both parties competing in the election had some version of an unconditional cash transfer in their platforms, although in neither case was it universal.

Many economists, going back at least to Milton Friedman, approve of UBI's hands-off attitude. As we discussed, many of them are acculturated to assume people know best what is good for themselves, and see no reason to believe a government bureaucrat would know better. For them, handing over cash to welfare recipients is obviously the right thing to do; the person knows what best to do with it. If buying food makes sense, they will buy food; but if clothes are more useful, they should have the right to decide. Programs like SNAP in the United States, which can only be spent on food, are overreaching. Likewise, doling the money out as a reward for some kind of "good behavior" as the conditional cash transfer programs, like the Progresa/Oportunidades/Prospera program in Mexico and its many imitators do, is just making people jump through hoops for no reason. If it is truly good behavior they would do it in any case and if they disagree, people are more likely to be right than the government. When the left-leaning Mexican government announced its intention to replace Prospera with an unconditional transfer in 2019, it cited that the "health seminars, medical checks (and other obligations) were a burden on women."[1]

There is also the very real attraction of a program that is universal and does not try to target and monitor people. Most social programs come with complicated screening and monitoring rules to make sure benefits are going to the right people. Making sure the conditions of educating children and getting their health checkups are met is not cheap: in Mexico, it costs about ten pesos to transfer a hundred pesos to a household. Of those ten pesos, 34 percent pays for the cost of identifying beneficiaries, and another 25 percent is used for ensuring compliance with the conditions for getting the conditional cash transfer.[2]

The proliferation of rules also makes it hard to sign up and, possibly as a result, take-up among the intended beneficiaries is much less than universal. In Morocco, Esther studied a program entitling households to a subsidized loan to get their homes connected to the water mains.[3] When she first visited the neighborhoods where the program was offered, the French company whose program they were evaluating, Veolia, proudly showed off the "Veolia bus" that went from neighborhood to neighborhood to provide information on the new program. Strangely, there was no one on the bus itself, and when Esther went from house to house, it was clear people often had a vague idea about the program but did not know what it would take to apply. The procedure, as it turns out, was not that simple. It could not be done on the bus. Potential customers had to go to the city hall with a number of papers certifying their residence and their right to the property. They had to fill out an application and come back some weeks later to see if it was approved. Esther and her colleagues offered a simple service: a field officer would come to your house, take photocopies of the relevant documents, fill out the application, and deliver it to the city hall. This was extremely effective; the sign-up rate increased by a factor of seven.

To make matters worse, those especially intimidated by the complexity of the sign-up process are often the neediest. In Delhi, widows and divorced women living in poverty are entitled to a monthly pension of Rs 1,500 (or $85 PPP, adjusting for the cost of living), a substantial amount for these women, but take-up is low: a World Bank survey found that two-thirds of eligible women were not enrolled in the program.[4] One reason may be the application process, which involves a complex set of rules most people would not understand or be able to navigate.

To understand the extent to which knowledge of the rules, or the rules themselves, prevent take-up, a study randomly divided a group of twelve hundred eligible Indian women into four groups.[5] One group was the control group; one group received information about the program; one group received information and some assistance with the process of signing up; and the last group got information, assistance, and was also accompanied by the local representative of the NGO to the office to sign up. Providing information increased the number of women who began the application process, but did not significantly increase the number of women who actually completed it. In contrast, helping them with the process resulted in more applications. Women who received help were six percentage points more likely to complete all the steps, and those taken to the office were eleven percentage points more likely to apply, almost double the base rate. Importantly, the most vulnerable women (illiterate, politically unconnected) benefitted the most from the intervention, consistent with the view they were the ones most likely to be excluded by the existing process. But even with the help, the take-up was only 26 percent for what was mostly free money, likely because the women had little faith in the government's ability to deliver, and thus did not see the value of jumping through the hoops.

The same goes for the United States. Between 2008 and 2014, millions of additional children got access to free lunch at school after it was decided that any children of parents who were obviously poor—those already covered by other anti-poverty programs—would be automatically enrolled. In fact, they had been eligible for free lunch ever since the rules were changed in 2004, but then it was up to the parents to claim the benefit, and that did not happen.[6]

Or take SNAP. Out of thirty thousand elderly people not enrolled in SNAP but who looked like they would be eligible, a randomly chosen group was told about their likely eligibility, and a random subgroup of those were actually helped to sign up. After nine months, only 6 percent of the control group signed up, but information increased the rate to 11 percent, and when help was added, it went up to 18 percent.[7]

It does not help that being identified as poor comes with a certain stigma in the US, a product of the continuing faith in the idea that anyone can succeed, very much in the face of the evidence, as we already discussed. Many people therefore resist having to admit to themselves or others that they are poor enough to deserve help. We encountered an interesting instance of this in our work with low-income workers in California. The label "food stamps," as one might imagine, comes from the fact that historically workers were paid in stamps. These days, "stamp recipients" receive government-issued electronic benefit transfer (EBT) cards that are swiped like a debit card in the checkout line, which avoids the stigma of handing over the stamps. But not everyone eligible for SNAP knows that. The experiment was carried out in the offices of H&R Block, a tax preparer. Most people who go to these offices in January are low-income workers who expect a tax refund. In some of these offices, chosen by lot, those likely to be eligible for SNAP received a pamphlet designed by a PR firm describing the local EBT card as the "Golden State Advantage Card." It was described as the way to "get more at the grocery shop" and the emphasis was on the fact that working families might be eligible. Members of the control group were asked instead whether they wanted to be screened for "food stamps" benefits and were given a pamphlet designed to reflect the more familiar language of the program. Banners in the office reinforced the messages in both cases. We found that clients were significantly more likely to be interested in SNAP if the label "food stamps" was not used.[8]

Conversely, belief that they will be unfairly excluded from a program can discourage those who need it the most from applying. This is why organizations that work with the extreme poor strongly affirm the need for universality of services. When Thierry Rauch, then a homeless person in France, heard the French government was going to help 30 percent of the poor to escape poverty, his reaction was "What is clear is that me and my family, we won't be in that number." He continued, "If the support is not for everyone, I am sure I will get thrown out." After a lifetime of being "thrown out," he had given up on trying to get selected.[9]

The same counterproductive pessimism was found at work in Morocco. Esther and her colleagues compared the performance of a program called Tayssir, a traditional conditional cash transfer that requires school attendance, with an unconditional cash transfer plan that claimed to help parents educate their children but did not actually require regular school attendance. During the fieldwork for the project, Esther visited a family that was not enrolled in the conditional cash transfer program. She asked why. They had three children of the right age, all enrolled in school. The father explained that he often worked as a daily laborer outside the village for the whole day, or even days on end, and therefore he could not make sure his children were attending regularly. He worried they would be absent too often and he would end up forfeiting the transfer, and looking like a bad parent.

The data suggest this family was not an exception. Some families where children were most at risk of dropping out of school opted out of the conditional cash transfer because they were not sure they would be able to meet the requirements. It seems they did not want the shame of being excluded for poor performance and preferred to exclude themselves instead. As a result, a nonconditional transfer presented as a *way to help families* educate their children, rather than a *condition*, was more effective in increasing education for those fragile families (and just as effective for everyone else).[10]

WHERE'S THE MONEY?

Given the downsides of existing transfer programs, where does the resistance to UBI come from? Why are there so few cash transfer programs, anywhere in the world, that are universal and come without strings attached?

One simple reason is money. Universal programs in which no one is excluded are expensive. The proposal to pay $1,000 a month for every American would cost $3.9 trillion a year. That's about $1.3 trillion more than all existing welfare programs, roughly the equivalent of the entire federal budget, or 20 percent of the US economy.[11] To finance it without cutting back all the traditional functions of government (defense, public education, etc.) would require eliminating all exiting welfare programs *and* raising the US tax level to the level of Denmark's. That is why even the enthusiastic supporters of UBI talk about a design where the transfer would be lower as people got richer, and would be zero above a certain income. So not, in fact, universal. If UBI were paid only to the poorer half of Americans it would cost a much more affordable $1.95 trillion. But that would require targeting, with all its pitfalls.

MIDDLE-CLASS MORALITY

Abhijit at the age of twelve, like many of his friends, was in love with Audrey Hepburn. He discovered her as Eliza Doolittle in the movie version of the Lerner and Loewe musical *My Fair Lady*, based on the play *Pygmalion* by George Bernard Shaw (a radical left-winger in his time). In the play her father, Alfred, makes this truly wonderful little philosophical speech (before more or less offering to sell his daughter for five pounds even):

> I ask you, what am I? I'm one of the undeserving poor: that's what I am. Think of what that means to a man. It means that he's up against middle class morality all the time. If there's anything going, and I put in for a bit of it, it's always the same story: "You're undeserving; so you can't have it." But my needs is as great as the most deserving widow's

that ever got money out of six different charities in one week for the death of the same husband. I don't need less than a deserving man: I need more. I don't eat less hearty than him; and I drink a lot more. I want a bit of amusement, cause I'm a thinking man. I want cheerfulness and a song and a band when I feel low. Well, they charge me just the same for everything as they charge the deserving. What is middle class morality? Just an excuse for never giving me anything.[12]

It was hard being poor in Victorian England where the play is set. To be deserving of charity one had to be abstemious, thrifty, church-going, and above all hard working. If not, it was off to the poorhouse where work was enforced and husbands and wives were kept apart, unless you happened to be in debt, in which case it was to debtor's prison or an enforced trip Down Under. An 1898 "map descriptive of London Poverty" classified some areas as "lowest class, vicious, semi-criminal."[13]

We are not very far from this today. Mention welfare in a well-heeled crowd in the United States, India, or Europe and there will always be a few shaking heads, worried that welfare turns the poor into "good for nothings," to use a Victorian expression still popular among a certain class of Indians. Give them cash and they will stop working or drink it up. Somewhere behind this is the suspicion the poor are poor because they lack the will to achieve; give them any excuse and they will check out.

In the United States, the economic catastrophe of the Depression during the 1930s temporarily gave poverty a more benign face because it was so ubiquitous. Everyone knew someone who suffered from sudden poverty. John Steinbeck's brave Okies fleeing the Dust Bowl are a staple of high school classes. Franklin D. Roosevelt's New Deal marked the beginning of an era where poverty was seen as something society could fight, and beat, with government intervention. This continued until the 1960s, culminating in Lyndon B. Johnson's "war on poverty." But when growth slowed and resources were tight, the war on poverty turned into war on the poor. Ronald Reagan would return time and again to the image of the so-called welfare queen, who was black, lazy, female, and fraudulent. The model for this was Linda Taylor, a woman from Chicago who had four aliases and was convicted of $8,000 in fraud, for which she spent several years in prison. This was one and a half years longer than onetime billionaire capitalist hero Charles Keating, the central figure in the most famous corruption scandal of the Reagan era (the Keating Five scandal), and the related savings and loans crisis that was to cost taxpayers over $500 billion in bailout money.

In a new twist, the moral turpitude of the poor was now presented as the consequence of welfare itself. In 1986, Reagan famously declared the war on poverty lost. It was welfare that made us lose the war, by discouraging work and encouraging dependency, which led to the "crisis of family breakdowns, especially among the welfare poor, both black and white."[14] In a radio address to the nation on February 15, 1986, Reagan declared:

> We're in danger of creating a permanent culture of poverty as inescapable as any chain or bond; a second and separate America, an America of lost dreams and stunted lives. The irony is that misguided welfare programs instituted in the name of compassion have actually helped turn a shrinking problem into a national tragedy. From the 1950's on, poverty in America was declining. American society, an opportunity society, was doing its wonders. Economic growth was providing a ladder for millions to climb up out of poverty and into prosperity. In 1964 the famous War on Poverty was declared and a funny thing happened. Poverty, as measured by dependency, stopped shrinking and then actually began to grow worse. I guess you could say, poverty won the war. Poverty won in part because instead of helping the poor, government programs ruptured the bonds holding poor families together.
>
> Perhaps the most insidious effect of welfare is its usurpation of the role of provider. In States where payments are highest, for instance, public assistance for a single mother can amount to much more than the usable income of a minimum wage job. In other words, it can pay for her to quit work. Many families are eligible for substantially higher benefits when the father is not present. What must it do to a man to know that his own children will be better off if he is never legally recognized as their father? Under existing welfare rules, a teenage girl who becomes pregnant can make herself eligible for welfare benefits

that will set her up in an apartment of her own, provide medical care, and feed and clothe her. She only has to fulfill one condition—not marry or identify the father . . . The welfare tragedy has gone on too long. It's time to reshape our welfare system so that it can be judged by how many Americans it makes independent of welfare.[15]

These ominous claims do not withstand scrutiny. One could line many long bookshelves with studies on the impact of welfare on fertility and family structure. The overwhelming conclusion of this literature is that those effects, if they are there at all, are very small.[16] Reagan's fears were unfounded.

But despite this overwhelming evidence, the idea that welfare causes poverty, and the tropes of "dependency," "welfare cultures," "crisis of family values," and the implicit association with race or ethnicity, is pervasive across different times and places. In June 2018, French president Emmanuel Macron taped himself preparing for a speech on his proposed reforms of the anti-poverty programs. The tape was made public by the administration as a candid "behind the curtains" view of the president, a window into his real style and unvarnished opinions. We see him, despite all the differences between the two, adopting very much a Reagan-like tone, repeating over and over that the current system is failing, and managing to talk about the need to make the poor more responsible six times in the space of a few minutes.[17]

In the United States, this spirit turned into action in 1996 when President Clinton passed, with bipartisan support, the Personal Responsibility and Work Opportunity Reconciliation Act. It replaced the Aid to Families with Dependent Children (AFDC) program with Temporary Assistance for Needy Families (TANF), which imposed new work requirements on the beneficiaries. Clinton also expanded the earned income tax credit (EITC), which supplements earnings for poor *workers* (making government assistance conditional on already having some work). In 2018, President Trump's Council of Economic Advisers issued a report advocating a work requirement as a condition of eligibility for the three major noncash assistance programs: Medicaid, SNAP (food stamps), and rental assistance.[18] In June of 2018, Arkansas became the first state to implement a work requirement for Medicaid adults. Interestingly, the Council of Economic Advisers' main argument was no longer that the war on poverty had failed but, on the contrary, that "our war on poverty is largely over and a success." The report argued that "the safety net—including government tax and [both cash and non-cash] transfer policies—has contributed to a dramatic reduction in poverty [correctly measured] in the United States. However, the policies have been accompanied by a decline in self-sufficiency [in terms of receipt of welfare benefits] among non-disabled working-age adults. Expanding work requirements in these non-cash welfare programs would improve self-sufficiency, with little risk of substantially reversing progress in addressing material hardship." In other words, people had to be made to work for their supper, so they were not cheated of "the American work ethic, the motivation that drives Americans to work longer hours each week and more weeks each year than any of our economic peers [which] is a long-standing contributor to America's success." Sure, it might cause some pain, but it was worth it to prevent a large number of poor people from succumbing to sloth, one of the seven deadly sins. The Puritans would have applauded.

GIVE US THIS DAY OUR DAILY BREAD

The Puritans would have also agreed with the reluctance to hand over cash, a reticence historically shared by the left and the right. In India, one of the more successful recent efforts by the left was the demand for a national food security act. Passed in 2013, it promises five kilos of subsidized food-grains every month to almost two-thirds of Indians, over seven hundred million people.[19] In Egypt, the food subsidy program cost 85 billion Egyptian pounds in 2017–2018 ($4.95 billion, or 2 percent of GDP).[20] Indonesia has Rastra (formerly called Raskin), which distributes subsidized rice to over thirty-three million households.[21]

Distributing grains is complicated and costly. The government has to buy the grains, store them, and transport them, often across many hundreds of miles. In India, the estimate is that transport and storage add 30 percent to the cost of the program. Moreover, there is the challenge of making sure the intended recipient gets the grains at the intended price. In 2012, eligible households received only a third of the amount they were due under the Indonesian Raskin program, and paid 40 percent more than the official price.[22]

In India, the government is now considering moving to what it calls direct benefit transfers, sending money to people's bank accounts rather than giving them food (or other material benefits), on the grounds that it would be much cheaper and less subject to corruption. However, there is considerable opposition, led mostly by left-wing intellectuals. One of them interviewed twelve hundred households throughout India about their preferences for cash versus food. Overall two-thirds of the households preferred food transfers to cash. In states where the food distribution system worked well (mainly in South India), this preference was even stronger. When asked why, 13 percent of households mentioned transaction costs (the bank and market are far, so it's hard to turn cash into food). But one-third of the households who prefer food argued that getting foodstuff protects them against the temptation to misuse cash. In Dharmapuri in Tamil Nadu, one respondent said, "Food is much safer. Money gets spent easily." Another said, "Even if you give ten times the amount I will prefer the ration shop since the goods cannot be frittered away."[23]

SHORT-SELLING THEMSELVES

And yet there is nothing in the data to suggest they are right to be so worried. As of 2014, 119 developing countries had implemented some kind of unconditional cash assistance program and 52 countries had conditional cash transfer programs for poor households. Together, one billion people in developing countries participated in at least one of these.[24] The initial phase of many of these programs was implemented as an experiment. What is very clear from all these experiments is that there is no support in the data for the view that the poor just blow the money on desires rather than needs. If anything, those who get these transfers *raise the share* of their total expenses that go to food (i.e., it is not just that they spend more on food when they have more money, but they might even spend so much more that the fraction of food spending goes up); nutrition improves and so does expenditure on schooling and health.[25] There is also no evidence that cash transfers lead to greater spending on tobacco and alcohol.[26] And cash transfers generally increase food expenditures as much as food rations.[27]

Even men do not seem to waste the money; when the transfers are given at random to either a man or a woman, there is no difference in how much is spent on food versus, say, alcohol or tobacco.[28] We are still in favor of giving the money to the woman, because it restores a little of the balance of power within the family and might allow her to do what she deems important (including working outside of the home[29]), but not so much because we think that the man will drink it up.

AVOIDING THE SNAKE PIT

There is no evidence that cash transfers make people work less.[30] Economists find this surprising —why would you work if you did not need the money to survive? What about the temptation of sloth, for which the biblical punishment is being thrown in a snake pit in hell?

It seems plausible that many (perhaps most) people genuinely aspire to do something with their lives, but the exigencies of surviving on very little paralyze them. Perhaps getting the extra cash encourages them to work harder and/or try new things. In Ghana, Abhijit and his colleagues carried out an experiment. Beneficiaries were offered a chance to make bags, which the experimenters then bought from them at very generous prices. Some of the women workers (chosen at random) were also part of a program that gave them a productive asset, most often goats, along with some training in how to make best use of the asset and some confidence boosting (these were very poor women, who did not necessarily believe they could be successful at anything). Despite the fact that tending the goats added to their workload (and also gave them some income, so that they were less desperately in need of extra cash), the women who got into the program produced more bags and earned more from them than those who were not included in the asset giveaway. Most interestingly, the big difference between those with and without an asset became evident when a bag had a complex design. Asset beneficiaries worked faster, yet met the necessary quality standards. The most plausible explanation is that getting the gift of the asset freed them up from worries of survival, giving them the bandwidth and the energy to focus on their work.[31]

It is also true that the typical poor person in the developing world cannot get a loan (or can only get one at some astronomical interest rate) and has no one to bail them out if their venture fails. Both these conditions make it much harder for them to start the business of their dreams. A cash transfer that goes on for some years both provides some extra finance and backstops consumption if the enterprise fails. Perhaps a guaranteed income would make the poor willing to go somewhere else to look for a better job, to learn a new skill, or to start a new business.

But maybe all of this applies only in developing countries, where the poor are very poor indeed and the cash actually *enables* them to work. Perhaps in the United States things are very different since everyone, however poor, is usually able to find work. Is it possible that the sloth effect dominates there? As it turns out, there is also evidence, going back to the 1960s, suggesting that sloth should not be a major concern in the US. In fact, the first-ever large-scale randomized experiment in the social sciences, the New Jersey Income Maintenance Experiment, was devised precisely to determine the impact of the "negative income tax." A negative income tax (NIT) implements the idea that the system of income taxation should be designed so everyone is guaranteed to receive at least a minimum income. The poor should pay negative taxes so they get paid more than they earn, but as they get richer they will get less in transfers until at some point they start paying into the system.

This is different from a UBI, because for people near the tipping point between being takers from and payers into the system, there is potentially a strong disincentive to work. In other words, in addition to the *income effect* (I do not need to work if I have enough money to survive on already) that most policy makers worry about, such schemes can have a *substitution effect* (working is less valuable since what I make in extra income is taken out as reduced welfare payments).

Many scholars and policy makers, in both political parties, were in favor of a negative income tax. On the left, the US Office of Economic Opportunity under Democrat president Lyndon Johnson heralded the idea and set forth a plan for replacing traditional welfare with an NIT. On the right, Milton Friedman advocated replacing most existing transfer programs with a single NIT. Republican president Richard Nixon proposed it in 1971 as part of his package of welfare reform, but Congress did not approve it. A key concern at the time was that beneficiaries would work less as a result of the program, and thus the government would end up paying people who would otherwise have earned their own living.

It was then that Heather Ross, a PhD student in economics at MIT, came up, arguably for the first time in economics, with the idea of an experiment to settle this issue. Ross was frustrated that politicians used anecdotes to justify economic policy, and that there was no factual basis to establish whether low-income people would stop working if they received help from this kind of program. In 1967, she submitted a proposal to the US Office of Economic Opportunity for an RCT. This was ultimately funded and, as Ross put it, she ended up with a "$5 million thesis."[32]

The outcome of this inspired proposal would be not just a New Jersey NIT experiment, but also a series of others. In the early 1970s, Donald Rumsfeld (yes, the same one) steered the NIT away from full implementation and toward a series of experiments. The first experiment took place in urban areas in New Jersey and Pennsylvania (1968–1972), with subsequent experiments in rural areas of Iowa and North Carolina (1969–1973), in Gary, Indiana (1971–1974), and the largest one, the Seattle-Denver Income Maintenance Experiment (SIME/DIME) experiment, in Seattle, Washington, and Denver, Colorado (1971–1982, covering forty-eight hundred households).[33]

The NIT experiments convincingly established the feasibility and usefulness of running RCTs for policy making. It would be decades before comparably intellectually ambitious projects would take center stage again in social policy. That said, these being the first experiments in the social sciences, it is not surprising their design and implementation were far from perfect. Participants were lost, samples were too small to get precise results, and, most worryingly, data collection was contaminated.[34] Moreover, because the experiment was short lived and small scale, it was also not easy to extrapolate what would happen in response to a more permanent and more universal program.

Nevertheless, taken together, the results suggest the NIT program did reduce labor supply a bit, but not nearly as much as was feared.

On average, the reduction in time worked was only between two and four weeks of full-time employment over a year.[35] In the largest experiment (SIME/DIME), husbands who received the NIT reduced their hours of work by only 9 percent compared to those who did not, although wives who received the NIT reduced their hours by 20 percent.[36] Overall, the official conclusion of the study was that the income maintenance program did not have large effects on the propensity for people, particularly the prime earners in the family, to work.[37]

There are also examples of local unconditional transfer programs, from various parts of the United States. The Alaska Permanent Fund has distributed, since 1982, a yearly dividend of $2,000 per person per year. It seems to have no adverse impact on employment.[38] Of course, the Alaska Permanent Fund, while universal and permanent (as its name indicates), is also quite small compared to the proposed UBI. If it had been sufficient to live off, people might have stopped working. A more UBI-like program is the payment of casino dividends on Cherokee lands to the members of the tribe. The transfers, about $4,000 per adult per year, represent a large boost in income, since the per capita household income for Native Americans is about $8,000. Comparing eligible and ineligible families in the Smoky Mountains before and after the payments, one study found no effect on work in the family, but large positive impacts on the education of the adolescents.[39]

UUBI (UNIVERSAL ULTRA BASIC INCOME)

So, there is no evidence that unconditional cash transfers lead to a life of dissolution. What does that tell us about the design of welfare policy?

In developing countries, where lots of people are at risk of finding themselves destitute from time to time, and where the safety nets, however imperfect, that exist in rich countries (emergency rooms, shelters, food banks) are missing, the value of having an assured fallback option like UBI could be enormous, both in dealing with bad luck and in making it easier to try something new.

One of the most common ways in which people safeguard themselves against income risk in many parts of the developing world is by holding on to land. We discussed the reluctance to migrate in chapter 2, and one reason is that those who migrate risk losing their land rights. Interestingly, for example, these days most rural land-owning households in India get a majority of their income from something other than agriculture. But land ownership is still valuable because it comes with the assurance that if all else fails, they can grow their own living.

This has the consequence that areas with a large fraction of small-holders tend to find it difficult to industrialize. This is partly due to the design of land reform; when the poor are given land rights, it is often inheritable but not saleable. But there is also a strong resistance to sell among the farmers themselves. In the Indian state of West Bengal, when the communists came to power after winning the 1977 elections, their first priority was to give the tenant farmers permanent rights on the land they tilled. The right could be inherited, but not sold. Thirty years later, the same communist government, conscious of the lack of industrial development in the state, tried to buy out the farmers (including the tenant farmers). That met with such furious resistance that the plans were shelved. The communists ended up getting booted out of power after massive protests against the land expulsions, and the bloody repression they were met with.

The one thing the farmers in West Bengal wanted in compensation for giving up their land was the promise of a job, a stable source of income. Perhaps if there had been some kind of UBI to provide this income, the resistance might have been much less and it might have been easier to move arable land into industrial use. In chapter 5, we mentioned poor use of land is a major source of misallocation in India, probably responsible for a significant loss of economic growth. If UBI alleviated the need to stick to your land at all costs, it would reduce this misallocation. It might also reduce labor misallocation by making it more palatable for the landed to sell their land and move where there are better labor market opportunities.

India, however, does not have anything like UBI right now. The current scheme proposed by the government applies only to farmers and is nowhere near a living. The minimum income guarantee proposed by the opposition is more akin to the negative income tax credit. The plan is that it should be targeted to the poor and progressively taxed away as incomes grow. In fact, very few countries have anything like a UBI, which is guaranteed to everyone and is not taxed away. If they have anything, they have transfers targeted to the poor that can be conditional or unconditional. But targeting the right people in the developing world tends to be especially difficult because most people work in agriculture or on tiny firms. It is almost impossible for the government to know how much they earn, making it very hard to isolate the poor and target them with the extra income.[40]

The alternative to targeting is self-targeting. India's National Rural Employment Guarantee Act (NREGA) is the largest of these self-targeted programs (and perhaps some sort of model for the federal job guarantee proposed in the United States). Every rural family is entitled to a hundred days of work per year at the official minimum wage, which is higher in most places than the actual wage. There is no official screening, but there is the requirement to work, usually on construction sites, which screens out anybody with something better to do than stand in the sun for eight hours a day.

The program is popular with the poor. So popular that the Modi government decided not to fight with it head-on after winning India's 2014 election, despite having campaigned against it. One advantage of a workfare program like NREGA is that it substitutes, at least partly, for a minimum wage in places where minimum wage cannot be enforced. Workers can use the NREGA wage to bargain with private-sector employers, and there is evidence they do.[41] Moreover, one study found that private employment actually went up, even though salaries went up. By colluding to pay too little, employers were actually reducing the number of jobs, perhaps because some people were unable or unwilling to work for very little money.

The main sticking point with any workfare program is that someone has to create millions of jobs. In India, this is meant to be the responsibility of the village governments (the *panchayats*). But there is a lot of mistrust between the central authorities and the village governments, with each side, often with some reason, accusing the other of corruption. The result is the kind of red tape and inefficiency that often arises when there is a lot of emphasis on fighting corruption. Approving a project proposal and getting work going takes several months and quite some effort by the head of the panchayat. This means the program is unable to respond effectively to sudden changes in need, say, an unexpected drought. It also means that if you happen to live in a village where the panchayat leadership has decided these projects are too much trouble, you are out of luck. In Bihar, India's poorest state, less than half of those who want work through NREGA get it.[42]

The program ends up being rather prone to corruption because the very people involved in monitoring the program can use their power to block payments and extract bribes. Cutting the number of layers of bureaucrats involved in the monitoring of the program reduced the wealth of the median NREGA functionaries by 14 percent.[43] And even when people get work, it often takes months to get paid.

All of this suggests there are many very good reasons to consider moving to a UBI in many developing countries. The problem of course is money. Most developing countries need to tax more, but that won't change quickly. Initially, most of the money will have to come from shutting down other programs, including some of the big and popular ones such as power subsidies. Cutting the number of programs potentially has the added advantage of concentrating the limited government capacity on just a few things. The government of India has hundreds of programs on its books. Many of these have essentially no funding, but they have an office dedicated to them and some staff who accomplish very little. Manish Sisodia, the deputy chief minister in the Delhi government, once joked that when he came to power there was a line item in the budget for opium purchases. He discovered this was the remnant of a long-defunct program to help opium-addicted refugees from Afghanistan who had settled in Delhi.

Any universal income that governments of poor countries can afford will be ultra basic. Hence UUBI. The Economic Survey of India proposed something like that in 2017. It estimated that an annual transfer of Rs 7,620 ($430 at PPP) to 75 percent of India's population would push all but India's absolute poorest above the 2011–2012 poverty line. Rs 7,620 is very little even by Indian standards (less than what several economists have proposed for an Indian UBI), but perhaps enough to survive on. The survey puts the cost of such a scheme at 4.9 percent of India's GDP. In 2014–2015, India's major fertilizer, petroleum, and food subsidies cost 2.07 percent of GDP, while the ten largest central welfare schemes cost 1.38 percent, so cutting these existing programs entirely would pay for about two-thirds of the UUBI.[44]

This proposal assumes it would be fairly easy to exclude 25 percent of people from the program. It may indeed be possible to introduce a mild form of self-selection. Requiring each beneficiary to visit an ATM every week and put their biometric ID into the system, whether or not they take out the money, would have the dual advantage of eliminating ghost claimants and making it too much of a hassle for the wealthy to want to claim the benefit. There should be fallback options that allow the disabled to get their money, or in case the technology malfunctions (as it often does, particularly for manual workers whose fingerprints get erased by working). But with the right framing ("come and get some extra money when you need it"), a mild requirement like having to visit an ATM once a week could potentially discourage at least 25 percent of the population to draw the transfer at any given time, while making sure those who really need it still get it.

While we are in favor of a UUBI based on what we know so far, there is no data yet on its long-term impact. Most of our evidence is from relatively short-lived interventions. We cannot be sure how people will react to being assured a basic income forever. When the novelty of the extra income wears off, will they go back to being discouraged and work less, or aspire higher and try harder? What will be the long-term impact on their families of being assured an income? This is what a large-scale RCT of a UBI in Kenya Abhijit is involved in will hopefully find out. In forty-four villages, every adult has been guaranteed $0.75 per day for twelve years. In eighty villages, every adult will receive the transfer for two years. In seventy-one villages, every adult will receive one onetime payment of $500 per adult. Finally, in a hundred more villages, no one is guaranteed any income, but data will be regularly collected. In total, almost fifteen thousand households are involved in the experiment. We will start seeing results in early 2020.

We can, however, already see long-term evidence from the conditional cash transfers that have been in place for many years in several countries. These programs started in the 1990s, and those who were children at the time are now young adults. There seems to be an enduring positive effect on their welfare. For example, in Indonesia, in 2007, the government introduced PKH, a conditional cash transfer program in 438 subdistricts across Indonesia (randomly selected from a pool of 736 subdistricts) to a total of about 700,000 households. The program had the standard features of most conditional cash transfer programs: households received a monthly transfer if they sent their children to school and obtained preventive care. Villages enrolled into the program in 2007 continue to receive the benefits even today, but due to bureaucratic inertia, the government never expanded the program to the control villages. Comparing treated and control villages shows some large persistent gains on health and education; there is a dramatic increase in births attended by a health professional and a halving of the number of children not in school. Over time, the program also affected the stock of human capital; there has been a reduction of 23 percent in the number of stunted children, and school completion increased. However, despite these gains in human capital and the transfers themselves, households are not measurably richer. This is an important warning about the long-term effects of purely financial transfers. It may be the case that the sums of money the governments can afford are too small to make a real difference to incomes (and the cost of large transfers is too much for the system to bear).[45]

Given all this, the best combination may be a UUBI everyone can access when they need it and larger transfers targeted to the very poor and linked to preventive care and children's education. The conditions for receiving transfers do not need to be very strictly enforced. In Morocco, we saw that a "labeled cash transfer," which merely encouraged the use of money to help with education costs but without enforcement, seems to have been just as effective at changing behavior as a traditional conditional cash transfer program.[46] Similarly, the PKH program in Indonesia did not strictly enforce conditionalities. In this sense, it also was a "labeled cash transfer." This lowers administrative costs and avoids excluding the most fragile families. Targeting can also be done relatively cheaply, by focusing on poor regions and relying on some identification by community leaders and readily available data. There will be errors. But as long as we are willing to be liberal in the application of the tests (so that those who need help don't get thrown out, even at the cost of giving it to some people who do not need it), and as long as the UUBI is there to provide a minimum, we might get the best of both worlds.

UBI FOR THE USA?

Welfare policy in the United States (and in most other rich countries) also needs a reset. There are too many angry people who feel that for too long things have not been going their way. And there is no immediate sign things will sort themselves out. So is UBI the answer for the United States?

If voters are persuaded government is on the right track, they may be less resistant to paying the increase in taxes necessary to fund it. According to a Pew Research Center study,[47] 61 percent of Americans are in favor of a government policy offering all Americans a guaranteed income that would meet their basic needs in case robots become capable of doing most human jobs. Among Democrats, 77 percent are in favor. Among Republicans, 38 percent are in favor. Sixty-five percent of Democrats (but only 30 percent of Republicans) say the government has a responsibility to help displaced workers, even if it involves raising taxes. Given this level of support and the fact that the United States is undertaxed by global standards, one can imagine taxes going up from 26 percent to 31.2 percent of GDP. This would allow every American to get $3,000 per year.[48] For a family of four, this would be $12,000 per year, half the poverty line. It is not a fortune, but is a significant amount of money for anyone in the poorest third. If it is financed by a tax on capital, and the share of capital in the economy grows because of automation, UBI could become more generous over time. In Europe, there is less space for taxes to be raised, but a whole range of social transfers (housing, income support, etc.) could be collapsed into a single payment with few restrictions on how it could be spent. This is in effect what was tried out in Finland in 2017 and 2018, where 2,000 *unemployed* workers were randomized to get a UBI replacing all traditional assistance programs (housing, employment assistance, etc.). The remaining 173,222 formed the control group. Early results suggest UBI recipients are happier. There is no difference in earnings between the two groups, perhaps consistent with everything we have seen until now.[49]

But would a UBI really make the left-behind people feel that much less angry? Many proponents of UBI, but not the poor, seem to see it as a way to buy off those who will be made unproductive by the new economy and won't be able to find work. If they had the UBI, they would be content to stop looking for work and do something else instead. But everything we know so far seems to say this is very unlikely. We asked those who responded to our survey this question: "Do you think that if there was a universal basic income of $13,000 a year (with no strings attached) you would stop working or stop looking for work?" Eighty-seven percent said they would not.[50] All the evidence scattered through this book suggests most people actually want to work, not just because they need the money; work brings with it a sense of purpose, belonging, and dignity.

In 2015, the Rand Corporation conducted an in-depth survey of the working conditions of about three thousand Americans.[51] Those surveyed were asked how often their work provides them with the following: "satisfaction of work well done," "feeling of doing useful work," "sense of personal accomplishment," "opportunity to make positive impact on community/society," "opportunities to fully use talents," and "goals to aspire to." They found four out of five US workers reported their job provides at least one of these sources of meaning always or most of the time.

Around the same time, the Pew Research Center collected data on Americans' satisfaction with their job and asked respondents whether they felt their job gave them a sense of identity.[52] About half (51 percent) of employed Americans said they got a sense of identity from their job, while the other half (47 percent) said their job is just what they do for a living.

It is not entirely clear how the numbers from these two studies fit together, but there is no question many people care about having a job in a way that goes beyond just getting paid. However, it is the workers with more education and those who earn more who tend to see their job as part of their identity; only 37 percent of those who make $30,000 per year or less report getting a sense of identity from their job. There are also some significant differences by industry. For example, 62 percent of adults working in the healthcare industry and 70 percent of those working in education say they get a sense of identity from their job, compared with 42 percent of people working in hospitality and 36 percent in retail or wholesale trade.

People think in terms of good jobs and bad jobs, or at least meaningful jobs and less meaningful jobs. Better-paid jobs are on average better jobs, but what you do matters as well. People may resist having to move from the job they love to a job they perceive as worthless, even if their income would be more or less unchanged. And, in fact, people do not really land on their feet when they lose a job they have had for many years. Many studies have found that, on average, displaced workers never fully recover in terms of earnings after a mass layoff. On average, the jobs they find are less well paid, less stable, and do not have the same benefits.[53]

This is probably partly related to the fact, which we discussed in chapter 2, that labor markets are a lot about finding the right match between employers and employees; finding an employer who trusts and values you and whom you trust and value is a matter of luck. Once you find one, it is natural to try to stay, leading to a more stable and rewarding career, both economically and otherwise. Once you lose that connection, it is hard to reestablish it, especially if you are older and set in your ways.

This explains something rather remarkable and frightening. A study found that when workers with long tenure get fired during mass layoffs, they are more likely to die in the years immediately afterward.[54] Losing a job seems to literally give people heart attacks. The estimated impact of job displacement on the mortality rate goes down over time but does not go back to zero, as more long-run problems like alcoholism, depression, pain, and addiction set in. Overall, the study found that workers displaced in middle age lost between one and one and a half years of life expectancy.

Transitions are costly in ways most economic analysis ignores. As economists, we worry about the income loss and the time and effort involved in finding a new job, but the cost of losing the job itself appears nowhere in our models. It is probably no surprise that UBI, an idea economists instinctively gravitate toward, also ignores it. It imagines a world in which laid-off workers see themselves as freed from the obligation of working. Young retirees living off UBI find new meaning in their lives, working at home, volunteering in their communities, taking up crafts, or exploring the world. Unfortunately, evidence suggests that it is actually difficult for people to find meaning outside the structure of their work. Since the start of the American Time Use Survey (ATUS) in the 1960s, time spent on leisure activities has increased quite a bit, both for men and women.[55] For young men, a sizeable part of this time, since 2004, has been devoted to video games.[56] For all the other groups, the bulk of this time has been absorbed by watching television. In 2017, men spent on average five and a half hours per day on leisure activities (including browsing the internet, watching TV, socializing, and volunteering), and women five hours. Watching TV was the leisure activity occupying the most time (2.8 hours per day). Socializing outside the home came a distant second at thirty-eight minutes.[57] During the Great Recession, when time spent on work outside the home declined, television and sleep took up half the slack.[58]

But apparently watching television and sleeping do not necessarily make us happy. Daniel Kahneman and Alan Krueger showed, using surveys where they asked people to reconstruct their day and how they felt about each moment, that among leisure activities, watching TV, using the computer, and napping gave the least immediate pleasure and the least sense of achievement. Socializing is one of the most pleasurable activities.[59]

It seems that it is very hard for people to individually figure out how to build meaning into their lives. Most of us need the discipline provided by a structured work environment, to which we then add significance or meaning. This is something that comes up when individuals worry about automation. In the Pew Research Center survey, 64 percent of respondents said they expect people will have a hard time finding things to do with their lives if forced to compete with advanced robots and computers for jobs.[60] Indeed, people who have more time on their hands (retirees, the unemployed, those outside the labor force) are if anything less likely to volunteer than those employed full time.[61] Volunteering is something we do *on top* of our regular activities, not *instead* of them.

In other words, if we are right that the real crisis in rich countries is that many people who used to think of themselves as the middle class have lost the sense of self-worth they used to derive from their jobs, UBI is not the answer. The reason we have different answers to the question in rich and poor countries is twofold. First, UBI is easy, and many poor countries lack the governance capacity to run more complicated programs. This is not true of the United States, and even less true of France or Japan.

Second, in most developing countries, the average person would also certainly like a stable job with a good income and benefits, but it is not what they *think they are entitled to*. A very large proportion of the world's poor and near-poor, who essentially all live in the developing world, are self-employed. They don't like being self-employed, but they are used to it. They know they might have to switch from one occupation to a very different one within the space of a month or even a day, depending on what opportunities are available. They sell snacks in the morning and work as seamstresses in the afternoon. Or work as farmers during the monsoon and as brick makers during the dry season.

Partly for that reason, they do not build their lives around their work; they are careful to maintain connections with their neighbors, their relatives, their caste and religious groups, their formal and informal associations. In Abhijit's native West Bengal, the club (or in Bangla pronunciation, the *klaab*) is a key institution; most villages and urban neighborhoods have at least one. The members are men between the ages of sixteen and thirty-five; they meet nearly every day to play cricket or soccer or cards or the uniquely South Asian tabletop sport *carrom*. They often describe themselves as social workers, and when, say, there is a death in some family, they show up and help. But they also practice a mild form of extortion in the name of "social work" or religious observances, and this, along with contributions from local politicians who use them as foot soldiers, pays for the club and its occasional celebrations. Mostly, however, it serves as a way to keep the local bloods from getting into more trouble, in a setting where most of them are either not working or working at a job they don't enjoy. It provides a modicum of meaning.

BEYOND FLEXICURITY

If UBI won't solve the disruption caused by our current economic model, what will? Economists and many policy makers like the Danish model of "flexicurity." It allows for full labor market flexibility, meaning people can be laid off quite easily whenever they aren't needed anymore, but the laid off are subsidized so they do not suffer much of an economic loss, and there is a concerted effort by the government to get the worker back into employment (perhaps after meaningful retraining). Compared to a system where workers are essentially on their own (like in the United States), flexicurity is meant to ensure job loss is not a tragedy, but a normal phase of life. Compared to a system that makes it difficult to fire workers on permanent contracts (like in France), flexicurity makes it possible for employers to adjust to changes in circumstances, and avoids the conflict between the "insiders," those lucky enough to have strongly protected jobs, and the "outsiders," who have no jobs at all.

This is consistent with the economist's basic reflex: we should let the market do its job and insure people who end up holding the short end of the stick. In the long run, preventing reallocation of labor from shrinking sectors to growing ones is both impractical and costly. For many people in the economy, particularly the younger worker, any help to seriously retrain is valuable. We saw earlier that the TAA program worked.

Nonetheless, we don't think that flexicurity is the entire answer. This is because of what we already discussed; job loss is clearly much more than income loss. It is all too often about being yanked from a settled life plan and a particular vision of the good life. In particular, older people and those who have worked in a particular location or for a particular firm for many years probably find it more difficult to switch to another career. Retraining them is costly, given they have relatively few years of work life left. They have a lot to lose and little to gain from moving to another career (and even more to another place). The only relatively easy transition would be to move to another role in the same area and in a similar position.

This is why at the end of chapter 3 we proposed the somewhat radical idea that some workers should be subsidized to stay in place. When a whole sector is disrupted by trade or by technology, the wages of the older workers could be partly or fully subsidized. Such a policy should only be triggered when a particular industry in an area is in decline, and reserved for older employees (above fifty or fifty-five) with at least ten (or eight or twelve) years of experience in a comparable position.

Economists are instinctively critical of opening up such a large space for governmental discretion. How will the government know what the declining industries are?

We don't doubt there will be some errors and some abuse. However, this has been the excuse for not intervening all these years when trade has been robbing people of their livings while claiming to make everyone better off. If we want to claim trade is good for everyone, we need to design mechanisms to make it actually so, and those will involve identifying losers and compensating them. In fact, trade economists (including those in government) have the numbers to know where imports are growing fast and where outsourcing is growing apace; the round of tariffs imposed by the United States in 2018 were computed from this data. A trade war risks hurting a lot of other people in the economy, whereas a much more targeted subsidy would protect the most vulnerable groups without creating new forms of disruption. A similar policy for identifying sectors and locations where automation is happening fastest, and intervening, could also be put together.

Prominent urban economists, like Moretti, are suspicious of place-based policies because they worry the policy will just end up redistributing activity from one region to the other, and possibly away from the most productive regions to less productive regions. But if people over a certain age cannot or will not move, then it is not clear what choice we have. Today, large pockets of left-behind people are dotted across the US landscape, with hundreds of towns blighted by anger and substance abuse, where everyone who can afford it has either left or is contemplating leaving. It will be very difficult to help people in these places. The goal of social policy, therefore, should be to help the distressed places that exist, but perhaps more importantly avoid ending up with many more.

In a sense, this is what Europe has done with its Common Agricultural Policy. Economists hate it, because a dwindling number of European farmers have gotten a great deal as a result of subsidies at the expense of everyone else. But they forget that by preventing many of the farms from shutting down, it has kept the countryside in many European countries much more verdant and vibrant. In the past, since farmers were paid more to produce more, they had a tendency to intensify agriculture, giving rise to large ugly fields. But since 2005–2006, the amount of assistance given to farmers has not been linked to production. It is based instead on environmental protection and animal welfare. The result is that small artisanal farms are able to survive, and from them we get high-quality produce and pretty landscapes. This is something most Europeans probably think is worth preserving and certainly contributes to the quality of their lives and the sense of what it is to be a European. Would French GDP be higher if agricultural production were more concentrated and farmhouses were replaced by warehouses? Possibly. Would welfare be higher? Probably not.

The analogy between protecting manufacturing employment in the United States and protecting nature in France may seem strange. But pretty countrysides attract tourists and keep young people around to take care of their aging parents. Similarly, the company town can ensure there is a high school, some sports teams, a main street with a few shops, and a sense of belonging somewhere. This is also the environment, something we all enjoy, and society should be ready to pay for it, just as it is willing to pay for trees.

SMART KEYNESIANISM: SUBSIDIZING THE COMMON GOOD

In 2018, a very different approach based on subsidizing work is gaining ground in the US Democratic party. In 2019, presidential candidates Cory Booker, Kamala Harris, Bernie Sanders, and Elizabeth Warren have all proposed some kind of federal guarantee, whereby any American who wanted to work would be entitled to a good job ($15 an hour with retirement and health benefits on par with other federal employees, childcare assistance, and twelve weeks of paid family leave) in community service, home care, park maintenance, etc. The Green New Deal proposed by Democratic members of Congress includes a federal job guarantee. The idea is of course not new; the Indian National Rural Employment Guarantee Act works along the same lines, as did the original New Deal.

Such a program is not easy to run well if the experience in India is any guide. Creating and organizing enough jobs would probably be even harder in the United States, given that very few people want to dig ditches or build roads, which is what they are asked to do in India. Also, the jobs would need to be useful. If they were transparently some form of make-work, they would not boost the employees' self-esteem. Between pretending to work and going on disability, they might still choose the latter. Finally, given the required scale of the program, it would have to be implemented by private companies bidding on government contracts, known for delivering low quality at a high price.

A more realistic strategy may be for the government to increase the demand for labor-intensive public services by increasing the budget for those services without necessarily providing them directly. An important consideration, especially in the developing world, is to not create jobs where people are underworked and overpaid. As we already saw, the presence of such jobs freezes up the labor market, because everyone queues up to get them. This has the result that overall employment may actually go down. The jobs need to be useful and compensation needs to be fair. There are many possibilities. Elder care, education, and childcare are all sectors where the productivity gains from automation are, at least for the moment, limited. Indeed, it seems likely that robots will never be completely able to replace the human touch in caring for the very young or the very old, though they may well complement it effectively.

Another reason why humans will be very hard to replace in schools and preschools is that if robots take over all the jobs requiring narrow technical skills (from screwing in bolts to accounting), people will be increasingly valued for flexibility and natural empathy. Indeed, research shows social skills have become more valued in the labor market in the last decade compared to cognitive skills.[62] There is very little research on how social skills can be taught, but it seems common sense that human beings will retain some comparative advantage over software in teaching social skills. Indeed, an experiment conducted in Peru shows boarding-school students who were randomly assigned beds near highly sociable students gained social skills themselves. In contrast, being assigned a neighboring student with good test scores did not help them get better grades.[63]

The comparative advantage of humans in care and teaching means the relative productivity of these sectors will increasingly lag behind as machines gain hold elsewhere, and they may also attract less private investment than sectors where more rapid productivity gains can be achieved. At the same time, the care of the elderly is definitely a worthwhile social goal that is currently underserved, and there are enormous potential gains for society from investing in better education and early-childhood care. This will cost money; these two sectors alone could probably absorb as much money as a government would be willing to spend. But if this is money spent paying people well for stable, well-respected jobs, it will achieve two important goals: producing something useful for society and providing a large number of meaningful occupations.

HEAD STARTS

The intergenerational mobility of children is tightly linked to the neighborhoods in which they grow up. A child born in the bottom half of the income distribution in the United States will on average reach the forty-sixth percentile of income if he grew up in Salt Lake City, Utah, but only the thirty-sixth percentile if he happened to be from Charlotte, North Carolina. These spatial differences emerge well before an individual starts working: children in the low-mobility zones are less likely to attend college and are more likely to have children of their own early.[64]

In 1994, the US department of Housing and Urban Development launched a program called Moving to Opportunity (MTO) that offered public housing residents the opportunity to participate in a lottery giving them the chance to move from high-poverty housing projects to lower-poverty neighborhoods. About half of the families who won the vouchers took advantage of it, and those who did ended up in much less poor neighborhoods.

A team of researchers was able to follow winners and losers of the voucher lottery to see if anything changed as a result. The early results for children were somewhat disappointing: while girls were in a better mental state and did better in school, the same was not true of boys.[65] However, in the longer term, some twenty-odd years after the initial lottery, large differences in their life outcomes were evident. Young adults whose parents won the vouchers earned $1,624 more per year than those whose parents did not. They were more likely to have gone to college, they lived in better neighborhoods, and the girls were less likely to be single mothers. Some of these effects will therefore likely transmit to the next generation as well.[66]

What explains why some neighborhoods are "better" than others for mobility? Researchers are far from settling this, but there are clearly features of the environment that seem to be correlated with higher mobility, including most importantly the quality of schools. The map of social mobility, it turns out, is closely related to the map of performance in standardized education tests.[67]

Thanks to decades of research on education, we know a fair amount about what can be done to improve learning outcomes. In 2017, a study summarized 196 randomized studies conducted in developed economies on interventions (both in schools and with parents) to improve school achievement.[68] While there was a wide variation in how effective these interventions were, a good preschool education and intensive tutoring in schools for disadvantaged children seemed to work best. Some children have a higher chance of falling behind grade level and then getting totally lost; preparing them ahead of time in preschool, and then being ready to identify and address any major gaps in their learning before they become too large, stops it from happening. This is entirely consistent with what we have found in our own work in developing countries.[69]

There is also evidence that short-term gains in school outcomes translate into long-term differences in opportunities. For example, an RCT in Tennessee that cut class sizes from 20–25 to 12–17 led to an increase in test scores in the short run and a higher chance of going to college later on. Students assigned to small classes had better lives later on, as measured by home ownership, their savings, their marital status, and the neighborhood they lived in.[70] High-dosage tutoring and small class sizes require staff, which would provide employment as well as helping kids throughout their school career.

The constraint in the United States comes from the local funding of education. This has the consequence that the places in the most desperate need of good public education have the least money to pay for it. A substantial financial effort could make a big difference. More generally, one consequence of the low levels of government funding in the US is that pre-kindergarten education is not federally subsidized, and as a result only 28 percent of children attend some sort of subsidized pre-K program in the United States,[71] in contrast with France, say, where pre-K is subsidized, attendance has been near universal for years,[72] and it was recently made mandatory.

The original evidence in support of pre-K programs came from some early randomized controlled trials that found large effects of high-quality preschool interventions both in the short and long term, leading Nobel Prize–winner James Heckman to advertise them as the best solution to reduce inequality.[73] However, some of these experiments were tiny, making it possible to ensure the programs were run exactly as they should be.

Two larger RCTs evaluating more realistic "at scale" pre-K programs (the national Head Start program and the Tennessee pre-K experiment) have been more disappointing; both of them found effects in the short run, but the effects on test scores faded or were even reversed after a few years.[74] This has led many to conclude pre-K programs are overrated.

But in fact a key finding of the national Head Start study is that the effectiveness of Head Start seems to vary tremendously with the quality of the program. In particular, programs that run for the full day are more effective than half-day programs, and those that include home visits and other forms of engagement with parents are also more effective. There is also separate evidence from RCTs in both the United States and other countries of the effectiveness of home visits, during which preschool teachers or social workers work with parents to show them how to play with their children.[75]

The general takeaway right now is that there needs to be more research so we know exactly what works in early childhood. But what we do know suggests resources matter; when Head Start was scaled up, many centers tried to reduce costs by cutting services, making them ineffective. Maintaining quality is crucial and has the added advantage of offering a massive expansion of what would surely be attractive jobs for many people, especially if they were adequately paid. These jobs would be both rewarding and impossible to robotize (one cannot really imagine a robot visiting parents at home).

Equally importantly, it seems possible to train someone to be an effective pre-K teacher cheaply and fairly quickly, as long as there are the necessary materials to support them. In India, we worked with Elizabeth Spelke, a psychology professor at Harvard, to create a pre-school math curriculum involving games that build on the intuitive knowledge of mathematics to prepare those who have not yet learned to read or write or even count for primary school. This was evaluated in an RCT in several hundred preschools in the slums of Delhi.[76] Liz was initially horrified by the conditions in Delhi—the tiny porches overcrowded with students of various ages and the teachers' low level of training, many of whom had barely completed high school. It was a far cry from the conditions in her lab at Harvard. But it turns out those teachers, with one week's worth of training and good materials, were able to sustain the slum children's attention, who played math games for several weeks, progressing through the games fast and with gusto, learning a good deal of math in the process.

Inadequate access to childcare is also one of the most severe disadvantages faced by both married and single low-income women in the United States. The lack of subsidized high-quality full-day care means they either do not work (since childcare often costs almost as much as they would make) or have to take the best available job close to family (close to their mothers, in particular) to get help with childcare. Women bear a substantial "child penalty" in the labor market, which is responsible for a large fraction of the remaining gender gap in earnings in advanced economies.[77] Even in progressive Denmark, while there is almost no difference in the earnings of men and women before childbirth, the arrival of a child creates a gender gap in earnings of around 20 percent in the long run. Women start falling behind men in terms of their occupational rank and their probability of becoming managers right after the birth of their first child. Moreover, new mothers switch jobs to join companies that are more "family friendly," as measured by the share of women with young children in the firm's workforce. About 13 percent permanently drop out of the labor force.[78] Expanding highly subsidized quality whole-day care is one very effective way to raise incomes among low-income women by, quite simply, making work pay.

Elder care is another area with tremendous scope for expansion, since the United States has very little in-home care of the elderly and very few publicly funded old-people's homes. Denmark and Sweden, in contrast, spend 2 percent of GDP on elder care.[79] A centralized e-health database where patient records are stored electronically helps hospitals and local authorities collaborate. All eighty-year-olds (not just the poor) are entitled to home visits and home help, and all widowed over-sixty-fives are monitored to see if they need help. Older people also get money for necessary improvements to make their homes safer. Those who need continuous care usually end up in publicly run nursing homes, paid for out of the public pension they are entitled to.

Working with the elderly can be challenging, and in the United States these jobs pay very little; in other words, they are not very attractive. But that again could change. We need to provide the money to hire enough people, train them adequately, ensure they have enough time to spend with each person, and pay them well enough to make them proud of the work they do.

HELP MOVING

Given the important role neighborhoods play, both for finding good jobs and for raising children, helping people to move is another important policy.

In the United States, scaling up Moving to Opportunity for the entire nation (making it possible for everyone to move to a good neighborhood) is not really possible, but supporting workers to change regions or jobs should be. There are actually several programs aimed at this, but many of them do little more than point workers to jobs and help them with the application process. The experience with these "active labor market" policies is fairly disappointing, both in Europe and the US. Their effects are positive but small, and they come largely at the expense of similar workers who are not helped.[80]

A more ambitious (and expensive) program would give displaced workers automatic access to a much longer period of unemployment insurance. They would have time to train and look for good jobs, and therefore not need to accept the first available low-paid job or go on disability. Such a program would give them access not just to short-term training options, but also to more advanced programs, perhaps in colleges or community colleges, with full scholarships. We need to start thinking of the challenge as not just of finding a job but rather of finding a career. An RCT in the United States recently evaluated three programs that tried to do just this. The core idea was to extend the training of unemployed workers to several months, to develop specialized skills in sectors where workers were in short supply (such as healthcare and computer maintenance), then match the workers with sectors that needed them. The results after two years are very promising. During the second year of the evaluation, after they had completed their training, participants were more likely to be employed, and when employed, in better jobs than comparable workers who did not participate in the programs. Overall, participants earned 29 percent more than nonparticipants.[81]

Importantly, these programs also helped with relocation. For disadvantaged job seekers and workers, they provided help with childcare or transportation or a referral for housing or legal services, either during training or at the beginning of the new job. Such help could be expanded to provide short-term housing, and finding schools and daycare for the children. Housing vouchers, smaller than those provided by Moving to Opportunity, could help make good neighborhoods more affordable.

It may also be important to help companies that need workers to look outside the immediate neighborhood and local referral networks. Most programs seeking to help facilitate the process of pairing workers and jobs focus on the workers. But for an employer the process of finding the right worker is also time consuming and costly. A survey suggests that recruitment costs (vacancy posting, screening, and training new workers) range between 1.5 percent and 11 percent of the yearly wage of a worker. Large companies often have a human resources department, but for small businesses those recruitment costs could be a real barrier. A recent study in France showed recruiting costs are big enough to slow down hiring. Researchers teamed up with the national unemployment agency to offer recruiting assistance to firms. They posted vacancies on behalf of the firm and generated and screened promising job applications; they found that companies offered these services posted more vacancies and hired 9 percent more permanent workers than those that were not.[82] Services like this could allow employers to move beyond the purely informal referral channel to an expanded pool of candidates.

Programs like these might pay for themselves—new skills and better matching between workers and employers are valuable to any economy—but even if they don't, the gains in terms of reducing anxiety and restoring dignity in our society would be profound. For it is not just the unemployed workers who would be touched by such a program, but all those who think their jobs may one day be at risk, or those who know someone who has been affected. Equally importantly, by shifting the narrative of such programs from "you are being bailed out" to "sorry this happened to you, but by acquiring new skills and/ or moving you are helping the economy stay robust" we might alter the sense many blue-collar workers have that they are victims of a war waged by the rest of us against them.

For example, the Obama administration's supposed "war on coal" was seen as a war against the coal *workers*. It may be that coal workers are particularly proud of their specific line of work and believe nothing could replace it, but it is worth remembering that until relatively recently coal workers fought against their employers, not alongside them as they do today. They have precisely the kind of physically dangerous and hazardous jobs most Americans think should be done by machines. The same goes for steelworkers; it must be possible to conceive of jobs less dangerous that carry the same level of pride.

Despite that, when, in March of 2016, Hillary Clinton icily announced that "we are going to put a lot of coal miners and coal companies out of business," coal workers perhaps not unreasonably felt this was callously undercutting their way of life without ever feeling the need to apologize or compensate them for the loss. Clinton immediately followed by talking about the need to take care of the miners, but the "we" opening this sentence clearly framed the debate as an "us" versus "them" issue. That sentence was aired in political ads for months afterward.

In fact, each and every transition can and should be a chance for government to signal its empathy for the workers who have to suffer it. Changing careers and moving are both difficult, but they are also an opportunity for the economy and for individuals to find the best match between talent and occupation. Everyone should be able, just as four out of five Americans do, to find meaning in their jobs. A program for better job transitions would be a universal right. But unlike UBI, which is just a universal right to an income, the program would link to what seems to be an integral part of social identity. We each should have a universal right to a productive life within society.

Many European countries invest much more in their job transition programs than the United States. For the 2 percent of GDP Denmark spends on active labor market policies (training, job finding assistance, etc.), it gets high job-to-job mobility (going straight from one job to another) as well as lots of transitions in and out of employment. The rate of involuntary displacement is similar to that in other OECD countries, but the rate at which displaced workers find a job is much more rapid: three in four displaced workers find a new job within one year. Importantly, the Danish model survived the 2008 crisis and recession, with no large increase in involuntary unemployment at that time. Germany spends 1.45 percent of its GDP on active labor market policies, and this went up to 2.45 percent during the crisis, when unemployment was much higher than usual.[83] In France, on the other hand, notwithstanding claims about how it wants to do more for the unemployed, expenditure on active labor market policies has been stuck at 1 percent of GDP for more than a decade. The corresponding measure for the United States is just 0.11 percent.[84]

In fact, the United States also has its own model it could follow. The Trade Adjustment Assistance program, discussed in chapter 3, provides workers at approved firms money to pay for training and extended unemployment insurance while they get the training. This program is quite effective, and furthermore it did exactly what a program of this type should do: it helped workers in the most disadvantaged places move. Its effect on future earnings was twice as large for workers whose original employer was located in a distressed region. And workers who received TAA assistance were also much more likely to change region and industry.[85] But instead of becoming a template of what could be done to help workers manage various kinds of difficult transitions, the TAA has remained tiny. How could that make sense?

TOGETHER IN DIGNITY

The reluctance to make use of available government programs, even when they work well, may be related to the fact that a majority of Republicans and a substantial fraction of Democrats are against the government starting a universal income program or a national job program to support those who lose their jobs to automation, even though many more are in favor of limiting the right of companies to replace people with robots.[86] Behind this is partly suspicion about the government's motives (they only want to help "those people") and partly exaggerated skepticism about the government's ability to deliver. But there is also something else that even people and organizations on the left share: a suspicion of handouts, of charity without empathy or understanding. In other words, they don't want to be patronized by the government.

When Abhijit was serving on a UN Panel of Eminent Persons to come up with what were to be new millennium development goals, he was often subjected to low-key lobbying by prominent international NGOs with views on what some of those goals should be. This was often a very pleasant way to learn about interesting initiatives, and Abhijit enjoyed the encounters. But the one meeting he remembers most vividly was with an organization called ATD Fourth World.

When he walked into the cavernous room in the EU headquarters where the meeting was held, he immediately noticed it was a very different crowd. No suits, no ties, no high heels; lined faces, scruffy winter jackets, and also an eagerness he associated with college freshmen in their first week. These were people, he was told, who had experienced extreme poverty and were still very poor. They wanted to participate in a conversation about what the poor wanted.

It turned out to be nothing like anything he had ever encountered before. People quickly intervened and talked about their lives and about the nature of poverty and the failings of policy, drawing on their own experiences. Abhijit tried to respond, trying at first to be as delicate as possible when he disagreed. He soon realized he was being patronizing; they were in no way less sophisticated or less able to argue back than he was.

He left with enormous respect for ATD Fourth World, and an understanding of why its slogan is "All Together in Dignity to Overcome

Poverty." It was an organization that put dignity first, if necessary even before basic needs. It had built an internal culture where everyone was taken seriously as a thinking human being, which is what gave the members the confidence Abhijit had not expected.

Travailler et Apprendre Ensemble ("Work and Learn Together"), or TAE, is a small business started by ATD Fourth World to provide people in extreme poverty with permanent jobs. One winter morning, we went to Noisy-le-Grand in the east of Paris to observe one of their team meetings. When we arrived, the group was preparing the schedule for the workweek across their different activities, assigning people to tasks and drawing up their plan on a whiteboard. When they were done with scheduling the work, they started discussing a company event. The atmosphere was relaxed but engaged, problems were discussed with seriousness, and everyone then went off to start their tasks. It could have been the weekly meeting of a small start-up in Silicon Valley.

What was different was the activities they were scheduling (cleaning services, construction, and computer maintenance) and the people around the table. After the meeting, we continued talking to Chantal, Gilles, and Jean-François. Chantal had been a nurse, but after an accident found herself seriously disabled. Unable to work for many years, she ended up homeless. This is when she reached out to ATD for help. ATD gave her housing and directed her to TAE when she was ready to work. She had been working there for ten years when we met her, first on the cleaning team and then on the software team, and had become a leader. She was now contemplating leaving to start a small NGO to help disabled people find work.

Gilles had also worked at TAE for ten years. After a period of severe depression, he found himself incapable of working in a stressful environment. TAE allowed him to work at his own rhythm and he progressively got better.

Jean-François and his wife had lost custody of their son, Florian, who suffered from ADHD, and Jean-Francois himself, who had temper issues, was placed under administrative custody of the state. They reached out to ATD, which was allowed to take Florian on a supervised basis in one of their centers, where he learned about TAE.

The CEO, Didier, had been the CEO of a "traditional" firm before joining TAE. Pierre-Antoine, his aide, had been a social worker in a job placement office. Pierre-Antoine explained the limits of the traditional job-placement model. When people have one difficulty, it is possible to help. When people accumulate problems, they don't conform to what regular jobs expect from them, and they often quickly give up or get rejected. What is different at TAE is that the business is designed around them.

The key, according to what Bruno Tardieu, an ATD leader who accompanied us to the meeting, told us, is that "all their lives people have given them things. No one has even asked them to contribute." In TAE, they are asked to contribute. They make decisions together, train each other, eat together every day, and take care of each other. When someone is missing, they are checked on. When someone needs time to deal with a personal crisis, they receive help getting it.

The spirit of TAE reflects well that of its mother organization. ATD Fourth World was founded by Joseph Wresinski, a Catholic priest, in France in the 1950s, out of the conviction that extreme poverty is not the result of the inferiority or inadequacy of a group of people, but of systematic exclusion. Exclusion and misunderstanding build on each other. The extreme poor are robbed of their dignity and their agency. They are made to understand that they should be grateful for help, even when they don't particularly want it. Robbed of their dignity, they easily become suspicious, and this suspicion is taken for ingratitude and obstinacy, which further deepens the trap in which they are stuck.[87]

What does a small business in France, employing less than a dozen ultra poor people and struggling to get by, teach us about social policy more generally?

First, given the right conditions, *everyone* can hold a job and be productive. This faith gave rise to a French experiment trying to create "zero long-term unemployed territories" where the government and civil society organizations commit to finding a job for everyone within a short period of time. To get there, the government is offering a subsidy of up to €18,000 per employee to any organization that agrees to hire *any* long-term unemployed who wants a job. At the same time,

NGOs are being engaged to find the long-term unemployed (including those who face multiple difficulties: mental or physical handicaps, prior convictions, etc.), match them to jobs, and offer them the assistance they need to be able to take the jobs.

Second, work is not necessarily what follows *after* all the other problems have been solved and people are "ready," but is part of the recovery process itself. Jean-François was able to take back custody of his son after he found a job and is inspired by the pride his son takes in him now that he is working.

Very far from Noisy-le-Grand, in Bangladesh, the enormous NGO BRAC arrived at the same conclusion. They noticed that the poorest of the poor in the villages where they worked were excluded (or self-excluded) from many of their programs. To solve this problem, they came up with the idea of the "graduation approach." After identifying the poorest people in the village with the help of the community, BRAC workers provided them with a productive asset (such as a pair of cows or a few goats) and for eighteen months, supported them emotionally, socially, and financially, and trained them to make best use of their assets. RCTs of this program in seven countries found a large impact.[88] In India, we have been able to follow the evaluation sample for ten years. Despite economic progress in the area, which lifted all households, we still find very large and persistent differences in how the beneficiaries live compared to the comparison group that did not get the program. They consume more, have more assets, and are healthier and happier; they have "graduated" from being the outliers to being the "normal poor."[89] This is quite different from the long-term follow-ups of pure cash transfer programs, which have so far been disappointing.[90] Putting these families squarely on track toward productive work required more than money. It required treating them as human beings with a respect they were not used to, recognizing both their potential and the damage done to them by years of deprivation.

The deep disregard for the human dignity of the poor is endemic in the social protection system. A particularly heart-wrenching instance is what happened to Chantal, one of the TAE employees we met. When Chantal and her husband, who are both disabled, asked for assistance at home with their four children, two of whom are also disabled, they were offered temporary placement for their children in foster care.

This "temporary" solution ended up lasting ten years, during which they were only allowed to see their children for one weekly supervised visit. The suspicion that poor parents are incapable of taking care of their children is widespread. Until the 1980s, tens of thousands of poor Swiss children were removed from their families and placed on farms. In 2012, the government of Switzerland formally apologized for the separations. This discrimination is in effect a form of racism against the poor, a reminder of the policy in Canada where scores of indigenous children were sent to boarding school and forbidden to speak their language, to ease their "assimilation" in mainstream Canadian culture.

A social protection system that treats anyone with this kind of callousness becomes punitive, and people will go to great lengths to avoid having anything to do with it. Make no mistake. This does not just affect some small sliver of the extreme poor that's very different from the rest of us. When part of the social system conveys punishment and humiliation, it is the entire society that recoils from it. The last thing a worker wants when he has just lost his job is to be treated like "those people."

STARTING FROM RESPECT

A different model is possible. We once drove to the *mission locale* office in the city of Sénart near Paris to observe a meeting of "young creators." The mission locale is a one-stop shop to serve all the needs (medical, social, employment) of disadvantaged youth. This program of young creators is for any young man or woman who is currently unemployed and wants to start a small business. Sitting around the table, the young people explained what they wanted to do. We heard about plans to start a gym, a beauty parlor, and an organic beauty products shop. We then asked them why they wanted to have their own businesses. Strikingly, none of them spoke about money. One after the other, they spoke about dignity, self-respect, and autonomy.

The approach of the young creators program is very different from the typical approach in unemployment agencies. In the traditional approach, the goal of the counselor is to quickly identify something

the youths, mostly high school dropouts or vocational school graduates, could do, usually some sort of training program, and direct them
there. The presumption is that the counselor knows what is good for
each person (the fashion these days is to do it with the help of some
machine-learning algorithm). The youths then have to conform or lose
their benefits.

Didier Dugast, who conceived the creators program, told us that
more often than not, the traditional approach fails entirely. The young
people who arrive have been told, all their lives, what to do. They
have also been told, in school and perhaps at home, that they are not
good enough. They arrive bruised and wounded, with extremely low
self-esteem (we verified this in our quantitative survey[91]), which often
translates into an instinctive suspicion of everything offered to them,
and a tendency to resist suggestions.

The idea behind the young creators program is to start with the
project the young man or woman proposes, and to take it very seriously. The first interview invites them to explain what they want to
do, why they want to do it, and where it fits into their personal life and
plans. We sat in on three interviews: a young woman who wanted to
start a pharmacy for Chinese medicine, a young man who wanted to
sell his graphic designs through an online shop, and a young woman
who wanted to set up a home care business for elderly people. In all
cases, these first interviews were long (about an hour each) and the
caseworker took time to understand the project, without ever obviously judging it. More in-depth interviews followed, as well as a few
group workshops. In the course of these conversations, the caseworker
started to focus on convincing the youths that they were in control of
their destinies and had what it took to succeed. At the same time, it
was also made clear there was more than one way to succeed; perhaps
the aspiring Chinese pharmacist could start training to become a nurse
or a paramedic.

We were involved in the RCT of this project. Nine hundred young
people who had applied for the program were assigned either to this
program or to the regular services. We found that those in the program
were more likely to be employed and earned more. The effects were
much larger for those who were the most disadvantaged to start with.
What was extremely surprising at first glance was that the program

actually *reduces* the probability of being self-employed, even though it begins with the applicant's idea for starting a business. The main value of the program (and its explicit philosophy) is that the self-employment project is a starting point, but not necessarily the end. The program is essentially a form of therapy aimed at restoring confidence. What matters is finding stable, rewarding occupations within six months to a year. In contrast, a competing program we also evaluated that simply cherry-picked the most promising candidates for a self-employment program and then focused on bringing their initial project idea to fruition had no effect whatsoever, mostly because it selected the type of people likely to succeed regardless of the help they got.[92]

In our view, the deep respect for the dignity of the young people is what made the Sénart young creators initiative work. Many of these young people had never experienced being taken seriously by anyone in an official position (teachers, bureaucrats, law enforcement officials). As we saw earlier, research in education shows that children quickly internalize their place in the pecking order, and teachers reinforce it. Teachers told that some children are smarter than others (even though they were simply chosen randomly) treat them differently, so that these children in fact do better.[93] In France, there was a randomized evaluation of an Énergie Jeunes intervention inspired by Angela Duckworth's idea of "grit."[94] It showed inspirational videos to students, to encourage them to think of themselves as strong and powerful, and this had positive effects on their regular attendance in school, their attitudes in class, and even their grades. The effect did not seem to be rooted in children's perceptions of their own grit or seriousness (if anything, children gave themselves low scores on those). It was more that the students became much more optimistic about the chances of success for someone like themselves.[95] ATD Fourth World, in collaboration with l'Institut Supérieur Maria Montessori in Paris, is attempting to break this vicious cycle of low expectations as early as possible. In the emergency housing projects it runs, ATD runs high-quality Montessori schools as shiny and well operated as the few private Montessori schools catering to upper classes in the center of Paris.

The same shift in attitude, from patronizing to respectful, was built into the program Becoming a Man, in inner-city Chicago. The program seeks to temper violence among young people. But instead of telling them it is wrong to be violent, it starts with recognizing that for teens in disadvantaged neighborhoods violence may be the norm, so being aggressive or even fighting may be necessary to avoid developing a reputation as a victim. Someone in this sort of neighborhood environment could develop a tendency to reflexively push back with violence whenever challenged. So instead of telling participants it was not the right thing to do, or punishing them when they did so, Becoming a Man asked kids from poor neighborhoods to participate in a series of activities, inspired by cognitive behavioral therapy, to help them identify when fighting was the appropriate reaction and when it might not be. Essentially, they were taught to just take a minute to gauge the environment and assess the proper course of action. Participation in the program reduced the total number of arrests during the intervention period by about a third, reduced violent crime arrests by half, and increased graduation rates by around 15 percent.[96]

What is common among a drought-affected farmer in India, a youth in Chicago's South Side, and a fifty-something white man who was just laid off? While they may *have* problems, they are not *the* problem. They are entitled to be seen for who they are and to not be defined by the difficulties besieging them. Time and again, we have seen in our travels in developing countries that hope is the fuel that makes people go. Defining people by their problems is turning circumstance into essence. It denies hope. A natural response is then to wrap oneself into this identity, with treacherous consequences for society at large.

The goal of social policy, in these times of change and anxiety, is to help people absorb the shocks that affect them without allowing those shocks to affect their sense of themselves. Unfortunately, this is not the system we have inherited. Our social protection still has its Victorian overlay, and all too many politicians do not try to hide their contempt for the poor and disadvantaged. Even with a shift in attitude, social protection will require a profound rethinking and an injection of lots of imagination. We have given some clues in this chapter on how to get there, but we clearly don't have all the solutions, and suspect nobody else does either. We have much more to learn. But as long as we understand what the goal is, we can win.

GOOD AND BAD
ECONOMICS

... In succession
Houses rise and fall, crumble, are extended,
Are removed, destroyed, restored, or in their place
Is an open field, or a factory, or a by-pass.
Old stone to new building, old timber to new fires,
Old fires to ashes, and ashes to the earth ...
—T. S. Eliot, *East Coker*

ECONOMICS IMAGINES A world of irrepressible dynamism. People get inspired, change jobs, turn from making machines to making music, quit and decide to wander the world. New businesses get born, rise, fail, and die, are replaced by timelier and more brilliant ideas. Productivity grows in staccato leaps, nations grow richer. What was made in Manchester mills moves to Mumbai factories and then to Myanmar and maybe, one day, to Mombasa or Mogadishu. Manchester is reborn as Manchester digital, Mumbai turns its mills into up-market housing and shopping malls, where those who work in finance spend their newly fattened paychecks. Opportunities are everywhere, waiting to be discovered and grabbed by those who need them.

As economists who study poor countries we have long known that things do not quite work that way, at least in the countries we have worked in and spend our time. The Bangladeshi would-be-migrant starves in his village with his family rather than brave the uncertainties of seeking a job in the city. The Ghanaian job seeker sits at home wondering when the opportunity he believed his education promised

323

him will drop into his empty lap. Trade shuts down factories in the Southern Cone of South America, but few new businesses arrive to take their place. Change seems all too often to benefit other people, unseen people, unreachable people. Those who lost their jobs in the Mumbai mills will not get to eat in those glittering eateries. Perhaps their children will get jobs serving—jobs they for the most part do not want.

What we realized over the last few years is that this is also the story of many places in the developed world. All economies are sticky. There are of course important differences. Small businesses in the United States grow much faster than those in India or Mexico, and those that fail to grow are shut down, forcing their owners to move on. Those in India and, to a lesser extent in Mexico, seem stuck in their place in time, neither growing to be the next Walmart nor exiting into something else more promising.[1] Yet this US dynamism conceals enormous geographical variations. Businesses shut down in Boise and show up in booming Seattle, but the workers who lost their jobs cannot afford to move to Seattle. Nor do they want to anyway, since so much of what they value—their friends and their families, their memories and their loyalties—will have to stay behind. But as the good jobs vanish and the local economy goes into a tailspin, the choices look more and more dire and anger mounts. This is what is happening in Eastern Germany, much of France outside the big cities, the Brexit heartland, and in the red states of the US, but also in large pockets of Brazil and Mexico. The rich and the talented step nimbly into the glittering pockets of economic success, but all too many of the rest have to hang back. This is the world that produced Donald Trump, Jair Bolsonaro, and Brexit and will produce many more disasters unless we do something about it.

And yet as development economists we are also keenly aware that the most remarkable fact about the last forty years is the pace of change, good and bad. The fall of communism, the rise of China, the halving and then halving again of world poverty, the explosion of inequality, the upsurge and downswing in HIV, the huge drop in infant mortality, the spread of the personal computer and the cell phone, Amazon and Alibaba, Facebook and Twitter, the Arab Spring, the spread of authoritarian nationalism and looming environmental catastrophes— we have seen them all in the last four decades. In the late 1970s, when

Abhijit was taking baby steps toward becoming an economist, the Soviet Union still commanded respect, India was figuring out how to
be more like it, the extreme left worshipped China, the Chinese worshipped Mao, Reagan and Thatcher were just beginning their assault
on the modern welfare state, and 40 percent of the world population
was in dire poverty. A lot has changed since then. A lot of it for the
better.

Not all the change was willed. Some good ideas just happened to
catch fire, some bad ones as well. Some of the change was accidental,
some the unanticipated consequences of something else. For example,
part of the increase in inequality was the flip side of the sticky economy, which makes it all the more lucrative to be in the right place at
the right time. In turn, the increase in inequality funded a construction
boom that created jobs for the unskilled in the cities of the developing
world, paving the way to the reduction in poverty.

But it would be wrong to underestimate just how much of the
change was driven by policy—the opening up of China and India to
private enterprise and trade, the slashing of taxes on the rich in the
UK, the US, and their imitators, the global cooperation to fight preventable deaths, the prioritization of growth over the environment,
the encouragement of internal migration through improvements in
connectivity or its discouragement through failure to invest in livable
urban spaces, the decline of the welfare state but also the recent rein-
vention of social transfers in the developing world, and so on. Policy is
powerful. Governments have the power to do enormous good but also
important damage, and so do large private and bilateral donors.

A lot of that policy stood on the shoulders of good and bad economics (and the social sciences more generally). Social scientists were
writing about the mad ambition of Soviet-style dirigisme, the need to
liberate the entrepreneurial genie in countries like India and China,
the potential for environmental catastrophe, and the extraordinary
power of network connections a long time before these became obvious to the wider world. Smart philanthropists were practicing
good social science when they pushed for giving away antiretroviral
medicines to HIV patients in the developing world to secure much
more widespread testing and save millions of lives. Good economics
prevailed over ignorance and ideology to ensure insecticide-treated

bed nets were given away rather than sold in Africa, thereby cutting childhood malaria deaths by more than half. Bad economics underpinned the grand giveaways to the rich and the squeezing of welfare programs, sold the idea that the state is impotent and corrupt and the poor are lazy, and paved the way to the current stalemate of exploding inequality and angry inertia. Blinkered economics told us trade is good for everyone, and faster growth is everywhere. It is just a matter of trying harder and, moreover, worth all the pain it might take. Blind economics missed the explosion in inequality all over the world, the increasing social fragmentation that came with it, and the impending environmental disaster, delaying action, perhaps irrevocably.

As John Maynard Keynes, who transformed macroeconomic policy with his ideas, wrote: "Practical men who believe themselves to be quite exempt from any intellectual influence, are usually the slaves of some defunct economist. Madmen in authority, who hear voices in the air, are distilling their frenzy from some academic scribbler of a few years back." Ideas are powerful. Ideas drive change. Good economics alone cannot save us. But without it, we are doomed to repeat the mistakes of yesterday. Ignorance, intuitions, ideology, and inertia combine to give us answers that look plausible, promise much, and predictably betray us. As history, alas, demonstrates over and over, the ideas that carry the day in the end can be good or bad. We know the idea that remaining open to migration will inevitably destroy our societies looks like it is winning these days, despite all evidence to the contrary. The only recourse we have against bad ideas is to be vigilant, resist the seduction of the "obvious," be skeptical of promised miracles, question the evidence, be patient with complexity and honest about what we know and what we can know. Without that vigilance, conversations about multifaceted problems turn into slogans and caricatures and policy analysis gets replaced by quack remedies.

The call to action is not just for academic economists—it is for all of us who want a better, saner, more humane world. Economics is too important to be left to economists.

NOTES

PREFACE TO THE PAPERBACK EDITION

1. Zidong An, João Tovar Jalles, and Prakash Loungani, "How Well Do Economists Forecast Recessions?," IMF working paper no. 18/39, March 5, 2018, www.imf.org/en/Publications/WP/Issues/2018/03/05/How-Well-Do -Economists-Forecast-Recessions-45672.

2. "Grippes: Un virus sous surveillance," *C'est pas sorcier*, May 22, 2013, www.youtube.com/watch?v=k9U-vSZnOyQ.

3. Lawrence Wright, "The Plague Year," *New Yorker*, December 28, 2020, www.newyorker.com/magazine/2021/01/04/the-plague-year.

4. IMF fiscal monitor, chapter 1, October 2020, www.imf.org/-/media /Files/Publications/fiscal-monitor/2020/October/English/ch1.ashx.

5. "Kerala: COVID-19 Battle," GoK Dashboard, accessed March 22, 2021, https://dashboard.kerala.gov.in/index.php.

6. Thomas J. Bollyky, Sawyer Crosby, and Samantha Kiernan, "Fighting a Pandemic Requires Trust," *Foreign Affairs*, October 23, 2020, www.foreignaffairs .com/articles/united-states/2020-10-23/coronavirus-fighting-requires-trust.

7. Qing Han et al., "Trust in Government and Its Associations with Health Behaviour and Prosocial Behaviour During the COVID-19 Pandemic," PsyArXiv, June 29, 2020, https://psyarxiv.com/p5gns/.

8. Noah Smith "No, Pandemic UI Did Not Kill Jobs," *Noahpinion*, December 8, 2020, https://noahpinion.substack.com/p/no-pandemic-ui-didnt -kill-jobs.

9. Corina Boar and Simon Mongey, "Dynamic Trade-Offs and Labor Supply Under the CARES Act," NBER Working Paper No. 27727, August 2020, www.nber.org/papers/w27727.

10. "Economists vs. Common Sense," *Wall Street Journal*, August 2, 2020, www.wsj.com/articles/economists-vs-common-sense-11596398926.

11. Anne Case and Angus Deaton, *Deaths of Despair and the Future of Capitalism* (Princeton, NJ: Princeton University Press, 2020).

12. Ellora Derenoncourt and Claire Montialoux, "Minimum Wages and Racial Inequality," *Quarterly Journal of Economics* 136, no. 1 (February 2021): 169–228.

13. Carlos Torres et al., "Comparison of Knowledge and Behavior Following Physician-Delivered COVID-19 Public Health Messages and Messages Acknowledging Racial Inequity: A Randomized Clinical Trial" (unpublished manuscript, 2021).

CHAPTER 1. MEGA: MAKE ECONOMICS GREAT AGAIN

1. Amber Phillips, "Is Split-Ticket Voting Officially Dead?," *Washington Post,* 2017, https://www.washingtonpost.com/news/the-fix/wp/2016/11/17/is-split-ticket-voting-officially-dead/?utm_term=.6b57fc114762.

2. "8. Partisan Animosity, Personal Politics, Views of Trump," Pew Research Center, 2017, https://www.people-press.org/2017/10/05/8-partisan-animosity-personal-politics-views-of-trump/.

3. "Poll: Majority of Democrats Think Republicans Are 'Racist,' 'Bigoted' or 'Sexist,'" *Axios,* 2017, https://www.countable.us/articles/14975-poll-majority-democrats-think-republicans-racist-bigoted-sexist.

4. Stephen Hawkins, Daniel Yudkin, Míriam Juan-Torres, and Tim Dixon, "Hidden Tribes: A Study of America's Polarized Landscape," *More in Common,* 2018, https://www.moreincommon.com/hidden-tribes.

5. Charles Dickens, *Hard Times*, *Household Words* weekly journal, London, 1854.

6. Matthew Smith, "Leave Voters Are Less Likely to Trust Any Experts—Even Weather Forecasters," YouGov, 2017, https://yougov.co.uk/topics/politics/articles-reports/2017/02/17/leave-voters-are-less-likely-trust-any-experts-eve.

7. This survey was done in collaboration with Stefanie Stantcheva and is described in Abhijit Banerjee, Esther Duflo, and Stefanie Stantcheva, "Me and Everyone Else: Do People Think Like Economists?," MIMEO, Massachusetts Institute of Technology, 2019.

8. "Steel and Aluminum Tariffs," Chicago Booth, IGM Forum, 2018, http://www.igmchicago.org/surveys/steel-and-aluminum-tariffs.

9. "Refugees in Germany," Chicago Booth, IGM Forum, 2017, http://www.igmchicago.org/surveys/refugees-in-germany (the answers are normalized by the number of people who give an opinion).

10. "Robots and Artificial Intelligence," Chicago Booth, IGM Forum, 2017, http://www.igmchicago.org/surveys/robots-and-artificial-intelligence.

11. Paola Sapienza and Luigi Zingales, "Economic Experts versus Average Americans," *American Economic Review* 103, no. 10 (2013): 636–42, https://doi.org/10.1257/aer.103.3.636.

12. "A Mean Feat," *Economist,* January 9, 2016, https://www.economist.com/finance-and-economics/2016/01/09/a-mean-feat.

13. Siddhartha Mukherjee, *The Emperor of All Maladies: A Biography of Cancer* (New York: Scribner, 2010).

CHAPTER 2. FROM THE MOUTH OF THE SHARK

1. United Nations International migration report highlight, accessed June 1, 2017, https://www.un.org/en/development/desa/population/migration/publications/migrationreport/docs/MigrationReport2017_Highlights.pdf; Mathias Czaika and Hein de Haas, "The Globalization of Migration: Has the World Become More Migratory?," *International Migration Review* 48, no. 2 (2014): 283–323.

2. "EU Migrant Crisis: Facts and Figures," News: European Parliament, June 30, 2017, accessed April 21, 2019, http://www.europarl.europa.eu/news/en/headlines/society/20170629STO78630/eu-migrant-crisis-facts-and-figures.

3. Alberto Alesina, Armando Miano, and Stefanie Stantcheva, "Immigration and Redistribution," NBER Working Paper 24733, 2018.

4. Oscar Barrera Rodriguez, Sergei M. Guriev, Emeric Henry, and Ekaterina Zhuravskaya, "Facts, Alternative Facts, and Fact-Checking in Times of Post-Truth Politics," *SSRN Electronic Journal* (2017), https://dx.doi.org/10.2139/ssrn.3004631.

5. Alesina, Miano, and Stantcheva, "Immigration and Redistribution."

6. Rodriguez, Guriev, Henry, and Zhuravskaya, "Facts, Alternative Facts, and Fact-Checking in Times of Post-Truth Politics."

7. Warsan Shire, "Home," accessed June 5, 2019, https://www.seekersguidance.org/articles/social-issues/home-warsan-shire/.

8. Maheshwor Shrestha, "Push and Pull: A Study of International Migration from Nepal," Policy Research Working Paper WPS 7965 (Washington, DC: World Bank Group, 2017), http://documents.worldbank.org/curated/en/318581486560991532/Push-and-pull-a-study-of-international-migration-from-Nepal.

9. *Aparajito*, directed by Satyajit Ray, 1956, Merchant Ivory Productions.

10. Using data from sixty-five countries, Alwyn Young finds that urban dwellers consume 52 percent more than rural dwellers. Alwyn Young, "Inequality, the Urban-Rural Gap, and Migration," *Quarterly Journal of Economics* 128, no. 4 (2013): 1727–85.

11. Abhijit Banerjee, Nils Enevoldsen, Rohini Pande, and Michael Walton, "Information as an Incentive: Experimental Evidence from Delhi," MIMEO, Harvard, accessed April 21, 2019, https://scholar.harvard.edu/files/rpande/files/delhivoter_shared-14.pdf.

12. Lois Labrianidis and Manolis Pratsinakis, "Greece's New Emigration at Times of Crisis," LSE Hellenic Observatory GreeSE Paper 99, 2016.

13. John Gibson, David McKenzie, Halahingano Rohorua, and Steven Stillman, "The Long-Term Impacts of International Migration: Evidence from a Lottery," *World Bank Economic Review* 32, no. 1 (February 2018): 127–47.

14. Michael Clemens, Claudio Montenegro, and Lant Pritchett, "The Place Premium: Wage Differences for Identical Workers Across the U.S. Border," Center for Global Development Working Paper 148, 2009.

15. Emi Nakamura, Jósef Sigurdsson, and Jón Steinsson, "The Gift of Moving: Intergenerational Consequences of a Mobility Shock," NBER Working Paper 22392, 2017, revised January 2019, DOI: 10.3386/w22392.

16. Ibid.

17. Matti Sarvimäki, Roope Uusitalo, and Markus Jäntti, "Habit Formation and the Misallocation of Labor: Evidence from Forced Migrations," 2019, https://ssrn.com/abstract=3361356 or http://dx.doi.org/10.2139/ssrn.3361356.

18. Gharad Bryan, Shyamal Chowdhury, and Ahmed Mushfiq Mobarak, "Underinvestment in a Profitable Technology: The Case of Seasonal Migration in Bangladesh," *Econometrica* 82, no. 5 (2014): 1671–1748.

19. David Card, "The Impact of the Mariel Boatlift on the Miami Labor Market," *Industrial and Labor Relations Review* 43, no. 2 (1990): 245–57.

20. George J. Borjas, "The Wage Impact of the *Marielitos*: A Reappraisal," *Industrial and Labor Relations Review* 70, no. 5 (February 13, 2017): 1077–1110.

21. Giovanni Peri and Vasil Yasenov, "The Labor Market Effects of a Refugee Wave: Synthetic Control Method Meets the Mariel Boatlift," *Journal of Human Resources* 54, no. 2 (January 2018): 267–309.

22. Ibid.

23. George J. Borjas, "Still More on Mariel: The Role of Race," NBER Working Paper 23504, 2017.

24. Jennifer Hunt, "The Impact of the 1962 Repatriates from Algeria on the French Labor Market," *Industrial and Labor Relations Review* 45, no. 3 (April 1992): 556–72.

25. Rachel M. Friedberg, "The Impact of Mass Migration on the Israeli Labor Market," *Quarterly Journal of Economics* 116, no. 4 (November 2001): 1373–1408.

26. Marco Tabellini, "Gifts of the Immigrants, Woes of the Natives: Lessons from the Age of Mass Migration," HBS Working Paper 19-005, 2018.

27. Mette Foged and Giovanni Peri, "Immigrants' Effect on Native Workers: New Analysis on Longitudinal Data," *American Economic Journal: Applied Economics* 8, no. 2 (2016): 1–34.

28. *The Economic and Fiscal Consequences of Immigration,* National Academies of Sciences, Engineering, and Medicine (Washington, DC: National Academies Press, 2017), https://doi.org/10.17226/23550.

29. Christian Dustmann, Uta Schönberg, and Jan Stuhler, "Labor Supply Shocks, Native Wages, and the Adjustment of Local Employment," *Quarterly Journal of Economics* 132, no. 1 (February 2017): 435–83.

30. Michael A. Clemens, Ethan G. Lewis, and Hannah M. Postel, "Immigration Restrictions as Active Labor Market Policy: Evidence from the Mexican Bracero Exclusion," *American Economic Review* 108, no. 6 (June 2018): 1468–87.

31. Foged and Peri, "Immigrants' Effect on Native Workers."

32. Patricia Cortés, "The Effect of Low-Skilled Immigration on US Prices: Evidence from CPI Data," *Journal of Political Economy* 116, no. 3 (2008): 381–422.

33. Patricia Cortés and José Tessada, "Low-Skilled Immigration and the Labor Supply of Highly Skilled Women," *American Economic Journal: Applied Economics* 3, no. 3 (July 2011): 88–123.

34. Emma Lazarus, "The New Colossus," in *Emma Lazarus: Selected Poems*, ed. John Hollander (New York: Library of America, 2005), 58.

35. Ran Abramitzky, Leah Platt Boustan, and Katherine Eriksson, "Europe's Tired, Poor, Huddled Masses: Self-Selection and Economic Outcomes in the Age of Mass Migration," *American Economic Review* 102, no. 5 (2012): 1832–56.

36. "Immigrant Founders of the 2017 Fortune 500," Center for American Entrepreneurship, 2017, http://startupsusa.org/fortune500/.

37. Nakamura, Sigurdsson, and Steinsson, "The Gift of Moving."

38. Jie Bai, "Melons as Lemons: Asymmetric Information, Consumer Learning, and Quality Provision," working paper, 2018, accessed June 19, 2019, https://drive.google.com/file/d/0B52sohAPtnAWYVhBYm11cDBrSmM/view.

39. "For the conversion of his money into capital, therefore, the owner of money must meet in the market with the free labourer, free in the double sense, that as a free man he can dispose of his labour-power as his own commodity, and that on the other hand he has no other commodity for sale, is

short of everything necessary for the realisation of his labour-power." From Karl Marx, *Das Kapital* (Hamburg: Verlag von Otto Meissner, 1867).

40. Girum Abebe, Stefano Caria, and Esteban Ortiz-Ospina, "The Selection of Talent: Experimental and Structural Evidence from Ethiopia," working paper, 2018.

41. Christopher Blattman and Stefan Dercon, "The Impacts of Industrial and Entrepreneurial Work on Income and Health: Experimental Evidence from Ethiopia," *American Economic Journal: Applied Economics* 10, no. 3 (July 2018): 1–38.

42. Girum Abebe, Stefano Caria, Marcel Fafchamps, Paolo Falco, Simon Franklin, and Simon Quinn, "Anonymity or Distance? Job Search and Labour Market Exclusion in a Growing African City," CSAE Working Paper WPS/2016-10-2, 2018.

43. Stefano Caria, "Choosing Connections. Experimental Evidence from a Link-Formation Experiment in Urban Ethiopia," working paper, 2015; Pieter Serneels, "The Nature of Unemployment Among Young Men in Urban Ethiopia," *Review of Development Economics* 11, no. 1 (2007): 170–86.

44. Carl Shapiro and Joseph E. Stiglitz, "Equilibrium Unemployment as a Worker Discipline Device," *American Economic Review* 74, no. 3 (June 1984): 433–44.

45. Emily Breza, Supreet Kaur, and Yogita Shamdasani, "The Morale Effects of Pay Inequality," *Quarterly Journal of Economics* 133, no. 2 (2018): 611–63.

46. Dustmann, Schönberg, and Stuhler, "Labor Supply Shocks, Native Wages, and the Adjustment of Local Employment."

47. Patricia Cortés and Jessica Pan, "Foreign Nurse Importation and Native Nurse Displacement," *Journal of Health Economics* 37 (2017): 164–80.

48. Kaivan Munshi, "Networks in the Modern Economy: Mexican Migrants in the U.S. Labor Market," *Quarterly Journal of Economics* 118, no. 2 (2003): 549–99.

49. Lori Beaman, "Social Networks and the Dynamics of Labor Market Outcomes: Evidence from Refugees Resettled in the U.S.," *Review of Economic Studies* 79, no. 1 (January 2012): 128–61.

50. George Akerlof, "The Market for 'Lemons': Quality Uncertainty and the Market Mechanism," *Quarterly Journal of Economics* 84, no. 3 (1970): 488–500.

51. Referees and editors apparently found Akerlof's paper difficult to understand. Essentially, the kind of circular reasoning that explains the unraveling requires a proper mathematical exposition to make sure it is watertight,

and in 1970 this particular style of mathematical argumentation was unfamiliar to most economists. Therefore, it took some time before a journal ventured to publish it. But once published, it became an instant classic and has remained one of the most influential papers of all time. The kind of mathematics it used, which is an application of the branch of applied math called "game theory," is now taught to economics undergraduates.

52. Banerjee, Enevoldsen, Pande, and Walton, "Information as an Incentive."

53. World air quality report, AirVisual, 2018, accessed April 21, 2019, https://www.airvisual.com/world-most-polluted-cities.

54. Abhijit Banerjee and Esther Duflo, "The Economic Lives of the Poor," *Journal of Economic Perspectives* 21, no. 1 (2007): 141–68.

55. Global Infrastructure Hub, *Global Infrastructure Outlook*, Oxford Economics, 2017.

56. Edward Glaeser, *Triumph of the City: How Our Greatest Invention Makes Us Richer, Smarter, Greener, Healthier, and Happier* (London: Macmillan, 2011).

57. Jan K. Brueckner, Shihe Fu Yizhen Gu, and Junfu Zhang, "Measuring the Stringency of Land Use Regulation: The Case of China's Building Height Limits," *Review of Economics and Statistics* 99, no. 4 (2017) 663–77.

58. Abhijit Banerjee and Esther Duflo, "Barefoot Hedge-Fund Managers," *Poor Economics* (New York: PublicAffairs, 2011).

59. W. Arthur Lewis, "Economic Development with Unlimited Supplies of Labour," *Manchester School* 22, no. 2 (1954): 139–91.

60. Robert Jensen and Nolan H. Miller, "Keepin' 'Em Down on the Farm: Migration and Strategic Investment in Children's Schooling," NBER Working Paper 23122, 2017.

61. Robert Jensen, "Do Labor Market Opportunities Affect Young Women's Work and Family Decisions? Experimental Evidence from India," *Quarterly Journal of Economics* 127, no. 2 (2012): 753–92.

62. Bryan, Chowdhury, and Mobarak, "Underinvestment in a Profitable Technology."

63. Maheshwor Shrestha, "Get Rich or Die Tryin': Perceived Earnings, Perceived Mortality Rate, and the Value of a Statistical Life of Potential Work-Migrants from Nepal," World Bank Policy Research Working Paper 7945, 2017.

64. Maheshwor Shrestha, "Death Scares: How Potential Work-Migrants Infer Mortality Rates from Migrant Deaths," World Bank Policy Research Working Paper 7946, 2017.

65. Donald Rumsfeld, *Known and Unknown: A Memoir* (New York: Sentinel, 2012).

66. Frank H. Knight, *Risk, Uncertainty, and Profit* (Boston: Hart, Schaffner, and Marx, 1921).

67. Justin Sydnor, "(Over)insuring Modest Risks," *American Economic Journal: Applied Economics* 2, no. 4 (2010): 177–99.

68. We will return to the idea of these motivated beliefs in chapter 4. For a reference, see Roland Bénabou and Jean Tirole, "Mindful Economics: The Production, Consumption, and Value of Beliefs," *Journal of Economic Perspectives* 30, no. 3 (2016): 141–64.

69. Alexis de Tocqueville, *Democracy in America* (London: Saunders and Otley, 1835).

70. Alberto Alesina, Stefanie Stantcheva, and Edoardo Teso, "Intergenerational Mobility and Preferences for Redistribution," *American Economic Review* 108, no. 2 (2018): 521–54, DOI: 10.1257/aer.20162015.

71. Benjamin Austin, Edward Glaeser, and Lawrence H. Summers, "Saving the Heartland: Place-Based Policies in 21st Century America," Brookings Papers on Economic Activity Conference Drafts, 2018.

72. Peter Ganong and Daniel Shoag, "Why Has Regional Income Convergence in the U.S. Declined?," *Journal of Urban Economics* 102 (2017): 76–90.

73. Enrico Moretti, *The New Geography of Jobs* (Boston: Houghton Mifflin Harcourt, 2012).

74. Ganong and Shoag, "Why Has Regional Income Convergence in the U.S. Declined?"

75. "Starbucks," Indeed.com, accessed April 21, 2019, https://www.indeed.com/q-Starbucks-l-Boston,-MA-jobs.html; "Starbucks," Indeed.com, accessed April 21, 2019, https://www.indeed.com/jobs?q=Starbucks&l=Boise percent2C+ID.

76. This example is worked out by Ganong and Shoag in Peter Ganong and Daniel Shoag, "Why Has Regional Income Convergence in the U.S. Declined?"

77. "The San Francisco Rent Explosion: Part II," Priceonomics, accessed June 4, 2019, https://priceonomics.com/the-san-francisco-rent-explosion-part-ii/.

78. According to RentCafé, the average rent in Mission Dolores is $3,728 for 792 square feet. "San Francisco, CA Rental Market Trends," accessed June 4, 2019, https://www.rentcafe.com/average-rent-market-trends/us/ca/san-francisco/.

79. "New Money Driving Out Working-Class San Franciscans," *Los Angeles Times*, June 21, 1999, accessed June 4, 2019, https://www.latimes.com/archives/la-xpm-1999-jun-21-mn-48707-story.html.

80. Glaeser, *Triumph of the City*.

81. Atif Mian and Amir Sufi have developed these arguments in their book *House of Debt: How They (and You) Caused the Great Recession, and How We Can Prevent It from Happening Again* (Chicago: University of Chicago Press, 2014), and many articles, including Atif Mian, Kamalesh Rao, and Amir Sufi, "Household Balance Sheets, Consumption, and the Economic Slump," *Quarterly Journal of Economics* 128, no. 4 (2013): 1687–1726.

82. Matthew Desmond, *Evicted: Poverty and Profit in the American City* (New York: Crown, 2016).

83. Mark Aguiar, Mark Bils, Kerwin Kofi Charles, and Erik Hurst, "Leisure Luxuries and the Labor Supply of Young Men," NBER Working Paper 23552, 2017.

84. Kevin Roose, "Silicon Valley Is Over, Says Silicon Valley," *New York Times,* March 4, 2018.

85. Andrew Ross Sorkin, "From Bezos to Walton, Big Investors Back Fund for 'Flyover' Start-Ups," *New York Times,* December 4, 2017.

86. Glenn Ellison and Edward Glaeser, "Geographic Concentration in U.S. Manufacturing Industries: A Dartboard Approach," *Journal of Political Economy* 105, no. 5 (1997): 889–927.

87. Bryan, Chowdhury, and Mobarak, "Underinvestment in a Profitable Technology."

88. Tabellini, "Gifts of the Immigrants, Woes of the Natives."

CHAPTER 3. THE PAINS FROM TRADE

1. "Steel and Aluminum Tariffs," Chicago Booth, IGM Forum, 2018, http://www.igmchicago.org/surveys/steel-and-aluminum-tariffs.

2. "Import Duties," Chicago Booth, IGM Forum, 2016, http://www.igmchicago.org/surveys/import-duties.

3. Abhijit Banerjee, Esther Duflo, and Stefanie Stantcheva, "Me and Everyone Else: Do People Think Like Economists?," MIMEO, Massachusetts Institute of Technology, 2019.

4. Ibid.

5. *The Collected Scientific Papers of Paul A. Samuelson*, vol. 3 (Cambridge, MA: MIT Press, 1966), 683.

6. Ibid.

7. David Ricardo, *On the Principles of Political Economy and Taxation* (London: John Murray, 1817).

8. Paul A. Samuelson and William F. Stolper, "Protection and Real Wages," *Review of Economic Studies* 9, no. 1 (1941), 58–73.

9. P. A. Samuelson, "The Gains from International Trade Once Again," *Economic Journal* 72, no. 288 (1962): 820–29, DOI: 10.2307/2228353.

10. John Keats, "Ode on a Grecian Urn," in *The Complete Poems of John Keats,* 3rd ed. (New York: Penguin Classics, 1977).

11. Petia Topalova, "Factor Immobility and Regional Impacts of Trade Liberalization: Evidence on Poverty from India," *American Economic Journal: Applied Economics* 2, no. 4 (2010): 1–41, DOI: 10.1257/app.2.4.1.

12. "GDP Growth (annual %)," World Bank, accessed March 29, 2019, https://data.worldbank.org/indicator/ny.gdp.mktp.kd.zg?end=2017&start=1988.

13. Of course, the trade optimists, among them Jagdish Bhagwati, T. N. Srinivasan, and their followers make the argument that pre-1991 growth was about to grind to a halt and the bailout and trade liberalization saved it.

14. Tractatus 7, in Ludwig von Wittgenstein, *Tractatus Logico-Philosophicus,* originally published by *Annalen der Naturphilosophie*, 1921. Published in the original edition by Chiron Academic Press in 2017, with an introduction by Bertrand Russell.

15. "GDP Growth (annual %)," World Bank.

16. The share of GDP for the top 1 percent (in terms of income) rose from a low of 6.1 percent in 1982 to 21.3 percent in 2015. World Inequality Database, accessed March 15, 2019, https://wid.world/country/india.

17. Diego Cerdeiro and Andras Komaromi, approved by Valerie Cerra, "The Effect of Trade on Income and Inequality: A Cross-Sectional Approach," International Monetary Fund Background Papers, 2017.

18. Pinelopi Koujianou Goldberg and Nina Pavcnik, "Distributional Effects of Globalization in Developing Countries," *Journal of Economic Literature* 45, no. 1 (March 2007): 39–82.

19. Thomas Piketty, Li Yang, and Gabriel Zucman, "Capital Accumulation, Private Property and Rising Inequality in China, 1978–2015," *American Economic Review*, forthcoming in 2019, working paper version accessed on June 19, 2019, http://gabriel-zucman.eu/files/PYZ2017.pdf.

20. Topalova, "Factor Immobility and Regional Impacts of Trade Liberalization."

21. Gaurav Datt, Martin Ravallion, and Rinku Murgai, "Poverty

Reduction in India: Revisiting Past Debates with 60 Years of Data," VOX CEPR Policy Portal, accessed March 15, 2019, voxeu.org.

22. Eric V. Edmonds, Nina Pavcnik, and Petia Topalova, "Trade Adjustment and Human Capital Investments: Evidence from Indian Tariff Reform," *American Economic Journal: Applied Economics* 2, no. 4 (2010): 42–75. DOI: 10.1257/app.2.4.42.

23. Orazio Attanasio, Pinelopi K. Goldberg, and Nina Pavcnik, "Trade Reforms and Trade Inequality in Colombia," *Journal of Development Economics* 74, no. 2 (2004): 331–66; Brian K. Kovak, "Regional Effects of Trade Reform: What Is the Correct Level of Liberalization?" *American Economic Review* 103, no. 5 (2013): 1960–76.

24. Pinelopi K. Goldberg, Amit Khandelwal, Nina Pavcnik, and Petia Topalova, "Trade Liberalization and New Imported Inputs," *American Economic Review* 99, no. 2 (2009): 494–500.

25. Abhijit Vinayak Banerjee, "Globalization and All That," in *Understanding Poverty,* ed. Abhijit Vinayak Banerjee, Roland Bénabou, and Dilip Mookherjee (New York: Oxford University Press, 2006).

26. Topalova, "Factor Immobility and Regional Impacts of Trade Liberalization."

27. Abhijit Banerjee and Esther Duflo, "Growth Theory Through the Lens of Development Economics," ch. 7, in *The Handbook of Economic Growth,* eds. Philippe Aghion and Stephen Durlauf (Amsterdam: North Holland, 2005), vol. 1, part A: 473–552.

28. Topalova, "Factor Immobility and Regional Impacts of Trade Liberalization."

29. Pinelopi K. Goldberg, Amit K. Khandelwal, Nina Pavcnik, and Petia Topalova, "Multiproduct Firms and Product Turnover in the Developing World: Evidence from India," *Review of Economics and Statistics* 92, no. 4 (2010): 1042–49.

30. Robert Grundke and Cristoph Moser, "Hidden Protectionism? Evidence from Non-Tariff Barriers to Trade in the United States," *Journal of International Economics* 117 (2019): 143–57.

31. World Trade Organization, "Members Reaffirm Commitment to Aid for Trade and to Development Support," 2017, accessed March 18, 2019, https://www.wto.org/english/news_e/news17_e/gr17_13jul17_e.htm.

32. David Atkin, Amit K. Khandelwal, and Adam Osman, "Exporting and Firm Performance: Evidence from a Randomized Experiment," *Quarterly Journal of Economics* 132, no. 2 (2017): 551–615.

33. "Rankings by Country of Average Monthly Net Salary (After Tax) (Salaries and Financing)," Numbeo, accessed March 18, 2019, https://www.numbeo.com/cost-of-living/country_price_rankings?itemId=105.

34. Abhijit V. Banerjee and Esther Duflo, "Reputation Effects and the Limits of Contracting: A Study of the Indian Software Industry," *Quarterly Journal of Economics* 115, no. 3 (2000): 989–1017.

35. Amos Tversky and Daniel Kahneman, "The Framing of Decisions and Psychology of Choice," *Science* 211 (1981): 453–58.

36. Jean Tirole, "A Theory of Collective Reputations (with Applications to the Persistence of Corruption and to Firm Quality)," *Review of Economic Studies* 63, no. 1 (1996): 1–22.

37. Rocco Machiavello and Ameet Morjaria, "The Value of Relationships: Evidence from Supply Shock to Kenyan Rose Exports," *American Economic Review* 105, no. 9 (2015): 2911–45.

38. Wang Xiaodong, "Govt Issues Guidance for Quality of Products," *China Daily*, updated September 14, 2017, accessed March 29, 2019, http://www.chinadaily.com.cn/china/2017-09/14/content_31975019.htm.

39. Gujanita Kalita, "The Emergence of Tirupur as the Export Hub of Knitted Garments in India: A Case Study," ICRIER, accessed April 21, 2019, https://www.econ-jobs.com/research/52329-The-Emergence-of-Tirupur-as-the-Export-Hub-of-Knitted-Garments-in-India-A-Case-Study.pdf.

40. L. N. Revathy, "GST, Export Slump Have Tirupur's Garment Units Hanging by a Thread," accessed April 21, 2019, https://www.thehindubusinessline.com/economy/gst-export-slump-have-tirupurs-garment-units-hanging-by-a-thread/article9968689.ece.

41. "Clusters 101," Cluster Mapping, accessed March 18, 2019, http://www.clustermapping.us/content/clusters-101.

42. Antonio Gramsci, "'Wave of Materialism' and 'Crisis of Authority,'" in *Selections from the Prison Notebooks* (New York: International Publishers, 1971), 275–76; Prison Notebooks, vol. 2, notebook 3, 1930, 2011 edition, SS-34, Past and Present 32–33.

43. According to the World Bank, India's openness ratio was 42 percent in 2015, compared to 28 percent in the United States and 39 percent in China. "Trade Openness—Country Rankings," TheGlobalEconomy.com., accessed March 8, 2019, https://www.theglobaleconomy.com/rankings/trade_openness/.

44. Pinelopi K. Goldberg, Amit K. Khandelwal, Nina Pavcnik, and Petia Topalova, "Imported Intermediate Inputs and Domestic Product Growth: Evidence from India," *Quarterly Journal of Economics* 125, no. 4 (2010): 1727–67.

45. Paul Krugman, "Taking on China," *New York Times*, September 30, 2010.

46. J. D. Vance, *Hillbilly Elegy: A Memoir of a Family and Culture in Crisis* (New York: Harper, 2016).

47. David Autor, David Dorn, and Gordon Hanson, "The China Syndrome: Local Labor Market Effects of Import Competition in the United States," *American Economic Review* 103, no. 6 (2013): 2121–68; David Autor, David Dorn, and Gordon Hanson, "The China Shock: Learning from Labor-Market Adjustment to Large Changes in Trade," *Annual Review of Economics* 8 (2016): 205–40.

48. Ragnhild Balsvik, Sissel Jensen, and Kjell G. Salvanes, "Made in China, Sold in Norway: Local Labor Market Effects of an Import Shock," *Journal of Public Economics* 127 (2015): 137–44; Wolfgang Dauth, Sebastian Findeisen, and Jens Suedekum, "The Rise of the East and the Far East: German Labor Markets and Trade Integration," *Journal of the European Economic Association* 12, no. 6 (2014): 1643–75; Vicente Donoso, Víctor Martín, and Asier Minondo, "Do Differences in the Exposure to Chinese Imports Lead to Differences in Local Labour Market Outcomes? An Analysis for Spanish Provinces," *Regional Studies* 49, no. 10 (2015): 1746–64.

49. M. Allirajan, "Garment Exports Dive 41 Percent in October on GST Woes," *Times of India*, November 16, 2017, https://timesofindia.indiatimes.com/business/india-business/garment-exports-dive-41-in-october-on-gst-woes/articleshow/61666363.cms.

50. Atif Mian, Kamalesh Rao, and Amir Sufi, "Housing Balance Sheets, Consumption, and the Economic Slump," *Quarterly Journal of Economics* 128, no. 4 (2013): 1687–1726.

51. The story is reported in an article from the *Atlantic* magazine. Alana Semuels, "Ghost Towns of the 21st Century," *Atlantic,* October 20, 2015.

52. Autor, Dorn, and Hanson, "The China Syndrome."

53. David H. Autor, Mark Duggan, Kyle Greenberg, and David S. Lyle, "The Impact of Disability Benefits on Labor Supply: Evidence from the VA's Disability Compensation Program," *American Economic Journal: Applied Economics* 8, no. 3 (2016): 31–68.

54. David H. Autor, "The Unsustainable Rise of the Disability Rolls in the United States: Causes, Consequences, and Policy Options," in *Social Policies in an Age of Austerity*, eds. John Karl Scholz, Hyunpyo Moon, and Sang-Hyop Lee (Northampton, MA: Edward Elgar, 2015) 107–36.

55. Aparna Soni, Marguerite E. Burns, Laura Dague, and Kosali I. Simon, "Medicaid Expansion and State Trends in Supplemental Security Income Program Participation," *Health Affairs* 36, no. 8 (2017): 1485–88.

56. See, for example, Enrico Moretti and Pat Kline, "People, Places and Public Policy: Some Simple Welfare Economics of Local Economic Development Programs," *Annual Review of Economics* 6 (2014): 629–62.

57. David Autor, David Dorn, and Gordon H. Hanson, "When Work Disappears: Manufacturing Decline and the Fall of Marriage Market Value of Young Men," *AER Insights,* forthcoming 2019, available as NBER Working Paper 23173, 2018, DOI: 10.3386/w23173.

58. Anne Case and Angus Deaton, "Rising Morbidity and Mortality in Midlife Among White Non-Hispanic Americans in the 21st Century," *PNAS* 112, no. 49 (2015): 15078–83, https://doi.org/10.1073/pnas.1518393112.

59. Arnaud Costinot and Andrés Rodríguez-Clare, "The US Gains from Trade: Valuation Using the Demand for Foreign Factor Services," *Journal of Economic Perspectives* 32, no. 2 (Spring 2018): 3–24.

60. Rodrigo Adao, Arnaud Costinot, and Dave Donaldson, "Nonparametric Counterfactual Predictions in Neoclassical Models of International Trade," *American Economic Review* 107, no. 3 (2017): 633–89; Costinot and Rodríguez-Clare, "The US Gains from Trade."

61. "GDP Growth (annual %)," World Bank, accessed March 29, 2019, https://data.worldbank.org/indicator/ny.gdp.mktp.kd.zg.

62. Costinot and Rodríguez-Clare, "The US Gains from Trade."

63. Sam Asher and Paul Novosad, "Rural Roads and Local Economic Development," Policy Research Working Paper 8466 (Washington, DC: World Bank, 2018).

64. Sandra Poncet, "The Fragmentation of the Chinese Domestic Market Peking Struggles to Put an End to Regional Protectionism," *China Perspectives*, accessed April 21, 2019, https://journals.openedition.org/chinaperspectives/410.

65. *Small Is Beautiful* was a book written by the German ecologist Schumacher in 1974 to defend the Gandhian idea of small farms in villages. E. F. Schumacher, *Small Is Beautiful: A Study of Economics as If People Mattered* (London: Blond & Briggs, 1973).

66. Nirmala Banerjee, "Is Small Beautiful?," in *Change and Choice in Indian Industry,* eds. Amiya Bagchi and Nirmala Banerjee (Calcutta: K. P. Bagchi & Company, 1981).

67. Chang-Tai Hsieh and Benjamin A. Olken, "The Missing 'Missing Middle,'" *Journal of Economic Perspectives* 28, no. 3 (2014): 89–108.

68. Adam Smith, *The Wealth of Nations* (W. Strahan and T. Cadell, 1776).

69. Dave Donaldson, "Railroads of the Raj: Estimating the Impact of Transportation Infrastructure," *American Economic Review* 108, nos. 4–5 (2018): 899–934.

70. Dave Donaldson and Richard Hornbeck, "Railroads and American Growth: A 'Market Access' Approach," *Quarterly Journal of Economics* 131, no. 2 (2016): 799–858.

71. Arnaud Costinot and Dave Donaldson, "Ricardo's Theory of Comparative Advantage: Old Idea, New Evidence," *American Economic Review* 102, no. 3 (2012): 453–58.

72. Asher and Novosad, "Rural Roads and Local Economic Development."

73. David Atkin and Dave Donaldson, "Who's Getting Globalized? The Size and Implications of Intra-National Trade Costs," NBER Working Paper 21439, 2015.

74. "U.S. Agriculture and Trade at a Glance," US Department of Agriculture Economic Research Service, accessed June 8, 2019, https://www.ers .usda.gov/topics/international-markets-us-trade/us-agricultural-trade/us -agricultural-trade-at-a-glance/.

75. Ibid.

76. "Occupational Employment Statistics," Bureau of Labor Statistics, accessed March 29, 2019, https://www.bls.gov/oes/2017/may/oes452099.htm.

77. "Quick Facts: United States," US Census Bureau, accessed March 29, 2019, https://www.census.gov/quickfacts/fact/map/US/INC910217.

78. Benjamin Hyman, "Can Displaced Labor Be Retrained? Evidence from Quasi-Random Assignment to Trade Adjustment Assistance," January 10, 2018, https://ssrn.com/abstract=3155386 or http://dx.doi.org/10.2139/ ssrn.3155386.

79. "Education and Training," Veterans Administration, accessed June 21, 2019, https://benefits.va.gov/gibill/.

80. Sewin Chan and Ann Huff Stevens, "Job Loss and Employment Patterns of Older Workers," *Journal of Labor Economics* 19, no. 2 (2001): 484–521.

81. Henry S. Farber, Chris M. Herbst, Dan Silverman, and Till von Wachter, "Whom Do Employers Want? The Role of Recent Employment and Unemployment Status and Age," *Journal of Labor Economics* 37, no. 2 (April 2019): 323–49, https://doi.org/10.1086/700184.

82. Benjamin Austin, Edward Glaesar, and Lawrence Summers, "Saving the Heartland: Place-Based policies in 21st Century America," Brookings Papers on Economic Activity conference draft 2018, accessed June 19, 2019, https://www.brookings.edu/wp-content/uploads/2018/03/3_austinetal.pdf.

CHAPTER 4. LIKES, WANTS, AND NEEDS

1. John Sides, Michael Tesler, and Lynn Vavreck, *Identity Crisis: The 2016 Presidential Campaign and the Battle for the Meaning of America* (Princeton, NJ: Princeton University Press, 2018).

2. George Stigler and Gary Becker, "De Gustibus Non Est Disputandum," *American Economic Review* 67, no. 2 (1977): 76–90.

3. Abhijit Banerjee and Esther Duflo, *Poor Economics: A Radical Rethinking of the Way to Fight Global Poverty* (New York: PublicAffairs, 2011).

4. Abhijit V. Banerjee, "Policies for a Better-Fed World," *Review of World Economics* 152, no. 1 (2016): 3–17.

5. Abhijit Banerjee, "A Simple Model of Herd Behavior," *Quarterly Journal of Economics* 107, no. 3 (1992): 797–817.

6. Lev Muchnik, Sinan Aral, and Sean J. Taylor, "Social Influence Bias: A Randomized Experiment," *Science* 341, no. 6146 (2013): 647–51.

7. Drew Fudenberg and Eric Maskin, "The Folk Theorem in Repeated Games with Discounting or with Incomplete Information," *Econometrica* 54, no. 3 (1986): 533–54; Dilip Abreu, "On the Theory of Infinitely Repeated Games with Discounting," *Econometrica* 56, no. 2 (1988): 383–96.

8. Elinor Ostrom, *Governing the Commons* (Cambridge: Cambridge University Press, 1990).

9. See, for example, E. R. Prabhakar Somanathan and Bhupendra Singh Mehta, "Decentralization for Cost-Effective Conservation," *Proceedings of the National Academy of Sciences* 106, no. 11 (2009): 4143–47; J. M. Baland, P. Bardhan, S. Das, and D. Mookherjee, "Forests to the People: Decentralization and Forest Degradation in the Indian Himalayas," *World Development* 38, no. 11 (2010): 1642–56. This does not mean community ownership always works. Indeed, even the theory makes it clear that it may not. Suppose for example, that you expect other people in the community will not always play by the rules. The temptation for you to cheat is then stronger, since with some other people overgrazing, the common pasture will not be that great; therefore, the threat of exclusion from it will be less daunting. In fact, the evidence on whether communally owned forest areas are less deforested is not overwhelming.

10. Robert M. Townsend, "Risk and Insurance in Village India," *Econometrica* 62, no. 3 (1994): 539–91; Christopher Udry, "Risk and Insurance in a Rural Credit Market: An Empirical Investigation in Northern Nigeria," *Review of Economic Studies* 61, no. 3 (1994): 495–526.

11. A recent very well-argued book that makes this case is Raghuram Rajan's *The Third Pillar*. Raghuram Rajan, *The Third Pillar: How Markets and the State Leave Community Behind* (New York: HarperCollins, 2019).

12. Harold L. Cole, George J. Mailath, and Andrew Postlewaite, "Social Norms, Savings Behavior, and Growth," *Journal of Political Economy* 100, no. 6 (1992): 1092–1125.

13. Constituent Assembly of India Debates (proceedings), vol. 7, November 4, 1948, https://cadindia.clpr.org.in/constitution_assembly_debates/volume/7/1948-11-04. The relationship between the two men has been widely written about, notably by the novelist Arundhati Roy in her 2017 book, *The Doctor and the Saint* (which focuses more on Ambedkar) and Ramachandra Guha's recent book *Gandhi* (told more from Gandhi's side). The two men did not get along. Gandhi thought Ambedkar was a hothead; Ambedkar implied the old man was a bit of a fraud. Despite their opposition, it is with Gandhi's blessing that Ambedkar ended up drafting the constitution. Arundhati Roy, *The Doctor and the Saint: Caste, War, and the Annihilation of Caste* (Chicago: Haymarket Books, 2017); Ramachandra Guha, *Gandhi: The Years That Changed the World,* 1914–1948 (New York: Knopf, 2018).

14. Viktoria Hnatkovska, Amartya Lahiri, and Sourabh Paul, "Castes and Labor Mobility," *American Economic Journal: Applied Economics* 4, no. 2 (2012): 274–307.

15. Karla Hoff, "Caste System," World Bank Policy Research Working Paper 7929, 2016.

16. Kanchan Chandra, *Why Ethnic Parties Succeed: Patronage and Ethnic Headcounts in India* (Cambridge: Cambridge University Press, 2004); Christophe Jaffrelot, *India's Silent Revolution: The Rise of the Lower Castes in North India* (London: Hurst and Company, 2003); Yogendra Yadav, *Understanding the Second Democratic Upsurge: Trends of Bahujan Participation in Electoral Politics in the 1990s* (Delhi: Oxford University Press, 2000).

17. Abhijit Banerjee, Amory Gethin, and Thomas Piketty, "Growing Cleavages in India? Evidence from the Changing Structure of Electorates, 1962–2014," *Economic & Political Weekly* 54, no. 11 (2019): 33–44.

18. Abhijit Banerjee and Rohini Pande, "Parochial Politics: Ethnic Preferences and Politician Corruption," CEPR Discussion Paper DP6381, 2007.

19. "Black Guy Asks Nation for Change," *Onion,* March 19, 2008, accessed June 19, 2019, https://politics.theonion.com/black-guy-asks-nation-for-change-1819569703.

20. Eileen Patten, "Racial, Gender Wage Gaps Persist in U.S. Despite Some Progress," Pew Research Center, July 1, 2016.

21. Raj Chetty, Nathaniel Hendren, Maggie R. Jones, and Sonya R. Porter, "Race and Economic Opportunity in the United States: An Intergenerational Perspective," NBER Working Paper 24441, 2018.

22. According to a study by the Stanford Center on Poverty and Inequality: "At the end of 2015, a full 9.1 percent of young black men (ages 20–34) were incarcerated, a rate that is 5.7 times that of young white men (1.6%). Fully 10 percent of black children had an incarcerated parent in 2015, compared with 3.6 percent of Hispanic children and 1.7 percent of white children." Becky Pettit and Bryan Sykes, "State of the Union 2017: Incarceration," Stanford Center on Poverty and Inequality.

23. In this sense, African Americans are more like Muslims in India than the scheduled castes. Muslims are simultaneously falling behind the Hindu population in economic terms and are the target of rising levels of violence from the majority Hindu population.

24. Jane Coaston, "How White Supremacist Candidates Fared in 2018," *Vox*, November 7, 2018, accessed April 22, 2019, https://www.vox.com/policy-and-politics/2018/11/7/18064670/white-supremacist-candidates-2018-midterm-elections.

25. Robert P. Jones, Daniel Cox, Betsy Cooper, and Rachel Lienesch, "How Americans View Immigrants and What They Want from Immigration Reform: Findings from the 2015 American Values Atlas," Public Religion Research Institute, March 29, 2016.

26. Leonardo Bursztyn, Georgy Egorov, and Stefano Fiorin, "From Extreme to Mainstream: How Social Norms Unravel," NBER Working Paper 23415, 2017.

27. Cited in Chris Haynes, Jennifer L. Merolla, and S. Karthik Ramakrishnan, *Framing Immigrants: News Coverage, Public Opinion, and Policy* (New York: Russell Sage Foundation, 2016).

28. Ibid.

29. Anirban Mitra and Debraj Ray, "Implications of an Economic Theory of Conflict: Hindu-Muslim Violence in India," *Journal of Political Economy* 122, no. 4 (2014): 719–65.

30. Daniel L. Chen, "Club Goods and Group Identity: Evidence from Islamic Resurgence During the Indonesian Financial Crisis," *Journal of Political Economy* 118, no. 2 (2010): 300–54.

31. Amanda Agan and Sonja Starr, "Ban the Box, Criminal Records, and Statistical Discrimination: A Field Experiment," *Quarterly Journal of Economics* 133, no. 1 (2017): 191–235.

32. Ibid.

33. Claude M. Steele and Joshua Aronson, "Stereotype Threat and the Intellectual Test Performance of African Americans," *Journal of Personality and Social Psychology* 69, no. 5 (1995): 797–811.

34. Steven J. Spencer, Claude M. Steele, and Diane M. Quinn, "Stereotype Threat and Women's Math Performance," *Journal of Experimental Social Psychology* 35, no. 1 (1999): 4–28.

35. Joshua Aronson, Michael J. Lustina, Catherine Good, Kelli Keough, Claude M. Steele, and Joseph Brown, "When White Men Can't Do Math: Necessary and Sufficient Factors in Stereotype Threat," *Journal of Experimental Social Psychology* 35, no. 1 (1999): 29–46.

36. Robert Rosenthal and Lenore Jacobson, "Pygmalion in the Classroom," *Urban Review* 3, no. 1 (1968): 16–20.

37. Dylan Glover, Amanda Pallais, and William Pariente, "Discrimination as a Self-Fulfilling Prophecy: Evidence from French Grocery Stores," *Quarterly Journal of Economics* 132, no. 3 (2017): 1219–60.

38. Ariel Ben Yishay, Maria Jones, Florence Kondylis, and Ahmed Mushfiq Mobarak, "Are Gender Differences in Performance Innate or Socially Mediated?," World Bank Policy Research Working Paper 7689, 2016.

39. Rocco Macchiavello, Andreas Menzel, Antonu Rabbani, and Christopher Woodruff, "Challenges of Change: An Experiment Training Women to Manage in the Bangladeshi Garment Sector," University of Warwick Working Paper Series No. 256, 2015.

40. Jeff Stone, Christian I. Lynch, Mike Sjomeling, and John M. Darley, "Stereotype Threat Effects on Black and White Athletic Performance," *Journal of Personality and Social Psychology* 77, no. 6 (1999): 1213–27.

41. Ibid.

42. Marco Tabellini, "Racial Heterogeneity and Local Government Finances: Evidence from the Great Migration," Harvard Business School BGIE Unit Working Paper 19-006, 2018, https://ssrn.com/abstract=3220439 or http://dx.doi.org/10.2139/ssrn.3220439; Conrad Miller, "When Work Moves: Job Suburbanization and Black Employment," NBER Working Paper No. 24728, June 2018, DOI: 10.3386/w24728.

43. Ellora Derenoncourt, "Can You Move to Opportunity? Evidence from the Great Migration," working paper, accessed April 22, 2019, https://scholar.harvard.edu/files/elloraderenoncourt/files/derenoncourt_jmp_2018.pdf.

44. Leonardo Bursztyn and Robert Jensen, "How Does Peer Pressure Affect Educational Investments?," *Quarterly Journal of Economics* 130, no. 3 (2015): 1329–67.

45. Ernst Fehr, "Degustibus Est Disputandum," Emerging Science of Preference Formation, inaugural talk, Universitat Pompeu Fabra, Barcelona, Spain, October 7, 2015.

46. Alain Cohn, Ernst Fehr, and Michel Andre Marechal, "Business Culture and Dishonesty in the Banking Industry," *Nature* 516 (2014): 86–89.

47. For an overview of their work, see Roland Bénabou and Jean Tirole, "Mindful Economics: The Production, Consumption, and Value of Beliefs," *Journal of Economic Perspectives* 30, no. 3 (2016): 141–64.

48. William Julius Wilson, *When Work Disappears: The World of the New Urban Poor* (New York: Knopf Doubleday, 1997).

49. J. D. Vance, *Hillbilly Elegy: A Memoir of a Family and Culture in Crisis* (New York: Harper, 2016).

50. Dan Ariely, George Loewenstein, and Drazen Prelec, "'Coherent Arbitrariness': Stable Demand Curves without Stable Preferences,"*Quarterly Journal of Economics* 118, no. 1 (2003): 73–106.

51. Daniel Kahneman, Jack L. Knetsch, and Richard H. Thaler, "Experimental Tests of the Endowment Effect and the Coase Theorem," *Journal of Political Economy* 98, no. 6 (1990): 1325–48.

52. Dan Ariely, George Loewenstein, and Drazen Prelec, "'Coherent Arbitrariness': Stable Demand Curves without Stable Preferences," *Quarterly Journal of Economics* 118, no. 1 (2003): 73–106.

53. Muzafer Sherif, *The Robber's Cave Experiment: Intergroup Conflict and Cooperation,* (Middletown, CT: Wesleyan University Press, 1998).

54. Gerard Prunier, *The Rwanda Crisis: History of a Genocide* (New York: Columbia University Press, 1997).

55. Paul Lazarsfeld and Robert Merton, "Friendship as a Social Process: A Substantive and Methodological Analysis," in *Freedom and Control in Modern Society,* eds. Morroe Berger, Theodore Abel, and Charles H. Page (New York: Van Nostrand, 1954).

56. Matthew Jackson, "An Overview of Social Networks and Economic Applications," *Handbook of Social Economics,* 2010, accessed January 5, 2019, https://web.stanford.edu/~jacksonm/socialnetecon-chapter.pdf.

57. Kristen Bialik, "Key Facts about Race and Marriage, 50 Years after Loving v. Virginia," Pew Research Center, 2017, http://www.pewresearch.org/fact-tank/2017/06/12/key-facts-about-race-and-marriage-50-years-after-loving-v-virginia/.

58. Abhijit Banerjee, Esther Duflo, Maitreesh Ghatak, and Jeanne Lafortune, "Marry for What? Caste and Mate Selection in Modern India," *American Economic Journal: Microeconomics* 5, no. 2 (2013), https://doi.org/10.1257/mic.5.2.33.

59. Cass R. Sunstein, Republic.com. (Princeton, NJ: Princeton University Press, 2001); Cass R. Sunstein, *#Republic: Divided Democracy in the Age of Social Media* (Princeton, NJ: Princeton University Press, 2017).

60. "Little Consensus on Global Warming: Partisanship Drives Opinion," Pew Research Center, 2006, http://www.people-press.org/2006/07/12/little-consensus-on-global-warming/.

61. R. Cass Sunstein, "On Mandatory Labeling, with Special Reference to Genetically Modified Foods," *University of Pennsylvania Law Review* 165, no. 5 (2017): 1043–95.

62. Matthew Gentzkow, Jesse M. Shapiro, and Matt Taddy, "Measuring Polarization in High-Dimensional Data: Method and Application to Congressional Speech," working paper, 2016.

63. Yuriy Gorodnickenko, Tho Pham, and Oleksandr Talavera, "Social Media, Sentiment and Public Opinions: Evidence from #Brexit and #US Election," National Bureau of Economics Research Working Paper 24631, 2018.

64. Shanto Iyengar, Gaurav Sood, and Yphtach Lelkes, "Affect, Not Ideology: A Social Identity Perspective on Polarization," *Public Opinion Quarterly*, 2012, http://doi.org/10.1093/poq/nfs038.

65. "Most Popular Social Networks Worldwide as of January 2019, Ranked by Number of Active Users (in millions)," Statista.com, 2019, accessed April 21, 2019, https://www.statista.com/statistics/272014/global-social-networks-ranked-by-number-of-users/.

66. Maeve Duggan, Nicole B. Ellison, Cliff Lampe, Amanda Lenhart, and Mary Madden, "Social Media Update 2014," Pew Research Center, 2015, http://www.pewinternet.org/2015/01/09/social-media-update-2014/.

67. Johan Ugander, Brian Karrer, Lars Backstrom, and Cameron Marlow, "The Anatomy of the Facebook Social Graph," Cornell University, 2011, https://arxiv.org/abs/1111.4503v1.

68. Yosh Halberstam and Brian Knight "Homophily, Group Size, and the Diffusion of Political Information in Social Networks: Evidence from Twitter," *Journal of Public Economics*, 143 (November 2016), 73–88, https://doi.org/10.1016/j.jpubeco.2016.08.011.

69. David Brock, *The Republican Noise Machine* (New York: Crown, 2004).

70. David Yanagizawa-Drott, "Propaganda and Conflict: Evidence from the Rwandan Genocide," *Quarterly Journal of Economics* 129, no. 4 (2014), https://doi.org/10.1093/qje/qju020.

71. Matthew Gentzkow and Jesse Shapiro, "Ideological Segregation Online and Offline," *Quarterly Journal of Economics* 126, no. 4 (2011), http://doi.org/10.1093/qje/qjr044.

72. Levi Boxell, Matthew Gentzkow, and Jesse Shapiro, "Greater Internet Use Is Not Associated with Faster Growth in Political Polarization among US

Demographic Groups," Proceedings of the National Academy of Sciences of the United States of America, 2017, https://doi.org/10.1073/pnas.1706588114.

73. Gregory J. Martin and Ali Yurukoglu, "Bias in Cable News: Persuasion and Polarization," *American Economic Review* 107, no. 9 (2017), http://doi.org/10.1257/aer.20160812.

74. Ibid.

75. Matthew Gentzkow, Jesse M. Shapiro, and Matt Taddy, "Measuring Polarization in High-Dimensional Data: Method and Application to Congressional Speech," working paper, 2016.

76. Julia Cagé, Nicolas Hervé, and Marie-Luce Viaud, "The Production of Information in an Online World: Is Copy Right?," Net Institute working paper, 2017, http://dx.doi.org/10.2139/ssrn.2672050.

77. "2015 Census," American Society of News Editors, https://www.asne.org/diversity-survey-2015.

78. "Sociocultural Dimensions of Immigrant Integration," in *The Integration of Immigrants into American Society,* eds. Mary C. Waters and Marissa Gerstein Pineau (Washington, DC: National Academies of Sciences Engineering Medicine, 2015).

79. Hunt Allcott and Matthew Gentzkow, "Social Media and Fake News in the 2016 Election," *Journal of Economic Perspectives* 31, no. 2 (2017), http://doi.org/10.1257/jep.31.2.211.

80. Donghee Jo, "Better the Devil You Know: An Online Field Experiment on News Consumption,"Northeastern University working paper, accessed June 20, 2019, https://www.dongheejo.com/.

81. Gordon Allport, *The Nature of Prejudice* (Cambridge, MA: Addison-Wesley, 1954).

82. Elizabeth Levy Paluck, Seth Green, and Donald P. Green, "The Contact Hypothesis Re-evaluated," *Behavioral Public Policy* (2017): 1–30.

83. Johanne Boisjoly, Greg J. Duncan, Michael Kremer, Dan M. Levy, and Jacque Eccles, "Empathy or Antipathy? The Impact of Diversity," *American Economic Review* 96, no. 5 (2006): 1890–1905.

84. Gautam Rao, "Familiarity Does Not Breed Contempt: Generosity, Discrimination, and Diversity in Delhi Schools," *American Economic Review* 109, no. 3 (2019): 774–809.

85. Matthew Lowe, "Types of Contact: A Field Experiment on Collaborative and Adversarial Caste Integration," OSF, last updated on May 29, 2019, osf.io/u2d9x.

86. Thomas C. Schelling, "Dynamic Models of Segregation," *Journal of Mathematical Sociology* 1 (1971): 143–186.

87. David Card, Alexandre Mas, and Jesse Rothstein, "Tipping and the Dynamics of Segregation," *Quarterly Journal of Economics* 123, no. 1 (2008): 177–218.

88. The French system of public housing is not a lottery, but in principle it should work to spread people around: a commission meets at the *departement* level (similar to a county) to allocate vacant units to applicant families across the entire departement, based on family size and other priority criteria, but not race. But subsidized housing in nice neighborhoods is so lucrative that the incentive to cheat is very powerful. In the mid-1990s, allocation of housing units in Paris was exposed as a key mechanism of clientelism, put in place and maintained by Jacques Chirac (the mayor of Paris, and later the president of France). Yann Algan, Camille Hémet, and David D. Laitin, "The Social Effects of Ethnic Diversity at the Local Level : A Natural Experiment with Exogenous Residential Allocation," *Journal of Political Economy* 124, no. 3 (2016): 696–733.

89. Joshua D. Angrist and Kevin Lang, "Does School Integration Generate Peer Effects? Evidence from Boston's Metco Program,"*American Economic Review* 94, no. 5 (2004): 1613–34.

90. Abhijit Banerjee, Donald Green, Jennifer Green, and Rohini Pande, "Can Voters Be Primed to Choose Better Legislators? Experimental Evidence from Rural India," Poverty Action Lab working paper, 2010, accessed June 19, 2019, https://www.povertyactionlab.org/sites/default/files/publications/105_419_Can%20Voters%20be%20Primed_Abhijit_Oct2009.pdf.

CHAPTER 5. THE END OF GROWTH?

1. Robert Gordon, *The Rise and Fall of American Growth* (Princeton, NJ: Princeton University Press, 2016).

2. C. I. Jones, "The Facts of Economic Growth," in *Handbook of Macroeconomics*, vol. 2, eds. John B. Taylor and Harald Uhlig (Amsterdam: North Holland, 2016), 3–69.

3. Angus Maddison, "Historical Statistics of the World Economy: 1-2008 AD," Groningen Growth and Development Centre: Maddison Project Database (2010).

4. Angus Maddison, "Measuring and Interpreting World Economic Performance 1500–2001," *Review of Income and Wealth* 51, no. 1 (2005): 1–35, https://doi.org/10.1111/j.1475-4991.2005.00143.x.

5. Robert Gordon, *The Rise and Fall of American Growth* (Princeton, NJ: Princeton University Press, 2016), 258.

6. J. Bradford DeLong, Claudia Goldin, and Lawrence F. Katz, "Sustain-

ing U.S. Economic Growth," in Henry J. Aaron , James M. Lindsay, Pietro S. Nivola, *Agenda for the Nation* (Washington, DC: Brookings Institution, 2003), 17–60.

7. Robert Gordon, *The Rise and Fall of American Growth* (Princeton, NJ: Princeton University Press, 2016), 575, figure 17.2. Annualized TFP growth in the US was 0.46 percent per year between 1880 and 1920 and 1.89 percent per year between 1920 and 1970.

8. Nicholas Crafts, "Fifty Years of Economic Growth in Western Europe: No Longer Catching Up but Falling Behind?," *World Economics* 5, no. 2 (2004): 131–45.

9. Robert Gordon, *The Rise and Fall of American Growth* (Princeton, NJ: Princeton University Press, 2016).

10. Annualized TFP growth in the US was 1.89 percent per year between 1920 and 1970 and 0.57 between 1970 and 1995; Robert Gordon, *The Rise and Fall of American Growth* (Princeton, NJ: Princeton University Press, 2016), 575, figure 17.2.

11. Robert Gordon, *The Rise and Fall of American Growth* (Princeton, NJ: Princeton University Press, 2016), 575, figure 17.2. Annual TFP growth was 0.40 from 2004 to 2014, even lower than the 0.70 annual TFP growth during the 1973–1994 period and the annual 0.46 TFP growth during the 1890–1920 period.

12. "Total Factor Productivity," Federal Reserve Bank of San Francisco, accessed June 19, 2019, https://www.frbsf.org/economic-research/indicators -data/total-factor-productivity-tfp/.

13. Robert Gordon and Joel Mokyr, "Boom vs. Doom: Debating the Future of the US Economy," debate, Chicago Council of Global Affairs, October 31, 2016.

14. Robert Gordon, *The Rise and Fall of American Growth* (Princeton, NJ: Princeton University Press, 2016), 594–603.

15. Robert Gordon and Joel Mokyr, "Boom vs. Doom: Debating the Future of the US Economy," debate, Chicago Council of Global Affairs, October 31, 2016.

16. Alvin H. Hansen, "Economic Progress and Declining Population Growth," *American Economic Review* 29, no. 1 (1939): 1–15.

17. Angus Maddison, *Growth and Interaction in the World Economy: The Roots of Modernity* (Washington, DC: AEI Press, 2005).

18. Thomas Piketty, *Capital in the Twenty-First Century* (Cambridge, MA: Harvard University Press, 2013), 73, table 2.1. The data Piketty uses for long-term growth originally comes from Angus Maddison, and can be found

on the Maddison project data base at https://www.rug.nl/ggdc/historical development/maddison/releases/maddison-project-database-2018.

19. For the interested reader who decides to peruse this literature, it will be useful to know that economists call well-being "welfare" (by which they are not referring to welfare programs). So this is what they would call a welfare calculation.

20. Chad Syverson, "Challenges to Mismeasurement Explanations for the US Productivity Slowdown," *Journal of Economic Perspectives* 31, no. 2 (2017): 165–86, https://doi.org/10.1257/jep.31.2.165.

21. Ibid.

22. Hunt Allcott, Luca Braghieri, Sarah Eichmeyer, and Matthew Gentzkow, "The Welfare Effects of Social Media," NBER Working Paper 25514 (2019).

23. Robert M. Solow, "A Contribution to the Theory of Economic Growth," *Quarterly Journal of Economics* 70, no. 1 (1956): 65–94, https://doi .org/10.2307/1884513.

24. "Estimating the U.S. Labor Share," Bureau of Labor Statistics, 2017, accessed April 15, 2019, https://www.bls.gov/opub/mlr/2017/article/estimating -the-us-labor-share.htm.

25. The Berkeley economist Brad DeLong is famous for making this point in J. Bradford De Long, "Productivity Growth, Convergence, and Welfare: Comment," *American Economic Review* 78, no. 5 (1988): 1138–54. He recently updated his graph using World Bank data at /www.bradford -delong.com/2015/08/in-which-i-once-again-bet-on-a-substantial-growth -slowdown-in-china.html.

26. Archimedes: "Give me a lever and a place to stand and I will move the earth." *The Library of History of Diodorus Siculus*, Fragments of Book XXVI, as translated by F. R. Walton, in *Loeb Classical Library*, vol. 11 (Cambridge: Harvard University Press 1957).

27. Robert E. Lucas Jr., "On the Mechanics of Economic Development," *Journal of Monetary Economics* 22, no. 1 (1988): 3–42.

28. Robert E. Lucas Jr., "Why Doesn't Capital Flow from Rich to Poor Countries?," *American Economic Review* 80, no. 2 (1990): 92–96.

29. Francesco Caselli, "Accounting for Cross-Country Income Differences," in *Handbook of Economic Growth*, vol. 1, part A, eds. Philippe Aghion and Steven N. Durlauf (Amsterdam: North Holland, 2005), 679–741.

30. Anne Robert Jacques Turgot, "Sur le Memoire de M. de Saint-Péravy," in *Oeuvres de Turgot et documents le concernant, avec biographie et notes*, ed. G. Schelle (Paris : F. Alcan, 1913).

31. Karl Marx, *Das Kapital* (Hamburg: Verlag von Otto Meisner, 1867). Fortunately for capitalism, there was a misstep in Marx's logic. As Solow pointed out, when the return on capital goes down, the speed of accumulation also goes down. Therefore, unless capitalists start saving more precisely when it is less rewarding to do so, accumulation will eventually slow down and the rate of profit will stop falling.

32. Julia Carrie, "Amazon Posts Record 2.5bn Profit Fueled by Ad and Cloud Business," *Guardian,* July 26, 2018. Part of the profits come from Amazon selling cloud storage. But cloud storage is itself a by-product of the excess capacity on the cloud they knew they had to build to remain the dominant market maker. So Amazon cloud business is part and parcel of their gigantic size.

33. Paul M. Romer, "Increasing Returns and Long-Run Growth," *Journal of Political Economy* 94, no. 5 (1986): 1002–37, https://doi.org/10.1086/261420.

34. Danielle Paquette, "Scott Walker Just Approved $3 billion Deal for a New Foxconn Factory in Wisconsin," *Washington Post,* September 18, 2017; Natalie Kitroeff, "Foxconn Affirms Wisconsin Factory Plan, Citing Trump Chat," *New York Times,* February 1, 2019.

35. Enrico Moretti, "Are Cities the New Growth Escalator?" in *The Urban Imperative: Towards Competitive Cities*, ed. Abha Joshi-Ghani and Edward Glaeser (New Delhi: Oxford University Press, 2015), 116–48.

36. Laura Stevens and Shayndi Raice, "How Amazon Picked HQ2 and Jilted 236 Cities," *Wall Street Journal,* November 14, 2018.

37. Amazon HQ2 RFP," September 2017, https://images-na.ssl-images-amazon.com/images/G/01/Anything/test/images/usa/RFP_3._V516043504_.pdf accessed June 14, 2019.

38. Adam B. Jaffe, Manuel Trajtenberg, and Rebecca Henderson, "Geographic Localization of Knowledge Spillovers as Evidenced by Patent Citations," *Quarterly Journal of Economics* 108, no. 3 (1993): 577–98, https://doi.org/10.2307/2118401.

39. Enrico Moretti. *The New Geography of Jobs.* (Boston: Mariner Books, 2012).

40. Michael Greenstone, Richard Hornbeck, and Enrico Moretti, "Identifying Agglomeration Spillovers: Evidence from Winners and Losers of Large Plant Openings," *Journal of Political Economy* 118, no. 3 (June 2010): 536–98, https://doi.org/10.1086/653714.

41. Of course, the question being asked in New York was not about the size of the gains (everybody agreed there would be some) but why Amazon was allowed to keep so much of it for themselves. After all, Alexandria offered much less, and Boston nothing at all (but then Boston did not win).

42. Jane Jacobs, "Why TVA Failed," *New York Review of Books*, May 10, 1984.

43.Patrick Kline and Enrico Moretti, "Local Economic Development, Agglomeration Economies, and the Big Push: 100 Years of Evidence from the Tennessee Valley Authority," *Quarterly Journal of Economics* 129, no. 1 (2014): 275–331, https://doi.org/10.1093/qje/qjt034.

44. Ten percent growth over the past decade will raise growth over the next decade by 20 percent of 10 percent, which is 2 percent. This will create additional growth of 20 percent of 2 percent, or 0.4 percent, over the following decade and so on. It is evident the additional rounds of growth are small to start with and get smaller pretty fast.

45. Patrick Kline and Enrico Moretti, "Local Economic Development, Agglomeration Economies and the Big Push: 100 Years of Evidence from the Tennessee Valley Authority," *Quarterly Journal of Economics* 129, no. 1 (2014): 275–331, https://doi.org/10.1093/qje/qjt034.

46. Enrico Moretti, "Are Cities the New Growth Escalator?," in *The Urban Imperative: Towards Competitive Cities*, ed. Edward Glaeser and Abha Joshi-Ghani (New Delhi: Oxford University Press, 2015), 116–48.

47. Peter Ellis and Mark Roberts, *Leveraging Urbanization in South Asia: Managing Spatial Transformation for Prosperity and Livability,* South Asia Development Matters (Washington, DC: World Bank, 2016), https://doi .org/10.1596/978-1-4648-0662-9. License: Creative Commons Attribution CC BY 3.0 IGO.

48. Paul M. Romer, "Endogenous Technological Change," *Journal of Political Economy* 98, no. 5, part 2 (1990): S71–S102, https://doi.org/10.1086/261725.

49. Philippe Aghion and Peter Howitt, "A Model of Growth Through Creative Destruction," *Econometrica* 60, no. 2 (1992): 323–51.

50. The Wikipedia entry for Schumpeter reads thus: "Schumpeter claimed that he had set himself three goals in life: to be the greatest economist in the world, to be the best horseman in all of Austria and the greatest lover in all of Vienna. He said he had reached two of his goals, but he never said which two, although he is reported to have said that there were too many fine horsemen in Austria for him to succeed in all his aspirations." See https:// en.wikipedia.org/wiki/Joseph_Schumpeter.

51. Philippe Aghion and Peter Howitt, "A Model of Growth Through Creative Destruction," *Econometrica* 60, no. 2 (1992): 323–51.

52. 'Real GDP Growth," US Budget and Economy, http://usbudget.blog spot.fr/2009/02/real-gdp-growth.html.

53. David Leonardt, "Do Tax Cuts Lead to Economic Growth?," *New York Times*, September 15, 2012, https://nyti.ms/2mBjewo.

54. Thomas Piketty, Emmanuel Saez, and Stefanie Stantcheva, "Optimal Taxation of Top Labor Incomes: A Tale of Three Elasticities," *American Economic Journal: Economic Policy* 6, no. 1 (2014): 230–71, https://doi.org/10.1257/pol.6.1.230.

55. William Gale, "The Kansas Tax Cut Experiment," Brookings Institution, 2017, https://www.brookings.edu/blog/unpacked/2017/07/11/the-kansas-tax-cut-experiment/.

56. Owen Zidar, "Tax Cuts for Whom? Heterogeneous Effects of Income Tax Changes on Growth and Employment," *Journal of Political Economy* 127, no. 3 (2019): 1437–72, https://doi.org/10.1086/701424.

57. Emmanuel Saez, Joel Slemrod, and Seth H. Giertz, "The Elasticity of Taxable Income with Respect to Marginal Tax Rates: A Critical Review," *Journal of Economic Literature* 50, no. 1 (2012): 3–50, https://doi.org/10.1257/jel.50.1.3.

58. "Tax Reform," IGM Forum, 2017, http://www.igmchicago.org/surveys/tax-reform-2.

59. "Analysis of Growth and Revenue Estimates Based on the US Senate Committee on Finance Tax Reform Plan," Department of the Treasury, 2017, https://www.treasury.gov/press-center/press-releases/Documents/TreasuryGrowthMemo12-11-17.pdf.

60. The signatories were Robert J. Barro, Michael J. Boskin, John Cogan, Douglas Holtz-Eakin, Glenn Hubbard, Lawrence B. Lindsey, Harvey S. Rosen, George P. Shultz, and John B. Taylor. See "How Tax Reform Will Lift the Economy," *Wall Street Journal:* Opinion, 2017, https://www.wsj.com/articles/how-tax-reform-will-lift-the-economy-1511729894?mg=prod/accounts-wsj.

61. Jason Furman and Lawrence Summers, "Dear colleagues: You Responded, but We Have More Questions About Your Tax-Cut Analysis," *Washington Post,* 2017, https://www.washingtonpost.com/news/wonk/wp/2017/11/30/dear-colleagues-you-responded-but-we-have-more-questions-about-your-tax-cut-analysis/?utm_term=.bbd78b5f1ef9.

62. "Economic Report of the President together with the Annual Report of the Council of Economic Advisers," 2016, https://obamawhitehouse.archives.gov/sites/default/files/docs/ERP_2016_Book_Complete%20JA.pdf.

63. Thomas Philippon *The Great Reversal: How America Gave up on Free Markets* (Cambridge: Harvard University Press, 2019).

64. David Autor, David Dorn, Lawrence F. Katz, Christina Patterson,

and John Van Reenen, "The Fall of the Labor Share and the Rise of Superstar Firms," NBER Working Paper 23396, 2017.

65. For powerful arguments that the rise in concentration has been bad for consumers, see Thomas Philippon *The Great Reversal: How America Gave Up on Free Markets* (Cambridge: Harvard University Press, 2019); Jan De Loecker, Jan Eeckhout, and Gabriel Unger, "The Rise of Market Power and the Macroeconomic Implications," working paper, 2018.

66. Esteban Rossi-Hansberg, Pierre-Daniel Sarte, and Nicholas Trachter, "Diverging Trends in National and Local Concentration,"NBER Working Paper 25066, 2018.

67. Alberto Cavallo, "More Amazon Effects: Online Competition and Pricing Behaviors," NBER Working Paper 25138, 2018.

68. Germán Gutiérrez and Thomas Philippon, "Ownership, Concentration, and Investment," *AEA Papers and Proceedings* 108 (2018): 432–37, https://doi.org/10.1257/pandp.20181010; Thomas Philippon, *The Great Reversal: How America Gave Up on Free Markets* (Cambridge: Harvard University Press, 2019).

69. Facundo Alvaredo, Lucas Chancel, Thomas Piketty, Emmanuel Saez, and Gabriel Zucman, "World Inequality Report 2018: Executive Summary," World Inequality Lab, 2018.

70. Mats Elzén and Per Ferström, "The Ignorance Survey: United States," Gapminder, 2013, https://static.gapminder.org/GapminderMedia/wp-uploads/Results-from-the-Ignorance-Survey-in-the-US..pdf.

71. "Poverty," World Bank, 2019, accessed April 14, 2019, https://www.worldbank.org/en/topic/poverty/overview#1.

72. "The Millennium Development Goals Report 2015: Fact Sheet," United Nations, 2015.

73. "Child Health," USAID.com, February 17, 2018, accessed April 14, 2019, https://www.usaid.gov/what-we-do/global-health/maternal-and-child-health/technical-areas/child-health.

74. "The Millennium Development Goals Report 2015: Fact Sheet," United Nations, 2015.

75. "Literacy Rate, Adult Total (% of People Ages 15 and Above)," World Bank Open Data, https://data.worldbank.org/indicator/se.adt.litr.zs.

76. "Number of Deaths Due to HIV/AIDS," World Health Organization, accessed April 14, 2019, https://www.who.int/gho/hiv/epidemic_status/deaths_text/en/.

77. Paul Romer "Economic Growth," in Library of Economics and Liberty: Economic Systems, accessed June 13, 2019, https://www.econlib.org/library/Enc/EconomicGrowth.html.

78. William Easterly, *The Elusive Quest for Growth* (Cambridge, MA: MIT Press 2001).

79. Ross Levine and David Renelt, "A Sensitivity Analysis of Cross-Country Growth Regressions," *American Economic Review* 82, no. 4 (September 1992): 942–63.

80. Daron Acemoglu, Simon Johnson, and James A. Robinson, "The Colonial Origins of Comparative Development: An Empirical Investigation, *"American Economic Review* 91, no. 5 (2001): 1369–1401, https://doi.org/10.1257/aer.91.5.1369; Daron Acemoglu, Simon Johnson, James A. Robinson, "Reversal of Fortune: Geography and Institutions in the Making of the Modern World Income Distribution," *Quarterly Journal of Economics* 117, no. 4 (November 2002): 1231–94, https://doi.org/10.1162/003355302320935025/.

81. Dani Rodrik, Arvind Subramanian, and Francesco Trebbi, "Institutions Rule: The Primacy of Institutions over Geography and Integration in Economic Development," *Journal of Economic Growth* 9, no. 2 (2004): 131–65, https://doi.org/10.1023/B:JOEG.0000031425.72248.85.

82. "Global 500 2014," *Fortune,* 2014, accessed June 13, 2019, http://fortune.com/global500/2014/.

83. William Easterly, "Trust the Development Experts—All 7 Billion," Brookings Institution, 2008, https://www.brookings.edu/opinions/trust-the-development-experts-all-7-billion/.

84. "The Impact of the Internet in Africa: Establishing Conditions for Success and Catalyzing Inclusive Growth in Ghana, Kenya, Nigeria and Senegal," Dalberg, 2013.

85. World Development Report 2016: Digital Dividends," World Bank, 2016, http://www.worldbank.org/en/publication/wdr2016.

86. Kenneth Lee, Edward Miguel, and Catherine Wolfram, "Experimental Evidence on the Economics of Rural Electrification," working paper, 2018.

87. Julian Cristia, Pablo Ibarrarán, Santiago Cueta, Ana Santiago, and Eugenio Severín, "Technology and Child Development: Evidence from the One Laptop per Child Program," *American Economic Journal: Applied Economics* 9, no. 3 (2017): 295–320, https://doi.org/10.1257/app.20150385.

88. Rema Hanna, Esther Duflo, and Michael Greenstone, "Up in Smoke: The Influence of Household Behavior on the Long-Run Impact of Improved Cooking Stoves," *American Economic Journal: Economic Policy* 8, no. 1 (2016): 80–114, https://doi.org/ 10.1257/pol.20140008.

89. James Berry, Greg Fischer, and Raymond P. Guiteras, "Eliciting and Utilizing Willingness-to-Pay: Evidence from Field Trials in Northern Ghana," CEnREP Working Paper 18-016, May 2018.

90. Rachel Peletz, Alicea Cock-Esteb, Dorothea Ysenburg, Salim Haji, Ranjiv Khush, and Pascaline Dupas, "Supply and Demand for Improved Sanitation: Results from Randomized Pricing Experiments in Rural Tanzania," *Environmental Science and Technology* 51, no. 12 (2017): 7138–47, https://doi.org/10.1021/acs.est.6b03846.

91. "India: The Growth Imperative," report, McKinsey Global Institute, 2001.

92. Robert Jensen, "The Digital Provide: Information (Technology), Market Performance, and Welfare in the South Indian Fisheries Sector," *Quarterly Journal of Economics* 122, no. 3 (August 2007): 879–924. https://doi.org/10.1162/qjec.122.3.879.

93. Robert Jensen and Nolan H. Miller, "Market Integration, Demand, and the Growth of Firms: Evidence from a Natural Experiment in India, "*American Economic Review* 108 no. 12 (2018): 3583–625, https://doi.org/10.1257/aer.20161965.

94. See, for example, the prospectus of one firm in Tirupur: "Prospectus," Vijayeswari Textiles Limited, February 25, 2007, http://www.idbicapital.com/pdf/IDBICapital-VijayeswariTextilesLtdRedHerringProspectus.pdf. accessed June 13, 2019.

95. Abhijit Banerjee and Kaivan Munshi, "How Efficiently Is Capital Allocated? Evidence from the Knitted Garment Industry in Tirupur," *Review of Economic Studies* 71, no. 1 (2004): 19–42, https://doi.org/10.1111/0034-6527.00274.

96. Nicholas Bloom and John Van Reenen, "Measuring and Explaining Management Practices Across Firms and Countries," *Quarterly Journal of Economics* 122, no. 4 (2007): 1351–1408.

97. Chris Udry, "Gender, Agricultural Production, and the Theory of the Household," *Journal of Political Economy* 104, no. 5 (1996): 1010–46.

98. Francisco Pérez-González, "Inherited Control and Firm Performance," *American Economic Review* 96, no. 5 (2006): 1559–88.

99. Chang-Tai Hsieh and Peter J. Klenow, "Misallocation and Manufacturing TFP in China and India,"*Quarterly Journal of Economics* 124, no. 4 (2009): 1403–48, https://doi.org/10.1162/qjec.2009.124.4.1403.

100. Chang-Tai Hsieh and Peter Klenow, "The Life Cycle of Plants in India and Mexico," *Quarterly Journal of Economics* 129, no. 3 (2014): 1035–84, https://doi.org/10.1093/qje/qju014.

101. Chang-Tai Hsieh and Peter Klenow, "Misallocation and Manufacturing TFP in China and India,"*Quarterly Journal of Economics* 124, no. 4 (2009): 1403–48, https://doi.org/10.1162/qjec.2009.124.4.1403.

102. Qi Liang,, Pisun Xu, Pornsit Jiraporn, "Board Characteristics and Chinese Bank Performance," *Journal of Banking and Finance* 37, no. 8 (2013): 2953–68, https://doi.org/10.1016/j.jbankfin.2013.04.018.

103. "Bank Lending Rates," Trading Economics, accessed April 15, 2019, https://tradingeconomics.com/country-list/bank-lending-rate.

104. "Interest Rates," Trading Economics, accessed April 15, 2019, https://tradingeconomics.com/country-list/interest-rate.

105. Gilles Duranton, Ejaz Ghani, Arti Grover Goswami, and William Kerr, "The Misallocation of Land and Other Factors of Production in India," World Bank Group Policy Research Working Paper 7547, (2016), https://doi.org/10.1596/1813-9450-7221.

106. Nicholas Bloom, Benn Eifert, Aprajit Mahajan, David McKenzie, and John Roberts, "Does Management Matter? Evidence from India,"*Quarterly Journal of Economics* 128, no. 1 (2013), https://doi.org/10.1093/qje/qjs044.

107. Jaideep Prabhu, Navi Radjou, and Simone Ahuja, *Jugaad Innovation: Think Frugal, Be Flexible, Generate Breakthrough Growth* (San Francisco: Jossey-Bass, 2012).

108. Emily Breza, Supreet Kaur, and Nandita Krishnaswamy, "Scabs: The Social Suppression of Labor Supply," NBER Working Paper 25880 (2019), https://doi.org/10.3386/w25880.

109. Authors' calculation from the National Sample Survey, 66h round, 2009–2010, accessed June 19, http://www.icssrdataservice.in/datarepository/index.php/catalog/89/overview.

110. Abhijit Banerjee and Gaurav Chiplunkar, "How Important Are Matching Frictions in the Labor Market? Experimental and Non-Experimental Evidence from a Large Indian Firm," working paper, 2018, accessed June 19, 2019, https://gauravchiplunkar.com/wp-content/uploads/2018/08/matchingfrictions_banerjeechiplunkar_aug18.pdf.

111. Esther Duflo, Pascaline Dupas, and Michael Kremer, "The impact of Free Secondary Education: Experimental Evidence from Ghana," MIMEO, Massachusetts Institute of Technology, accessed April 18, 2019, https://economics.mit.edu/files/16094.

112. "Unemployment, Youth Total (% of total labor force ages 15–24) (national estimate)," World Bank Open Data, accessed April 15, 2019, https://data.worldbank.org/indicator/SL.UEM.1524.NE.ZS.

113. Abhijit Banerjee and Gaurav Chiplunkar, "How Important Are Matching Frictions in the Labor Market? Experimental and Non-Experimental Evidence from a Large Indian Firm," working paper, 2018.

114. "Labour Market Employment, Employment in Public Sector, Employment in Private Sector Different Categories-wise," Data.gov.in, accessed April 15, 2019, https://data.gov.in/resources/labour-market-employ ment-employment-public-sector-employment-private-sector-different.

115. Sonalde Desai and Veena Kulkarni, "Changing Educational Inequalities in India in the Context of Affirmative Action," *Demography* 45, no. 2 (2008): 245–70.

116. Abhijit Banerjee and Sandra Sequeira, "Spatial Mismatches and Beliefs about the Job Search: Evidence from South Africa," MIMEO, MIT, 2019.

117. Neha Dasgupta, "More Than 25 Million People Apply for Indian Railway Vacancies," Reuters, March 29, 2018, accessed June 19, 2019, https://www.reuters.com/article/us-india-unemployment-railways/more -than-25-million-people-apply-for-indian-railway-vacancies-idUSKBN1 H524C.

118. Frederico Finan, Benjamin A. Olken, and Rohini Pande, "The Personnel Economics of the States," in *Handbook of Field Experiments*, vol. 2, eds. Abhijit Banerjee and Esther Duflo (Amsterdam: North Holland, 2017).

119. Ezra Vogel, *Japan as Number One* (Cambridge, MA: Harvard University Press, 1979), 153–54, 204–205, 159, 166.

120. Ernest Liu, "Industrial Policies in Production Networks," working paper, 2019.

121. Albert Bollard, Peter J. Klenow, and Gunjan Sharma, "India's Mysterious Manufacturing Miracle," *Review of Economic Dynamics* 16, no. 1 (2013): 59–85.

122. Pierre-Richard Agénor and Otaviano Canuto, "Middle-Income Growth Traps," *Research in Economics* 69, no. 4 (2015): 641–60, https://doi.org /10.1016/j.rie.2015.04.003.

123. "Guidance Note for Surveillance under Article IV Consultation," International Monetary Fund, 2015.

124. In fact, the under-five child mortality in 2017 was only 8.8 deaths per 1,000 live births, much lower than in Guatemala (27.6), but also quite similar to that in the United States (6.6). "Mortality Rate, under-5 (per 1,000 Live Births)," World Bank Data, accessed April 15, 2019, https://data.worldbank.org/ indicator/SH.DYN.MORT?end=2017&locations=GT-LK-US&start=2009. "Maternal Mortality Rate (National Estimate per 100,000 Live Births)." World Bank Data, accessed April 15, 2019, https://data.worldbank.org/ indicator/SH.STA.MMRT.NE?end=2017&locations=GT-LK-US&start

=2009. "Mortality Rate, Infant (per 1,000 Live Births)," World Bank Data, accessed April 15, 2019, https://data.worldbank.org/indicator/SP.DYN.IMRT.IN?end=2017&locations=GT-LK-US&start=2009.

125. "Mortality Rate, under-5 (per 1,000 Live Births)," World Bank Data, accessed April 16, 2019, https://data.worldbank.org/indicator/SH.DYN.MORT?end=2017&locations=GT-LK-US&start=2009.

126. Taz Hussein, Matt Plummer, and Bill Breen (for the *Stanford Social Innovation Review*), "How Field Catalysts Galvanise Social Change," SocialInnovationExchange.org., 2018, https://socialinnovationexchange.org/insights/how-field-catalysts-galvanise-social-change.

127. Christian Lengeler, "Insecticide-Treated Bed Nets and Curtains for Preventing Malaria," *Cochrane Database of Systematic Reviews* 2, no. 2 (2004), https://doi.org/10.1002/14651858.CD000363.pub2.

128. Abhijit Banerjee and Esther Duflo, *Poor Economics* (New York: PublicAffairs, 2011).

129. Jessica Cohen and Pascaline Dupas, "Free Distribution or Cost-Sharing? Evidence from a Randomized Malaria Prevention Experiment," *Quarterly Journal of Economics* 125, no. 1 (2010): 1–45.

130. "World Malaria Report 2017," World Health Organization, 2017.

131. S. Bhatt, D. J. Weiss, E. Cameron, D. Bisanzio, B. Mappin, U. Dalrymple, K. Battle, C. L. Moyes, A. Henry, P. A. Eckhoff, E. A. Wenger, O. Briët, M. A. Penny, T. A. Smith, A. Bennett, J. Yukich, T. P. Eisele, J. T. Griffin, C. A. Fergus, M. Lynch, F. Lindgren, J. M. Cohen, C. L. J. Murray, D. L. Smith, S. I. Hay, R. E. Cibulskis, and P. W. Gething, "The Effect on Malaria Control on *Plasmodium falciparum* in Africa between 2000 and 2015," *Nature* 526 (2015): 207–11, https://doi.org/10.1038/nature15535.

132. William Easterly, "Looks like @JeffDSachs got it more right than I did on effectiveness of mass bed net distribution to fight malaria in Africa," tweet, August 18, 2017, 11:04 a.m.

CHAPTER 6. IN HOT WATER

1. "Global Warming of 1.5°C," IPCC Special Report, Intergovernmental Panel on Climate Change, 2008, accessed June 16, 2019, https://www.ipcc.ch/sr15/.

2. As the October 2018 report of the IPCC states, "Human activities are estimated to have caused approximately 1.0°C of global warming above pre-industrial levels, with a likely range of 0.8°C to 1.2°C. Global warming is likely to reach 1.5°C between 2030 and 2052 if it continues to increase at the current rate."

3. CO_2 equivalent emissions refer to the emissions of greenhouse gas (CO_2, methane, etc.) expressed in a common unit by converting amounts of other gases to the equivalent amount of CO_2 with the same effect on global warming. For example, 1 million metric tonnes of methane represents 25 million metric CO_2e.

4. Lucas Chancel and Thomas Piketty, "Carbon and Inequality: from Kyoto to Paris," report, Paris School of Economics, 2015, accessed June 16, 2019, http://piketty.pse.ens.fr/files/ChancelPiketty2015.pdf.

5. Robin Burgess, Olivier Deschenes, Dave Donaldson, and Michael Greenstone, "Weather, Climate Change and Death in India," LSE working paper, 2017, accessed June 19, 2018, http://www.lse.ac.uk/economics/Assets/Documents/personal-pages/robin-burgess/weather-climate-change-and-death.pdf.

6. Orley C. Ashenfelter and Karl Storchmann, "Measuring the Economic Effect of Global Warming on Viticulture Using Auction, Retail, and Wholesale Prices," *Review of Industrial Organization* 37, no. 1 (2010): 51–64.

7. Joshua Graff Zivin and Matthew Neidell, "Temperature and the Allocation of Time: Implications for Climate Change," *Journal of Labor Economics* 32, no. 1 (2014): 1–26.

8. Joshua Goodman, Michael Hurwitz, Jisung Park, and Jonathan Smith, "Heat and Learning," NBER Working Paper 24639, 2018.

9. Achyuta Adhvaryu, Namrata Kala, and Anant Nyshadham, "The Light and the Heat: Productivity Co-benefits of Energy-saving Technology," NBER Working Paper 24314, 2018.

10. Melissa Dell, Benjamin F. Jones, and Benjamin A. Olken, "What Do We Learn from the Weather? The New Climate-Economy Literature," *Journal of Economic Literature* 52, no. 3 (2014): 740–98.

11. Olivier Deschenes and Michael Greenstone, "Climate Change, Mortality, and Adaptation: Evidence from Annual Fluctuations in Weather in the US," *American Economic Journal: Applied Economics*, 3 no. 4 (2011): 152–85.

12. Robin Burgess, Olivier Deschenes, Dave Donaldson and Michael Greenstone, "Weather, Climate Change and Death in India," LSE working paper, 2017 accessed June 16, 2019, http://www.lse.ac.uk/economics/Assets/Documents/personal-pages/robin-burgess/weather-climate-change-and-death.pdf.

13. Melissa Dell, Benjamin F. Jones, and Benjamin A. Olken, "What Do We Learn from the Weather? The New Climate-Economy Literature," *Journal of Economic Literature* 52, no. 3 (2014): 740—98.

14. Nihar Shah, Max Wei, Virginie Letschert, and Amol Phadke, "Ben-

efits of Leapfrogging to Superefficiency and Low Global Warming Potential Refrigerants in Room Air Conditioning," U.S. Department of Energy: Ernest Orlando Lawrence Berkeley National Laboratory Technical Report, 2015, accessed June 16 2019, https://eta.lbl.gov/publications/benefits-leap frogging-superefficiency.

15. Maximilian Auffhammer and Catherine Wolfram, "Powering Up China: Income Distributions and Residential Electricity Consumption," *American Economic Review: Papers & Proceedings* 104, no. 5 (2014): 575–80.

16. Nicholas Stern, *The Economics of Climate Change: The Stern Review* (Cambridge, UK: Cambridge University Press, 2006).

17. Daron Acemoglu, Philippe Aghion, Leonardo Bursztyn, and David Hemous, "The Environment and Directed Technical Change," *American Economic Review* 102, no. 1 (2012): 131–66.

18. Daron Acemoglu and Joshua Linn, "Market Size in Innovation: Theory and Evidence from the Pharmaceutical Industry," *Quarterly Journal of Economics* 119, no. 3 (2004): 1049–90.

19. Hannah Choi Granade et al., "Unlocking Energy Efficiency in the U.S. Economy," executive summary," McKinsey & Company, 2009, accessed June 16, 2019, https://www.mckinsey.com/~/media/mckinsey/dotcom/client _service/epng/pdfs/unlocking%20energy%20efficiency/us_energy_ efficiency_exc_summary.ashx.

20. "Redrawing the Energy-Climate Map," technical report, International Energy Agency, 2013. Accessed June 16, 2019, https://www.iea.org/ publications/freepublications/publication/WEO_Special_Report_2013_ Redrawing_the_Energy_Climate_Map.pdf.

21. Meredith Fowlie, Michael Greenstone, and Catherine Wolfram, "Do Energy Efficiency Investments Deliver? Evidence from the Weatherization Assistance Program," *Quarterly Journal of Economics* 133, no. 3 (2018): 1597–1644.

22. Nicholas Ryan, "Energy Productivity and Energy Demand: Experimental Evidence from Indian Manufacturing Plants," NBER Working Paper 24619, 2018.

23. Meredith Fowlie, Catherine Wolfram, C. Anna Spurlock, Annika Todd, Patrick Baylis, and Peter Cappers, "Default Effects and Follow-on Behavior: Evidence from an Electricity Pricing Program," NBER Working Paper 23553, 2017.

24. Hunt Allcott and Todd Rogers, "The Short-Run and Long-Run Effects of Behavioral Interventions: Experimental Evidence from Energy Conservation," *American Economic Review* 104, no. 10 (2014): 3003–37.

25. David Atkin, "The Caloric Costs of Culture: Evidence from Indian Migrants," *American Economic Review* 106, no. 4 (2016): 1144–81.

26. In Bangladesh, a study found that providing incentives to wash your hands for before meals for a few weeks increases handwashing even after the incentives are removed. Furthermore, people warned that they would get incentives in the future started washing their hands in anticipation of the program, to prepare themselves. Hussam, Reshmaan, Atonu Rabbani, Giovanni Regianni, and Natalia Rigol, "Habit Formation and Rational Addiction: A Field Experiment in Handwashing," Harvard Business School BGIE Unit Working Paper 18-030, 2017.

27. Avraham Ebenstein, Maoyong Fan, Michael Greenstone, Guojun He, and Maigeng Zhou, "New Evidence on the Impact of Sustained Exposure to Air Pollution on Life Expectancy from China's Huai River Policy," *PNAS* 114, no. 39 (2017): 10384–89.

28. WHO Global Ambient Air Quality Database (update 2018), https://www.who.int/airpollution/data/cities/en/.

29. Umair Irfan, "How Delhi Became the Most Polluted City on Earth," Vox, November 25, 2017.

30. "The Lancet Commission on Pollution and Health," *Lancet* 391 (2017): 462–512.

31. "The Lancet: Pollution Linked to Nine Million Deaths Worldwide in 2015, Equivalent to One in Six Deaths," *Lancet*, public release, 2018.

32. Achyuta Adhvaryu, Namrata Kala, and Anant Nyshadham, "Management and Shocks to Worker Productivity: Evidence from Air Pollution Exposure in an Indian Garment Factory," IGC working paper, 2016, accessed June 16, 2019, https://www.theigc.org/wp-content/uploads/2017/01/Adhvaryu-et-al-2016-Working-paper.pdf.

33. Tom Y. Chang, Joshua Graff Zivin, Tal Gross, and Matthew Neidell, "The Effect of Pollution on Worker Productivity: Evidence from Call Center Workers in China," American Economic Journal: Applied Economics 11, no. 1 (2019): 151–72.

34. A short-lived "odd-even" restriction, where cars with license plates ending in odd and even numbers were allowed out on alternate days led to a decline in particulate matter, but was brought down by a cabal of irate elites and environmental experts with "better" plans. Michael Greenstone, Santosh Harish, Rohini Pande, and Anant Sudarshan, "The Solvable Challenge of Air Pollution in India," in *India Policy Forum* volume conference volume 2017 (New Delhi: Sage Publications, 2017).

35. Kevin Mortimer et al., "A Cleaner-Burning Biomass-Fuelled Cookstove Intervention to Prevent Pneumonia in Children under 5 Years Old in Rural Malawi (the Cooking and Pneumonia Study): A Cluster Randomised Controlled Trial," *Lancet* 389, no. 10065 (2016): 167–75.

36. Theresa Beltramo, David L. Levine, and Garrick Blalock, "The Effect of Marketing Messages, Liquidity Constraints, and Household Bargaining on Willingness to Pay for a Nontraditional Cook-stove," Center for Effective Global Action Working Paper Series No. 035, 2014; Theresa Beltramo, Garrick Blalock, David I. Levine, and Andres M. Simons, "Does Peer Use Influence Adoption of Efficient Cookstoves? Evidence from a Randomized Controlled Trial in Uganda," *Journal of Health Communication: International Perspectives* 20 (2015): 55–66; David I. Levine, Theresa Beltramo, Garrick Blalock, and Carolyn Cotterman, "What Impedes Efficient Adoption of Products? Evidence from Randomized Variation of Sales Offers for Improved Cookstoves in Uganda," *Journal of the European Economic Association* 16, no. 6 (2018): 1850–80; Ahmed Mushfiq Mobarak, Puneet Dwivedi, Robert Bailis, Lynn Hildemann, and Grant Miller, "Low Demand for Nontraditional Cookstove Technology," *Proceedings of the National Academy of Sciences* 109, no. 27 (2012): 10815–20.

37. Rema Hanna, Esther Duflo, and Michael Greenstone, "Up in Smoke: The Influence of Household Behavior on the Long-Run Impact of Improved Cooking Stoves," *American Economic Journal: Economic Policy* 8, no. 1 (2016): 80–114.

38. Abhijit V. Banerjee, Selvan Kumar, Rohini Pande, and Felix Su, "Do Voters Make Informed Choices? Experimental Evidence from Urban India," working paper, 2010.

CHAPTER 7. PLAYER PIANO

1. Kurt Vonnegut, *Player Piano* (New York: Charles Scribner's Sons, 1952).

2. Kurt Vonnegut, *God Bless You, Mr. Rosewater* (New York: Holt, Rinehart and Winston, 1965).

3. Erik Brynjolfsson and Andrew McAfee, *The Second Machine Age* (New York: W. W. Norton & Company, 2014).

4. David H. Autor, "Why Are There Still So Many Jobs? The History and Future of Workplace Automation," *Journal of Economic Perspectives* 29, no. 3 (2015): 3–30.

5. Ellen Fort, "Robots Are Making $6 Burgers in San Francisco," *Eater San Francisco*, June, 21, 2018.

6. Michael Chui, James Manyika, and Mehdi Miremadi, "How Many of Your Daily Tasks Could Be Automated?," *Harvard Business Review*, December

14, 2015 and "Four Fundamentals of Business Automation," *McKinsey Quarterly*, November 2016, accessed June 19, 2019, https://www.mckinsey.com/business-functions/digital-mckinsey/our-insights/four-fundamentals-of-workplace-automation.

7. "Automation, Skills Use and Training," Organisation for Economic Co-operation and Development Library, accessed April 19, 2019, https://www.oecd-ilibrary.org/employment/automation-skills-use-and-training_2e2f4eea-en.

8. "Robots and Artificial Intelligence," Chicago Booth: The Initiative on Global Markets, IGM Forum, June 30, 2017.

9. Robert Gordon, *The Rise and Fall of American Growth* (Princeton, NJ: Princeton University Press, 2016).

10. Databases, Tables, and Calculators by Subject, Series LNS14000000, Bureau of Labor Statistics, accessed April 11, 2019, https://data.bls.gov/timeseries/lns14000000.

11. Robert Gordon, *The Rise and Fall of American Growth* (Princeton, NJ: Princeton University Press, 2016); "Labor Force Participation Rate, Total (% total population ages 15+) (national estimate)," World Bank Open Data, https://data.worldbank.org/indicator/SL.TLF.CACT.NE.ZS?locations=US.

12. Daron Acemoglu and Pascual Restrepo, "Artificial Intelligence, Automation and Work," NBER Working Paper 24196, 2018.

13. N. F. R. Crafts and Terence C. Mills, "Trends in Real Wages in Britain 1750–1913," *Explorations in Economic History* 31, no. 2 (1994): 176–94.

14. Robert Fogel and Stanley Engerman, *Time on the Cross* (New York: W. W. Norton & Company, 1974).

15. Daron Acemoglu and Pascual Restrepo, "Robots and Jobs: Evidence from United States Labor Markets," NBER Working Paper 23285, 2017.

16. Daron Acemoglu and Pascual Restrepo, "The Race Between Machine and Man: Implications of Technology for Growth, Factor Shares and Employment," NBER Working Paper 22252, 2017.

17. David Autor, "Work of the Past, Work of the Future," Richard T. Ely Lecture, *American Economic Association: Papers and Proceedings,* 2019.

18. Daron Acemoglu and Pascual Restrepo, "Artificial Intelligence, Automation and Work," NBER Working Paper 24196, 2018.

19. Ibid.

20. Ibid.

21. Aaron Smith and Monica Anderson, "Americans' Attitudes towards a Future in Which Robots and Computers Can Do Many Human Jobs," Pew

Research Center, October 4, 2017, accessed April 3, 2019, http://www.pew internet.org/2017/10/04/americans-attitudes-toward-a-future-in-which -robots-and-computers-can-do-many-human-jobs/.

22. Jean Tirole and Olivier Blanchard, for example, have argued that the uncertainty in the outcome of a firing could in fact exacerbate unemployment. (David Blanchard and Olivier Tirole, "The Optimal Design of Unemployment Insurance and Employment Protection. A First Pass," NBER Working Paper 10443, 2004.) However, it does not appear that European countries that have loosened employment protection have lower unemployment. Overall, there seems to be no relationship. Giuseppe Bertola, "Labor Market Regulations: Motives, Measures, Effects," International Labor Organization, Conditions of Work and Employment Series No. 21, 2009.

23. Kevin J. Delaney, "The Robot That Takes Your Job Should Pay Taxes, Says Bill Gates," *Quartz,* February 17, 2017, accessed April 13, 2019, https:// qz.com/911968/bill-gates-the-robot-that-takes-your-job-should-pay-taxes/.

24. "European Parliament Calls for Robot Law, Rejects Robot Tax," Reuters, February 16, 2017, accessed April 12, 2019, https://www.reuters.com /article/us-europe-robots-lawmaking/european-parliament-calls-for-robot -law-rejects-robot-tax-idUSKBN15V2KM.

25. Ryan Abbott and Bret Bogenschneider, "Should Robots Pay Taxes? Tax Policy in the Age of Automation," *Harvard Law & Policy Review* 12 (2018).

26. John DiNardo, Nicole M. Fortin, and Thomas Lemieux, "Labor Market Institutions and Distribution of Wages, 1973–1990: A Semiparametric Approach," *Econometrica* 64, no. 5 (1996): 1001–44; David Card, "The Effect of Unions on the Structure of Wages: A Longitudinal Analysis," *Econometrica* 64, no. 4 (1996): 957–79; Richard B. Freeman, "How Much Has Deunionization Contributed to the Rise of Male Earnings Inequality?," in eds. Sheldon Danziger and Peter Gottschalk *Uneven Tides: Rising Income Inequality in America* (New York: Russell Sage Foundation, 1993), 133–63.

27. See "UK Public Spending Since 1900," https://www.ukpublicspend ing.co.uk/past_spending.

28. John Kenneth Galbraith. "Recession Economics." *New York Review of Books,* February 4, 1982.

29. Facundo Alvaredo, Lucas Chancel, Thomas Piketty, Emmanuel Saez, and Gabriel Zucman, "World Inequality Report 2018: Executive Summary," Wid.World, 2017, accessed April 13, 2019, from the World Inequality Lab website: https://wir2018.wid.world/files/download/wir2018-summary -english.pdf.

30. "United Kingdom," World Inequality Database, Wid.World, accessed April 13, 2019, https://wid.world/country/united-kingdom/.

31. Thomas Piketty, Emmanuel Saez, and Stefanie Stantcheva, "Optimal Taxation of Top Labor Incomes: A Tale of Three Elasticities," *American Economic Journal: Economic Policy* 6, no. 1 (2014): 230–71, DOI: 10.1257/pol.6.1.230.

32. Facundo Alvaredo, Lucas Chancel, Thomas Piketty, Emmanuel Saez, and Gabriel Zucman, "World Inequality Report 2018," Wid.World, retrieved from the World Inequality Lab website: https://wir2018.wid.world/files/download/wir2018-full-report-english.pdf.

33. David Autor, "Work of the Past, Work of the Future," Richard T. Ely Lecture, *American Economic Review: Papers and Proceedings,* 2019.

34. David Autor, David Dorn, Lawrence F. Katz, Christina Patterson, and John Van Reenen, "The Fall of the Labor Share and the Rise of Superstar Firms," NBER Working Paper 23396, issued in May 2017, DOI: 10.3386/w2339.

35. Thomas Piketty, *Capital in the Twenty-First Century,* trans. Arthur Goldhammer (Cambridge, MA: Harvard University Press, 2014).

36. World Bank Data, accessed April 19, 2019, https://data.worldbank.org/indicator/ne.trd.gnfs.zs.

37. Claudia Goldin and Lawrence F. Katz, *The Race between Education and Technology* (Cambridge, MA: Harvard University Press, 2010).

38. Thomas Piketty, *Capital in the Twenty-First Century,* trans. Arthur Goldhammer (Cambridge, MA: Harvard University Press, 2014).

39. David Autor, David Dorn, Lawrence F. Katz, Christina Patterson, and John Van Reenen, "The Fall of the Labor Share and the Rise of Superstar Firms," NBER Working Paper 23396 10.3386/w2339, 2017.

40. Jason Furman and Peter Orszag, "Slower Productivity and Higher Inequality: Are They Related?," Peterson Institute for International Economics Working Paper 18-4, 2018.

41. Jae Song, David J Price, Fatih Guvenen, Nicholas Bloom, Till von Wachter, "Firming Up Inequality," *Quarterly Journal of Economics*, Volume 134, no. 1 (2019): 1–50, https://doi.org/10.1093/qje/qjy025.

42. Sherwin Rosen, "The Economics of Superstars," *American Economic Review* 71, no. 5 (1981): 845–58.

43. Xavier Gabaix and Augustin Landier, "Why Has CEO Pay Increased So Much?," *Quarterly Journal of Economics* 123, no. 1 (2008): 49–100.

44. Facundo Alvaredo, Lucas Chancel, Thomas Piketty, Emmanuel Saez, and Gabriel Zucman, "World Inequality Report 2018," Wid.World,

2017, retrieved from the World Inequality Lab website: https://wir2018.wid .world/files/download/wir2018-full-report-english.pdf.

45. World Inequality Database, Wid.World, https://www.wid.world.

46. Robin Greenwood and David Scharfstein, "The Growth of Finance," *Journal of Economic Perspectives* 27, no. 2 (2013): 3–28.

47. Thomas Philippon and Ariell Reshef, "Wages and Human Capital in the U.S. Finance Industry: 1909–2006," *Quarterly Journal of Economics* 127, no. 4 (2012): 1551–1609.

48. Brian Bell and John Van Reenen, "Bankers' Pay and Extreme Wage Inequality in the UK," CEP Special Report, 2010.

49. Jon Bakija, Adam Cole, and Bradley T. Heim, "Jobs and Income Growth of Top Earners and the Causes of Changing Income Inequality: Evidence from U.S. Tax Return Data," working paper, Williams College, 2012, accessed June 19, 2019, https://web.williams.edu/Economics/wp/BakijaCole HeimJobsIncomeGrowthTopEarners.pdf.

50. Bertrand Garbinti, Jonathan Goupille-Lebret, and Thomas Piketty, "Income Inequality in France, 1900–2014: Evidence from Distributional National Accounts (DINA)," WID.world Working Paper Series No. 2017/4, 2017.

51. Olivier Godechot, "Is Finance Responsible for the Rise in Wage Inequality in France?," *Socio-Economic Review* 10, no. 3 (2012): 447–70.

52. Eugene F. Fama and Kenneth R. French, "Luck Versus Skill in the Cross-Section of Mutual-Fund Returns," *Journal of Finance* 65, no. 5 (2010): 1915–47.

53. Thomas Philippon and Ariell Reshef, "Wages and Human Capital in the U.S. Finance Industry: 1909–2006, *Quarterly Journal of Economics* 127, no. 4 (2012): 1551–1609.

54. Robin Greenwood and David Scharfstein, "The Growth of Finance," *Journal of Economic Perspectives* 27, no. 2 (2013): 3–28.

55. Claudia Goldin and Lawrence F. Katz, "Transitions: Career and Family Life Cycles of the Educational Elite," *American Economic Review* 98, no. 2 (2008): 363–69.

56. Marianne Bertrand and Sendhil Mullainathan, "Are CEO's Rewarded for Luck? The Ones Without Principals Are," *Quarterly Journal of Economics* 116, no. 3 (2001): 901–32.

57. Scharfstein and Greenwood showed that in most continental European countries the share of finance in the economy either did not grow much in the 1990s and 2000s, or it even declined. Robin Greenwood and David Scharfstein, "The Growth of Finance," *Journal of Economic Perspectives* 27, no. 2 (2013): 3–28.

58. Thomas Piketty, *Capital in the Twenty-First Century,* trans. Arthur Goldhammer (Cambridge, MA: Harvard University Press, 2014), 550–51, and Emmanuel Saez and Gabriel Zucman, "Alexandria Ocasio-Cortez's Idea Is Not about Soaking the Rich," accessed April 20, 2019, https://www.nytimes.com/2019/01/22/opinion/ocasio-cortez-taxes.html.

59. Thomas Piketty, Emmanuel Saez, and Stefanie Stantcheva, "Optimal Taxation of Top Labor Incomes: A Tale of Three Elasticities," *American Economic Journal: Economic Policy* 6, no. 1 (2014): 230–71.

60. Maury Brown, "It's Time to Blowup the Salary Cap Systems in the NFL, NBA, and NHL," *Forbes,* March 10, 2015, accessed April 11, 2019, https://www.forbes.com/sites/maurybrown/2015/03/10/its-time-to-blowup-the-salary-cap-systems-in-the-nfl-nba-and-nhl/#1e35ced969b3.

61. Our discussion in this section and the next draws heavily on the work of Thomas Piketty, Emmanuel Saez, and Gabriel Zucman. A reader who wants to go deeper is enjoined to read Thomas Piketty, *Capital in the Twentieth Century,* trans. Arthur Goldhammer (Cambridge, MA: Harvard University Press, 2014); Gabriel Zucman's *The Hidden Wealth of Nations* (Chicago: University of Chicago Press, 2015); and Saez's and Zucman's forthcoming book, *The Triumph of Injustice*.

62. Emmanuel Saez, Joel Slemrod, and Seth H. Giertz, "The Elasticity of Taxable Income with Respect to Marginal Tax Rates: A Critical Review," *Journal of Economic Literature* 50, no. 1 (2012): 3–50.

63. Pian Shu, "Career Choice and Skill Development of MIT Graduates: Are the 'Best and Brightest' Going into Finance?," Harvard Business School Working Paper 16-067, 2017.

64. David Autor, "Skills, Education, and the Rise of Earnings Inequality among the 'Other 99 Percent,'" *Science* 344, no. 6168 (2014): 843–51.

65. Henrik J. Kleven, Camille Landais, and Emmanuel Saez. 2013. "Taxation and International Migration of Superstars: Evidence from the European Football Market," *American Economic Review* 103, no. 5: 1892–1924.

66. Annette Alstadsæter, Niels Johannesen, and Gabriel Zucman, "Tax Evasion and Inequality," NBER Working Paper 23772, 2018.

67. Thomas Piketty, *Capital in the Twenty-First Century,* trans. Arthur Goldhammer (Cambridge, MA: Harvard University Press, 2014).

68. Ibid.

69. The other part is that investment income is taxed at a lower rate anyway. An alternative to a wealth tax would be to tax investment income even when it is not distributed, but it is technically very difficult to account for that income.

70. Ben Casselman and Jim Tankersly, "Democrats Want to Tax the Wealthy. Many Voters Agree." *New York Times*, February 19, 2019, https://www.nytimes.com/2019/02/19/business/economy/wealth-tax-elizabeth-warren.html.

71. H. J. Kleven, Knudsen, M. B., Kreiner, C. T., Pedersen, S. and E. Saez, "Unwilling or Unable to Cheat? Evidence from a Tax Audit Experiment in Denmark," *Econometrica* 79 (2011): 651–92, doi:10.3982/ECTA9113.

72. Gabriel Zucman, "Sanctions for Offshore Tax Havens, Transparency at Home," *New York Times,* April 7, 2016; Gabriel Zucman, "The Desperate Inequality behind Global Tax Dodging," *Guardian,* November 8, 2017.

73. Henrik Jacobsen Kleven, Camille Landais, Emmanuel Saez, and Esben Schultz, "Migration and Wage Effects of Taxing Top Earners: Evidence from the Foreigners' Tax Scheme in Denmark," *Quarterly Journal of Economics* 129, no. 1 (2013): 333–78.

74. Ben Casselman and Jim Tankersly, "Democrats Want to Tax the Wealthy. Many Voters Agree," *New York Times*, February 19, 2019, https://www.nytimes.com/2019/02/19/business/economy/wealth-tax-elizabeth-warren.html.

75. Abhijit Banerjee, Esther Duflo, and Stefanie Stantcheva, "Me and Everyone Else: Do People Think Like Economists?," MIMEO, Massachusetts Institute of Technology, 2019.

76. Erzo F. P. Luttmer, "Neighbors as Negatives: Relative Earnings and Well-Being," *Quarterly Journal of Economics* 120, no. 3 (2005): 963–1002.

77. Ricardo Perez-Truglia, "The Effects of Income Transparency on Well-Being: Evidence from a Natural Experiment," NBER Working Paper 25622, 2019.

78. Leonardo Bursztyn, Bruno Ferman, Stefano Fiorin, Martin Kanz, Gautam Rao, "Status Goods: Experimental Evidence from Platinum Credit Cards," *Quarterly Journal of Economics* 133, no. 3 (2018): 1561–95, https://doi.org/10.1093/qje/qjx048.

79. Alberto Alesina, Stefanie Stantcheva, and Edoardo Teso, "Intergenerational Mobility and Preferences for Redistribution," *American Economic Review* 108, no. 2 (2018): 521–54.

80. Ibid.

81. Ibid.

82. Anne Case and Angus Deaton, "Rising Midlife Morbidity and Mortality, US Whites," Proceedings of the National Academy of Sciences, December 2015, 112 (49) 15078-15083; DOI:10.1073/pnas.1518393112; Anne

Case and Angus Deaton, "Mortality and Morbidity in the 21st Century," Brookings Papers on Economic Activity, 2017.

83. Tamara Men, Paul Brennan, and David Zaridze, "Russian Mortality Trends for 1991–2001: Analysis by Cause and Region," *BMJ: British Medical Journal* 327, no. 7421 (2003): 964–66.

84. Anne Case and Angus Deaton, "Mortality and Morbidity in the 21st Century," Brookings Papers on Economic Activity, 2017.

85. Alberto Alesina, Stefanie Stantcheva, and Edoardo Teso, "Intergenerational Mobility and Preferences for Redistribution," *American Economic Review* 108, no. 2 (2018): 521–54.

86. Emily Breza, Supreet Kaur, and Yogita Shamdasani, "The Morale Effects of Income Inequality." *Quarterly Journal of Economics* 133, no.2 (2017): 611–63.

87. David Autor, David Dorn, Gordon Hansen, and Kaveh Majlesi, "Importing Political Polarization. The Electoral Consequences of Rising Trade Exposure," NBER Working Paper 22637, September 2016, revised December 2017.

CHAPTER 8. LEGIT.GOV

1. "Revenue Statistics 2018 Tax Revenue Trends in the OECD," Organisation for Economic Co-operation and Development, December 5, 2018, accessed June 18, 2018, https://www.oecd.org/tax/tax-policy/revenue-statistics-highlights-brochure.pdf.

2. Emmanuel Saez and Gabriel Zucman to Elizabeth Warren, January 18 2019, http://gabriel-zucman.eu/files/saez-zucman-wealthtax-warren.pdf.

3. Ben Casselman and Jim Tankersly, "Democrats Want to Tax the Wealthy. Many Voters Agree," *New York Times,* February 19, 2019, https://www.nytimes.com/2019/02/19/business/economy/wealth-tax-elizabeth-warren.html.

4. Abhijit Banerjee, Esther Duflo, and Stefanie Stantcheva, "Me and Everyone Else: Do People Think Like Economists?," MIMEO, Massachusetts Institute of Technology, 2019.

5. Cited in *Conservatives Betrayed: How George W. Bush and Other Big Government Republicans Hijacked the Conservative Cause,* by Richard A. Viguerie (Los Angeles: Bonus Books, 2006), 46.

6. Emmanuel Saez, Joel Slemrod, and Seth H. Giertz, "The Elasticity of Taxable Income with Respect to Marginal Tax Rates: A Critical Review," *Journal of Economic Literature* 50, no. 1 (2012): 3–50.

7. Isabel Z. Martinez, Emmanuel Saez, and Michael Seigenthaler, "Intertemporal Labor Supply Substitution? Evidence from the Swiss Income Tax Holidays," NBER Working Paper 24634, 2018.

8. Emmanuel Saez, Joel Slemrod, and Seth H. Giertz, "The Elasticity of Taxable Income with Respect to Marginal Tax Rates: A Critical Review," *Journal of Economic Literature* 50, no. 1 (2012): 3–50.

9. Abhijit Banerjee, Esther Duflo, and Stefanie Stantcheva, "Me and Everyone Else: Do People Think Like Economists?," MIMEO, Massachusetts Institute of Technology, 2019.

10. Ronald Reagan, Inaugural Address, Washington, DC, 1981.

11. Alberto Alesina, Stefanie Stantcheva, and Edoardo Teso, "Intergenerational Mobility and Preferences for Redistribution," *American Economic Review* 108, no. 2 (2018): 521–54.

12. Anju Agnihotri Chaba, "Sustainable Agriculture: Punjab Has a New Plan to Move Farmers Away from Water-Guzzling Paddy," *Indian Express,* March 28 2018, accessed March 4, 2019, https://indianexpress.com/article/india/sustainable-agriculture-punjab-has-a-new-plan-to-move-farmers-away-from-water-guzzling-paddy-5064481/.

13. "Which States Rely Most on Federal Aid?," Tax Foundation, accessed April 19, 2019, https://taxfoundation.org/states-rely-most-federal-aid/.

14. An often-cited stock quote of Milton Friedman, who was an inspiration to generations of economists, especially those on the right, popular on twitters and found in all quote repositories said: "The great achievements of civilization have not come from government bureaus." He went on to add: "Einstein didn't construct his theory under order from a bureaucrat." The choice of the example is odd. Einstein was a bureaucrat (in the Swiss Patent Office) when he did his early research, and had he not actually delivered what he delivered, he would be a prime example of waste in government. Milton Friedman Quotes, BrainyQuote.com, BrainyMedia Inc., 2019, accessed June 18, 2019, https://www.brainyquote.com/quotes/milton_friedman_412621.

15. Abhijit Banerjee, Rema Hanna, Jordan Kyle, Benjamin A. Olken, and Sudarno Sumarto, "Tangible Information and Citizen Empowerment: Identification Cards and Food Subsidy Programs in Indonesia," *Journal of Political Economy* 126, no. 2 (2018).

16. Karthik Muralidharan and Venkatesh Sundararaman, "The Aggregate Effect of School Choice: Evidence from a Two-Stage Experiment in India," *Quarterly Journal of Economics* 130, no. 3 (2015): 1011–66.

17. Luc Behaghel, Bruno Crépon, and Marc Gurgand, "Private and Public Provision of Counseling to Job Seekers: Evidence from a Large Controlled

Experiment," *American Economic Journal: Applied Economics* 6, no. 4 (2014): 142–74.

18. Mauricio Romero, Justin Sandefur and Wayne Sandholtz, "Outsourcing Service Delivery in a Fragile State: Experimental Evidence from Liberia," working paper, ITAM, accessed June 18, 2019, https://www.dropbox.com/s/o82lfb6tdffedya/MainText.pdf?dl=0.

19. Finlay Young, "What Will Come of the More Than Me Rape Scandal?," ProPublica, May 3, 2019, accessed June 18, 2019 https://www.propublica.org/article/more-than-me-liberia-rape-scandal.

20. Oriana Bandiera, Andrea Prat, and Tommaso Valletti, "Active and Passive Waste in Government Spending: Evidence from a Policy Experiment," *American Economic Review* 99, no. 4 (2009): 1278–1308.

21. Abhijit Banerjee, Rema Hanna, Jordan Kyle, Benjamin A. Olken, and Sudarno Sumarto, "Tangible Information and Citizen Empowerment: Identification Cards and Food Subsidy Programs in Indonesia," *Journal of Political Economy* 126, no. 2 (2018): 451–91

22. Abhijit Banerjee, Esther Duflo, and Stefanie Stantcheva, "Me and Everyone Else: Do People Think Like Economists?," MIMEO, Massachusetts Institute of Technology, 2019.

23. Alain Cohn, Ernst Fehr, and Michel Andre Marechal, "Business Culture and Dishonesty in the Banking Industry," *Nature* 516: (2014) 86–89.

24. Reman Hanna and Shing-Yi Wang, "Dishonesty and Selection into Public Service: Evidence from India," *American Economic Journal: Economic Policy* 9 no. 3 (2017): 262–90.

25. Sebastian Baufort, Nikolaj Harmon, Frederik Hjorth, and Asmus Leth Olsen et al., "Dishonesty and Selection into Public Service in Denmark: Who Runs the World's Least Corrupt Public Sector?," Discussion Papers 15–12, University of Copenhagen, Department of Economics, 2015.

26. Oriana Bandiera, Michael Carlos Best, Adnan Khan, and Andrea Prat, "Incentives and the Allocation of Authority in Organizations: A Field Experiment with Bureaucrats," CEP/DOM Capabilities, Competition and Innovation Seminars, London School of Economics, London, May 24 2018.

27. Clay Johnson and Harper Reed, "Why the Government Never Gets Tech Right," *New York Times,* October 24, 2013, accessed March 4, 2019, https://www.nytimes.com/2013/10/25/opinion/getting-to-the-bottom-of-healthcaregovs-flop.html?_r=0.

28. Bertrand Garbinti, Jonathan Goupille-Lebret, and Thomas Piketty, "Income Inequality in France, 1900–2014: Evidence from Distributional National Accounts (DINA)," *Journal of Public Economics* 162 (2018): 63–77.

29. Thomas Piketty and Nancy Qian, "Income Inequality and Progressive Income Taxation in China and India, 1986–2015," *American Economic Journal: Applied Economics* 1 *no.* 2 (2009): 53–63, *DOI:* 10.1257/app.1.2.53.

30. World Inequality Database, accessed June 19, 2019, https://wid.world/country/india/ and https://wid.world/country/china/.

31. Luis Felipe López-Calva and Nora Lustig, *Declining Inequality in Latin America: A Decade of Progress?* (Washington, DC: Brookings Institution Press, 2010), 1–24.

32. Santiago Levy, *Progress Against Poverty: Sustaining Mexico's PROGRESA-Oportunidades Program* (Washington, DC: Brookings Institution Press, 2006).

33. Dozens of studies have documented various aspects of the Progresa experiment. The first working paper was Paul J. Gertler and Simone Boyce, "An Experiment in Incentive-Based Welfare: The Impact of Progresa on Health in Mexico," working paper, 2003. The studies of this and subsequent experiments are summarized in *Conditional Cash Transfers: Reducing Present and Future Poverty,* ed. Ariel Fizsbein and Norbert Schady, accessed on April 19, 2019, http://documents.worldbank.org/curated/en/914561468314712643/Conditional-cash-transfers-reducing-present-and-future-poverty.

34. World Inequality data base, accessed on June 18, 2019, https://wid.world/country/colombia, https://wid.world/country/chile, https://wid.world/country/brazil.

CHAPTER 9. CASH AND CARE

1. Quote by Laticia Animas, who heads the new program. Benjamin Russell, "What AMLO's Anti-Poverty Overhaul Says About His Government," *Americas Quarterly,* February 26, 2019, accessed April 17, 2019, https://www.americasquarterly.org/content/what-amlos-anti-poverty-overhaul-says-about-his-government.

2. David Raul Perez Coady and Hadid Vera-Llamas, "Evaluating the Cost of Poverty Alleviation Transfer Programs: An Illustration Based on PROGRESA in Mexico," IFRPI discussion paper, http://ebrary.ifpri.org/utils/getfile/collection/p15738coll2/id/60365/filename/60318.pdf. See also Natalia Caldes, David Coady, and John A. Maluccio, "The Cost of Poverty Alleviation Transfer Programs: A Comparative Analysis of Three Programs in Latin America," *World Development* 34, no. 5 (2006): 818–37.

3. Florencia Devoto, Esther Duflo, Pascaline Dupas, William Parienté, and Vincent Pons, "Happiness on Tap: Piped Water Adoption in Urban Morocco," *American Economic Journal: Economic Policy* 4 no. 4 (2012): 68–99.

4. Maria Mini Jos, Rinku Murgai, Shrayana Bhattacharya, and Soumya Kapoor Mehta, "From Policy to Practice: How Should Social Pensions Be Scaled Up?," *Economic and Political Weekly* 50, no. 14 (2015).

5. Sarika Gupta, "Perils of the Paperwork: The Impact of Information and Application Assistance on Welfare Program Take-Up in India," Harvard University, November 2017, accessed June 19, 2019, https://scholar.harvard.edu/files/sarikagupta/files/gupta_jmp_11_1.pdf.

6. Esther Duflo, "The Economist as Plumber," *American Economic Review: Papers & Proceedings* 107, no. 5 (2017): 1–26.

7. Amy Finkelstein and Matthew J. Notowidigdo, "Take-up and Targeting: Experimental Evidence from SNAP," NBER Working Paper 24652, 2018.

8. Diane Whitmore Schanzenbach, "Experimental Estimates to the Barriers of Food Stamp Enrollment," Institute for Research on Poverty Discussion Paper no. 1367-09, September 2009.

9. Bruno Tardieu, *Quand un people parle: ATD, Quarte Monde, un combat radical contre la misère* (Paris: Editions La Découverte, 2015).

10. Najy Benhassine, Florencia Devoto, Esther Duflo, Pascaline Dupas, and Victor Pouliquen, "Turning a Shove into a Nudge? A 'Labeled Cash Transfer' for Education," *American Economic Journal: Economic Policy* 7, no. 3 (2015): 86–125.

11. These key numbers are summarized in Robert Reich's review of two books on the UBI https://www.nytimes.com/2018/07/09/books/review/annie-lowrey-give-people-money-andrew-yang-war-on-normal-people.html and can also be found in the books themselves. Annie Lowrey, *Give People Money: How a Universal Basic Income Would End Poverty, Revolutionize Work, and Remake the World*, 2018, and Andrew Yang, *The War on Normal People: The Truth About America's Disappearing Jobs and Why Universal Basic Income Is Our Future,* 2018.

12. George Bernard Shaw, *Pygmalion* (London: Penguin Classics, 2013).

13. Map Descriptive of London Poverty 1898–9, accessed April 21, 2019, https://booth.lse.ac.uk/learn-more/download-maps/sheet9.

14. "Radio Address to the Nation on Welfare Reform," Ronald Reagan Presidential Library and Museum, accessed March 20, 2019, https://www.reaganlibrary.gov/research/speeches/21586a.

15. Ibid.

16. For the reader who wants more, this literature is summarized in several books: James P. Ziliak, "Temporary Assistance for Needy Families," in *Economics of Means-TestedTransfer Programs in the United States*, vol. 1, ed. Robert A. Moffitt (National Bureau of Economic Research and University

of Chicago Press, 2016), 303–93; Robert Moffitt "The Temporary Assistance for Needy Families Program," in *Means-Tested Transfer Programs in the U.S.,* ed. R. Moffitt (University of Chicago Press and NBER, 2003); Robert Moffitt, "The Effect of Welfare on Marriage and Fertility: What Do We Know and What Do We Need to Know?," in *Welfare, the Family, and Reproductive Behavior*, ed. R. Moffitt (Washington, DC: National Research Council, National Academy of Sciences Press, 1998).

17. Sibith Ndiaye (@SibithNdiaye), "Le Président? Toujours exigeant. Pas encore satisfait du discours qu'il prononcera demain au congrès de la Mutualité, il nous précise donc le brief! Au boulot!," tweet, June 12, 2018, 3:28 p.m., accessed June 19, 2019, https://twitter.com/SibethNdiaye/status /1006664614619308033.

18. "Expanding Work Requirements in Non-Cash Welfare Programs," Council of Economic Advisors, July 2018, https://www.whitehouse.gov/wp -content/uploads/2018/07/Expanding-Work-Requirements-in-Non-Cash -Welfare-Programs.pdf.

19. Shrayana Bhattacharya, Vanita Leah Falcao, and Raghav Puri, "The Public Distribution System in India: Policy Evaluation and Program Delivery Trends," in *The 1.5 Billion People Question: Food, Vouchers, or Cash Transfers?* (Washington, DC: World Bank, 2017).

20. "Egypt to Raise Food Subsidy Allowance in Bid to Ease Pressure from Austerity," Reuters, June 20, 2017, accessed June 19, 2019, https://www.reuters .com/article/us-egypt-economy/egypt-to-raise-food-subsidy-allowance-in -bid-to-ease-pressure-from-austerity-idUSKBN19B2YW.

21. Peter Timmer, Hastuti, and Sudarno Sumarto, "Evolution and Implementation of the Rastra Program in Indonesia," in *The 1.5 Billion People Question: Food, Vouchers, or Cash Transfers?* (Washington, DC: World Bank, 2017).

22. Abhijit Banerjee, Rema Hanna, Jordan Kyle, Benjamin A. Olken, and Sudarno Sumarto, "Tangible Information and Citizen Empowerment: Identification Cards and Food Subsidy Programs in Indonesia," *Journal of Political Economy* 126, no. 2 (2018): 451–91.

23. Reetika Khera, "Cash vs In-Kind Transfers: Indian Data Meets Theory," *Food Policy* 46 (June 2014): 116–28, https://doi.org/10.1016/j.foodpol .2014.03.009.

24. Ugo Gentilini, Maddalena Honorati, and Ruslan Yemtsov, "The State of Social Safety Nets 2014 (English)," World Bank Group, 2014, accessed June 19, 2019, http://documents.worldbank.org/curated/en/302571468320707386/ The-state-of-social-safety-nets-2014.

25. Abhijit V. Banerjee, "Policies for a Better Fed World," *Review of World Economics* 152, no. 1 (2016): 3–17.

26. David K. Evans and Anna Popova "Cash Transfers and Temptation Goods," *Economic Development and Cultural Change* 65, no. 2 (2917), 189–221.

27. Abhijit V. Banerjee, "Policies for a Better Fed World," *Review of World Economics* 152, no. 1 (2016): 3–17.

28. Johannes Haushofer and Jeremy Shapiro, "The Short-Term Impact of Unconditional Cash Transfers to the Poor: Experimental Evidence from Kenya," *Quarterly Journal of Economics* 131, no. 4 (2016): 1973–2042.

29. Ercia Field, Rohini Pande, Natalia Rigol, Simone Schaner, and Charity Troyer Moore, "On Her Account: Can Strengthening Women's Financial Control Boost Female Labor Supply?," working paper, Harvard University, Cambridge, MA, 2016, accessed June 19, 2019, http://scholar.harvard.edu/files/rpande/files/on_her_account.can_strengthening_womens_financial_control_boost_female_labor_supply.pdf.

30. Abhijit Banerjee, Rema Hanna, Gabriel Kreindler, and Ben Olken, "Debunking the Stereotype of the Lazy Welfare Recipient: Evidence from Cash Transfer Programs," *World Bank Research Observer* 32, no. 2 (August 2017) 155–84, https://doi.org/10.1093/wbro/lkx002.

31. Abhijit Banerjee, Karlan Dean and Chris Udry, "Does Poverty Increase Labor Supply? Evidence from Multiple Income Effects," MIMEO, Massachusetts Institute of Technology, 2019.

32. David Greenberg and Mark Shroder, "Part 1: Introduction. An Overview of Social Experimentation and the Digest," *Digest of Social Experiments,* accessed March 25, 2019, https://web.archive.org/web/20111130101109/http://www.urban.org/pubs/digest/introduction.html#n22.

33. Philip K. Robins, "A Comparison of the Labor Supply Findings from the Four Negative Income Tax Experiments,"*Journal of Human Resources* 20, no. 4 (Autumn 1985): 567–82.

34. Orley Ashenfelter and Mark W. Plant, "Nonparametric Estimates of the Labor Supply Effects of Negative Income Tax Programs," *Journal of Labor Economics* 8, no. 1, Part 2: Essays in Honor of Albert Rees (January 1990): S396–S415.

35. Philip K. Robins, "A Comparison of the Labor Supply Findings from the Four Negative Income Tax Experiments," *Journal of Human Resources* 20, no. 4 (Autumn, 1985): 567–82.

36. Ibid.

37. Albert Rees, "An Overview of the Labor-Supply Results," *Journal of Human Resources* 9, no. 2 (Spring 1974): 158–180.

38. Damon Jones and Ioana Marinescu, "The Labor Market Impacts of Universal and Permanent Cash Transfers: Evidence from the Alaska Permanent Fund," NBER Working Paper 24312.

39. Randall K .Q. Akee, William E. Copeland, Gordon Keeler, Adrian Angold, and E. Jane Costello, "Parents' Income and Children's Outcomes: A Quasi-Experiment Using Transfer Payments from Casino Profits," *American Economic Journal: Applied Economics* 2, no. 1 (2010): 86–115.

40. Vivi Alatas, Abhijit Banerjee, Rema Hanna, Matt Wai-poi, Ririn Purnamasari, Benjamin A. Olken, and Julia Tobias, "Targeting the Poor: Evidence from a Field Experiment in Indonesia," *American Economic Review* 102, no. 4 (2012): 1206–40, DOI: 10.1257/aer.102.4.1206.

41. Clément Imbert and John Papp, "Labor Market Effects of Social Programs: Evidence from India's Employment Guarantee," *American Economic Journal: Applied Economics* 7, no. 2 (2015): 233–63; Muralidharan Karthik, Paul Niehuas, and Sandip Sukhtankar, "General Equilibrium Effects of (Improving) Public Employment Programs: Experimental Evidence from India," NBER Working Paper 23838, 2018 DOI: 10.3386/w23838.

42. Martin Ravalion, "Is a Decentralized Right to Work Policy Feasible?," NBER Working Paper 25687, March 2019.

43. Abhijit Banerjee, Esther Duflo, Clement Imbert, Santhos Mattthews, and Rohini Pande, "E-Governance, Accountability, and Leakage in Public Programs: Experimental Evidence from a Financial Management Reform in India," NBER Working Paper 22803, 2016.

44. "Economic Survey 2016–17," Government of India, Ministry of Finance, Department of Economic Affairs, Economic Division, 2017, 188–90.

45. Nur Cahyadi, Rema Hanna, Benjamin A. Olken, Rizal Adi Prima, Elan Satriawan, and Ekki Syamsulhakim, "Cumulative Impacts of Conditional Cash Transfer Programs: Experimental Evidence from Indonesia," NBER Working Paper 24670, 2018.

46. Najy Benhassine, Florencia Devoto, Esther Duflo, Pascaline Dupas, and Victor Pouliquen, "Turning a Shove into a Nudge? A "Labeled Cash Transfer" for Education," *American Economic Journal: Economic Policy* 7, no. 3 (2015): 86–125.

47. Aaron Smith and Monica Anderson, "Americans' Attitudes towards a Future in Which Robots and Computers Can Do Many Human Jobs," Pew Research Center, October 4, 2017, accessed April 3, 2019, http://www.pew internet.org/2017/10/04/americans-attitudes-toward-a-future-in-which-robots -and-computers-can-do-many-human-jobs/.

48. Robert B. Reich, "What If the Government Gave Everyone a Paycheck?," July 9, 2018, https://www.nytimes.com/2018/07/09/books/review/annie-lowrey-give-people-money-andrew-yang-war-on-normal-people.html.

49. Olli Kangas, Signe Jauhiainen, Miska Simanainen, Mina Ylikännö, eds., "The Basic Income Experiment 2017–2018 in Finland. Preliminary Results," Reports and Memorandums of the Ministry of Social Affairs and Health, 2019, 9.

50. Abhijit Banerjee, Esther Duflo, and Stefanie Stantcheva, "Me and Everyone Else: Do People Think Like Economists?," MIMEO, Massachusetts Institute of Technology, 2019.

51. Nicole Maestas, Kathleen J. Mullen, David Powell, Till von Wachter, and Jeffrey B. Wenger, "Working Conditions in the United States: Results of the 2015 American Working Conditions Survey," Rand Corporation, 2017.

52. "The State of American Jobs: How the Shifting Economic Landscape Is Reshaping Work and Society and Affecting the Way People Think about the Skills and Training They Need to Get Ahead," ch. 3, Pew Research Center, October 2016, accessed April 21, 2019, http://www.pewsocialtrends.org/2016/10/06/3-how-americans-view-their-jobs/#fn-22004-26.

53. See Steve Davis and Till Von Wachter, "Recession and the Costs of Job Loss," Brookings Papers on Economic Activity, Brookings Institution, Washington, DC, 2011, https://www.brookings.edu/wp-content/uploads/2011/09/2011b_bpea_davis.pdf, and references therein.

54. Daniel Sullivan and Till Von Wachter, "Job Displacement and Mortality: An Analysis Using Administrative Data," Quarterly Journal of Economics 124, no. 3 (2009): 1265–1306.

55. Mark Aguiar and Erik Hurst, "Measuring Trends in Leisure: The Allocation of Time over Five Decades," Quarterly Journal of Economics 122, no. 3 (2007): 969–100.

56. Mark Aguiar, Mark Bils, Kerwin Kofi Charles, and Erik Hurst, "Leisure Luxuries and the Labor Supply of Young Men," NBER Working Paper 23552, June 2007.

57. "American Time Use Survey—2017 Results," news release, Bureau of Labor Statistics, US Department of Labor, June 28, 2018, accessed June 19, 2019, https://www.bls.gov/news.release/atus.nro.htm.

58. Mark Aguiar, Erik Hurst, and Loukas Karabarbounis, "Time Use During the Great Recession," American Economic Review 103, no. 5 (2013): 1664–96.

59. Daniel Kahneman and Alan G. Krueger, "Developments in the Measurement of Subjective Well-Being," Journal of Economic Perspectives 20, no. 1 (2006): 3–24.

60. Aaron Smith and Monica Anderson, "Americans' Attitudes towards a Future in Which Robots and Computers Can Do Many Human Jobs," Pew Research Center, October 4, 2017, accessed April 3, 2019, http://www.pew internet.org/2017/10/04/americans-attitudes-toward-a-future-in-which-robots -and-computers-can-do-many-human-jobs/.

61. "Volunteering in the United States, 2015," Economic News Release, February 25, 2016, accessed April 21, 2019, https://www.bls.gov/news.release /volun.nro.htm.

62. David Deming, "The Growing Importance of Social Skills in the Labor Market," *Quarterly Journal of Economics* 132, no. 4 (2017): 1593–1640, https://doi.org/10.1093/qje/qjx022.

63. Román Zárate, "Social and Cognitive Peer Effects: Experimental Evidence from Selective High Schools in Peru," MIT Economics, 2019, accessed June 19, 2019, https://economics.mit.edu/files/16276.

64. Raj Chetty, Nathaniel Hendren, Patrick Kline, and Emmanuel Saez, "Where Is the Land of Opportunity? The Geography of Intergenerational Mobility in the United States," *Quarterly Journal of Economics* 129, no. 4 (2014): 1553–1623, https://doi.org/10.1093/qje/qju022.

65. Lawrence F. Katz, Jeffrey R. Kling, and Jeffrey B. Liebman, "Moving to Opportunity in Boston: Early Results of a Randomized Mobility Experiment," *Quarterly Journal of Economics* 116 no. 2 (2001): 607–54, https://doi .org/10.1162/00335530151144113.

66. Ra Chetty, Nathaniel Hendren, and Lawrence F. Katz, "The Effect of Exposure to Better Neighborhoods and Children: New Evidence from the Moving to Opportunity Experiment," *American Economic Review* 106, no. 4 (2016): 855–902.

67. Raj Chetty and Nathaniel Hendren, "The Impacts of Neighborhoods on Intergenerational Mobility II: County-Level Estimates," *Quarterly Journal of Economics* 133, no. 3 (2018): 1163–1228.

68. Roland G. Fryer Jr., "The Production of Human Capital in Developed Countries: Evidence from 196 Randomized Field Experiments," in *Handbook of Economic Field Experiments* 2 (Amsterdam: North-Holland, 2017): 95–322.

69. Abhijit Banerjee, Rukmini Banerji, James Berry, Esther Duflo, Harini Kannan, Shobhini Mukerji, Marc Shotland, and Michael Walton, "From Proof of Concept to Scalable Policies: Challenges and Solutions, with an Application," *Journal of Economic Perspectives* 31, no. 4 (2017): 73–102.

70. Raj Chetty, John Friedman, Nathaniel Hilger, Emmanuel Saez, Diane Whitmore Schanzenbach, and Danny Yagan, "How Does Your Kindergarten Classroom Affect Your Earnings? Evidence from Project Star," *Quarterly Journal of Economics* 126, no. 4 (2011): 1593–1660.

71. Ajay Chaudry and Rupa Datta, "The Current Landscape for Public Pre-Kindergarten Programs," in *The Current State of Scientific Knowledge on Pre-Kindergarten Effects,* Brookings Institution, Washington, DC, 2017, accessed June 19, 2019 https://www.brookings.edu/wp-content/uploads/2017/04/duke_prekstudy_final_4-4-17_hires.pdf.

72. Maria Stephens, Laura K. Warren, and Ariana L. Harner, "Comparative Indicators of Education in the United States and Other G-20 Countries: 2015. NCES 2016-100," National Center for Education Statistics, 2015.

73. All the references to Heckman's research on the long-term impact of preschool education can be found at https://heckmanequation.org/. Among other references, see Jorge Luis García, James J. Heckman, Duncan Ermini Leaf, and María José Prados, "The Life-Cycle Benefits of an Influential Early Childhood Program," NBER Working Paper 22993, 2016.

74. Michael Puma, Stephen Bell, Ronna Cook, and Camilla Heid, "Head Start Impact Study Final Report," US Department of Health and Human Services, Administration for Children and Families, 2010, https://www.acf.hhs.gov/sites/default/files/opre/executive_summary_final.pdf; Mark Lipsey, Dale Farran, and Kelley Durkin, "Effects of the Tennessee Prekindergarten Program on Children's Achievement and Behavior through Third Grade," *Early Childhood Research Quarterly* 45 (2017): 155–76.

75. R. M. Ford, S. J. McDougall, and D. Evans, "Parent-Delivered Compensatory Education for Children at Risk of Educational Failure: Improving the Academic and Self-Regulatory Skills of a Sure Start Preschool Sample," *British Journal of Psychology* 100, no. 4 (2009), 773–97. A. J. L. Baker, C. S. Piotrkowski, and J. Brooks-Gunn, "The Effects of the Home Instruction Program for Preschool Youngsters on Children's School Performance at the End of the Program and One Year Later," *Early Childhood Research Quarterly* 13, no. 4 (1998), 571–86. K. L. Bierman, J. Welsh, B. S. Heinrichs, R. L. Nix, and E. T. Mathis, "Helping Head Start Parents Promote Their Children's Kindergarten Adjustment: The REDI Parent Program," *Child Development,* 2015. James J. Heckman, Margaret L. Holland, Kevin K. Makinom Rodrigo Pinto, and Maria Rosales-Rueda, "An Analysis of the Memphis Nurse-Family Partnership Program," NBER Working Paper 23610, July 2017, http://www.nber.org/papers/w23610. Orazio Attanasio, C. Fernández, E. Fitzsimons, S. M Grantham-McGregor, C. Meghir, and M. Rubio-Codina, "Using the Infrastructure of a Conditional Cash Transfer Programme to Deliver a Scalable Integrated Early Child Development Programme in Colombia: A Cluster Randomised Controlled Trial," *British Medical Journal* 349 (September 29, 2014): g5785. Paul Gertler, James Heckman, Rodrigo Pinto, Arianna Zan-

olini, Christel Vermeerch, Susan Walker, Susan Chang-Lopez, and Sally Grantham-McGregor, "Labor Market Returns to an Early Childhood Stimulation Intervention in Jamaica," *Science* 344, no. 6187 (2014): 998–1001.

76. Moira R. Dillon, Harini Kannan, Joshua T. Dean, Elizabeth S. Spelke, and Esther Duflo, "Cognitive Science in the Field: A Preschool Intervention Durably Enhances Intuitive but Not Formal Mathematics," *Science* 357, no. 6346 (2017): 47–55.

77. Henrik Kleven, Camille Landais, Johanna Posch, Andreas Steinhauer, and Josef Zweimüller, "Child Penalties Across Countries: Evidence and Explanations," no. w25524, National Bureau of Economic Research, 2019.

78. Henrik Kleven, Camille Landais, and Jakob Egholt Søgaard, "Children and Gender Inequality: Evidence from Denmark," no. w24219, National Bureau of Economic Research, 2018.

79. "Denmark: Long-term Care," Organisation for Economic Co-Operation and Development, 2011, http://www.oecd.org/denmark/47877588.pdf.

80. Bruno Crépon and Gerard van den Berg, "Active Labor Market Policies," *Annual Review of Economics*, https://doi.org/10.1146/annurev-economics -080614-115738; Bruno Crépon, Esther Duflo, Marc Gurgand, Roland Rathelot, and Philippe Zamora, "Do Labor Market Policies Have Displacement Effects? Evidence from a Clustered Randomized Experiment," *Quarterly Journal of Economics* 128, no. 2 (2013): 531–80.

81. Sheila Maguire, Joshua Freely, Carol Clymer, Maureen Conway, and Deena Schwartz, "Tuning In to Local Labor Markets: Findings from the Sectoral Employment Impact Study," Public/Private Ventures, 2010, accessed April 21, 2019, http://ppv.issuelab.org/resources/5101/5101.pdf.

82. Yann Algan, Bruno Crépon, Dylan Glover, "The Value of a Vacancy: Evidence from a Randomized Evaluation with Local Employment Agencies in France," J-PAL working paper, 2018, accessed April 21, 2019, https:// www.povertyactionlab.org/sites/default/files/publications/5484_The-Value_ of_a_vacancy_Algan-Crepon-Glover_June2018.pdf.

83. "Employment Database—Labour Market Policies And Institutions," Organisation for Economic Co-operation and Development.

84. "Active Labour Market Policies: Connecting People with Jobs," Organisation for Economic Co-operation and Development, http://www.oecd .org/employment/activation.htm.

85. Benjamin Hyman, "Can Displaced Labor Be Retrained? Evidence from Quasi-Random Assignment to Trade Adjustment Assistance," January 10, 2018, https://ssrn.com/abstract=3155386 or http://dx.doi.org/10.2139/ssrn.3155386.

86.Aaron Smith and Monica Anderson, "Automation in Everyday Life: Chapter 2," Pew Research Center, 2017, accessed April 21, 2019, https://www .pewinternet.org/2017/10/04/americans-attitudes-toward-a-future-in-which -robots-and-computers-can-do-many-human-jobs/.

87. Bruno Tardieu, *Quand un people parle* (Paris: La Découverte, 2015).

88. Abhijit Banerjee, Esther Duflo, Nathanael Goldberg, Dean Karlan, Robert Osei, William Parienté, Jeremy Shapiro, Bram Thuysbaert, and Christopher Udry, "A Multifaceted Program Causes Lasting Progress for the Very Poor: Evidence from Six Countries," *Science* 348, no. 6236 (2015): 1260799.

89. Esther Duflo, Abhijit Banerjee, Raghabendra Chattopadyay, Jeremy Shapiro, "The Long Term Impacts of a 'Graduation' Program: Evidence from West Bengal," MIMEO, Massachusetts Institute of Technology, 2019.

90. Christopher Blattman, Nathan Fiala, and Sebastian Martinez, "The Long Term Impacts of Grants on Poverty: 9-Year Evidence from Uganda's Youth Opportunities Program," April 5, 2019, https://ssrn.com/abstract =3223028 or http://dx.doi.org/10.2139/ssrn.3223028.

91. Bruno Crépon, Esther Duflo, Éllise Huillery, William Pariente, Juliette Seban, and Paul-Armand Veillon, "Cream Skimming and the Comparison between Social Interventions Evidence from Entrepreneurship Programs for At-Risk Youth in France," 2018.

92. Ibid.

93. Robert Rosenthal and Lenore Jacobson, "Pygmalion in the Classroom," *Urban Review* 3, no. 1 (1968): 16–20.

94. Angela Duckworth, *Grit: The Power of Passion and Perseverance* (New York; Scribner, 2016).

95. Yann Algan, Adrien Bouguen, Axelle Charpentier, Coralie Chevallier, and Élise Huillery, "The Impact of a Large-Scale Mindset Intervention on School Outcomes: Experimental Evidence from France," MIMEO, 2018.

96. Sara B. Heller, Anuj K. Shah, Jonathan Guryan, Jens Ludwig, Sendhil Mullainathan, and Harold A. Pollack, "Thinking, Fast and Slow? Some Field Experiments to Reduce Crime and Dropout in Chicago," *Quarterly Journal of Economics* 132k, no. 1 (2017): 1–54.

CONCLUSION: GOOD AND BAD ECONOMICS

1. Chang-Tai Hsieh and Peter J. Klenow, "The Life Cycle of Plants in India and Mexico," *Quarterly Journal of Economics* 129, no. 3 (August 2014): 1035–84, https://doi.org/10.1093/qje/qju014.

ACKNOWLEDGMENTS

All books are the product of many minds but this one more so than most. Chiki Sarkar encouraged us to pursue this project before we had any idea of where we were headed. Her enthusiasm, lively intelligence, and faith in our abilities led us and supported us throughout this project. A little bit later in the project Andrew Wylie joined in. The backing of his vast experience gave us the confidence to proceed. Neel Mukherjee read the entire manuscript in its first, raw, version and gave us direction, style advice, and above all reassurance that this was a book worth writing and perhaps even reading. Maddie McKelway did extraordinary work to ensure that every fact in the manuscript was correctly checked and cited, and that every sentence made (at least some) sense. Clive Priddle, as with our previous book, understood exactly where we were trying to go, often before we did so ourselves. His edits made this a book.

In writing a book that ventures much beyond our "core competence," we had to rely heavily on the wisdom of many of our economist friends. Being surrounded by so many brilliant people, it is impossible to remember where every idea came from. Listing some risks excluding many others, but we feel compelled to name (without implicating, of course) Daron Acemoglu, David Atkin, Arnaud Costinot, Dave Donaldson, Rachel Glennerster, Penny Goldberg, Michael Greenstone, Bengt Holmstrom, Michael Kremer, Ben Olken, Thomas Piketty, Emma Rothschild, Emmanuel Saez, Frank Schilbach, Stefanie Stantcheva, and Ivan Werning. Thank you so much for educating us. Thank you also to our PhD advisors, Josh Angrist, Jerry Green, Andreu Mas Colell, Eric Maskin, and Larry Summers; and our many teachers, collaborators, friends, and students, all of whose imprints are everywhere in the book. Again at the risk of being grossly unfair, the book would not be the way it is without the influence of, among others,

Philippe Aghion, Marianne Bertrand, Arun Chandrasekhar, Daniel Cohen, Bruno Crepon, Ernst Fehr, Amy Finkelstein, Maitreesh Ghatak, Rema Hanna, Matt Jackson, Dean Karlan, Eliana La Ferrara, Matt Low, Ben Moll, Sendhil Mullainathan, Kaivan Munshi, Andrew Newman, Paul Niehaus, Rohini Pande, Nancy Qian, Amartya Sen, Bob Solow, Cass Sunstein, Tavneet Suri, and Robert Townsend.

Our year of leave at the Paris School of Economics was a godsend. It was a pleasant and fun place to work, both collegial and lively. We are especially grateful to Luc Behagel, Denis Cogneau, Olivier Compte, Hélène Giacobino, Mark Gurgand, Sylvie Lambert, and Karen Macours; and to Gilles Postel-Vinay and Katia Zhuravskaya for their always-welcoming smiles, much fun conversation, and many sweaty games of tennis. Our MIT colleagues Glenn and Sara Ellison, who coordinated their sabbaticals with us, made the year all the more wonderful. We gratefully acknowledge financial support from the Région Île-de-France (Chaire Blaise Pascal), the Axa Research Fund, the ENS Foundation, Paris School of Economics, and MIT. We thank them for their support.

For over 15 years, the J-PAL crew has not only fed our research fire, but also kept us optimistic about both economics and humankind. We are infinitely fortunate to work with kind, generous and dedicated people every day, year after year. Thank to Iqbal Dhaliwal who steers the ship and to John Floretta, Shobhini Mukherjee, Laura Poswell and Anna Schrimpf, who are our daily companions, seen and unseen. And, of course, to Heather McCurdy and Jovanna Mason for valiantly attempting to put some semblance of order into our lives.

Esther's parents, Michel and Violaine Duflo, and her brother Colas and his family were a huge part of why we had such a lovely time in Paris. Thank you for everything you do for us, year after year.

Abhijit's parents, Dipak and Nirmala Banerjee, are for him always the ideal readers for what he writes. He thanks them for teaching him so much of the economics he knows and, perhaps more importantly, the reasons why he should care.

INDEX

absolute advantage, 53
Acemoglu, Daron, 183, 200
Acumen Fund, 187
ATD Fourth World, 315
adverse selection, 33
affirmative action
  merit, 138–139
  purpose of, 137
  resentment of, 140
  shared schools, 142–143
  Students for Fair Admission v.
    Harvard, 139
Affordable Care Act of 2010
  (Obamacare), 85, 127, 144
Africa, impact of climate change on,
  211–212
African-American population in US,
  discrimination against, 108–109
Aghion, Philippe, 172, 178
agricultural marketing boards, 48
Aid for Trade initiative, 66
Aid to Artisans (ATA), 67, 68, 70
Akerlof, George, 32–33
Alaska Permanent Fund, 292
Alibaba, 77
Allport, Gordon, 136
Amazon, 69, 163, 167, 178
Amazon Marketplace, 77
Ambedkar, B. R., 106
American Time Use Survey (ATUS),
  300–301
Americans
  American dream, 42
  heredity, role of in fortunes, 42

mobility of, 42–43
segregation by skill level, 43–44
anti-immigrant attitudes, experiment
  on, 109–110
Aparajito (Ray), 14
arbitrariness experiments, 122–123
Arcidiacono, Peter, 139
Argentina, lowered tariffs and
  increased inequality in, 59–30
artificial intelligence, 150, 227–232
Atlantic magazine, on impact of China
  shock in Tennessee, 82
ATUS. *See* American Time Use
  Survey
automation
  college education, value of, 232, 240
  computerization, 240
  displacement effect, 230
  excessive, 232
  impact on UK from 1755–1820, 231
  industry concentration and
    monopolies, 233
  inequality increase, 232
  labor laws, 234
  limiting, 234
  R&D resources and, 233–234
  replacement of human actions with
    robots, 235
  robots' effect on employment,
    231–232
  tax on robots, 235
  US jobs at risk, 229
  US tax code and, 233
Autor, David, 80, 83

ABOUT THE AUTHORS

 **Abhijit V. Banerjee** is the Ford Foundation International Professor of Economics at the Massachusetts Institute of Technology, and a co-founder and co-director of the Abdul Latif Jameel Poverty Action Lab (J-PAL). He is a co-recipient of the Sveriges Riksbank Prize in Economic Sciences in Memory of Alfred Nobel 2019 for his work on alleviating global poverty. In 2011, he was named one of *Foreign Policy* magazine's top one hundred global thinkers. Banerjee served on the UN Secretary-General's High-level Panel of Eminent Persons on the Post-2015 Development Agenda. *Poor Economics*, his previous book with Esther Duflo, won the *Financial Times* and Goldman Sachs Business Book of the Year award and was translated into seventeen languages. He lives in Cambridge, Massachusetts.

 **Esther Duflo** is the Abdul Latif Jameel Professor of Poverty Alleviation and Development Economics in the Department of Economics at the Massachusetts Institute of Technology and a co-founder and co-director of the Abdul Latif Jameel Poverty Action Lab (J-PAL). The youngest and only second woman to be awarded the prize, she is a co-recipient of the Sveriges Riksbank Prize in Economic Sciences in Memory of Alfred Nobel 2019 for her work on alleviating global poverty. Duflo won the 2010 John Bates Clark Medal for best American economist under forty and received a 2009 MacArthur "Genius" Fellowship. In 2011 she was part of *Time* magazine's 100 most influential people. She lives in Cambridge, Massachusetts.

403

PublicAffairs is a publishing house founded in 1997. It is a tribute to the standards, values, and flair of three persons who have served as mentors to countless reporters, writers, editors, and book people of all kinds, including me.

I. F. Stone, proprietor of *I. F. Stone's Weekly*, combined a commitment to the First Amendment with entrepreneurial zeal and reporting skill and became one of the great independent journalists in American history. At the age of eighty, Izzy published *The Trial of Socrates*, which was a national bestseller. He wrote the book after he taught himself ancient Greek.

Benjamin C. Bradlee was for nearly thirty years the charismatic editorial leader of *The Washington Post*. It was Ben who gave the *Post* the range and courage to pursue such historic issues as Watergate. He supported his reporters with a tenacity that made them fearless and it is no accident that so many became authors of influential, best-selling books.

Robert L. Bernstein, the chief executive of Random House for more than a quarter century, guided one of the nation's premier publishing houses. Bob was personally responsible for many books of political dissent and argument that challenged tyranny around the globe. He is also the founder and longtime chair of Human Rights Watch, one of the most respected human rights organizations in the world.

•   •   •

For fifty years, the banner of Public Affairs Press was carried by its owner Morris B. Schnapper, who published Gandhi, Nasser, Toynbee, Truman, and about 1,500 other authors. In 1983, Schnapper was described by *The Washington Post* as "a redoubtable gadfly." His legacy will endure in the books to come.

Peter Osnos, *Founder*